D0754582

HF

WITHDRAWN

The Emotionally Disturbed Child
in the Classroom

Frank M. Hewett
University of California, Los Angeles

Frank D. Taylor
Santa Monica Unified School District

ALLYN AND BACON, INC.
BOSTON   LONDON   SYDNEY   TORONTO

The Emotionally Disturbed Child in the Classroom

The Orchestration of Success

Second Edition

The previous edition was published under the title *The Emotionally Disturbed Child in the Classroom,* Copyright © 1968 by Allyn and Bacon, Inc.

Library of Congress Cataloging in Publication Data

Hewett, Frank M
 The emotionally disturbed child in the classroom.

 Bibliography: p.
 Includes index.
  1. Problem children—Education. 2. Emotional problems of children. 3. Role playing. I. Taylor, Frank D., joint author. II. Title.
 LC480l.H49 1980 371.9'4 79-23973
 ISBN 0-205-06725-5

Printed in the United States of America.

Drawings which open chapters, and some within chapters, by Steve McAdam

Production Editor: Nancy Doherty
Preparation Buyer: Linda Card
Series Editor: Miggy Hopkins

Contents

chapter 9

The Resource Specialist Program at Elementary and Secondary Levels   *272*

chapter 10

The Severely Disturbed Child   *288*

chapter 11

Working with Parents   *332*

References   *351*

Index   *367*

Preface

In the twelve years since the publication of the first edition of this book, the emotionally disturbed child has come to be viewed more and more as a child with a learning problem teachers can do something about and only secondarily as a complex psychiatric casualty. The first edition opened with: "This book is about educational deeds"; we so introduce the second edition to you.

The educational deeds of this second edition are preceded by a two-chapter introduction concerned with defining emotional disturbance and the roles teachers and disturbed children play. Starting with Chapter 3, we become "deed oriented," sharing an approach for conceptualizing emotionally disturbed behavior, functionally describing emotionally disturbed children, and finally presenting a step-by-step procedure for writing an Individual Education Program for any exceptional child. We have chosen not to confine ourselves only to emotionally disturbed children since emotional and behavioral problems cut across exceptionalities so frequently. More and more we should be talking about *any* child whose behavior, or lack of it, is standing in the way of his or her receiving an effective education. The remaining chapters present an update of educational activities and programs presented in the first edition. We close with a chapter on working with parents, an area of somewhat minor consequence twelve years ago but, fortunately, of vital concern today.

Our orientation is still basically behavioral-educational, but we have replaced the concept of the "engineering" of success with that of the "orchestration" of success. We have also broadened our philosophy to include more concern with disturbed children's attitudes, feelings, and self-concepts.

This second edition represents the culmination of over fourteen years of collaboration between the authors; the University of California, Los Angeles; and the Santa Monica Unified School District. We gratefully acknowledge the contributions made by the staff and students in both settings. Our thanks also to Steve McAdam for his original and provocative artwork which seems particularly fitting for a field that sometimes takes itself a bit too seriously. Finally, we are particularly appreciative of the contributions made by our editorial assistants, Carol Reynard and Scott Tomblin, and of Mary Hunt who managed and prepared the entire manuscript.

F. M. H.

F. D. T.

The Emotionally Disturbed Child in the Classroom

chapter 1

What Is Emotional Disturbance?

I t was the school lunch period. The door to the teachers' lounge opened quickly and slammed shut. The three teachers sitting around the table looked up. They saw Sue Billings, a third grade teacher, who appeared very upset. She stood by the door a moment, shaking her head slowly. Then she walked over to the wall rack where her coffee cup hung with those for each of the teachers at the Woodside Elementary School.

Margaret Wilson, a fourth grade teacher, looked at the two teachers sitting with her at the table—Betty Simpson, who teaches kindergarten, and Bill Edwards, a teacher at the sixth grade level. She raised her eyebrows slightly in a questioning manner. Sue Billings filled her cup with coffee from a large urn and slowly sat down at the table with the others.

"I've had it," she said grimly. "Either Bobby Myron goes or I do."

Betty Simpson knew the name. She had had Bobby in kindergarten. He was a handful even then—very active, easily distracted, and constantly disrupting the class. While Bobby seemed quite bright, his lack of attention had seriously interfered with his learning. Bobby had somehow made it through the first and second grades, but not without earning a school-wide reputation as a learning and behavior problem.

"What's happened this time?" Betty Simpson asked.

Sue Billings shook her head. "He's got to go, that's all there is to it." Then, settling back in her chair, she described a morning of Bobby Myron's exploits. Early in the morning he had hidden in the supply cabinet leaving an entire shelf of writing and drawing paper in rumpled disarray. Then he took Mary Riley's lunch money, punching her in the stomach when she threatened to tell the teacher.

"Mary Riley is such a sweet girl and probably my best student," said Sue Billings. "She was very upset."

Then during the morning Bobby was constantly out of his seat, swearing loudly each time he was reprimanded.

"He has a filthy mouth," said Sue Billings. "And it's beginning to influence the other children."

Finally, Bobby was sent to the principal's office for the remainder of the morning. However, he returned to go to lunch with the class. Sue Billings thought about making him stay in the classroom until she took the other children to the cafeteria, but he promised to be good so she put him at the end of the line in front of her.

Things went all right with only minimal pushing and shoving on Bobby's part until the class reached the entrance to the cafeteria. It was at this time that he attained his crowning achievement of the morning.

Sue Billings' voice quavered, and her face reddened with anger as she described it.

"Suddenly, Bobby Myron pulled away from me and pushed his way to the front of the line shouting he was going to be first. I was determined he was not going to get away with this, and I chased after him."

Things went from bad to worse as Sue Billings tried to catch Bobby.

He darted across the middle of the cafeteria where many children were seated at tables eating their lunches. When he saw his teacher closing in on him, Bobby jumped up on one of the tables and ran down the middle of it.

"It was the first grade table," said Sue Billings, "and he managed to step into almost every child's tray as he ran. You should have seen those poor frightened children. There was spilled milk and spaghetti everywhere."

With the entire cafeteria in an uproar by now, Bobby disappeared out the door and onto the playground.

Bill Edwards started to smile but suppressed it when he saw how genuinely upset Sue Billings was about the incident. As far as he was concerned all eight-year-old Bobby needed was a firm hand. The boy had learned how to get his teacher's goat, and Sue Billings' overreaction to his misbehavior was only making things worse. He had seen boys like Bobby grow out of their problems by the time they reached sixth grade. With proper handling, there was every reason to believe Bobby would do the same. Margaret Wilson shared Bill Edwards' appraisal of the situation; Betty Simpson remembered her days with Bobby and felt he was really an emotionally disturbed child who probably should be referred to a psychologist.

"He is a mean, destructive little boy," Sue Billings concluded, "and I intend to see he is taken out of my class at once. He should be receiving some sort of psychological treatment."

Without saying anything else, she got up from the table, rinsed out her coffee cup, and left the teachers' lounge.

"Poor Sue," said Margaret Wilson. "Bobby Myron has really gotten through to her this time."

The three teachers chatted for a while about Bobby and the problems he had caused in the school. Sue Billings seemed to be having more difficulty with him than any of his earlier teachers. Bill Edwards, Margaret Wilson, and Betty Simpson each had their own way of viewing children like Bobby who manifest behavior problems in the classroom, and each of them had their own way of dealing with such problems. They were much more in agreement regarding the problems caused by Martin Greenwood, a six-year-old, autistic boy who was recently enrolled in the school district's special education program for autistic children which had been placed at the Woodside School.

"Have you seen what those teachers in the autistic program have to deal with?" asked Margaret Wilson. "Imagine having a child like Martin Greenwood in your classroom."

"When he has a tantrum, you can hear it all over the school," said Betty Simpson. "I didn't believe a child that age could scream so loudly."

"I often see him walking into the playground from the school bus," said Bill Edwards. "He has to be physically restrained or he runs away. And he's constantly flapping his hands in front of his face and rolling his head from side to side."

"Give me Bobby Myron any day," said Margaret Wilson.

The other two teachers smiled and nodded in agreement.

This brief interlude in the teachers' lounge of the Woodside School serves to introduce us to some of the issues involved in the field of educating emotionally disturbed children.

One of the issues is deciding with some degree of certainty whether or not a child like Bobby Myron qualifies for the label *emotionally disturbed* or *behaviorally disordered*. With Martin Greenwood, the decision might be clear-cut due to the severity of his problems. But Bobby Myron's behavior is not as severe or predictable. Let's consider some of the reasons why classifying children like Bobby Myron is often difficult.

Teachers' Ranges of Tolerance

We all have preferences for the type of people with whom we enjoy working, and we differ with respect to our abilities for working effectively with certain types of individuals. Teachers often have definite preferences for the types of children they like to teach. They also differ in their abilities for dealing with the individual differences they encounter in teaching. These preferences and abilities can be conceived of as constituting two ranges of tolerance. The first range of tolerance relates to behavioral differences found among children in school. There was no question that "sweet" Mary Riley fit well within Sue Billings' range of tolerance for behavioral differences and that "mean" Bobby Myron clearly fell outside. Based on her earlier experiences with Bobby, Betty Simpson may have had a similar range of tolerance.

Bill Edwards and Margaret Wilson viewed Bobby quite differently. He appeared to fit within their ranges of tolerance for behavioral differences. However, it is likely we could describe children who would not be acceptable to them. Perhaps a "whiny" and dependent child would fall outside their ranges of tolerance. Or perhaps a child who cheated on tests would not be tolerated.

Martin Greenwood, the autistic child given to screaming and tantrums, may fall outside the ranges of tolerance for behavioral difference for all of the teachers in our example. Such a child may definitely need to be taught by a specially trained teacher who has developed a range of tolerance for accepting, understanding, and working with severely disturbed children.

The second range of tolerance concerns the differences in academic achievement level found among children in every classroom. While the designation *fifth grade* may communicate a homogeneity of academic functioning levels, this is very seldom the case. In a classroom at the "fifth grade" level, children will be found functioning in reading anywhere from a first or second grade level to an eighth or ninth grade level. Among those functioning at the lowest levels will often be children like Bobby Myron who also have behavior problems.

In our experience, teachers' ranges of tolerance for academic differences among their children are usually much broader than those for behavioral differences. If a child fits the teacher's range of tolerance for behavioral difference, he or she may be maintained in the classroom even though exhibiting serious academic problems. In a study concerned with why teachers differentially referred mildly retarded students with similar IQ's for special education assistance (Mercer, 1971), it was found that academic functioning level *was not* a determining factor. Teachers tended to maintain mildly retarded children in their regular classrooms if they were not behavior problems even though they functioned on a low academic level.

In trying to understand why similar behavior disorders are perceived differentially by teachers, and why some teachers have narrower ranges of tolerance for individual differences than others, we need to consider the *frequency of occurrence* of problem behaviors, their *degree of severity,* their *duration,* and their *clustering.*

Frequency of Occurrence

The child who has an occasional "bad" Monday morning or Friday afternoon in the classroom is perceived quite differently from the child who can be counted on to routinely disrupt the class. In the former case, the teacher may decide "it just wasn't one of his better days"; in the latter case, the cumulative effect of disruptive behavior may cause the teacher to react with, "Oh no, here he goes again!" Bobby Myron could be counted on to be a rather consistent behavior problem. Yet, the frequency of his misbehavior was reacted to differently by the teachers in our example. On the one hand, this frequency was viewed by Sue Billings and Betty Simpson as indicative of a serious emotional problem that required psychological treatment. If Bobby only had an occasional outburst, perhaps their reaction would be quite different. On the other hand, Bill Edwards and Margaret Wilson tended to view the frequency of Bobby's misbehavior as resulting from poor handling by his teacher. They were not as quick to diagnose Bobby as emotionally disturbed.

Thus, whether or not a given child's problem behavior falls within a given teacher's range of tolerance for behavioral differences depends in part on how frequently the behavior occurs and how the teacher reacts to that frequency. With respect to Martin Greenwood, his incessant self-stimulating behavior and efforts to run away would probably guarantee him a place outside all four teachers' ranges of tolerance.

Degree of Severity

Calling Mary Riley a "tattletale" or even using more unacceptable language when she threatened to tell the teacher that he took her lunch money, would have been a less severe act on Bobby Myron's part than punching her in the stomach. Physical aggression constitutes a particularly upsetting problem behavior for most teachers. One study concerned with singling out the special competencies needed by teachers of disturbed children over and above those needed by regular classroom teachers found only two competencies that were seen as unique for the special teachers: (1) "the ability to accept pupils who are violent" and (2) "experience on a clinical team with psychiatrists, psychologists, and social workers" (Dorward, 1963). Displays of physical aggression may place a child outside the range of tolerance for most regular classroom teachers, particularly if that aggression is directed toward the teacher. At moments like that, something is very seriously wrong with the teacher-pupil relationship and the effectiveness of the classroom program.

Yet there will be teachers like Bill Edwards who may not be threatened by such aggression and who may feel competent in handling outbursts like the one involving Bobby Myron. But he might be unique with respect to teachers in general. It is interesting how some teachers will immediately react to physically aggressive behavior but largely ignore severely withdrawn behavior. We can recall a fifth grade boy in a regular classroom who sat at his desk for most of the day with his coat pulled up over his head so that he could hide from the class. The teacher considered him a nice but shy boy and would not have necessarily referred him for help if the school psychologist had not happened to learn of the boy and his behavior.

Again, the bizarreness of Martin Greenwood's behavior, the severity of his tantrums, and the loudness of his screams would probably guarantee his placement outside most regular teachers' ranges of tolerance for behavioral differences.

Duration

Once a given problem behavior occurs, how long it continues is also a determining factor regarding whether it falls within a teacher's range of tolerance. The child who is a pencil or foot tapper may go unnoticed if the tapping is relatively brief. But if it goes on for long periods of time, sooner or later it will bring a reaction from someone, probably the teacher. A playful poke or two is part of the normal give and take of social interaction in the classroom, but repetitive and continuous poking is another matter. Name calling or teasing are additional examples.

In the next chapter we will review approaches for dealing with problem behaviors. One approach is to simply ignore a problem behavior, hoping the child will decrease and stop it because nobody pays any attention. However well this is supposed to work theoretically, when the duration of the behavior reaches a certain point the teacher can no longer afford to ignore it because of its possible contagious effect on the rest of the class.

Clustering

Clustering refers to the exhibition of two or more types of problem behaviors by a child thereby increasing the probability that the child's behavior will exceed the teacher's range of tolerance. In the case of Bobby Myron, we saw destruction of school supplies, stealing, physical aggression, defiance of the teacher, obscene language, and disregard for the rights and property of others all rolled into one infamous morning. Any one of these problems may have been enough to exceed Sue Billings' range of tolerance, but in combination there was no question about it.

Examples of the clustering of problem behaviors, where collectively several such behaviors exceed the teacher's range of tolerance, have been numerous in our experience. One very talented teacher with whom we worked tolerated a nine-year-old boy in her remedial classroom even though he had serious learning problems, got into fights frequently, was often late, and used profanity. In fact, she seemed to consider him a challenge. However, one day he became sexually provocative using gestures and language that completely disrupted the class. The teacher's reaction was very much like that of Sue Billings in our earlier example. Sexual misconduct tipped the scale and sent the boy far out of this teacher's range of tolerance, whereas up to that time he had been acceptable. As a result, the teacher refused to work with him any longer and demanded that he be removed from her class.

In the case of severely disturbed children like Martin Greenwood, the clustering of their problem behaviors makes them difficult pupils to teach. Self-care and toileting skills may be lacking, little or no communicative speech may be present, they may actively seek to distance themselves from others, and they may engage in tantrums and self-stimulating behavior that seriously interfere with attempts to teach them.

What is emotional disturbance? Up to this point we have defined it largely with reference to the range of tolerance of the teacher which in turn is determined by the frequency, degree of severity, duration, and clustering of the child's behavior. And we have used such terms as *problem behavior, behavior disorders,* and *emotional disturbance* interchangeably. Before continuing our discussion, let's reflect on these terms and what they mean.

Emotional Disturbance Versus Behavior Disorders

One of the first special classes for the type of children we are concerned with in this book was set up in New Haven, Connecticut in 1871 (Kauffman, 1977). The students were "truant, disobedient, and insubordinate." In 1874, New York City initiated a special class for "unruly or truant boys" (Wallin, 1955). Thus, the early emphasis in labeling children who presented behavior problems in school was on "breaking the rules" and "nonconformity." Perusal of the *Review of Educational Research* published by the American Educational Research Association with periodic issues devoted to research on exceptional children reveals some interesting trends in labeling. From 1941 to 1969, the titles of the chapters devoted to children with behavior or emotional problems were as follows:

1941   Socially maladjusted

1944   Socially maladjusted

1953   Socially maladjusted

1959   Emotional factors and academic achievement

1963   Emotionally and socially handicapped

1966   Emotionally and socially handicapped

1969   Behavior disorders

While use of the term, *emotional disturbance,* has been traced back fifty (Despert, 1965) to seventy-five years (Reinert, 1976), the titles of these research reviews suggest a shift in emphasis in education from social maladjustment, to emotional factors, and finally to behavior disorders. The shift to emotional disturbance no doubt reflects the influence of Freudian psychology in the United States in the 1940s and 1950s. We will discuss this influence and some of the individuals who applied psychoanalytic principles to education in a later section. The emphasis on behavior disorders in the late 1960s would appear to be the direct result of the impact of behavior modification approaches on special education during that decade. We will be discussing what such shifts in emphasis actually mean educationally later, but at this point let's examine the advantages of the two terms, *emotional disturbance* and *behavior disorders.*

Emotional Disturbance

1. The term is still in common use in special education literature particularly with reference to the severely disturbed.

2. The term is in common use in school programs for children with behavior problems.

3. Public Law 94–142, the Education for All the Handicapped Act of

1975, does not address itself to the needs of children with behavior disorders but rather to "seriously emotionally disturbed children." Thus, it would appear that children must qualify for this label rather than that of *behavior disordered* to be covered by the law. In a later section, we will present the definition of seriously emotionally disturbed that appears in PL 94–142. In addition, the Bureau for Education of the Handicapped in the United States Office of Education reports incidence or prevalence estimates for "emotionally disturbed children."

Behavior Disorders
1. The term has more practical usefulness in special education. Teachers can do something directly about disordered behavior that they cannot do about disturbed emotions.

2. The term probably does not constitute as ominous a label as *emotional disturbance,* and the latter term may be more socially harmful to the child.

3. Many of the research studies being done in special education that are concerned with children with behavior problems reflect a behavioral orientation and define their subject populations from a behavior disordered point of view.

What appears to be happening in the field of special education today is children like Bobby Myron are more apt to be described as having a "behavior disorder," while severely handicapped children like Martin Greenwood are being considered "severely emotionally disturbed." However, we will not make this distinction in this book, instead we'll consider the terms interchangeable and use *disturbed child* as a general reference. Actually, selection of one or the other of the terms is really an academic issue. It is the intent of this book to develop the idea that only one term is necessary to describe Bobby and Martin for educational purposes. That term is *learner,* and it applies with equal relevance to all normal and exceptional individuals. As teachers, the most important information we need relates to what the child is ready to learn, not reasons why he or she may encounter difficulties in learning based on concepts of emotional disturbance or behavior disorders. This establishes the orientation of this book as behavioral-educational. We will consider contrasting orientations in Chapter 4 and develop the concept of each and every child as first and foremost a learner ready at all times to learn something and of each and every teacher as an "orchestrator of success."

In our initial efforts to address the question, "What is emotional disturbance," we have discussed a number of issues that relate to who gets labeled emotionally disturbed and why. At this point, let's back up and consider how and when emotions develop and how they become disturbed according to several points of view.

How and When Do Emotions Develop?

What accounts for children developing fears, becoming angry, or displaying affection? What is the source of these emotions? Are we born with them or do they develop during our early life? Concern with the source of emotional behavior can be traced back to Hippocrates during the fourth and fifth centuries B.C. (Coleman, 1972). According to that great Greek physician, humans develop mental illness as a direct result of the imbalance of four basic bodily humors—blood, black bile, yellow bile, and phlegm.

> Depravement of the brain arises from phlegm and bile; those mad from phlegm are quiet, depressed, and oblivious; those from bile excited, noisy, and mischievous.

Emotions as Innate

In the twentieth century, John Watson, the so-called father of behaviorism, concluded that the newborn infant was born with three primary emotions: love, fear, and anger. These could be elicited at birth by means of specific environmental stimuli (Thompson, 1952). It was thought that the newborn expressed the innate emotion of love as the result of gentle stroking of the body. The newborn expressed the emotion of fear at the sound of a loud noise nearby or when experiencing a sudden loss of support (e.g., being dropped a short distance and then caught). Finally, the newborn expressed anger when physically restrained by tight clothing that restricted movement. Watson considered all other emotional responses to be built through the conditioning process on these three primary emotions.

Unfortunately, it was difficult to distinguish between these three emotional states unless one observed the actual stimuli utilized to elicit them. One investigator took movies of two infants, one three days old and the other approximately six days old, who were under conditions of hunger, who were dropped two to three feet and caught, who had their heads restrained, and who were pricked with a needle on the cheek (Sherman, 1927). Three versions of the movies were shown to nurses, medical students, and undergraduate and graduate students in psychology. In one version the source of eliciting stimuli was shown; in the second version this source was deleted; and in the third version the various eliciting stimuli were transposed. When the first version was shown there was considerable agreement regarding the emotion being displayed, but when versions two and three were shown there was very little agreement.

As a result of this and other studies, the idea that an innate emotional repertoire is present at birth waiting to be expressed as very specific emotions came to be considered untenable. Watson was accused of naive anthropomorphism, that is attributing specific emotional characteristics to newborn infants on the basis of adult beliefs regarding emotions rather

than according to scientific evidence. The emotion of love, supposedly produced by stroking the infant's body, is today seen as a state of homeostasis or quiescence. The so-called fear response elicited by loud noises or loss of support has come to be recognized as the Moro or startle reflex. And the response of anger thought to be elicited by restraint is a generalized response produced in infants by any intense stimulus.

Emotions as Developmentally Acquired

Once the idea that we are born with clearly differentiated emotions was discarded, child psychologists turned to a developmental explanation. That is, as is the case with all other aspects of a child's growth, emotions develop as the result of the ongoing interaction between heredity and environmental experience. While at birth we do not arrive with differentiated emotions, we do arrive with the potential for developing these emotions.

It was Bridges in 1932 who advanced the idea that specific emotions evolve out of an undifferentiated state of excitement that characterizes the infant's reaction to various stimuli at birth (Bridges, 1932). This idea retains validity today and has received further support although Bridges' undifferentiated state of excitement is now seen as consisting of undifferentiated distress and nondistress states (Sroufe & Mitchell, 1977). From a

developmental perspective, there should be a logical and orderly process in the unfolding of later emotions from these early undifferentiated distress and nondistress states. According to Sroufe and Mitchell (1977), the developmental literature suggests certain ages at which specific emotional reactions are common. However, it does not specify the age of first appearance or peak occurrence. With these qualifications in mind, let's consider the development of some basic human emotions during the first year of life:

Pleasure–Joy

0 months	Endogenous smile (not in response to external stimuli)
1 month	Turning toward
3 months	Pleasure
4–5 months	Delight and active laughter
7 months	Joy
12 months	Elation

Wariness–Fear

0 months	Startle, pain
4–5 months	Wariness
9 months	Fear (stranger aversion)
12 months	Anxiety, immediate fear

Rage–Anger

0 months	Distress due to covering of the face, physical restraint, extreme discomfort
3 months	Rage (as the result of disappointment)
7 months	Anger
12 months	Angry mood, petulance

Thus, by age one, children are emotional beings with the potential for common patterns of expression in relation to interacting with the environ-

ment around them. But not all children display the same patterns of emotional expression. Indeed, there are wide individual differences with respect to the frequency and degree to which such emotions as fear and anger are expressed.

Emotions as Influenced by Temperament

One area of study in developmental psychology that has important implications for our understanding individual differences in emotionality concerns temperament or behavioral style. *Temperament* is not synonymous with *emotion.* Temperament refers to such attributes as the quickness with which children move; the ease with which they approach a new physical environment, social situation, or task; the intensity and character of their mood expression; and the effort required by others to distract them when they are involved and absorbed in an activity (Thomas & Chess, 1977).

Temperament is a phenomenological term and does not imply a specific etiology or immutability. Like any individual human characteristic such as height, weight, or intellectual skill, its expression and even its nature are

influenced by environmental factors as the developmental process proceeds.

Thomas, Chess, and Birch (1969) have conducted longitudinal research studies which have identified nine categories and three constellations of temperament. The emergence of studies of temperament in recent years has been in reaction to the trend from the 1920s through the 1950s that assumed the child's environment was almost totally responsible for eventual personality development. While differences in temperament cannot be considered genetically determined characteristics, their appearance in the very early days and weeks of life suggests that they are not simply the result of environmental experience and child-rearing practices. Temperamental individuality is considered well established by the time the infant is two to three months old (Thomas & Chess, 1977).

The nine categories of temperament and their definitions are as follows:

1. *Activity Level*. The level of motor activity the child displays during bathing, eating, playing, dressing, and handling, as well as sleep-wake patterns and reaching, crawling, and walking behavior.

2. *Rhythmicity (Regularity)*. The predictability and/or unpredictability of sleeping, hunger, feeding patterns, elimination schedule, etc.

3. *Approach or Withdrawal*. How the child reacts to a new stimulus such as a new food, toy, or person.

4. *Adaptability*. This goes beyond initial approach and withdrawal and is concerned with the ease with which the child modifies behavior in desired directions.

5. *Threshold of Responsiveness*. The intensity level that is necessary to elicit a particular response from the child regardless of the sensory modality (e.g., visual, auditory).

6. *Intensity of Reaction*. The child's energy level in responding regardless of the quality or direction of the response.

7. *Quality of Mood*. The amount of the child's pleasant and friendly behavior compared with unpleasant and unfriendly behavior.

8. *Distractibility*. How extraneous environmental stimuli interfere with or alter the direction of the child's behavior.

9. *Attention Span and Persistence*. The length of time the child pursues a particular activity and how persistent the child is in continuing an activity in the face of obstacles to maintenance of the activity.

See page 24 for a description of the three constellations of temperament.

Emotions as Determined by the Id

In addition to a developmental approach to emotions and one concerned with differences in temperament found among young children, psychodynamic theory offers an explanation regarding the source of human emotion (Freud, 1949; Erikson, 1963). Psychodynamic theory has undergone and continues to undergo continuous revision since Sigmund Freud first published his psychoanalytic papers in the 1890s. The theory is psychodynamic in that it focuses on the "workings" of the mind and postulates three mental structures which underlie all mental activity: the *id*, *ego*, and *superego*.

The *id*, the most primitive of the three structures, is the source of human emotions and is thought to determine human personality development. The id is the only structure present at birth and is the reservoir for two basic instinctual drives: *libido*, a fixed quantity of sexual energy available to the individual from birth onward, and *aggression*. These drives underlie emotional behavior expressed by the child. Because of its close connection with these instinctual drives, the id contains powerful forces and energies and is devoted to the pleasure principle (the seeking of pleasure and the avoiding of pain). The mental representatives of the instinctual life of a child are in the form of unconscious wishes, urges, and feeling states. Such unconscious activity is made known in fantasy life, dream life, symptoms, inhibitions, slips of the tongue, mistakes, and impulses.

The other two mental structures are the *ego* and the *superego*. The ego acts as an arbitrator between the child's inner needs and wishes found in the id and the external demands of the environment. It is the center of adaptation and learning. The ego judges situations according to circumstances. It gathers and weighs data. Early Freudian theory emphasized the power and strength of the id, while later psychodynamic theory has emphasized the importance and strength of the ego.

The superego is a specialized part of the ego containing the conscience and the ego ideal, the construct concerned with how we measure our own individual worth. The conscience is the policymaker of the mind; it formulates permissible action from a moral viewpoint and is the source of the "Thou shalts" and "Thou shalt nots." The superego continues to grow and develop throughout life reflecting expectations of the key individuals and institutions in a person's life beginning with mother and then moving to the family, the peer group, the school, and the church among other sources of influence.

The id, ego, and superego make up a psychodynamic system which Freud called "the psychic apparatus." Their interrelationships are described in the following simplified example:

> On a dark night one walks down a street passing a jewelry store. No one is around. In the window showcase is a beautiful diamond ring. The id says: "I want that diamond. I want it because I love myself, because it would make me beautiful and would thus make other people love me, because I am angry at others having what I have not, and because I am uncomfortable under the tension of wanting what I do not have." The superego says arbitrarily, "No, you can't break the window and take it." The ego solves the impasse by advising. "But you shall have it if you will save your money until you can buy it." (Josselyn, 1948, p. 24).

Personality development actually occurs as the child encounters a series of psychosexual stages. Each of these involves a locus for pleasurable activities and certain tasks and experiences the child must successfully deal with if later problems are to be avoided. The first of these is an *oral* stage. During this stage, the child's initial contact with the environment is through the feeding process, early interpersonal relationships are initiated, and basic attitudes such as trust versus mistrust are established.

Next, the child moves to an *anal* stage. This stage centers on the elimination processes, and confrontation with demands for control and adher-

ence to routine occurs. This stage may result in the child developing feelings of autonomy or feelings of shame and doubt.

The *phallic* stage begins as the child becomes increasingly interested in the feelings of pleasure associated with the genital region of the body and with fantasies about his or her parents. The major task of this stage involves resolving the Oedipal conflict. This conflict begins when the child seeks to establish an affectionate relationship with the opposite-sexed parent and *unconsciously* wishes to have exclusive possession of that parent. There is also fear of retaliation from the parent of the same sex. Resolution of this conflict is usually accomplished through the child's identification with the like-sexed parent. Vicarious gratification in relation to this wish for possession of the opposite-sexed parent is thus achieved. At this time the child's own identity becomes established. In addition, the superego crystalizes as the child, through the process of identification, takes the values of the parents and applies them to himself or herself sometimes in a very strict fashion.

The next stage of development, called *latency,* usually covers the time the child is in elementary school. During this period, the Oedipal wishes are repressed and the child's energies are channeled into learning. Interests are typically directed toward the peer group, and teachers become substitutes for parents.

As the child moves into adolescence and further shifts his or her interests away from the family and toward the process of selecting an appropriate partner for life, the *genital* stage of psychosexual development occurs. It is during this time that all previous identities become consolidated. Instinctual pressures from the id become greater, but they are usually met with expanding ego and superego capacities.

This has been only a brief and simplified summary of psychodynamic theory. More complete accounts may be found elsewhere (Munroe, 1955; Rezmierski & Kotre, 1974).

To sum up the theories of where emotions originate that have been discussed here, within a developmental framework, we have described children's emotions as emanating in a more or less orderly sequence from undifferentiated distress and nondistress states. By the end of the first year of life, most children have evidenced the emotions of pleasure-joy, fear, and anger. Studies of individual differences with respect to temperament suggest that by two to three months of age, many children manifest unique activity and adjustment patterns that can affect the nature and degree of their emotional expression. According to psychodynamic theory, human emotions develop from two basic instinctual drives, libido and aggression, which are present at birth. Positive and negative aspects of emotional behavior are determined by our successes and failures in adjusting to the demands of a series of psychosexual stages in early childhood.

With this introduction to some possible origins of human emotions, let's now turn to the next logical question and consider "How do emotions become disturbed?"

How Do Emotions Become Disturbed?

As we saw earlier, the year-old child is an emotional being with discernible patterns of expression and behavior that can be reliably labeled as variations of pleasure-joy, fear, and anger (Sroufe & Mitchell, 1977). What happens to these patterns in the second year of life and beyond? We all know from our own experiences that great variability exists among children. Some are more fearful than others, some are more readily given to angry outbursts, and some are more loving and pleasant to be with.

Developmental Factors

To underscore this common observation, let's review a longitudinal study conducted by the Institute of Child Welfare at the University of California (Macfarlane, Allen, & Honzik, 1955). This study focused on the development of behavior problems among children from twenty-one months to fourteen years of age. Children in the study were chosen by a chance drawing from a birth certificate registry. They were not selected because of any high risk condition surrounding their births or any other problems they might have presented. As a result they were representative of typical children in their community.

Beginning at age twenty-one months, the children's mothers visited

the institute and were questioned regarding the types of problems the children showed. Exactly what constituted a problem had been determined in advance by the investigators, and these criteria were followed rigorously during all subsequent visits made by the mothers. The most striking finding when reviewing the problems these children displayed over the childhood years and into adolescence was their persistence, variety, and magnitude. For these were "normal" children, not emotionally disturbed children, although among their randomly selected population we would expect a certain percent to eventually develop problems that might later cause them to be labeled *disturbed*. But we would never expect such large percentages! Table 1–1 illustrates these findings for several behavior problems reported in the study.

Table 1–1. Percentages of children with selected problem behaviors from infancy to adolescence.

Problem	Sex	Age in Years						
		1¾	4	6	8	10	12	14
Specific fears	Boys	30%	47%	38%	34%	22%	17%	6%
	Girls	33%	45%	41%	35%	26%	21%	17%
Oversensitiveness	Boys	9%	42%	32%	50%	59%	39%	17%
	Girls	18%	51%	53%	49%	38%	48%	52%
Temper tantrums	Boys	59%	53%	59%	53%	44%	39%	22%
	Girls	43%	47%	51%	28%	32%	29%	9%
Destructiveness	Boys	14%	20%	24%	11%	11%	4%	0%
	Girls	2%	12%	8%	5%	6%	2%	0%

Data taken from Macfarlane, Allen, & Honzik, 1955.

From the percentages reported in this study, over one third of both boys and girls could be described as *fearful* between ages four and eight. The label *oversensitive* would apply to from one third to one half of all of the children from ages four to twelve. With only two exceptions, the same percentages of boys and girls had temper tantrums from ages 1¾ years to twelve years. Almost one fourth of the boys could be called *destructive* between ages four and eight; far fewer girls could be eligible for such a label.

What can we conclude from these findings? Were all of these children described by their mothers as fearful, oversensitive, given to tantrums, or destructively emotionally disturbed? Most certainly not. The following conclusions will help us understand why not.

1. Emotionally disturbed children do not have a monopoly on problem behaviors.

2. Problem behaviors considered indicative of emotional disturbance are commonly found among most normal children.

3. The problem behaviors manifested by normal children are not generally different in kind from those shown by disturbed children but are different in frequency of occurrence, degree of severity, duration, and clustering.

In attempts to explain why such large numbers of boys and girls developed problem behaviors and why undoubtedly some of them ended up being labeled *emotionally disturbed,* we would have to examine their family, social, school, and community experiences as well as their nutrition, health care, and physical condition over the years covered in the study. Their emotions became "disturbed" because of stress, conflicts, and problems in one or more of these areas during the course of growing up. Fortunately for most of the children, the disturbances were temporary. But it is for those for whom the problem behaviors were frequent, severe, of long duration, and clustered that this text is being written.

Temperamental Factors

Some of the children in the Macfarlane et al. study were no doubt evidencing differences in temperament that were present at birth and that contributed to the stress, conflicts, and problems experienced. The work of Thomas, Chess, and Birch (1969) cited earlier has revealed that patterns of temperament are commonly found among children in early life. The original sample of children studied by these investigators was collected from 1956 to 1962 and consisted of 141 children who are still being followed. These children provided the behavioral data that yielded three temperamental constellations of functional significance. These three constellations were designated: (1) the easy child, (2) the difficult child, and (3) the slow-to-warm-up child.

The Easy Child

These children are characterized by many positive qualities such as regularity, positive approach to new stimuli, good adaptability to change, and mild to moderately intense moods which are mostly positive. Among these children, sleeping and feeding schedules are quickly developed, new foods easily accepted, strangers approached with smiles, school adjustment causes little difficulty, frustration produces little fuss, and rules of new games are accepted with little trouble. These children are usually a joy to parents and teachers. They made up about 40 percent of the original sample.

The Difficult Child

Children in this group are characterized by many negative qualities such as irregularities in biological functions, withdrawal from new stimuli, poor adaptability to change, and intense moods which are frequently negative. They have irregular sleeping and feeding schedules; accept new foods slowly; require prolonged adjustment periods to new routines, people, or situations; and are given to frequent loud periods of crying. Frustration typically produces a violent tantrum. This group of children was referred to as "mother killers" by the more informal of the researchers. Approximately 10 percent of the sample were classified as difficult children.

The Slow-to-Warm-Up Child

Still another type of child that emerged from the studies is characterized by a combination of negative responses of mild intensity to new stimuli and slow adaptability even after repeated contact. This child evidences both mildly positive and mildly negative reactions and has less of a tendency to irregularity of biological

functions than the difficult child. While initially mildly negative to the bath, a new food, a stranger, a new place, or a new school situation, if given enough time to reexperience new situations without pressure, such a child gradually comes to show quiet and positive interest and involvement. The slow-to-warm-up child made up about 15 percent of the sample.

Altogether, about 65 percent of the 141 children could be classified into one of these three temperamental constellations. Some 35 percent of the children in the study did not fit into one of these three temperamental groups since they demonstrated variable and different combinations of temperamental traits.

Of particular interest to our discussion is the number of children in this study who developed behavior disorders during the early childhood years and how development of a behavior disorder related to temperamental characteristics. Thirty-nine percent of the total sample were identified as having a behavior disorder. This figure is the approximate rate found in other prevalence studies (Glidewell & Swallow, 1968) and is similar to the percentages of boys and girls who had certain adjustment problems in the Macfarlane et al. study cited earlier. The investigators divided the children with behavior disorders into "active" and "passive" types. The active group was characterized by temper tantrums and aggressive behavior while those in the passive group were largely nonparticipants standing on the sidelines and not joining group activities.

Both groups were compared with normal children who did not evidence behavior disorders in order to discern the unique temperamental characteristics of the behavior disordered group. The active group was found to differ significantly in excessive frequency of high activity, irregularity, low-threshold, nonadaptability, intensity, persistence, and distractibility. The passive group differed significantly in mood, activity level, approach/withdrawal, and persistence. Both the active and passive groups demonstrated differences in the direction of the difficult child constellation. But while 70 percent of the difficult children developed behavior disorders, 30 percent did not. It appeared that the development of a behavior disorder by a difficult child was related to parents who were inconsistent, impatient, or pressuring in their approach. Demands for conformity to rules imposed by the family, the school, and the peer group were particularly stressful for them.

Easy children adapted more readily to a wide range of parental attitudes and practices, but they could also experience excessively stressful situations that could lead to behavior disorders. They did, however, develop fewer such disorders in proportion to their representation in the total sample. One source of stress for easy children was found to be conflicts between expectations in the home and those in the peer group. For example, one very easy child became upset and was reduced to tears when the polite, formal manner he had learned at home only earned him ridicule and scapegoating among his more informal friends.

For slow-to-warm-up children, rigid demands for quick adaptation to new situations appeared to create considerable stress.

Overall, the investigation did not find any given pattern of temperament as such that always resulted in the development of a behavior disorder. This underscores the fact that temperament, alone, whatever its source, cannot be viewed as solely responsible for the development of behavior problems. It is always the interaction between the child's temperamental uniqueness and the uniqueness of his or her environment that must be considered.

An interesting illustration of this emerged in a comparison of middle-class, New York families and Puerto Rican families living in East Harlem (Thomas & Chess, 1977). When a sample of children drawn from both backgrounds was compared, it was found that by age nine, 31 percent of the middle-class children were diagnosed as having behavior problems, while only 10 percent of the Puerto Rican children were so diagnosed. When the two types of family environments were examined, it was found that the middle-class parents became much more alarmed at early behavioral difficulties, while the Puerto Rican parents were more relaxed, often saying: "He's a baby. He'll outgrow it." The middle-class parents pressed for early mastery of skills such as those associated with educational toys. The Puerto Rican parents, on the other hand, saw toys as a source of amusement and were not particularly concerned with mastery of skills ("If I do it for him, I get it done faster."). After age nine, the incidence of behavior problems among the middle-class children dropped considerably. There were no comparable follow-up data for the Puerto Rican children, but the investigators suspected they might develop more behavior problems as the result of increasing pressures at home and in school.

The work of Thomas, Chess, and Birch has clearly established temperamental uniqueness as an important variable in the development of behavior disorders. But as we attempt to explain why such large percentages of so-called normal children developed adjustment problems in the Macfarlane et al. study, we must look beyond single variables. Classification as a difficult child is not enough to guarantee the development of a behavior disorder. The temperament of the child is only a partial determiner. It is the interaction between this temperament and the "temperaments" of the family climate, the peer group, and other environmental agents with their sources of aggravation and support that is responsible.

Biological Factors

In addition to an interest in the possible relationship between temperamental uniqueness and the development of behavior disorders, biological factors such as genetic misfortune, brain damage, malnutrition, and disease have been studied. Schizophrenia appears to have a definite inherited component. If an identical twin has schizophrenia, some studies have reported that the chances are as high as 85 percent that the other twin will become schizophrenic (Meehl, 1969). This expectancy rate is four times higher than the rate for fraternal twins (Buss, 1966). Using a constitutional-predispositional explanation, schizophrenic children have been viewed as predisposed by heredity to develop the disorder; but some environmental stimulus, either physical or psychosocial, is required to activate it (Rosenthal, 1963). Studies of schizophrenic children have revealed evidence of irregularities in many biological processes such as pulse, temperature control, sleep patterns, and respiratory and elimination functions (Ritvo, Ornitz, Tanguay, & Lee, 1970; Bender, 1968).

Rimland has proposed that infantile autism is the result of neurological impairment, not experience (Rimland, 1969). He has cited as evidence: (1) most siblings of autistic children are normal; (2) autistic children are behaviorally unusual from birth; (3) in most reported cases of autism in identical twins, both twins are autistic; and (4) the symptomatology of au-

tism is highly unique and specific. According to Rimland, infantile autism is the result of a neurological deficit in the reticular formation in the brainstem which governs the integration of current perception with memory. The autistic child, therefore, is unable to relate current to past experience and integrate and attach meaning to his or her sensation. The insistence on sameness, ritualistic behavior, and failure to establish relationships with people that are commonly observed with autistic children are seen as reflections of this inability to integrate experiences meaningfully.

Hyperactivity is a frequently observed problem behavior among children considered emotionally disturbed or behaviorally disordered. In a study of contrasting characteristics between so-called hyperactive children and nonhyperactive children (Stewart, Pitts, Craig, & Dieruf, 1966), a large percentage of the hyperactive group exhibited disturbed behavior. Fifty-nine percent were described as fighting with other children (compared to 3 percent of the nonhyperactive), 51 percent had temper tantrums, and 41 percent were seen as destructive (none of the normals was so described).

Interest in the hyperactive child goes back to the work of Alfred Strauss (Strauss & Lehtinen, 1947) who studied mentally retarded children, some of whom had known brain damage. The brain-damaged retarded children in the Strauss & Lehtinen study differed from retarded children with no record of brain injury in that they were more distractible and manifested emotional lability or wide variation in mood. As a result of this study, children who were hyperactive and demonstrated the behaviors Strauss found among the brain-damaged retardates came to be known as being affected with the Strauss syndrome, the hyperkinetic impulse disorder, or minimal brain dysfunction (synonymous terms)—even though they were not mentally retarded.

Are all hyperactive children brain damaged? A review of the research literature led Keogh to conclude that "hyperactivity and cerebral dysfunction are neither synonymous nor mutually exclusive" (Keogh, 1971, p. 102). It has been found that some hyperactive children do evidence signs of brain damage, but many do not; and conversely some children evidencing brain damage are not hyperactive. Some type of minimal brain dysfunction may underlie the problem behavior exhibited by some hyperactive children and some emotionally disturbed children, but we cannot assume this from our current level of knowledge with any degree of certainty.

In general, evidence linking biological factors to the development of emotional disturbance is strongest with respect to the severely emotionally disturbed. There is no conclusive evidence linking such factors to the vast majority of mildly disturbed or behavior disordered children (Kauffman, 1977). As we stated with respect to the effects of temperament on the development of behavior disorders, no single variable will suffice as an explanation. It is the interaction between the child's physical and biological givens and the range and nature of his or her experiences that must always be considered.

Psychodynamic Factors

While psychodynamic theory has been influential in educational programs for disturbed children, it has not translated as directly into practice as some of the other approaches we shall consider. Rather than relying primarily on observational data in implementing such programs, it relies on assumptions or interpretations related to the child's early experiences and present behavior.

From a psychodynamic perspective, the development of a behavior disorder or emotional disturbance is viewed as the result of the child's failure to withstand the emotional strain produced by confrontation with critical psychosexual stages. Central to this view is the investment of libidinal energy during each stage. This investment is made first in the oral and then in the anal and genital zones of the body. These investments are not permanent, however, and normal personality development involves freeing up the libidinal energy invested during one stage so that it might be available to overcome obstacles in subsequent stages. According to Freudian theory, problems arise when libidinal energy is fixated during one or more stages. Such fixation is the result of excessive gratification during a particular stage, excessive deprivation, the prospect of too severe a transition to the next level, and/or even to constitutional factors (Rezmierski & Kotre, 1974).

Fixation at the oral stage may cause an individual to be passive and dependent or argumentative and negative. Erikson (1963), a proponent of ego psychology, has views similar to Freud's, but he is less extreme. He views emotional disturbance as the result of conflicts with significant others

during psychosexual development. At the oral stage such a conflict may instill a basic mistrust of others. Fixation during the anal stage may produce excessive orderliness, obstinacy, defiance, or miserliness depending on the nature of the conflict. According to Erikson, "shame" and "doubt" may develop during this stage as a result of the battle between mother and child for autonomy centered around toilet training. During the phallic or Oedipal stage, according to Erikson, boys may develop exaggerated masculinity and girls vindictiveness toward males as they seek to establish their unique identities. Excessive guilt may also be a by-product of conflicts at this stage.

The latency stage is supposedly a time when the child is freed from the necessity for making psychosexual adjustments and turns to the demands of learning and school. Erikson, however, sees these demands as resulting in a sense of inferiority if the child is unprepared to deal with them. Once the individual has reached the genital stage, problems of adjustment are not peculiar to this stage, but are rooted in conflicts at earlier stages. Erikson views this stage as involving a search for an identity and a role in young adult life and he also links problems encountered in this search to earlier conflicts.

It is difficult and somewhat unfair to attempt to summarize classical and more contemporary psychodynamic theory's explanation for the de-

velopment of emotional disturbance in such a brief section. It is also difficult to delineate a single explanation since there are wide differences
among proponents of the theory. However, when we set aside the complex
structures, concepts, and dynamics of the theory, we find that the fundamental explanation for the development of emotional disturbance is very
similar to those we cited earlier—faulty relationships between children and
their interpersonal environments during the critical early years.

Behavioral Factors

We turn now to an explanation for the development of emotional disturbance that focuses on observable disturbed behavior itself and on the
environmental conditions that may be responsible for initiating and maintaining such behavior. It, too, is concerned with faulty relationships between the child and the environment, but this explanation approaches
these on an extra-child, rather than an intra-child, basis. This explanation
emanates from learning theory.

According to Skinner (Skinner, 1953), there are two types of learned
behavior, *respondent* behavior and *operant* behavior. There are also two
types of conditioning that underlie the establishment of respondent and
operant behavior. These two types of conditioning can be used to explain
why children develop emotional problems such as those involving excessive
fear and aggression.

Respondent conditioning emanates from the work of Pavlov.
Through repeated pairings of a conditioned stimulus (buzzer) with an unconditioned stimulus (food), an unconditioned response (salivation) that
previously could only be elicited by the unconditioned stimulus comes under the control of the conditioned stimulus. Thus, a dog is conditioned to
salivate when the buzzer sounds.

John Watson, whom we discussed earlier as having postulated a theory
of innate emotions, made use of respondent conditioning to illustrate how
children can acquire fears (Watson & Rayner, 1920). An eleven-month-old,
healthy, normal boy named Albert was the subject in this classic experimental demonstration. Albert was tested for fear reactions to various stimuli, and it was found he only showed fear when he heard a loud sound
(striking a metal bar). In the experiment, a white rat (which he did not fear
at all) served as the conditioned stimulus. After only seven pairings of the
rat with the loud sound made by striking the bar, Albert showed fear of the
rat when it was presented alone. Thus, a previously neutral stimulus acquired the aversive properties of a previously feared stimulus. It was found
that Albert's fear soon generalized to other white and furry objects such as
a rabbit, a dog, a fur coat, cotton, and a Santa Claus mask. The fear was
observed to last for at least one month, and it occurred in different exper-

imental situations. We'll encounter Albert again in Chapter 4 when we discuss this experiment in more detail.

In operant conditioning as formulated by Skinner, we are concerned with the effects reinforcement and punishment have on behavior. Reinforcement is defined in terms of its effect on an individual's behavior. If we give the individual something after a response and the response increases in frequency, we say this is the result of positive reinforcement. If the same thing occurs when we remove something, we say this is the result of negative reinforcement. While positive reinforcement is sometimes interpreted as being something good or desirable, and negative reinforcement is sometimes interpreted as something bad and undesirable, this is not the case. They are mathematical rather than affective terms, *positive* meaning to "add something," and *negative* meaning "to take something away." Punishment is also defined in terms of its effect on an individual's behavior. But the effect is the opposite of reinforcement. If we give or take away something after a response, and the response *decreases* in frequency, we say this is the result of punishment.

The following are some examples of the use of positive and negative reinforcement and punishment with children.

Johnny turns in a perfect arithmetic paper and receives verbal praise from his teacher. He works harder than ever to continue turning in perfect papers. We say this is the result of positive reinforcement.

Jimmy turns in a perfect arithmetic paper and is told by the teacher that he doesn't have to do any homework for two days. He works harder than ever to continue turning in perfect arithmetic papers. We say this is the result of negative reinforcement.

Mike is out of his seat, and the teacher scolds him in front of the class. Mike is very careful not to be out of his seat again when he is not supposed to. We say this is the result of punishment.

Todd is out of his seat, and the teacher tells him that as a result he will have to stay in during recess. Todd is very careful not to be out of his seat again. We say this is also the result of punishment.

However, we might review two contrasting examples and speculate on how behavior disorders can develop as the result of operant conditioning.

Nicky talks out whenever he wants the teacher's attention. The teacher always stops what she is doing and responds to him. Nicky's talking out is on the increase. We say this is the result of positive reinforcement.

During the first part of the semester, Bill raised his hand to answer questions posed by the teacher. But whenever he gave the wrong answer, the teacher gave him an angry look and called him "stupid." Now Bill has become withdrawn and fearful in the class, never raising his hand. We say this is the result of punishment.

WACK!

Does Nicky's talking out in class or Bill's withdrawal constitute a serious behavior disorder? We cannot tell from these examples without knowing more regarding frequency, severity, and clustering. But if Nicky's parents have always rewarded his impulsive and demanding behavior and lack of respect for the rights of others, or if they have been excessively inconsistent, the boy may have a difficult problem getting along in school. And if Bill's parents have been excessively punitive when he attempted to please them but couldn't meet their standards, a serious emotional problem may also be developing (Bijou, 1963). While not concerned with emotions per se in attempting to explain how behavior disorders develop, learning theorists do recognize the emotional byproducts of inconsistent or excessive punishment. These are fear, anxiety, anger or rage, and depression (Russ, 1974). We will discuss the issue of punishment in educational programs for disturbed children in detail in Chapter 4.

Social Learning Factors

Social learning theory (Bandura, 1973) combines a number of the basic tenets of learning theory with cognitive variables. That is, in addition to concern with stimuli, responses, reinforcement, and punishment, how the individual perceives what is happening and what he or she thinks or feels about it become important in considering why behavior disorders develop. A major premise of social learning theory is we learn from observing others and frequently imitate their behavior. Hence, the child may learn to be aggressive by watching family members, friends, or other individuals in the community. The likelihood of such modeling occurring increases when the model has high status, is positively rewarded, and avoids punishment for practicing the modeled behavior.

As with learning theory, punishment that is inconsistent, unfair, or severe may heighten or serve to maintain aggressive behavior, and the punisher may actually provide a model of aggression. Families of children who are aggressive are often characterized by high rates of aggression among parents and other members (Patterson, Reid, Jones, & Conger, 1975).

Ecological Factors

Perhaps the broadest, most all-encompassing explanation for the development of behavior disorders or emotional disturbance is provided by the ecological approach (Hobbs, 1969; Lewis, 1967; Rhodes, 1967, 1970). Essentially, ecology is the study of the interaction between organism and environment. Ecological views have been formalized in biology. Human ecology views individuals only within the context of their environments and studies the effects of the individual on the environment and the effects of the environment on the individual. Emotional disturbance, therefore, is not conceived of or studied as an intra-child characteristic or as emanating from a negative aspect of the environment. It is conceived and studied in the context of the interaction between the child and the family, the school, the neighborhood, the peer group, the community, and even society-at-large.

The disturbed child is viewed as a behaver or an exciter whose behavior or life-style elicits "reciprocating emotive reactions" from a community of responders (Rhodes, 1970). The child considered most disturbed may be the one who violates the largest number of behavioral codes of the community of responders. We presented this perspective to a degree when we earlier discussed teachers' ranges of tolerance as determiners of whether or not a child was considered emotionally disturbed. According to ecological theory, we must locate the "state of discordance" (Lewis, 1967) between the emotionally disturbed child and his or her primary agents of socialization and view this state as the underlying cause of the disturbance.

Ecological theory can embrace all of the positions we presented earlier in this section. We can view the problem behaviors seen among large numbers of so-called normal children from ages twenty-one months to fourteen years in the Macfarlane et al. study as expressions of a state of discordance between the child and the total environment. We may even locate the primary source of the discordance in a parent, the family, or the child's nutrition or health, and not in the child's behavior per se. We worked with an adolescent boy with an IQ of approximately 80. He had the misfortune to be born into a family of extremely high achievers who expected him to follow in his father's footsteps and go to Princeton University. He was attempting an academic program in high school and failing miserably. From the father's point of view, he was just lazy. His mother babied him. His older brother teased him. His teachers criticized and demeaned him. He stayed up long hours to study but still couldn't keep up. His health began to suffer. Finally, he became deeply depressed and attempted suicide. Fortunately, following this episode, a careful examination of this boy's ecosystem resulted in greater understanding and acceptance on the part of all parties concerned.

The studies of temperament by Thomas, Chess, and Birch (1969) offer ideal illustrations of the ecological approach and have been utilized for that purpose (Feagans, 1974). Whatever the temperamental characteristics of the child from early life, it is the interaction between these characteristics and the characteristics of the environment that must be considered when attempting to explain the development of a behavior disorder.

When we are concerned with serious biological irregularities such as those thought to possibly underlie infantile autism, this interactional approach may shift focus primarily to intra-child characteristics. But even the most serious biological irregularity can be aggravated or improved to a certain extent by the nature of the child's experiences. Thus, an ecological perspective is still valid even with severely handicapped individuals.

Psychodynamic theory is very ecological in its view of the development of emotional disturbance. It is the child's interaction with the environment's inevitable demands for adjustment (e.g., weaning, toilet training, establishment of a sexual identity) during the critical early years of life that underlies the development of emotional and behavioral difficulties.

Finally, learning theory is compatible with the ecological perspective. It provides us with an understanding of how the child's experience and interaction with the environment lawfully results in learning both adaptive and maladaptive behavior.

How do emotions become disturbed? While proponents of the various approaches we have discussed in this section might differentially select and weight intra-child versus extra-child characteristics, in the final analysis all would be forced to respect the interaction of child and the environment as a major factor in determining type of problem behavior and its frequency of occurrence, degree of severity, and clustering.

With this introduction to the source of human emotions and the development of behavior disorders and emotional disturbance, let's turn to the issue of definition and classification.

How Can Emotional Disturbance and Behavior Disorders Be Defined and Classified?

Definitions of emotional disturbance and behavior disorders often use terms and concepts that reflect a particular orientation toward the nature and origin of behavior problems. For example, one definition proposed from the psychodynamic viewpoint is as follows:

> Impairment of emotional growth during some stage of development with resultant distrust toward self and others and hostility generated from anxiety. (Moustakas, 1953, p. 19).

Another definition is conceived within a behavioral perspective:

> Disorders that consist of inadequate or inappropriate behavior that is learned and can therefore be changed through application of learning procedures. (Dupont, 1969, p. 6).

The ecological orientation is reflected in the following definition:

> Behavioral disabilities are defined as a variety of excessive, chronic, deviant behaviors ranging from impulsive and aggressive acts to depression and withdrawal acts (1) which violate the perceiver's expectations of appropriateness, and (2) which the perceiver wishes to see stopped. (Graubard, 1973, p. 246).

Ideally a definition should help us pinpoint the type of child we are concerned with so we can diagnose the problem and communicate meaningfully with individuals in other disciplines such as medicine and psychiatry. Definitions also permit us to communicate with individuals who determine policies for meeting the educational needs of disturbed children and who are a part of the educational system or the local, state, or federal government. In addition, definitions should help us in research endeavors with disturbed children, enabling us to specify the populations of children we are studying, to replicate studies, and eventually to generalize findings. Unfortunately, these ideals have not been achieved in the field of special education at the present time. The three examples presented above place disturbed children in "conceptual ballparks," but due to their vagueness, they may have little value for diagnostic, communicative, and research purposes.

Psychiatric Definitions

Similar problems arise with traditional and psychiatric definitions and classifications of emotional disturbance and behavior disorders. One scheme reflecting various sources (Watson, 1959) classifies children with behavior disorders as follows:

Primary Behavior Disorders
> *Habit Disturbances.* Problems in the performance of some major biological function such as eating, sleeping, elimination, and sex. These may include thumbsucking, nail biting, eating too much or too little, vomiting, bedwetting, soiling, inability to sleep, night terror, faulty speech development, and sexual disturbances.
> *Conduct Disturbances.* Problems involving aggressive, destructive, nonconforming, and delinquent behavior.
> *Neurotic Traits.* Problems involving a conflict with the self and manifested by jealousy, withdrawal, inhibition of aggression, phobias, and intense anxiety.

Psychotic Disorders
Psychosomatic Disorders

The Group for the Advancement of Psychiatry (GAP, 1966) has proposed a classification system covering ten categories of children's behavior:

1. Healthy responses
2. Reactive disorders
3. Developmental deviation
4. Psychoneurotic disorders
5. Personality disorders
6. Psychotic disorders
7. Psychophysiologic disorders
8. Brain syndromes
9. Mental retardation
10. Other disorders

These ten behavioral categories are further subdivided, and descriptions of the specific types of behavior covered by each are presented. For example with respect to childhood psychotic disorders, the GAP classification scheme includes nine descriptive characteristics in its definition:

1. Severe and continued impairment of emotional relationships with persons, associated with an aloofness
2. A tendency toward preoccupation with inanimate objects
3. Loss of speech or failure in its development
4. Disturbances in sensory perception
5. Bizarre or stereotyped behavior and motility patterns
6. Marked resistance to change in environment or routine
7. Outbursts of intense and unpredictable panic
8. Absence of a sense of personal identity
9. Blunted, uneven, or fragmented intellectual development
(GAP, 1966, p. 251)

A review of studies reporting symptomatology found among children diagnosed as psychotic (Goldfarb, 1970) revealed that virtually all of the behavioral symptoms reported were included within the nine points. Only a very few children, however, manifested all of the symptoms, and no symptom by itself could be regarded as diagnostic of psychosis. The GAP scheme appears a useful tool, but it still presents us with problems of reliability (e.g., deciding just how "severe" impairment of emotional relationship has to be in order to qualify a child as psychotic; in other words, so that two or more observers would reach similar conclusions).

Behavioral Definitions

One attempt to describe emotional disturbance from a behavioral point of view is the Behavior Problem Checklist or BPC (Quay, 1972). Arguing that terms such as *emotionally disturbed* cover such a heterogeneity of behaviors that they are meaningless in describing individual children or in aiding the formulation of intervention, Quay set out to identify subsets of behavior that would be more specific and homogeneous. The BPC grew out of the work of Peterson (1961) who selected 400 representative case folders from the files of a child guidance clinic. The referral problems of each child were noted and some 58 items descriptive of deviant behavior were chosen. Then teachers of 831 children in kindergarten through sixth grade rated their students with respect to whether or not they displayed any of these deviant behaviors (e.g., disruptive in class, daydreaming, etc.).

A factor analysis revealed two factors, or clusters, of related behaviors: conduct problems and personality problems. A subsequent study of seventh and eighth graders revealed another cluster, inadequacy–immaturity (Quay & Quay, 1965). Examples of the characteristics associated with each of these dimensions are as follows:

Conduct Problem
Restlessness, attention-seeking, disruptiveness, rowdiness, dislike for school, jealousy, fighting, irresponsibility, disobedience, hyperactivity, destructiveness, cursing, hot-temperedness, negativism

Personality Problem
Not knowing how to have fun, behaving like an adult, being easily embarrassed, feelings of inferiority, crying easily, social withdrawal, being flustered easily, secretiveness, hypersensitivity, anxiety, depression, aloofness

Inadequacy–Immaturity
Preoccupation, "in a world of his or her own," short attention span, laziness in school, excessive daydreaming, passivity, suggestibility, sluggishness, drowsiness

Another type of child defined by the BPC research was the socialized delinquent. The traits of such a child, however, did not make up a single distinguishing factor.

The BPC has proven to be a reliable means of classifying children with behavior disorders according to descriptions of observable behavior. One disadvantage of relying on defined clusters of behaviors or traits to categorize a child, however, is that not all children may meet the criteria for inclusion in any one specific cluster. Recall that in the Thomas, Chess, and Birch study cited earlier, only 65 percent of the children fit one of the three temperament clusters—easy, difficult, or slow-to-warm-up. The other 35 percent were variable and manifested different combinations of temperamental traits.

Behavioral rating scales have been useful in dispelling some of the vagueness and elusiveness of the term *emotional disturbance.* Based on what people actually see and experience with disturbed children, rather than on what people speculate is going on inside such children's heads, these scales are particularly important for research purposes when subject populations must be defined in a reliable manner. While behavioral rating scales provide an important means for better defining and selecting subject populations for research, however, they, along with the other approaches cited, would appear to have only limited usefulness when it comes to specific educational planning for disturbed children. We get a general picture of a conduct-problem child challenging authority, a personality-problem child having major social adjustment problems, and an inadequacy-immaturity child being given to daydreaming. But what does one actually do in the classroom with such children? And what about the autistic child or other severely emotionally disturbed children? How do we translate "bizarre or stereotyped behavior and motility pattern" or "absence of a sense of personal identity" into a specific course of action for the teacher?

The definition and classification issue with respect to disturbed children is further clouded by Public Law 94–142. Earlier we pointed out that this law, the Education for All the Handicapped Act of 1975, does not make provision for children with behavior disorders but only for "seriously emotionally disturbed" children.

Seriously emotionally disturbed is defined as follows:
(i) The term means a condition exhibiting one or more of the following characteristics over a long period of time and to a marked degree, which adversely affects educational performance.
  (a) An inability to learn which cannot be explained by intellectual, sensory, and health factors;
  (b) An inability to build or maintain satisfactory interpersonal relationships with peers and teachers;
  (c) Inappropriate types of behavior or feelings under normal circumstances;
  (d) A general pervasive mood of unhappiness or depression; or
  (e) A tendency to develop physical symptoms or fears associated with personal or school problems.
(ii) The term includes children who are schizophrenic or autistic. The term does not include children who are socially maladjusted unless it is determined that they are seriously emotionally disturbed. *(Federal Register,* Vol. 42, No. 163, August 23, 1977, p. 42478).

This definition appears to cover milder forms of emotional disturbance in its specific components. Many nonpsychotic children exhibit "inappropriate types of behavior under normal circumstances." Therefore, we are probably going to find such nonpsychotic children, considered by many to have behavior disorders, actually called seriously emotionally disturbed to meet the specification of the law. The definition is also somewhat contradictory in excluding "children who are socially maladjusted," but including those who manifest "an inability to build or maintain satisfactory interpersonal relationships with peers and teachers." The issue could be raised that the two types of children being described are identical. The definition of emotional disturbance in PL 94–142 is rather vague and quite broad. Applying it will depend largely on the interpretation and ranges of tolerance of individuals referring children for special educational services. It may be that this vagueness reflects both the lack of consensus of a definition of mild disturbance in the field as well as a deliberate attempt to avoid opening the "flood gates" and allowing any child with a minor behavioral or interpersonal problem to be identified for special education services. At any rate, there will probably be a wide variety of interpretations of the PL 94–142 definition among the states.

In an effort to move toward an approach for describing emotionally disturbed children and children with behavior disorders in terms that lead more directly to the setting of educational goals and the formulation of educational methodology, we will combine many of the characteristics cited in this section into a functional classification approach in Chapter 3.

Incidence and Transience

Now that we have introduced the disturbed child, we might consider the question: How many children are there like Bobby Myron and Martin Greenwood in the United States today? The U.S. Office of Education estimates that 2 percent of the nation's school children are emotionally disturbed, making no distinction between mild and severe conditions. In a 1971 survey (Schultz, Hirshoren, Manton, & Henderson, 1971), it was found that eighteen states used this 2 percent estimate, seven used a 3 percent estimate, and six others, 5 percent. Overall, we have found a range of incidence estimates from .05 percent to 15 percent. If one surveys the literature related to incidence from the early 1940s to the present, the upper estimate has gone as high as 25 percent (Hewett & Blake, 1973). A report for the Joint Commission on Mental Health estimated that some 30 percent of school-aged children have some degree of intrapersonal or interpersonal difficulties (Glidewell & Swallow, 1968). With respect to gender, boys have consistently been found in greater numbers in populations of disturbed children. Estimates are that 66 percent (McCaffrey, Cumming, & Pausley, 1963) to 80 percent (Quay, Morse, & Cutler, 1966) of all disturbed children are boys. Boys also exhibit more aggressive conduct disturbances than girls (Quay, 1972).

There have been fewer estimates in the literature of the incidence of severe emotional disturbance (e.g., childhood schizophrenia and infantile autism). The range suggested is from 2 to 6 children per 10,000 of the child population (Mosher, Gunderson, & Buchsbaum, 1973).

Based on our earlier discussion of the crucial importance of the observer's range of tolerance for behavioral differences in determining who gets the label *emotionally disturbed* or *behaviorally disordered,* the wide discrepancies between incidence estimates should come as no surprise. When we survey the .05 to 30 percent range of estimation, we can speculate on the many criteria and the individual biases that are reflected. While it would be interesting to know the actual number of children experiencing enough difficulty in schools across the country to be singled out as "disturbed," we will probably never know. For, in addition to range of tolerance differences, another issue complicates the picture—mild emotional disturbance may be a most transient condition with large numbers of children "growing out" of their problems during the childhood years.

Earlier, we examined the large number of children exhibiting problem behavior in the Macfarlane et al. study. Most of those children were exhibiting transient disorders, and only a few probably qualified in school for the label *emotionally disturbed.* In a study done in Tennessee in 1972, 100 out of 773 children screened in grades two through five were rated by their teachers and peers as having behavior disorders (Glavin, 1972). Three years later, a second screening was undertaken. Only 30 percent of the children originally rated as having a behavior disorder in grades two through five were so rated when they were in grades five through eight. Seventy percent had improved over time without psychological treatment of any kind. This spontaneous improvement percentage is in line with the findings of other studies (McCaffrey, Cumming, & Pausley, 1963).

In our experience, when you walk into any elementary classroom, you can usually pick out two or three children who are "not with it" and who are visible enough to stand out from other members of the class in terms of their problem behavior. And if you stay long enough, you can usually determine if they "fit" within the teacher's range of tolerance for behavioral differences. Whether they would be the same children a week or semester later is debatable. Thus, we get almost no meaning from incidence figures. The U.S. Office of Education's 2 percent is undoubtedly very conservative and may be most accurate in relation to the moderately and severely emotionally disturbed. In general, the more severe the problem behavior the child exhibits, the more likely we are to obtain accurate, stable, and reliable estimates.

In this chapter we have addressed the question, "What is emotional disturbance?" We have seen that the answer to a large degree depends on who is considering the question and that person's range of tolerance for behavioral differences. Frequency of occurrence, degree of severity, duration, and clustering of the problem behaviors are additional determiners. Human emotions appear to originate during the first year of life. Specific emotions develop from early distress and nondistress states in infancy and are not innate. Differences in temperament among children are seen in the first two to three months and are related to the type of emotional behavior the child exhibits. Psychodynamic theory postulates an elaborate explanation for emotional and personality development involving the child's investment of instinctual energy during critical psychosexual stages of development.

Large numbers of so-called normal children exhibit problem behaviors during the childhood years. The cause for these behaviors relates to the interaction of environmental (family, peers, school, community) and physical (health, nutrition) influences. Most are transient in nature and diminish by early adolescence. Studies of temperamental differences among children have established a "difficult child" pattern that has been found to often result in the development of a behavior disorder. So-called hyperactive children often exhibit behavior disorders, but there is no conclusive evidence that their problems are the result of brain dysfunction. Severe emotional disturbance appears to have a definite genetic component and severely disturbed children often exhibit numerous biological irregularities.

Psychodynamic theory views the development of emotional disturbance as stemming from fixation during oral, anal, and/or phallic periods of development that occur in the first five years of life. Learning theorists have demonstrated how children can acquire fears through respondent conditioning and maladaptive behavior as the result of reinforcement and punishment. Social learning theory considers cognitive and affective variables important and considers the development of aggression the result of imitating social models. Ecological theory views the development of disturbed behavior as resulting from the complex interplay of relationships between the child and his or her social and psychological environments.

The definition and classification of emotional disturbance is a cloudy issue. Definitions in general establish "conceptual ballparks" for defining problem behavior. Behavioral descriptions of severely emotionally disturbed children have approached consensus and have been useful for classification purposes.

Incidence estimates of emotionally disturbed children and children with behavior disorders are largely meaningless due to differential criteria and the fact that the majority of children with milder problems tend to improve over time without any psychological assistance.

This concludes our introduction to emotionally disturbed children and children with behavior disorders. In the next chapter we'll consider how the different approaches to explaining the development of emotional problems and behavior disorders translate into contrasting educational strategies.

chapter 2

The Roles People Play

J ust as teachers differ with respect to their ranges of tolerance for problem behavior, so they differ with respect to their points of view regarding the best educational approach for dealing with it. In the last chapter
we examined contrasting explanations regarding the sources of emotional
development and emotional disturbance. These contrasting explanations
are the basis for various educational strategies that have been formulated
for helping the disturbed child in the school. Each of these strategies assigns both the teacher and the emotionally disturbed child a role. We will
draw upon role theory in our discussion in this chapter.

Role theory is a field of study concerned with real life behavior as it is
displayed in genuine, on-going social situations (Biddle & Thomas, 1966).
We all assume a variety of roles in our daily lives. These roles are determined by social norms, demands, and rules; by the role performances of
others; by those who observe and react to our role performances; and by
our own particular capabilities and personalities. The kind of parents we
are will therefore be determined by what we have learned parents should
be like, by what we have seen our own parents and the parents of others say
and do, by our friends and relatives who make judgments regarding our
parenting, and finally by our own unique characteristics. In a similar fashion what we do as teachers—our role performances in the classroom—is
defined by what we were taught in school at all levels; by what we have seen
various teachers say and do; by our fellow teachers, administrators, parents, and others who evaluate our performances; and by our individual
abilities, competencies, and personality characteristics. Somehow as a result
of all these varied influences we become teachers assuming particular roles
in our classrooms. Since these influences vary so markedly from individual
to individual, it is not surprising that as we visit a variety of classrooms we
will see markedly different teaching styles or roles.

Teachers also bring *expectations* regarding their roles and the roles of
their children into the classroom. In our earlier example, Sue Billings saw
herself as a teacher of third-grade curriculum to pupils who were obedient
and conforming. Bobby Myron fell far short of meeting her expectations,
and the discordance was most evident. It should be apparent that our discussion here and our previous discussion regarding teachers' ranges of
tolerance are closely related.

One concept in role theory that we will draw upon in this chapter is *role
perspective*. Role perspective is a particular viewpoint about what factors are
influential in governing human behavior (Biddle & Thomas, 1966). Exactly what were the underlying reasons for Bobby Myron's behavior? Depending on their role perspective, some might consider Bobby physically
ill; others, emotionally disturbed; and still others, as a boy who had learned
more wrong things than right things to do. In part, we were discussing role
perspectives in the previous chapter as we contrasted various explanations
for emotional disturbance.

Teachers often have contrasting role perspectives when approaching
the disturbed child in the classroom. And these role perspectives will often

determine the type of educational program provided the child, the priority ranking given various goals in the program, and the methodology used to achieve these goals. Thus, the role of the teacher who works with disturbed children may be largely determined by the role perspective he or she takes toward the nature and source of emotional disturbance.

As a means of illustrating the various viewpoints or role perspectives that have been taken regarding emotional disturbance, we will begin with an analogy. This analogy concerns the reactions of four art gallery visitors to an abstract sculpture that has been put on display for the first time. We will then relate their reactions to four role perspectives regarding Bobby Myron's behavior.

The first visitor approaches the sculpture and examines it very closely. He is interested in its physical structure and thinks:

> The most impressive aspect of this work relates to the materials it is made of. The artistic value of the sculpture is largely determined by its physical properties.

A teacher applying this viewpoint to the behavior of Bobby Myron may also be primarily interested in physical factors and think:

> This boy undoubtedly has neurological impairment. His hyperactivity and distractibility are diagnostic signs of some underlying physical disorder.

The second visitor approaches the sculpture and walks around it several times. She is interested in what it is supposed to represent.

> What is the message the artist is trying to convey? What is the underlying meaning of the sculpture?

From this role perspective, a teacher viewing the problem behavior of Bobby Myron might be influenced by psychodynamic theory and ask:

> This boy is experiencing serious inner conflicts. His behavior is symptomatic of intense anxiety and mistrust toward others probably related to faulty relationships with his parents.

The third visitor takes yet another approach. He stands back and views the sculpture from a distance and is concerned with how it fits into the gallery setting into which it has been placed.

> I'm not sure the sculpture is properly placed. It doesn't seem to go with the other works of art around it.

A teacher might consider Bobby Myron from a behavioral perspective and conclude:

> The boy simply has not learned to behave appropriately in the classroom. His behavior is maladaptive and sets him apart from other students who meet the expectations of the school.

Finally, the fourth visitor arrives. She takes a look at the sculpture, its surroundings, other works of art in the gallery rooms, and then walks outside to view the art gallery building itself.

This sculpture can only be considered in the context of the entire art gallery in which it has been placed and in relation to all of the other works of art. In addition, we need to consider the location of the gallery in the city, how it is managed by its board of trustees, and the community support it receives. We may even want to investigate the cultural importance of the arts on a national level.

From this ecological viewpoint, a teacher might approach Bobby Myron's behavior as follows:

Bobby Myron cannot be understood or helped by merely examining his problem behavior in school. We must learn more about his family relationships, the neighborhood where he lives, the children he plays with and their reactions to him, and the types of activities he engages in in the community.

In approaching Bobby Myron's problem behavior from these four role perspectives, teachers would be both assigning particular roles to Bobby and assuming particular roles themselves. These reciprocal role assignments can be described as follows:

1. The child as neurologically impaired
   The teacher as diagnostician-trainer

2. The child as emotionally disturbed
   The teacher as therapist

3. The child as a maladaptive behaver
   The teacher as behavior modifier

4. The child as a victim of discordance in his or her ecosystem
   The teacher as part of the child's ecosystem

For the remainder of this chapter we will discuss each of these child and teacher roles and examine the contrasting educational strategies, including goals and methods, that are associated with them. Where possible, we will also cite research findings regarding the effectiveness of each strategy.

☆ The Child as Neurologically Impaired

☆ The Teacher as Diagnostician–Trainer

The Child as Neurologically Impaired

There may be a great deal of uncertainty regarding whether or not Bobby Myron is *actually* neurologically impaired. But if the inference is made that he *may* be, and the label *presumed neurological dysfunction* is given to him, the result may not be in his best interests. To begin with such a label is ominous for the educator. It implies a defective child who may lack the capacity to learn. Thus, three unfortunate consequences may ensue:

1. We may teach to Bobby's label rather than to Bobby himself. What we give him to do and what we expect him to learn may have far more to do with a stereotyped notion of what children with neurological impairment can and cannot do rather than with Bobby's actual individuality and potential.

2. Even though we don't pin a badge on Bobby's shirt that states "I am brain damaged," it is amazing how children become aware of the labels others "pin" on them in discussions and reports. As the child realizes he or she is considered "retarded," "disturbed," or "handicapped," this may contribute greatly to the development of a negative self-concept.

3. If it turns out that Bobby Myron makes no progress in his educational program over the year, the label initially given him serves as a convenient means for explaining his failure. After all, the teacher may conclude, how can anyone expect a neurologically impaired child to make progess anyway?

Thus, labels can alter our expectations regarding a child's potential for learning, affect the child's self-concept directly, and become self-fulfilling prophecies allowing us to explain lack of learning as the result of a child failure rather than as the result of a teaching failure. As far as we are concerned, any child, whatever the label given him or her, who learns nothing in school over a period of time is very clearly not a child failure but a teaching failure.

The Teacher as Diagnostician–Trainer

From this role perspective, a teacher may consider three possible approaches for helping Bobby: (1) refer his parents to a physician who may prescribe certain medication that could have a "calming" influence on him, (2) administer various diagnostic tests and attempt to pinpoint visual and auditory perceptual problems as well as problems in coordination that might underlie his learning problems, (3) place him in a structured program of training in which he will be given exercises aimed at remediating his perceptual and coordination problems.

Behavior Disorder or Learning Disability?

To some readers the previous paragraph may seem out of place in a book on emotional disturbance and behavior disorders. The child being described is hyperactive with a learning disability, not emotionally disturbed. We could devote considerable space to the knotty issue of exactly

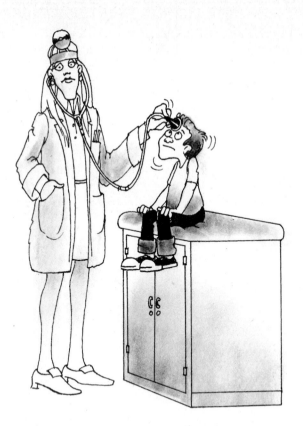

how one separates the child with a learning disability from the child who is disturbed. But we shall refrain and state our position briefly as follows:

1. Very often the child with a learning disability and the disturbed child are one and the same, particularly if we include hyperactivity, distractibility, emotional lability, and impulsivity as behavior problems.

2. Children who have encountered continual frustration and failure in school because of perceptual, coordination, and language difficulties are very apt to have poor self-concepts and negative attitudes toward school and learning. These will almost certainly be expressed in some form of problem behavior.

3. Does it really make a difference anyway to worry about making a differential diagnosis between a learning disability and emotional disturbance? Shouldn't we approach every child with learning and/or behavior problems in school and teach to the uniqueness of the child rather than the uniqueness of some assigned label?

Thus, whether Bobby Myron is an emotionally disturbed child, or a

child with a learning disability, or an emotionally disturbed child with a learning disability is academic. But what about the three approaches to helping him we discussed earlier?

The Use of Medication

In our experience, many special educators have had a special fondness for allying themselves with the professions of medicine, neurology, and psychiatry. While interdisciplinary communication and cooperation is essential if we are to help children with behavior and learning problems, it is unfortunate when teachers prefer to focus on a glamorous alliance with other professionals rather than to firmly establish their own unique identity as educators. Such an identity is every bit as professional and important as those associated with medicine. Actually, teachers have much more primary significance in "treating" most children with behavior disorders. We are not suggesting that teachers yearn to wear white coats as physicians do (although in the Soviet Union, where special education is called *defectology*, many teachers do just that). But some prefer the medical model for viewing children's learning and behavior problems with its emphasis on disease, impairment, diagnosis, and treatment by drugs.

Another disturbing aspect of prescribing drugs to hyperactive children is the drug, rather than the primary agent of influence in the child's life (e.g., home, school), is assigned the responsibility for solving the child's problem. It may be too easy to single out children with behavioral disorders as obvious candidates for drugs instead of taking a careful and critical look at the quality of instruction they are receiving in school and the adequacy of family relationships at home (Sroufe, 1975).

As early as 1937, hyperactive children were treated with amphetamine drugs (Bradley, 1937). Initially, it was thought that stimulant drugs which would normally produce an increase in activity level or a "high" in adults actually had a calming effect on hyperactive children. This "paradoxical" effect, however, has recently been discounted (Sroufe, 1975). It has been found that children treated with drugs are more active in open play situations than non drug-treated children. But from 50 to 80 percent have also been found to become more attentive, vigilant, and less given to irrelevant behavior when presented with learning tasks (Safer & Allen, 1976).

Studies of the effects of drug dosage levels on learning and behavior suggest that achieving social-behavioral control may require dosage at levels beyond those optimal for learning (Sprague & Sleator, 1976). That is, the child may actually learn more effectively at a dosage level that is less than that necessary to bring his or her behavior in line with the expectations of the school and the parents. Since physicians often rely on reports from parents and teachers with respect to determining dosage level, controlled behavior rather than learning effectiveness may be the criteria utilized in prescribing dosage level. Keogh and Barkett (in press) have concluded that the major effect of medication is on social behaviors and psychological processes involving selected attentional and visual-perceptual abilities. They have noted that there is little evidence of direct drug effects on academic achievement which might be expected in light of findings in studies of drug dosage.

Perhaps one of the most disturbing aspects of the wholesale prescribing of drugs to hyperactive children is that they learn that they cannot really control themselves and that there is something wrong with their brains or bodies (Sroufe, 1975). Stewart and Olds (1973) have reported hearing comments such as this from medicated children: "I can't help being bad today. I haven't had my pill." Wender (1971) has reported hearing, "My magic pills make me into a good boy and make everybody like me." Teachers may ask children on medication if they have "had their pill" and even have been quoted as saying, "Peter will be sent home today if he doesn't take his pill" (Stewart & Olds, 1973).

Teachers don't prescribe pills for children, but some may lean heavily in the direction of referring parents of hyperactive children to physicians who do. As in so many issues in the field of special education, we cannot make conclusive statements. Drugs are good and they are not good, drugs work and they do not work depending on the individual child. Much more research is needed in every area related to the pros and cons of the use of medication. Perhaps the most important point for teachers to consider is that even when hyperactive children do evidence a positive response to medication, their learning and behavior problems in school or elsewhere have in no way been "cured." All that has really been done is to positively "set the stage" for such improvement. Drugs do not teach children to read, teachers do. Drugs do not teach children how to get along with others and how to succeed, teachers and parents do. Drugs may make children more accessible to teaching efforts, but if those efforts are inept, all the drugs have done is to change the children so that they can fail to learn, come to hate school even more, and develop negative self-concepts in a calmer and quieter manner.

Diagnosis

The term *perceptual-motor handicap* has almost become a synonym for unconfirmed neurological impairment (Achenbach, 1974). The same may be said for the term *hyperactivity*. While hyperactivity may be quite easy to diagnose from an educational point of view (although we still have the ranges-of-tolerance issue to contend with), diagnosis of perceptual-motor handicaps often involves the administration of tests. Many of these tests have grown out of the early work of Strauss and Lehtinen (Strauss & Lehtinen, 1947). These pioneers were particularly concerned with pinpointing the specific effects of brain damage on behavior related to learning.

Among the test tasks they constructed was one that required children to visually separate foreground and background stimuli. For example, a picture of a hat with jagged lines across it would be flashed in front of the child for one fifth of a second, then the child would be asked to report what was shown. If the child reported seeing a hat, he was responding to the foreground stimuli; if he or she reported jagged lines, to background stimuli. While very few normal and non-brain-damaged retarded children reported seeing jagged lines, 75 percent of the brain injured retardates reported they saw lines instead of that hat. Normal and non-brain-injured individuals were found to visually focus on the obvious foreground figure, while brain injured children were very easily distracted by background patterns.

The diagnostic tests of Frostig (Frostig & Horne, 1964) and Kephart (Kephart, 1971) are examples of contemporary efforts to diagnose specific perceptual-motor problems. The Frostig Developmental Test of Visual Perception assesses five areas of visual perception: eye-motor coordination, figure-ground perception, constancy of shape, position in space, and spatial relationships. The Perceptual Motor Rating Scale developed by Kephart is also concerned with five areas: balance and posture, body image and differentiation, perceptual-motor match, ocular control, and form perception. By evaluating a child's performance on these tests, specific training exercises are prescribed in an effort to improve perceptual-motor functioning.

An instrument that aims at assessing an individual's competence in receptive, associative, and expressive language is the Illinois Test of Psycholinguistic Abilities or ITPA (Kirk, McCarthy, & Kirk, 1968). It purports to measure such basic linguistic abilities as auditory and visual reception, association, expression, memory, and closure (i.e., the ability to automatically grasp the whole of a visual pattern or verbal expression when only part of it is presented). Kirk and Kirk (1971) have prepared a set of specific guidelines to remedy problems in these areas.

What do such tests have to do with children who are disturbed or who exhibit learning disorders? As stated earlier, problems of distractibility and impulsivity cut across all categories of exceptionality and particularly accompany emotional disturbance and learning disabilities. The teacher who notices that a child whom we might call disturbed is also easily distracted, confuses letters such as *b* and *d*, has poor handwriting, and has difficulty verbalizing what is seen or heard may decide that the disturbed behavior is the result of a perceptual-motor language problem and greatly rely on diagnostic testing in determining instructional priorities.

Training

Approaching the child who manifests hyperactivity, distractibility, and impulsivity from this role perspective usually leads to a definite plan of training exercises. It may also lead to specific alterations of the classroom environment such as those prescribed by Cruickshank (Cruickshank, 1975). According to Cruickshank, hyperactive and neurologically impaired children (we have already stated that to exhibit hyperactivity and/or a perceptual-motor handicap often leads to the automatic diagnosis of unconfirmed or presumed neurological impairment) are often unable to refrain from reacting to stimuli around them. In order to help them direct their energies toward the learning tasks they are assigned, the teacher should therefore remove as much extraneous stimuli as possible. Walls, furniture, and woodwork should be painted the same color. Bulletin boards should be removed, and windows replaced with translucent glass to screen out outdoor stimuli. Cupboards should be equipped with solid wooden doors, and carpets and acoustical ceiling tiles installed.

In addition to reducing stimuli, Cruickshank views the reduction of space as an important consideration. Small cubicles, each approximately 2 ¼ × 3 ¼ feet in size, within which a child may work totally closed off from what is going on in the rest of the classroom, are advocated by Cruickshank. Application of this approach was studied over a two-year period with four small classes of hyperactive and distractible children (Cruickshank, Bentzen, Ratzeberg, & Tannhauser, 1961). Two classes rigidly adhered to reduction of stimuli and space, while two maintained a more traditional program. At the end of the study, there were no significant differences between the two programs, and children in all four classes made significant gains in achievement, visual perception, and social behavior. Other studies of the effects of cubicles on the performance of brain-injured and emotionally disturbed children have found no superiority in functioning in a stimulus-control condition (Cruse, 1970). Increases in attention span have been observed, but not progess in reading while working in a cubicle (Shores & Haubrich, 1969; Haubrich & Shores, 1976).

One of the attractive aspects of the diagnostician-trainer orientation relates to the specificity and concreteness of curriculum tasks. The Frostig program work sheets, developed to remediate problems found on the Frostig and Horne diagnostic tests, consist of exercises designed to improve the child's basic perceptual-motor abilities. The child may be given a sheet with a series of parallel lines. The parallel lines at the beginning are quite far apart, and the child may have little difficulty drawing a line in the center of the two lines without touching either. But the lines gradually narrow in later sections of the exercise, and a greater degree of hand-eye coordination is required to draw a line between them without touching them. On other sheets, figures (e.g., circles, diamonds) surrounded by distractive background lines and shadings have to be recognized and outlined by the child, thus strengthening visual-perceptual skills related to figure-ground or foreground-background discrimination.

Kephart's Perceptual-Motor Rating Scale leads directly to training procedures. The procedures emphasize the correction of underlying basic perceptual-motor skills rather than attacking hand-eye coordination problems on a direct basis. Thus, the child who cannot adequately draw a square is seen as a candidate for training in laterality (left-right) orientation, directionality, ocular control, dexterity, temporal-spatial translation (e.g., repeating tapped rhythms), and form percepts rather than for repeated drill in square drawing. Chalkboard, sensorimotor, and ocular control training are included in the Kephart program. At the chalkboard the child may move from random scribbling to exercises that teach a left-right orientation. Forms may be directly copied and then later drawn from memory. Large muscle activity is central to sensorimotor training. The child is taught bilateral, unilateral, and cross-lateral movements through activities such as angels-in-the-snow, rabbit hop, crab walk, measuring worm, and elephant walk. In addition, the trampoline and walking and balance boards are used. During ocular control training, the child is first taught to follow an object such as a small pen-shaped flashlight with his or her eyes as it is moved first laterally, then vertically, diagonally, and in a rotary fashion. Later the child will follow the penlight with both a finger and the eyes. In the final stages of training, variously sized balls are held jointly by teacher and child. As with the flashlight stage, the child's task is to keep the ball in sight as it is moved.

In addition to the Frostig and Kephart programs, there are approaches by Barsch (1965) and Cratty (1974) that involve a wide variety of activities to improve perceptual-motor skills. As can be seen from our examples, these training exercises are apt to be quite motivating for both teacher and child. From the teacher's perspective, there is a definite plan: (1) a visual-motor worksheet first thing in the morning, (2) practice on a balance beam for twenty minutes later on, (3) ocular training with a flashlight for ten minutes before prereading activities, etc. From the child's perspective, many of these tasks are just plain fun to do. And what about all the individual attention the child receives from the teacher, and the praise received for his or her efforts? For children who are seldom candidates for success and praise, such training exercises may be highly reinforcing.

While there can be no question about the potential motivational appeal of perceptual-motor training programs for both teacher and child, research has tended not to support the notion that training in basic underlying skills such as visual discrimination leads to improvement in academic skills such as reading (Bryan & Bryan, 1975). This does not mean the training is useless. Children who are given visual-perceptual training often do improve on tests of visual perception, but children who participate in activities more directly related to reading gain most in reading.

The following is a consideration of the implications for: (1) the setting of educational goals, and (2) the implementation of methodology for the child-as-neurologically-impaired and teacher-as-diagnostician–trainer role perspectives. Each role perspective discussed in this chapter will be summarized in this way.

Goals

Emotionally disturbed children often present a variety of puzzling problems. They may be quiet and withdrawn or loud and impulsive. They may be well-coordinated or clumsy, attentive to what they like best and inattentive to what teachers think is best for them. They may be underactive or overactive. Just exactly what should you do with them in the classroom? Because their behavioral, academic, and motivational problems are often very difficult to understand, it is no easy task to select THE curriculum goals that are most appropriate. We have worked with autistic children who have been enrolled in intensive programs of perceptual-motor training to the virtual exclusion of emphasis on language and social development. It appeared that the goal of improving an autistic child's motor coordination and spatial orientation was a definable and tangible one that held promise for at least making an observable difference in some aspect of the child's functioning. And indeed these children became better coordinated in their bodily movements after training, but a broader range of goals was certainly necessary to deal with the complex problems of autism. While such one-sidedness in goal setting may not be common in the field today (although it has by no means disappeared), it underscores the fact that when confronted with the behavioral and educational chaos often associated with emotionally disturbed children, some degree of specificity and definition is most reassuring—even at the expense of broader and more balanced goal setting.

Methodology

Setting aside reliance on medication, which constitutes a method for dealing with hyperactivity from this perspective, the specificity of goal setting is matched by the specificity of the methodology used to train the child. If you want to teach "square drawing," break the drawing of a square down into its basic component parts: teach line drawing, horizontal then vertical, then teach left-right line drawing, and finally up-down line drawing. Start with large chalkboard drills and drills involving broad, sweeping movements of the hands and arms. You can communicate directly to the child what you want him or her to do, participate directly in it yourself, and measure improvement over time through observation and testing.

While it may always be difficult at the end of the school year to answer the question, "Is Johnny less emotionally disturbed than he was in the fall," it is reassuring and gratifying to report he can walk fourteen feet down a balance beam without falling off, copy basic geometric designs with acceptable accuracy, and distinguish subtle differences in words (e.g., bat-bad). And who knows? Those kinds of accomplishments with their attendant praise from others and possible effect on bolstering self-esteem may very well add up to the answer, "Johnny is probably less emotionally disturbed at the end of the school year than he was at the beginning."

☆ The Child as Emotionally Disturbed

☆ The Teacher as Therapist

As we discussed in the previous chapter, the influence of Freudian psychology has been considerable in advancing theoretical explanations regarding the development of emotional disturbance. It has also had a major impact on what has been done with emotionally disturbed children in educational programs. In this section we will examine the evolution of psychodynamic influence in special education from the more traditional Freudian sources to contemporary psychoeducational approaches.

The Child as Emotionally Disturbed

Let's begin our discussion by first discussing the role of the child. The child is emotionally disturbed. Exactly what has that come to mean to special educators with this particular role perspective? Historically, one of the earliest answers was provided by August Aichhorn (Aichhorn, 1925/1965) who, in the late 1910s, was among the first to apply Freudian psychoanalytic principles to the management and treatment of aggressive delinquent male and female adolescents. Aichhorn viewed their aggressive, destructive behavior as the result of severe conflicts between the children and one or both of their parents. All of Aichhorn's adolescents were described as having been "brought up without affection," "to have suffered unreasonable severity and brutality," "to have been beaten unmercifully," and as a result to have developed a "strong hate reaction." Aichhorn concluded that none of his delinquents had ever had their needs for affection satisfied.

As we saw in Chapter 1, Erikson (1963) views emotional disturbance as the result of inadequate resolution of various critical conflicts during childhood. Such inadequate resolution may produce mistrust of others, shame, doubt, defiance, suspicion, inhibition, extreme guilt, lack of feelings of self-worth, and identity conflict. A humanistic psychologist, Carl Rogers (1969), while not identified with traditional psychodynamic approaches, also views emotional disturbance as the result of psychic conflict within the child. This conflict comes about when there is a discrepancy between the child's experiences and his or her self-concept. Rather than considering healthy development as being dependent on the meeting and overcoming of crises during childhood, Rogers sees it as being dependent on allowing the innate tendencies of the organism to be fulfilled. From early infancy, the infant is viewed as desiring self-growth, health, and self-actualization if allowed to choose experiences in accordance with these goals. When life experiences are not in accordance with these goals and conflict arises between the child's actualizing tendency and real-life experience, behavior disorders or emotional disturbance may develop.

Thus, according to sources reflecting psychodynamic and humanistic viewpoints, we may explain Bobby Myron's behavior in school as the result of one or more of the following:

1. Previous unsatisfactory interpersonal and affective relationships with others

2. Anger and hate toward others

3. Mistrust and suspicion toward others

4. Self-doubt and guilt

5. Withdrawal, fearfulness, and anxiety

6. Lack of feelings of self-worth

7. Conflict between previous experience and innate actualizing tendencies

8. Poor sense of identity

These problems result from conflicts between the child and the environment, particularly the interpersonal environment. They are psychological in nature as compared to the presumed neurological basis for problem behavior discussed earlier. As psychological problems, they are often treated by psychiatrists, clinical psychologists, social workers, counselors, and other "therapists." It is not surprising, then, that as the teacher oriented from a psychodynamic perspective begins to work with children evidencing such psychological problems, the role of therapist is often assumed.

The Teacher as Therapist

In the introduction to August Aichhorn's classic book describing his work with delinquent children, *Wayward Youth,* Sigmund Freud wrote that the educator working with such children "should be psychoanalytically trained otherwise the child remains an inaccessible enigma to him" (1925/ 1965, p. vi). The approach Aichhorn used in attempting to reach his delinquents reflected application of psychoanalytic principles. How does one help adolescents who are filled with hate for others and who have never had their needs for love met? Aichhorn answered this by stating, "As far as possible, let the boys alone" (1925/1965, p. 172).

Aichhorn and his staff maintained a consistently friendly and accepting atmosphere and provided opportunities for "wholesome occupations," for repeated talks with staff members, and for plenty of play in an attempt to prevent aggression. Gradually, "and with great caution," demands were made on the boys by the staff. The results? At first, acts of aggression increased with great intensity. Practically all the furniture in the living quarters was destroyed. Windows were broken and doors kicked to pieces. According to Aichhorn, "Screams and howls could be heard from afar" (p. 173). After a time, the wild acting-out behavior diminished and "a bond developed between the boys and the workers" (p. 175). Once this aggressive behavior stopped, Aichhorn reported that many of the boys demonstrated "superior mental performance" (p. 177) and were able to make up lost school work. In summarizing the eventual success of his program, Aichhorn stated:

> Perhaps part of our success was due to our willingness to take a chance, our fearlessness and also to the fact we did not allow ourselves to be drawn into guerrilla warfare. More important still, we were not afraid to let the boys grow up. (p. 180).

One of the concepts used by Aichhorn was transference, a psychoanalytic term referring to the patient's transferring of emotional feelings normally felt for a parent or loved one to the therapist. Aichhorn stressed the importance of the child identifying with the teacher:

> The personality of the worker is very important. The source of traits needed to be taken over by the child is in the worker. It is the tender feelings for the teacher that give the pupil the incentive to do what is prescribed and not to do what is forbidden. (p. 211).

When we consider the punitive orientation toward young criminal offenders which prevailed in Aichhorn's day, his "fearlessness" was truly remarkable in replacing harsh treatment with acceptance and love.

The importance of establishing a positive relationship between teacher and child was further underscored by Berkowitz and Rothman some forty years later:

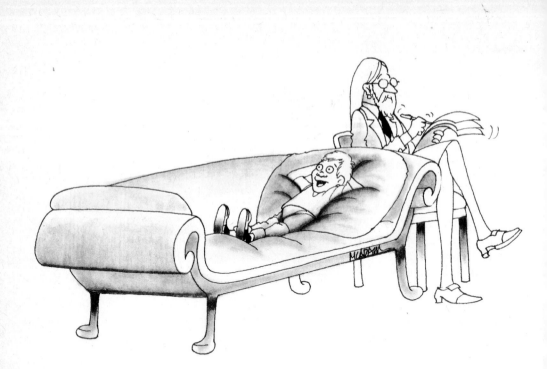

The role of the teacher-academician concerned with skills and discipline has given way to a new concept of teaching concerned with education of the emotions. In order to accomplish this goal, the teacher has to accept the behavior of the child from his first moment in class, no matter how unacceptable that behavior may be. The disturbed child who is aggressive is permitted to express his aggression without harming himself or others, while the withdrawn child is not pressured into socializing, but treated with intelligent neglect. Every child is made to feel that the teacher accepts him as an individual and that his behavior will be met with understanding. Because this is such an unusual role for a teacher to assume, the disturbed child meets the teacher with great suspicion and hostility. He will attempt at every opportunity to test the limits of the teacher's patience. The teacher, while trying to break down the child's concept of authority as a threatening force, maintains a constant emotional climate of returning good for evil. Little by little, the child begins to realize that perhaps nothing he can do will break the relationship, while at the same time he becomes aware that his behavior is socially unacceptable. The teacher makes it quite clear that no matter what the child does, he is accepted and liked as an individual. (Berkowitz & Rothman, 1960, pp. 119–120).

Berkowitz and Rothman further recommended that the teacher assume the blame for problems that frustrate the child (e.g., *Teacher:* "I made a mistake. I must be stupid today.") and become a subservient figure who

can be bullied by a child who needs to bully. Above all, these authors cautioned that the disturbed child who is impulsive, disorganized, aggressive, and negativistic must not be sacrificed to meet the teacher's need for order, conformity, and passivity.

Finally, Rogers (1969) also supports the positive teacher-child relationship. According to him, teachers should be facilitators, not instructors, who genuinely trust and prize their students. They should function as therapists in nondirective therapy, not as authorities or evaluators, and should provide a warm and accepting climate that facilitates significant learning.

In summary, what we encounter in these descriptions of the ideal teacher for disturbed children are the following:

1. Initial unconditional acceptance of the child and his or her behavior and gradual establishment of limits

2. Allowing aggressive behavior to be expressed as a means of "letting it run its course"

3. Development of trust in the teacher-pupil relationship before making demands on the child

4. Creation of a warm and accepting climate for learning rather than one concerned with formal academics

One of the most visible and controversial aspects of this approach relates to the role of permissiveness in helping children improve their behavior and learn. In the first role perspective discussed in this chapter, we found a great deal of emphasis on structure and teacher direction in the educational program. Here we see that the child is, in essence, in charge of things until he or she develops a trusting and positive relationship with the teacher.

Fenichel (1974) has written of his initial experience attempting to implement an educational program that was very permissive in allowing the child to do what he or she wanted. However, one day an acting-out, aggressive child yelled out "in helpless panic," "Why doesn't someone stop me from doing this?" After that, Fenichel began to change his philosophy, reasoning that teachers need to help protect children from their own impulses.

The notion of permitting or encouraging children to express aggressive feelings or channel them in some way such as participation in athletic competition or punching a punching bag as a means of catharsis has been challenged by research findings (Bandura, 1973; Berkowitz, 1973). Instead of draining off aggressive impulses, viewing and participating in aggression has been found to actually *increase* aggressive behavior (Eron, Huesmann, Lefkowitz, & Walder, 1972; Friedrich & Stein, 1973; Stein & Friedrich, 1975).

In the next section we'll consider the question of what type of educational program is provided the child when the teacher is cast in this accepting and therapeutic role.

Educational Programs

We have already established that concern for acceptance of the child and the development of a trusting relationship between teacher and child may result in a fairly permissive classroom environment. But once this trusting relationship develops, how does the teacher go about teaching the child?

Berkowitz (1974) considers learning in and of itself therapeutic since gratification of a successful academic experience can reduce tension and contribute to further learning success. She advocates the encouragement of fantasy "rather than dull reality" in classroom activities. A tape recorder may be provided so that the child can record thoughts regarding "What did I dream last night?" or "What kind of family would I like to have?" Word association lists beginning with neutral words (e.g., table, chair) and later with emotional words (e.g., late, teacher, right, homework, test) can be given to the child with the instruction to provide additional associations (Berkowitz & Rothman, 1960). Sentence completion activities (When teacher _____, My friend _____, I feel that school _____) are another suggestion. Drawing pictures and telling stories are additional creative arts that can be a part of a fantasy-oriented curriculum.

It has been argued that such stimulation of disturbed children's fantasies may be upsetting and undesirable. A technique of "neutralization" or selecting activities that are nonconflictual has been suggested by Jacobson and Faegre (1959). Newman (1959) has stated that activities and content concerned with happy family life, naughty pranks, and tender emotional themes may be too threatening and are best avoided with disturbed children.

Rothman (1974) questions the common practice of rewarding disturbed children for appropriate behavior or success and withholding rewards for problem behavior or failure. She feels the child who makes an incorrect response is in fact the one who needs to be rewarded because he or she may be frustrated, defeated, unhappy, or depressed. Therefore, she suggests the free use of rewards, particularly in the form of love, in the classroom. Rewards should not have to be earned and obtained only through success.

Rogers (1969) views programmed instruction as ideal for disturbed children, since they can set their own pace of learning rather than have it imposed on them by the teacher. He also sees small-group work as valuable in promoting experiential learning.

The point of view we are discussing here has its roots in Freudian psychology, but it has evolved considerably over the years. More recently a psychoeducational approach has been defined (Long, Morse, & Newman, 1971). It is a broader strategy for working with disturbed children and relies less on Freudian tradition. It has been defined as including "all psychological and educational strategies for helping children" (Long, Morse, & Newman, 1971). While considering children as mentally ill or emotionally disturbed, the psychoeducational approach is concerned with describing them in educationally relevant terms that highlight areas of strength and pinpoint areas of weakness for remediation. Among the major considerations of the psychoeducational approach are the following. Many of these overlap with the list on page 61 presented earlier, but they are more "school" and "education" oriented.

1. Cognitive and affective processes are in continuous interaction so that some children can't read because of emotional problems; others have emotional problems because they can't read.

2. Concentrate on how each pupil perceives, feels, thinks, and behaves by listening to what he or she says and focusing on that feeling.

3. Everything that happens to, with, for, and against the child is important and can have therapeutic value.

4. Even if you can't change home and community conditions, remember school can become an important island of support for the child.

5. Adults must establish themselves as allies not punishers.

6. Setting behavioral limits can be a form of love and demonstrate a caring and protective attitude toward the child.

7. Teaching social and academic skills can be important in helping the child cope with a stressful environment.

A counseling technique called "life space interviewing" has evolved as a part of the psychoeducational approach (Redl, 1959). The Life Space Interview, or LSI, is conducted following a problem the child has experienced. It may be a fight with a classmate, a teary tantrum because an assignment is too hard, or a refusal to share some physical education equipment with someone else. Redl views the LSI as either a "clinical exploitation of life events" or "emotional first-aid on the spot." As a clinical exploitation, Redl uses terms like *"reality-rub-in"* (helping the child face the facts), *"massaging numb value areas"* (appealing to the child's sense of fairness), and *"new tool salesmanship"* (helping the child to see alternatives) to describe the ingredients of the interview. As emotional first-aid, the LSI may provide a *"drain-off of frustration acidity"* (letting the child know the listener is sympathetic), *"support for the management of panic, fury, and guilt"* (the mere presence of an understanding adult), and *"umpire services"* (helping the child reach a decision in a crisis or difficult situation). The focus of the LSI is on the here-and-now and, in contrast to formal psychotherapy, it does not probe into the underlying dynamics of the child's problem or rely excessively on interpretation or insight.

Another psychoeducational approach involves the crisis- or helping-teacher (Morse, 1976). This teacher works in a small class that is divided so that two individual children or two small groups of children can be worked with at the same time. When a child becomes unmanageable in a regular classroom, the crisis-teacher may appear and escort him or her to the small classroom. Here the child may be engaged in a Life Space Interview, be given a nonacademic task such as a puzzle, or be individually tutored. Some children may go to work with the teacher on a planned basis, and here the concept of the helping-teacher becomes identical with the current concept of resource teacher or resource specialist. We will be discussing this type of special educator in some detail later in the book.

Glasser (1976) has proposed creating a more trusting atmosphere for learning by means of open-ended class meetings where children learn to express their feelings, develop communication skills, and experience more success in school. Programs focused on affective development that include very specific curricular plans have increased in recent years. One such program, Rational-Emotive Education, or REE, provides a variety of lesson plans that are designed to help the child learn to handle emotional troubles and worries more effectively (Kraus & McKeever, 1977).

Knobloch at Syracuse University has been instrumental in developing an integrated school with a broad psychoeducational orientation for both typical and atypical children. The school is called Jowonio: The Learning Place (Knobloch, 1977). It was named by the children after studying the Onondaga Indian culture and learning that *jowonio* means "to set free." The school program serves forty-six children with a ratio of one disturbed to two normal individuals. The school staff consists of seven teachers and eight teaching trainees enrolled in a graduate program in special education. In addition, professors in social work, physical therapy, movement therapy, instructional technology, and school psychology may participate in the program.

The basic grouping in the school is the "family group." Nine children (six normal and three handicapped) are assigned to a family group with three teachers. The age spread in the group is from three to four years, and there is an effort to balance the number of boys and girls as much as possible. The children remain in these groups for the majority of the school day, although they may join other groups part-time for special activities. An individual learning plan is developed for each child, and during the day each special child is worked with individually or paired with another child with similar needs. Group and independent activities are also provided.

A look at a typical family group's morning schedule provides an example of the school's orientation. School begins at 9:00 AM. Thirty minutes are devoted to "individual skill time." One child may be in play therapy at a community facility during this time. The others may sit around a table together, each working on some independent task. From 9:30 to 9:50 it is "free choice time." Some children may select what they want to do, while others may have limited choices such as activities involving relationship building with a significant adult that emphasizes sharing, trust, and stimulation; playing with considerable adult support and building relationships with other children; or playing with minimal adult support—alone or with other children. From 9:50 to 10:30 once a week, "dramatic movement" is offered. "Controlled movement skills, group social studies, and science group" occur on the other days. The remainder of the morning may involve entire class discussions devoted to "problem solving through cross-sensory processing," or it may include the planning of field trips, sharing news and problems, or swimming.

The Jowonio approach has many facets but it appears to be committed to a total child orientation with much emphasis on improving interpersonal relationships. The integration of both normal and disturbed children together in a close-knit class group appears to offer many advantages particularly for the disturbed group. When disturbed children only relate to other disturbed children in school, it is difficult to see how they can acquire more typical behavior patterns. From the normal child's point of view, the integrated experience may be very helpful with respect to learning about individual differences and learning to work with and help children with problems.

The Jowonio School models much of its curriculum after the developmental therapy program of Wood (Wood, 1977). This program, which is at the Rutland Center in Georgia, is a psychoeducational approach to the treatment of severely emotionally disturbed and autistic children aged from three to fourteen years. It is based on the assumption that young disturbed children go through the same stages of development as normal children, but at a different pace. It has been described as a "growth model" rather than "deficit model," and it blends psychodynamic constructs such as feelings, ego function, guilt, conflict, and self-concept with behavioral principles such as drives, reinforcement, task analysis, and operant behavior.

The disturbed children who participate in the developmental therapy program are grouped by stage of development rather than by type of problem or chronological age. If at all possible, the children participate part-time in an integrated setting with normal children and remain at home with their families rather than living in a residential facility. The developmental therapy program consists of four curriculum areas each of which involves five stages of development. The curriculum areas are: behavior, communication, socialization, and (pre)academics. Stage 1 for each of these curriculum areas is concerned with getting the child "responding to the environment with pleasure." Thus, at Stage 1, the behavior curriculum would invoke learning "to trust own body and skills;" the communication curriculum, "to use words to gain needs"; the socialization curriculum, "to trust an adult enough to respond to him"; and the academic curriculum, "to respond to the environment with processes of classification, discrimination, basic receptive language concepts, and body coordination."

As a means of further illustrating the developmental therapy model, we will include the four subsequent stage levels for the socialization curriculum.

Stage Two: Responding to the environment with success
Socialization goal: To participate in activities with others

Stage Three: Learning skills for successful group participation
Socialization goal: To find satisfaction in group activities

Stage Four: Investing in group processes
Socialization goal: To participate spontaneously and successfully as a group member

Stage Five: Apply individual/group skills in new situations
Socialization goal: To initiate and maintain effective peer group relationship independently
(Wood, 1977)

As can be seen, the five stages reflect emphasis on increasing degrees of social, behavioral, cognitive, and affective maturity. This developmental approach lends itself to the setting of specific behavioral objectives and the planning of *Individual Education Programs,* or IEP's, required by Public Law 94–142. We'll discuss the IEP in the next chapter.

We will summarize the approach we have been discussing by considering goals and methods.

Goals

Although there are differences between the more traditional psychodynamic approach and the more recent psychoeducational approach, they share basic goals. To begin with, they are concerned with "why" the disturbed child behaves the way he or she does. Basic to explaining why children become angry, mistrustful, fearful, guilty, and negative toward themselves is the kind of relationships they have had in their childhood and the type of stressful situations with which they have had to cope. Therefore, establishing trust between teacher and child and creating a stress-free, accepting learning environment become the primary goals. Formal academic goals are of secondary importance.

Methodology

In attempting to accomplish the goals of the psychodynamic and psychoeducational strategies, a unique teacher with unusual sensitivity, intuition, and clinical skills may be required. In fact, one proponent has stated that "the artistry of the teacher is more important than the trainable competencies" (Rabinow, 1960). While total permissiveness such as is found in Aichhorn's program with delinquents is probably rare today, these approaches rely a great deal on children leading the teachers, telling the teachers by various means what their problems are, and deciding if and when they are ready to work and learn in school. And they rely on a teacher who is sensitive to the cues they are providing. Thus, specifics of the methodology are difficult to define. Training a teacher to use life space interviewing will involve more than cookbook directions. The concepts of "reality-rub-in" and "massaging numb value areas" are subject to many interpretations and are far more difficult to communicate to a teacher than the ten steps required to help children write alphabet letters beginning with drawing horizontal and vertical lines on the chalkboard.

The psychodynamic and psychoeducational strategies are concerned with developing relationships, changing attitudes, encouraging emotional growth, creating accepting climates, developing trust, and improving self-concepts. These are critically important areas of concern for all educators working with disturbed children. However, as conceived and stated within these strategies, they are nebulous and somewhat elusive goals when it comes to specifying instructional methodologies for achieving them.

☆ **The Child as Maladaptive Behaver**

☆ **The Teacher as Behavior Modifier**

The previous two role perspectives were concerned with neurological and psychological variables which are "inside" the child. We come now to an approach that is more concerned with variables "outside" the child. These variables are the determiners of behavior and include the processes of reinforcement, punishment, and observational learning (e.g., modeling and imitation). We focus on the child's problem behaviors, attempt to ascertain what environmental events may be responsible for initiating and maintaining them, and then set out to modify the environment so that these problem behaviors decrease.

The Child as Maladaptive Behaver

One of the advantages of focusing on disturbed children as maladaptive behavers is that we do not have to conjure up medically or psychiatrically oriented labels for use in describing them. Bobby Myron who is a maladaptive behaver is a different Bobby Myron than Bobby Myron who is neurologically impaired or emotionally disturbed. The latter terms are outside our educational ballpark and may lead to concentration on what Bobby Myron *cannot* do rather than what he *can* do. They also tend to allow explanation of Bobby's failure to learn by referring to his "impairment" or "disturbance" rather than by seriously considering the instructional adequacy of the teacher or the program.

From the behavioral perspective, our description of Bobby Myron is a description of what he is or is not doing that is interfering with his being successful in school. If we focus on his hyperactivity, we may describe him as "being out of his seat excessively." As teachers we are then in a position to do something about "seat-sitting" in a way we never could about neurological impairment.

The Teacher as Behavior Modifier

Just as assigning the child the role of maladaptive behaver moves us closer to conceptualizing problem behavior in educationally relevant terms, so assigning the teacher the role of behavior modifier more specifically capitalizes on the teacher *as a teacher* rather than as a pseudo-neurologist or junior psychiatrist. The teacher who uses behavior modification in a class program for Bobby Myron will consider the following:

1. What are the specific problem behaviors that are interfering with Bobby's being successful in school?

2. What order of priority can be assigned these problem behaviors (e.g., seat sitting before remedial reading)?

3. What events in the classroom are related to the initiation and maintenance of these problem behaviors?

For example, when Bobby gets out of his seat is he:

a) Avoiding a school task he doesn't like or can't do?
b) Just plain bored?
c) Gaining the attention of the teacher?
d) Gaining the attention of his classmates?
e) Moving to another part of the room where there is something he likes (e.g., animal cages)?

4. How can we alter these events so that the frequency of the problem behavior declines?

For example, what would happen if we:

a) Were careful to see that all assigned tasks were at Bobby's level?
b) Were careful to see that assigned tasks were interesting to him?
c) Ignored him for as long as possible when he was out of his seat?
d) Praised him while he was working at his desk?
e) Quietly praised his classmates for ignoring Bobby?
f) Assigned him responsibility for feeding and caring for the animals?
g) Allowed him to care for and feed the animals and play with them only after certain assigned tasks at his desk were complete?
h) Punished him for being out of his seat by taking away privileges (e.g., recess)?
i) Punished him by sending him outside the room to the principal's office or home?

5. Consider recording the frequency of Bobby's "out of seat" behavior before making any changes (baseline) and then record the effects of possible interventions on the rate of problem behaviors.

Among the advantages of the behavioral orientation is its usefulness for research. By specifying certain behaviors that can be seen and measured in terms of frequency or degree, we can study the effects of various instructional approaches in a scientific manner that is not possible with other approaches. In the next section we will attempt to summarize what research has established regarding the use of behavioral techniques in educational programs with children who have behavior disorders. Our discussion will consider studies that have been done to assess behavioral approaches for reducing disruptive behavior in the classroom and for increasing attention.

Reduction of Disruptive Behavior

When a child is being disruptive in the classroom, the teacher's natural tendency may be to pay attention to the disruption, react to it, and perhaps scold the child. However, such attention is often positively reinforcing to the child and may increase the frequency of disruptive behavior (Madsen,

Becker, Thomas, Koser, & Plager, 1968; Thomas, Becker, & Armstrong, 1968). Simply ignoring out-of-seat behavior has been found to decrease its frequency (Madsen, Becker, & Thomas, 1968). But ignoring is easier with some problem behaviors than with others. The class may literally fall apart while certain problem behaviors are ignored. Other children may actually model the problem behavior because they get the message that the teacher doesn't really mind what the problem child is doing (MacMillan, Forness, & Trumbull, 1973).

What about rewarding the child for appropriate behavior rather than dealing directly with problem behaviors? In general, this has been found to be an effective approach (Kuypers, Becker, & O'Leary, 1968; Hall, Fox, Willard, Goldsmith, Emerson, Owen, Davis, & Procia, 1971). In one study (Hall, Lund, & Jackson, 1968), teachers praised children, moved close to them, and patted them on the back when they were studying appropriately and ignored them when they were not. This produced a reduction of non-study behaviors. The practice of accentuating the positive, while generally effective, may have only limited success if children with behavior disorders have serious academic problems. Such children may have difficulty being successful with any classroom task because of such problems (MacMillan & Morrison, 1979).

Games organized around behavioristic principles have been effective in reducing disruptive behavior on a total classroom basis. In one study (Wolf, Hanley, King, Lachowicz, & Giles, 1970), a kitchen timer set by the teacher for varying times went off periodically. All children in their seats when the bell sounded earned rewards. In another study (Barrish, Saunders, & Wolf, 1969), an elementary class was organized into two teams with

the instructions that when members of either team exhibited disruptive behavior, they would lose points for the team. The team losing the fewest points would then be rewarded. The game had a positive effect on overall classroom behavior, although two children had to be eliminated since they appeared positively reinforced by causing their team to lose points.

Most research focused on reducing disruptive behavior has been concerned with interactions between the teacher and the problem child. However, it has been found that the child's peers also may be potential sources of reinforcement (Buehler, Patterson, & Furness, 1966; O'Leary & O'Leary, 1972). Getting peers to withhold their attention when a given child is being disruptive has been shown to cause such behavior to decrease (Solomon & Wahler, 1973).

One interesting study investigated the effects of "loud" versus "soft" reprimands on the behavior of children who were being disruptive (O'Leary, Kaufman, Kass, & Drabman, 1970). Loudly calling out to the child may be a punishing experience because of the visibility that results, while a soft, personal reprimand heard only by the child may be less aversive. For whatever reason, the study demonstrated that soft reprimands were more effective in reducing disruptive behavior than were loud reprimands.

Increasing Attention

When attempting to teach children to read, it is essential to have their attention. Inattention is one of the most widely reported problems interfering with a child's learning in school. It has been found that praising and rewarding a child for paying attention will reduce nonattentive behavior (Shutte & Hopkins, 1970; Kazdin & Klock, 1973). As with disruptive behavior just discussed, the possibility exists that paying attention to the child's inattention has the effect of increasing the inattention.

In the Santa Monica Project (Hewett, Taylor, & Artuso, 1969), six classes of emotionally disturbed children, eight to eleven years of age, were studied under varying conditions. The model for the experimental classes was the classroom design which will be discussed in Chapter 7. Teachers of both control and experimental classes had knowledge of the design, but they were only expected to maintain it under the experimental condition. Control teachers could do anything they pleased, except administer a check mark system of rewards. Thus, giving check marks to students for appropriate behavior became the independent variable in the study.

Measures were taken at four-week intervals for two semesters of all the children's task attention, and reading and arithmetic achievement. Table 2–1 presents the class assignments to either experimental or control conditions during the fall and spring semesters. As can be seen in Figures 2–1, 2–2, 2–3, and 2–4, one class maintained the experimental condition all year, and one likewise maintained the control condition. Two classes started as experimental in the fall and changed to control in the spring. Two others reversed this, starting as control in the fall and becoming experimental in the spring. Figures 2–1 to 2–4 present the mean task attention percentages for the classes over the year. The presence of the experimental condition resulted in superior task attention except in the case of the class that was experimental in the fall and then became control in the spring. This class actually improved in task attention when the check mark system was removed. It appeared that through the systematic giving of check marks for the fall semester, the teacher in this class had firmly established herself as an effective social reinforcer and therefore could rely on this alone to motivate and manage her students. Although improvement in reading was not associated with the presence of the experimental condition, progress in arithmetic was.

Table 2–1. The assignment of project classes to experimental and control conditions.

Class	Fall Semester	Spring Semester
1 (E)	Experimental	Experimental
2(C)	Control	Control
3 and 4 (CE)	Control	Experimental
5 and 6 (EC)	Experimental	Control

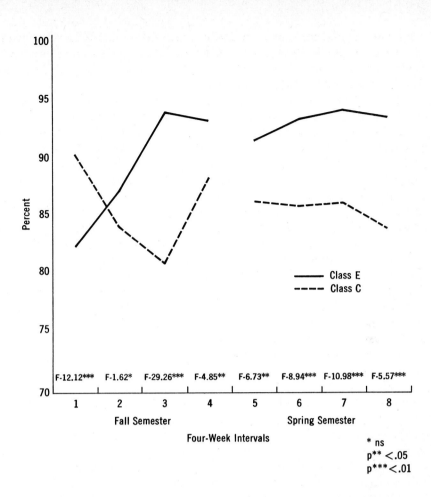

Figure 2–1. A graph of Class E and Class C mean task attention percentages—averaged for four-week intervals during the fall and spring semesters.

Other Studies

Self-recording procedures have successfully reduced disruptive behavior in a number of studies. Children with behavior disorders have been required to record a tally on a card each time a particular problem behavior occurs or to rate themselves for "good behavior" on a scale from one to five (Lovitt, Lovitt, Eaton, & Kirkwood, 1973; Drabman, Spitalnik, & O'Leary, 1973).

Academic response rate was found to accelerate among students with behavior disorders when they were allowed to decide how and when they would be rewarded for their efforts (Lovitt & Curtiss, 1969). Amount of

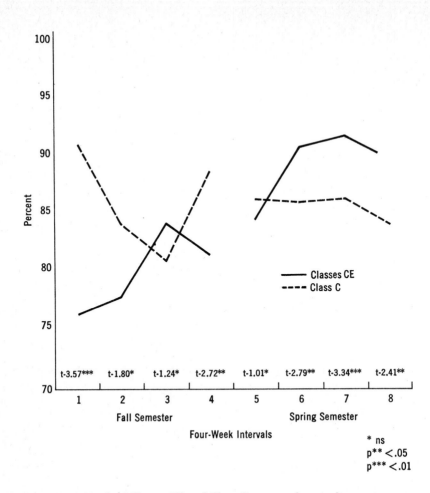

Figure 2–2. A graph of Classes CE and Class C mean task attention percentages—averaged for four-week intervals during the fall and spring semesters.

reinforcement did not appear to be a determining variable, although in some cases there was a tendency for students to gradually decrease the requirements they imposed on themselves for reward (Lovitt, 1973). Students have been reported to rate their classroom experience as more enjoyable when they were permitted to select their own rewards (Karraker, 1977).

In Chapter 1, we discussed how some problem behaviors actually develop as the result of a child imitating or modeling another individual. In attempting to change given problem behaviors, it has been found useful to encourage children to model appropriate behavior. Delinquent adolescents have been found to improve in social adjustment after a ten-week training period of thirty hours. During that time they created skits depicting problems they faced (e.g., being "put down" by an adult), acted these

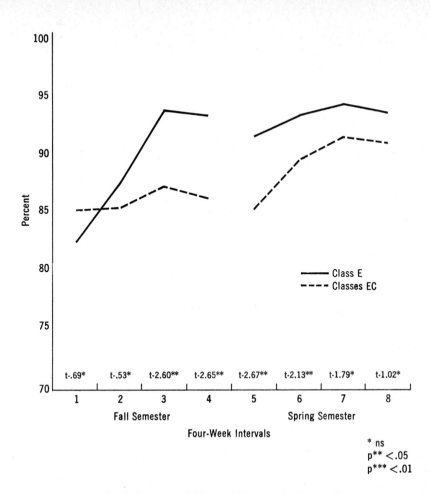

Figure 2–3. A graph of Class E and Classes EC mean task attention percentages—averaged for four-week intervals during the fall and spring semesters.

out, and videotaped them for later viewing (Chandler, Greenspan, & Barenboim, 1974).

In another study, an attempt was made to get a group of socially isolated children to interact more with their peers. A twenty-three-minute film depicting eleven examples of a child entering a group of other children was shown to the isolated children (O'Connor, 1972). A narrator in the film called attention to what was happening. The children who viewed the film increased in their interactions, while a control group who saw a film on dolphins did not. This increase was maintained several weeks later, and in a related study, exposure to a model in a training film produced increased interactions that lasted one month (Evers & Schwarz, 1973).

In still another study, six children with behavior disorders were paired with six peers who were exemplary models of desirable social behavior

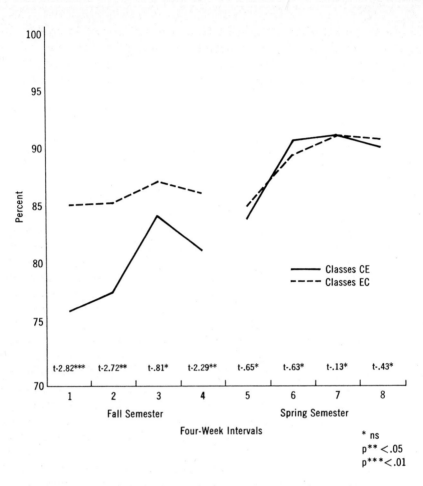

Figure 2–4. A graph of Classes CE and Classes EC mean task attention percentages—averaged for four-week intervals during the fall and spring semesters.

(Csapo, 1972). The problem children sat next to the models and were told to do what the models did so that they could learn to get along better in class. Socially appropriate behavior on the part of the subjects increased and was maintained ten days after the training had stopped.

It is interesting to note that the film-modeling procedure has proven more effective in maintaining positive interactions than direct social reinforcement of appropriate social behavior or directed modeling. Perhaps by specifying the relevant and significant elements of the socially well-adjusted in the children's behavior film, the narrator made these elements more vivid and meaningful to the poorly adjusted children.

The behavioral approach has been more effective in bringing about changes in children's social- and task-oriented behavior than it has been in fostering academic gains (O'Leary & Drabman, 1971). With increased emphasis on integrating exceptional children into regular classrooms wherever possible, the goals of special education must be both improving social and task behaviors and remediating academic deficits. However, in our experience and in line with the ranges of tolerance discussions in the previous chapter, improving social and task behaviors should be given first priority.

We will conclude our discussion of the child as a maladaptive behaver and the teacher as a behavior modifier with a survey of goals and methods.

Goals

An interesting contrast emerges when we compare the provision for goals by the behavioral approach with those of the two previously discussed role perspectives. The neurological approach is very specific regarding "what" should be emphasized with the child based on both theoretical and psychometric considerations. The psychodynamic and psychoeducational approaches emphasize more nebulous goals, but they are quite specific regarding development of trust and maintaining an accepting climate. What about the behavioral approach? Because it is concerned with the application of a set of principles and procedures derived from learning theory, it takes no position regarding the setting of educational goals. This is left up to the teacher. In essence, the message is, "You decide what isn't working for you or any of your children, and we will provide the technology to make it work." In the humanistically oriented realm of education, a technology on the loose with no clearly specified statement of goals or philosophy may well be viewed with suspicion; even worse, it may be totally rejected. Powerful techniques for influencing human behavior that do not clearly specify values and goals all too quickly conjure up associations with "brainwashing" and *"1984."* Proponents of the behavioral approach need to face up to this dilemma and begin to declare where they stand regarding what is good for children and why.

The use of behavioral methodology in the classroom has been met by differing degrees of acceptance by both regular and special educators. Perhaps some of this is due to the fact that psychologists and experimentally oriented special educators, rather than the teachers themselves, have done the research related to the application of behavioral approaches. And the findings of this research have appeared in journals quite obscure and remote as far as the teacher is concerned. In addition, most classroom teachers do not demonstrate an interest in doing research simply because of the heavy demands made on them by their teaching.

We're reminded of a situation in which one of us spoke before a large gathering of teachers regarding the importance of getting teachers to be more research-oriented. Attention was called to a study of ratings made by teachers on the competencies needed by a teacher working with emotionally disturbed children. The competence, "should engage in research activities," received almost the lowest rating, while "should know how to run a slide projector" was very high on the list. After the audience was gently chided regarding this discrepancy in ratings, one teacher got up and angrily stated that slide projectors helped one survive with difficult children, while research studies were a waste of time. Such a stand-off between the "real world" and the "applied world," and the "research laboratory" and the "scholarly laboratory" will undoubtedly continue for some time. However, more regular and special teachers are probably influenced by research now than ever before. And greater efforts are underway to do more educationally relevant research in the real world of the classroom and school and to disseminate such research findings to teachers.

The goal setter in the behavioral approach is the teacher. When appropriate, the child may also participate in selecting goals. No pre-set priorities are established because of inferred "intra-child" charactertistics such as neurological impairment or disturbed emotions. However, known limitations that the child possesses will certainly be taken into account. Despite the fantasies of some extreme antibehaviorists, a child with a broken leg will not be forced into running a race and only be rewarded if he or she wins or be punished if he or she loses because some cold-blooded behaviorist has decided the goal of "race running" is appropriate.

Methodology

We have already devoted considerable space to discussion of the methodology of the behavioral approach. There can be no question that it is the most specific of any methodology applied to the problems of disturbed children. It is based on established principles of scientific learning theory, and it works in the classroom. It is also the most widely studied, documented, and validated approach.

Some teachers see very little that is new in the behavioral approach. They may exclaim, "Why, I've been rewarding children if they were correct and nonrewarding if they were incorrect for years!" No doubt they have, but it is not the mere presence of aspects of this methodology in the classroom that is essential, but rather their *systematic application*. The child finds himself or herself in a highly predictable environment. What is expected is clearly presented, and the rewards the child receives are contingent upon meeting expectations operating in the classroom.

The role assigned the teacher in this approach is not mere emulation of an automaton or teaching machine. In the setting of educational goals and in the application of appropriate instructional strategies, the teacher relies on a knowledge of child development, a degree of clinical judgment, and a familiarity with sound educational practices.

To complete this chapter on roles children and teachers play, we turn to the ecological approach.

☆ **The Child as a Victim of Discordance in His or Her Ecosystem**

☆ **The Teacher as Part of the Child's Ecosystem**

We come now to an approach that does not assign separate roles to teacher or child but argues for examination of the relationship between the two as well as the relationship between all other aspects of the child's environment and the individual child's own uniqueness. We introduced the notion of human ecology in Chapter 1. We will expand on it here with specific consideration of how it may influence treatment and educational practices with disturbed children.

The Child as a Victim of Discordance in His or Her Ecosystem

A concept central to understanding human ecology is the *ecosystem*. Human ecologists do not discuss emotional disturbance; rather they speak of a disturbance within the *ecosystem*. This disturbance is not centered in the child as is assumed by the neurological and psychodynamic approaches, nor is it centered in the environment as assumed by the behavioral approach. It is centered in the interaction between the idiosyncratic individual and his or her unique environment—the ecosystem.

The school is one part of the child's unique environment or ecosystem. The teacher is another. As individual children come to school, they bring with them behaviors learned in another part of their ecosystem—in their homes and families. As children advance through grades in school, they bring to each new classroom, new teacher, and new curriculum, the influences of all previous interactions in the ecosystem of the school and elsewhere. When we single out an individual child as being emotionally disturbed or exhibiting a behavior disorder, we are using descriptive terms that really mean there is not a good fit—a discordance—between the child and his or her environment. What is wrong now probably relates to discordance during other times in the child's life.

It is difficult to argue with this approach to conceptualizing emotional disturbance. As was pointed out in Chapter 1, within the ecological framework, we can subsume all other approaches since the reciprocal relationship between the individual with his or her unique biological and psychological characteristics and the environment is a basic statement of the process of human development. But how can we formulate and implement an educational strategy based on the concept of human ecology? In 1961, one such effort, Project Re-ED, was initiated. We will review it as an illustration of the ecological approach (Lewis, 1967).

The Teacher as Part of the Child's Ecosystem

Project Re-ED

Project Re-ED was formulated as an alternative to costly, traditional, psychotherapeutic treatment approaches in closed settings that primarily relied on professionals in psychiatry, clinical psychology, and social work and that had a questionable record of effectiveness. Obviously, the psychotherapeutic idea that you need to treat a "sick" child by concentrating

on his or her intra-psychic conflicts is dramatically opposite to the concept of emotional disturbance as a state of discordance between child and environment and environment and child.

One of the most significant aspects of the Project Re-ED alternative is that educators, not psychiatrists or psychologists, are assigned primary responsibility for working with the children. These educators are specially trained and instead of "treating" they "re-educate" emotionally disturbed children. They also provide an "engaging, good-oriented, educational climate during all of a child's waking hours." This is in contrast to programs in traditional, residential treatment centers where for a few hours each week highly skilled and highly paid professionals provide "therapy," and during the rest of the time the children spend long periods of inactivity and idleness since the remainder of the staff is often of marginal competence.

Project Re-ED is more concept than readily definable fact. According to Hobbs, "One of the important early ideas in Project Re-ED was that there should be no orthodoxy, no fixed explanation, no set ways of doing things, no dogma" (1977, p. 65). He further stated after visiting a number of Re-ED schools:

> And while there are characteristics which the schools have in common, perhaps reflecting "a philosophy of Re-ED," each school is distinctive. Each has invented some unique way to translate Re-ED ideas into a living program and to take maximum advantage of local resources and opportunities. (p. 66).

A typical Project Re-ED school has forty children divided into five groups of eight children each. Each group is the responsibility of two teacher-counselors and a liaison teacher. The children live at the school five days a week and return home on weekends. In addition, other consultants participate in the program in each school. Children are referred by a community agency such as a child guidance clinic, family service agency, or school. But the referral does not involve assigning total responsibility for the child and his or her family to Project Re-ED. In most cases, the referring agency continues to work with the child's family. The ages of children referred range from six to twelve years with a modal age of ten. Approximately 75 percent of the children are boys. The average stay for a child is six to seven months.

Enrollment begins with an admission conference between the agency and the liaison teacher during which the child's problems and treatment to date are reviewed as well as the current status of the child, the family, and the community school. Preliminary Re-ED goals are set during this conference. In general, these tend to be quite specific and concrete, and they reflect changes that are realistic to expect in a relatively brief period. From the start, the intent is to return the child home as quickly as possible. A further example of this intent is the planning for the child's release during the admission conference and the identification of additional community resources that may need to be mobilized at that time. The criteria for accepting a child is not based on diagnostic labels, but rather on the potential the child appears to have for profitting from a group-centered educational program. As a result, a wide range of types of "disturbed" children have been included in the program.

Following this conference, the child is assigned to a Project Re-ED school and visits it with his or her parents. The teacher-counselors begin to plan an individualized program of remedial education and social living experiences for the child. In addition, they prepare the other children for the arrival of the new child into their living group.

The school day in a Project Re-ED school corresponds to a regular public-school day. It runs from 9:00 in the morning to 3:00 in the afternoon. After 3:00 the recreation period begins. During the school day there is heavy emphasis on basic academic skills and use of language. However, since placement of the child is based more on level of social skills than school achievement, provisions are made to individualize emphasis in the areas of the child's greatest need. In other words, what is taught is what is viewed as having the greatest social utility for the child.

After school, sports and recreation skills are taught since proficiency in these skills is viewed as being as useful socially as academics. The evening program emphasizes skills required to live harmoniously and may involve rap sessions and group discussion of problems that have arisen as well as evaluations of each other. Much of the "re-education" goes on during meal time, dressing, and bed time when the specially trained adults who live with the children must deal with refusals to eat or to go to bed, or such problems as physical aggression. There is much self-evaluation by the children, and tokens and other rewards may be earned for self-improvement.

During the time the child is enrolled, the goals are periodically reviewed along with progress being made in planning with the child's family, home (or regular) school, and other community agencies that will be critical in relation to the child's chances for successful readjustment. We see the ecological approach clearly expressed here. After attempting to identify the sources of discordance between the child, the family, the home school, and other persons or agencies in the community, Project Re-ED sets its goals in an effort to reduce the discordance, works intensively with the child, and coordinates its efforts with the people and places to whom the child will return. According to Lewis (1967):

> As soon as a judgment can be made that the child is functioning just well enough, and/or the systems in his community are changing their tolerance thresholds enough to support his behavior without undue conflict, and with reasonable prognosis for his continued healthy development, plans will be made to return him to his own home and school. (p. 357).

The role of the two teacher-counselors is to help the child learn to cope and adjust more adequately. The teacher-counselors are recruited from classroom teachers who are qualified to teach basic tool subjects to elementary-aged children and who hold promise for being counselors, recreation supervisors, campers, parent surrogates, and general "handy persons." In addition to teaching in the classroom, the teacher-counselors frequently take their children on camping trips. These trips provide unique opportunities for teaching the children to take responsibility and to cooperate with each other.

Once assigned, the two teacher-counselors must work as a team, setting goals for their eight children, evaluating progress, and coordinating their efforts with others outside in the community. They must be particularly skilled in identifying goals that are truly critical to the social milieu to which the child will return and that are feasible to accomplish during a brief period of time. Although both teachers may have similar backgrounds and qualifications, they assume slightly different roles. One actually teaches the children in the classroom; the other works with the group during after-school and evening activities and emphasizes the informal counseling and group-work aspects of the teacher-counselor role.

The liaison teacher is a unique individual on the Project Re-ED staff. This individual provides the link between the project and the home school to which the child will eventually return. Before the child is enrolled, the liaison teacher carefully appraises the sources of conflict between the child and the school, including academic deficits and behaviors that are annoying to teachers and classmates. This appraisal is extremely important to assist the teacher-counselor in setting goals for the child. While the children are living at the Project Re-ED school, the liaison teacher helps them maintain contact with their home schools by holding conferences with their home teachers, by informing the teacher-counselor of typical assignments the child would be getting in the home school, and by having the children correspond with their classmates on occasion. When the child is to be returned, the liaison teacher informs the home-school teacher and provides a description of the remedial techniques that have been found successful with the child, any special management problems that may be anticipated, and program modification in the public school that may be desirable. Once the child has returned to his or her home and home school, the liaison teacher eases the transition by serving as an educational consultant on a regular basis with the home-school teacher.

In one study (Bower, Lourie, Strother, & Sutherland, 1969), teacher ratings of a group of Re-ED children were made before and after the children participated in the program. Prior to participation, 75 percent of the children were rated as having fairly severe or very severe behavioral or emotional problems. Six months after the children left the Re-ED program, 75 percent were rated in the normal range or as having mild problems. Parents and professionals who had worked with the children rated 80 percent as moderately or greatly improved after Re-ED.

Project Re-ED is an innovative approach that has been successful in helping disturbed children learn more successful ways of functioning and relating in their normal environments. It has helped pave the way for this success through constant work with the settings and individuals in these environments to which the child must eventually return. While we have closed the previous three sections in this chapter with a discussion of provision for goals and methods, these topics have been covered in our general discussion here.

Achievement Place

Another illustration of an ecological approach is seen in the model environment called Achievement Place. This was developed by Phillips, Fixsen, and Wolf of the University of Kansas (Trotter, 1973). Although conceived of from a rather strict behavioral point of view, it aims at a total life influence for children from eleven to sixteen years of age who are juvenile delinquents or who have behavior disorders. Hence, it reflects an ecological orientation.

The Achievement Place model consists of a residential home, two teaching-parents, and seven or eight boys and girls. The home is run according to principles of behavior modification, and it aims to educate the children in academic, social, self-care, and vocational skills. Most of the Achievement Place youths are having serious problems in school that have led to suspension or dropping out. Thus, one of the major goals of the program is to return the children to school and improve their chances for success. Each child lives at Achievement Place but goes back to his or her regular community school. Upon leaving in the morning, the child is given a daily report card by the teaching-parents that will be used by the teachers in school to note whether or not the child behaved appropriately in class, completed homework, or performed adequately on tests or exams.

Upon returning home with the daily report card, the child is given points based on these grades. These points can be used to purchase a variety of privileges such as free time, trips, and spending money. Before introducing the daily report card, children in Achievement Place homes spent about 25 percent of their time in appropriate study behavior. Once the card was introduced, this percentage rose to 90 and a one-letter-grade increase was common for most students after a nine-week period. As the child demonstrates he or she has learned appropriate study behavior, the daily report card may be phased out.

In addition to school concerns, the teaching-parents of Achievement Place (trained in human development at the University of Kansas) instruct their young residents in proper social interactions, personal cleanliness, and community involvement. Specific behavioral goals are selected for each child based on behavior that family members, the school, the community, and the teaching-parents themselves believe should be changed. Desired behaviors earn points while undesired behaviors (e.g., speaking aggressively, arguing, disobeying, being late, stealing, lying, and cheating) lose points.

The boys and girls assigned to Achievement Place spend up to one year in the program. A comparison of Achievement Place youths with their counterparts who had been placed in state institutions revealed some interesting results once the two groups were on their own. One year after release, the institutional group had committed an average of 2.4 offenses, while the Achievement Place group had committed only 0.7. These figures dropped after two years to 1.4 for the institutional group and 0.0 for the other. As far as recidivism was concerned, after two years 53 percent of the institutional group had gotten into trouble with the law compared to only 19 percent of the Achievement Place group. A striking comparison emerges with respect to school attendance. Two semesters after release only 9 percent of the institutional group was still in school compared to 90 percent for their Achievement Place counterparts.

One of the most important aspects of Achievement Place is that it is a relatively inexpensive program to operate. State institutions spend about $22,000 per bed to open a new unit, while Achievement Place spends approximately $5,800. The yearly operating costs for the state institution are $9,800 per child, while Achievement Place operates with a yearly-per-child cost of $4,100.

The concept of Achievement Place and the ties with community life it maintains are exciting. How much more constructive and therapeutic it is to help children work out their problems in a close-knit, family-like group with complete community involvement rather than to isolate them in an alien, institutional environment.

Emotionally disturbed children and their teachers have assumed a variety of roles. Probably none of these is as distinct and specific as we have made them sound in this discussion, although undoubtedly we could find examples of them in the field today. While the roles we discussed may not involve "union card" status, they do involve differential selection of goals based on beliefs regarding the cause and nature of emotional disturbance and the most critical priorities for an effective educational program with disturbed children.

For some, diagnosis and training will take precedence over broader concerns with social relationships and motivation. The child will be suspected of evidencing a neurological problem. This may have a variety of effects on the teacher ranging from immense involvement in providing the child with structured exercises to explaining the failure of efforts to help him or her on the basis of a "damaged brain."

Some will give top priority to the building of relationships and the establishing of trust between teacher and child. Formal training and teaching will receive only secondary emphasis. The role of the teacher as educator will be overshadowed by the role of therapist in an attempt to formulate the important ingredients of an educational program with disturbed children. Phrases like "strengthen the ego," "develop trust," and "improve self-concept" may be stated as goals and provide more inspirational than substantive guidance for the teacher.

Some will envisage disturbed children as socialization failures who simply haven't learned how to get along. These people will resist considerations of "how" a child's central nervous system may affect behavior or "why" a child's life is in conflict. Methodology will overshadow concern with goals. This may create uncertainty and suspicion among those concerned with child development and humanistic psychology.

Finally, the boldest and most comprehensive approach views all previous approaches as overly narrow. It builds its case on the merits of as total and specific an intervention into all aspects of the child's life as possible. It creates new professional roles and can include the focus of any of the other approaches.

What is the ideal role for the teacher of emotionally disturbed children and what is the most logical role for the disturbed child? What are the methods and approaches that are most promising? In attempting to answer these questions, it is fitting to close this chapter on contrasting philosophies and methodologies with a discussion of the importance of open-mindedness among those concerned with disturbed children—teachers, other professionals, and parents.

Attempting to understand and effectively deal with emotional disturbance is often extremely frustrating. In the classroom, a teacher's fondest hope may be for a sure-fire remedy to bring order out of the educational chaos created by disturbed children. In a similar manner, at home parents may search desperately for "the answer" to solving the perplexing puzzle presented by their child. The concerns of both teacher and parents may approach desperation and herein lies a serious problem. Desperation breeds vulnerability, and vulnerability invites exploitation by both commercial and professional interests, some of whom promise, or seem to promise, that they have THE answer. It may be a program of training exercises; it may be a regimen of medication or special food supplements; it may be a "handy-dandy" kit with 101 ways to teach reading, spelling, or arithmetic; it may be a set of recordings guaranteed to improve language functioning; it may be an expensive piece of equipment that can be set up at home to foster improvement in motor coordination; it may be a private school with a mysterious one-of-a-kind teaching or treatment approach; it may be a manual with cookbook specifications for dealing with motivation and behavior problems; it may be fancy blocks, peg-boards, crawl-through playground equipment, or flashcards; in short, the possibilities are almost endless. Witness the increase year by year in the amount of floorspace given to displays of commercially available special education materials and equipment at the national convention of the Council for Exceptional Children.

We have briefly discussed Public Law 94–142 and will discuss it in more detail in the next chapter. This law has the potential for funneling large amounts of money into the states for improved and increased educational services for handicapped children, adolescents, and young adults. Some of this money will go into instructional materials, and the race to get on the commercial bandwagon and sell everything from kits, to performance objectives for Individual Education Programs, to colorful plastic counters for teaching arithmetic is on.

Some of these commercial materials are based on research and knowledge, but most are not. Many have a kind of obvious logic to their use and will differ in their degree of effectiveness. Similarly, the contrasting approaches to teaching emotionally disturbed children that have been discussed in this chapter are based on varying degrees of research and study. However, only the behavioral approach has really amassed any body of knowledge regarding its effectiveness. The others appeal to logic, belief systems of teachers, and teachers' actual experiences with children. Thus, we have varying degrees of knowledge to draw upon in philosophically developing educational programs for disturbed children and in selecting instructional materials to include in those programs. We have no certainty, however, that any program philosophy, educational methodology, or instructional material will *always* work with *all* disturbed children.

To bolster our plea for open-mindedness and resistance to those who promise or appear to promise certainty, we will draw upon a quotation from a well-known television commentator. This statement was made as he entered into retirement after thirteen years of attempting to make sense of the news on a nightly basis. Eric Sevareid stated that prominent among the lessons he had learned was the following: "To retain one's doubts as well as one's convictions, in this world of dangerously passionate certainties" (1977, p. 111). In our experience, the field of special education concerned with disturbed children, as well as that concerned with every other type of handicapping condition, has been influenced by some individuals who have manifested "dangerously passionate certainties." It has also been influenced by many others who retained their doubts as well as their convictions and lived comfortably and profitably with notions of open-mindedness, relativity, and uncertainty.

With respect to the psychodynamic and behavioral positions which we have discussed as separate approaches to educating disturbed children, Morse sees a blending of the two:

> The leaders in the field have finally gotten around to realizing that the human being behaves in a more diverse way than either of these positions alone [can explain]. Both positions imply things about human nature and about learning. The psychodynamic position certainly has had to expand its horizon about human nature and how behaviors change, and I think the same thing is true in behaviorism. The reason teachers sometimes grab onto one of these positions is because somebody sells it to them as the solution to everything. (1977, p. 164).

There are probably not as many "card carrying" extremists in the field of educating disturbed children today as there were in the 1950s and 1960s. What seems to be happening is a movement toward a "critical eclecticism" in which individual children are more and more studied with an open mind and whatever seems to hold promise for most effectively helping them on an individual basis is readily turned to. It is our conviction that one hundred years from now we will more likely have learned to use what we presently know in a wiser and more individualized manner rather than have discovered a breakthrough approach that will be appropriate for every disturbed child. Matching the individual child and his or her individual needs with the teaching strategy and instructional materials that will do the best possible job—whether this means walking a balance beam, engaging in a Life Space Interview, providing M & M's for appropriate behavior, or enrolling the child, the family, and the community into a total treatment effort—should be our continuing goal.

chapter 3

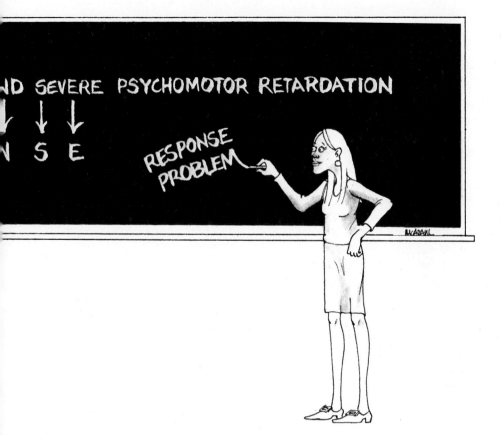

A Functional Description
of Emotional Disturbance

The issue of how to translate emotional disturbance or behavior disorders into educationally relevant concepts and terms has come up several times in our previous discussion. It is a critical issue in the entire field of special education. Children who are learning disabled, visually handicapped, hearing handicapped, physically handicapped, mentally retarded, or severely handicapped are no more helped educationally by terms such as *blindness, crippled,* or *mentally deficient* than is the child who is called *emotionally disturbed.* In fact, all such children may be adversely affected by labels, particularly if the label, not what the child has learned, needs to learn, and is ready to learn, receives primary focus. Descriptions of children in terms of their learning characteristics, accomplishments, and needs are "functional" (they tell the teacher where to go to work), while descriptions in terms of medical and psychiatric diagnoses and test scores are "nonfunctional" (they tell the teacher what the child can't do).

Over the years there has been increasing disenchantment with the educationally nonfunctional "medical model" and increasing concern with developing approaches that are truly functional in nature. A striking example of the movement from nonfunctional to functional descriptions is provided by events in the area of the visually handicapped. In 1935, the Social Security Act required that a legal definition of blindness be formulated so that eligibility for federal aid could be determined. For this reason, a definition based on visual acuity as measured by a wall chart was adopted for both the blind and the partially seeing. People were legally blind if they could only read from twenty feet a letter size that could be read by normally seeing individuals from a distance of two hundred feet (20/200). Children who were measured as "legally blind" were considered "educationally blind" as well and were given braille instruction; children with visual handicaps not so measured were given instruction by means of large print or optical magnification devices.

While this may sound like a logical approach, it wasn't long until teachers found that some "blind" children who were learning braille were not learning it through the sense of touch at all. In fact, they were "reading" it with their eyes since they actually had residual vision. Thus, instead of learning to read the alphabet, they were *visually* learning to read another symbol code, one of raised dots. Arbitrary interpretation of the definition of legal blindness was therefore found to be nonfunctional for many children in school. Today, a simple functional approach is generally utilized. Partially seeing children are those who can learn to read print; blind children are those who cannot read print but who need instruction in braille.

Recently, a more comprehensive, functional approach for describing visually handicapped children has been devised (Scholl, 1975). Instead of a numerical rating of visual acuity, a system is proposed that describes how effectively an individual can use whatever residual he or she possesses in not only reading and writing but in moving through the environment. The most severely visually handicapped individual is *unable* to read or write even with the aid of optical or other visual enlarging devices, *unable* to identify familiar objects in the environment, and *unable* to maneuver safely through an unfamiliar environment without the aid of a dog, cane, or sighted person. Less severely handicapped individuals are *able* to do one or more of these tasks. How much more useful for the teacher to be given this sort of information about a visually handicapped child rather than be told the child's visual acuity is 20/200.

We could provide numerous additional examples of similar problems with other exceptional children. How many children with such-and-such an IQ score have been expected to act retarded rather than to learn, just as children called legally blind were once expected not to be able to see at all? The authors have witnessed a Down's syndrome child with a tested IQ of 40 reading at third grade level which, according to expectations once considered valid, was impossible. Fortunately for this child, the teacher hadn't come across these expectations in any textbook on reading instruction. It is hoped we are moving from a time when labels and scores often determined our expectations to a time when the children themselves determine them.

The contrasting role perspectives we discussed in the last chapter varied with respect to potential for generating functional descriptions of emotional disturbance. In general, this potential ranged from the rather narrow (e.g., "He has a visual-perceptual problem"—training approach) to the very global (e.g., "She is in a state of discordance with her ecosystem"—ecological approach). In between we encountered such descriptions as "lack of self-esteem" (psychodynamic approach) and "exhibits maladaptive behavior" (behavioral approach). Of the four approaches, the behavioral translates most readily into a functional description of emotional disturbance. We will use this approach in this book, but as will soon be apparent, we will not lose sight of the idea of critical eclecticism along the way.

Although we are oriented in a behavioral direction, one of the most educationally meaningful and practical statements about emotionally disturbed children we have encountered comes from a psychodynamically oriented special educator:

1. The school is not one school, but many schools; in the final analysis it is for each child a different school.

2. What may be taught is only what the child is ready to learn and despite apparent uneducability, all children are ready to learn *something*.

3. Normal children on entering school already have had a childhood which has prepared them for the culture of the school; for most of our (emotionally disturbed) boys and girls this is not so. The teacher and other staff become the primary persons, the people on whom the youngsters may build new concepts of worthwhile life; they incorporate our goals and purposes for them and through us, somewhat late, get *ready* for school while attending school.

4. It is possible to do a tremendous amount of individualization if the adult really believes in it; the youngsters catch on to the greater justice of different *right* things for everybody rather than the same things for all. (Rabinow, 1955, p. 691).*

Rabinow was not speaking solely about emotionally disturbed children at all. He was talking about *learners,* each of whom is ready at all times to learn something. This is the fundamental orientation of this book toward emotional disturbance. It is an orientation completely compatible with all the ideas of the teacher as a diagnostician-trainer, as a therapist, as a behavior modifier, or as a part of the child's ecosystem. It is compatible with all the views of children as neurologically impaired, as emotionally disturbed, as maladaptive behavers, or as individuals who are experiencing discordance in their ecosystems. We are proposing an eclectic approach based on the behavioral perspective. Considering all children—normal and exceptional—first and foremost as learners may seem obvious and simplistic. However, it is the cornerstone upon which an effective educational program can be built. Furthermore, it is one answer to the effects-of-labeling dilemma special educators have suffered with for so long.

The term *learner* is exciting and dynamic. It is optimistic. It overshadows the negative and sidetracking aspects of the term *handicapped.* It suggests change. It directs us to look at what children can do, not at what some ominous label says they can't do. Teachers can *teach* learners, while they may have second thoughts about being able to teach autistic, psychotic, sociopathic, or neurotic children.

What Can Teachers Contribute in a Psychiatric Hospital?

If we conceptualize all emotionally disturbed children first and foremost as learners who are ready at all times to learn "something," our task in developing a functional-descriptive approach becomes one of defining the somethings such children need to learn. The framework for the approach we will present here was first formulated by the staff of the Neuropsychiatric Institute (NPI) School at UCLA.† The NPI School provides a full-time school program for emotionally disturbed and mentally retarded children and adolescents who are hospitalized in the UCLA Neuropsychiatric Institute and participate in diagnostic, training, research, and treatment programs there. When the school first opened, it was largely viewed as a

---

*Reprinted, with permission, from the *American Journal of Orthopsychiatry.* Copyright 1955 by the American Orthopsychiatric Association, Inc.
†The authors would like to acknowledge the valuable contribution to this approach made by Juanita Ferjo, Wallie Kass, Frank Langdon, Don Mayhew, Howard Richer, Jan Siegel, and Jim Simmons.

babysitting service by a psychodynamically oriented staff whose major concern was to uncover the deep-seated origins of the children's emotional problems. School was fine, but, after all, these children were psychiatrically ill and in a psychiatric hospital to receive a psychiatric evaluation and psychiatric treatment. Teachers were fine too, but, after all, they couldn't really be considered a part of that all-knowing professional triumvirate made up of the psychiatrist, the clinical psychologist, and the psychiatric social worker.

During case conferences when individual children were being discussed, the school staff might or might not be asked to comment on what was happening in the classroom. And when they were asked, the teachers' remarks were often limited to "he enjoys water play" for a child at the preschool level, to "she's reading in a second grade book" at the elementary level, to "he likes to read war stories" at the secondary level. Over time the school staff became concerned and frustrated with the role apparently assigned them in the NPI program. Why wasn't education viewed as more critical in the overall therapeutic program? Why didn't the psychiatrists, psychologists, and social workers pay more attention to the school's efforts? Why wasn't the school staff asked to participate on a more equal basis with representatives of other disciplines during case conferences?

While it was easy to wallow in self-pity, it soon became apparent that the truth of the matter was quite simple: even if the school had been invited to more fully participate in the NPI program, when it came to being asked about the unique role of education in the treatment of emotional disturbance, the school staff really had little to say. Thus, the problem was not one of a multidisciplinary conspiracy to "put down" education, but rather it was a failure on the part of the school staff to conceptualize emotional disturbance in distinctly educational- and learning-oriented terms so that the school's goals and contributions could be formulated and communicated. After all, the psychiatrists had their psychiatric classification system and the psychosexual stages of development, the clinical psychologists had their IQ tests and projective personality instruments, and the social workers had their framework of family dynamics to use as references to give them a unique identity and to allow them to discuss emotional disturbance from their own particular point of view. What did the school staff have? Actually, very little.

During a series of discussions with NPI psychiatrists, the school staff began to explore ways of conceptualizing emotional disturbance in an educational and learning context. When a child, any child, came into a classroom, what were the competencies required for success? Could we describe the problems of the emotionally disturbed child in school with reference to these competencies? The introduction of Donald is appropriate here.

Donald was an eleven-year-old boy brought into the NPI in a completely immobilized state. He would not walk, talk, eat, move, or care for himself. He was fed with a stomach tube initially, but later he would swallow juice—his only visible movement. As he regained strength, his psychiatrist felt going to school might help him in some way. He came to the NPI school one day—a seemingly lifeless, fragile robot whose power source had run down. The psychiatrist in charge of the case introduced him to the teacher: "This is Donald. He is in a catatonic schizophrenic stupor with severe psychomotor retardation. Good luck."

Such a description was a bit unsettling for the teacher and is an excellent example of the alien and essentially useless contribution such labels and diagnostic terms have to make in educational settings. As long as the teacher was intimidated by this pathetic little boy in a "catatonic schizophrenic stupor," it was doubtful that any worthwhile program could be provided by the school. But once she set aside the psychiatric jargon and took a long, hard look at Donald, things got better. Here was this immobilized student. We had heard what his psychiatric problem was. Now, what was his educational problem? Simple. Donald was a *severe response problem* in educational and learning terms. He did not move. To learn you must respond. Donald was a candidate for a response curriculum. He was no longer a mysterious alien with catatonic schizophrenia. He was now a learner, and it would be the role of the school to teach him to respond as the initial educational task. We will describe the response curriculum that was developed in the next chapter. The important point we want to make with the story of Donald is that we were in a position to really help him as a learner when we swept aside the meaningless diagnostic labels and functionally described him in learning and educational terms.

Levels of Learning Competence

Thus we had made a start in developing a functional classification approach. One basic competency we needed to include was "responding." What were others? During conversations with the psychiatric staff, we reviewed other approaches that had been used to describe emotionally disturbed children. We discussed one such approach in Chapter 1—the psychosexual stages of development emanating from the work of Freud and Erikson. Essentially what the oral, anal, phallic, and latency stages are describing are tasks and experiences children encounter as they develop their unique personalities beginning at birth and moving through the elementary years. Could we translate these psychosexual stages related to personality development into a series of basic competencies needed by all children from birth onward if they are going to be successful learners? If we could, perhaps these competencies would provide a developmental framework for describing emotional disturbance in learning and educational terms. By broadly translating the psychosexual stages into such terms, we arrived at six levels of learning competence for our framework.

Attention

Response

Order

Exploratory

Social

Mastery

The *attention* level is concerned with children making contact with the environment; the *response* level with getting them to actively participate motorically and verbally; the *order* level with teaching them to follow routines; the *exploratory* level with helping them become accurate and thorough explorers of their environments; the *social* level with aiding them in gaining the approval and avoiding the disapproval of others; and finally the *mastery* level with helping them learn skills related to self-care, academics, and vocational pursuits.

In their original form, these levels were called " a hierarchy of educational tasks" (Hewett, 1964). Later they were referred to as "a developmental sequence of educational goals" (Hewett, 1968); finally they were described as "levels of learning competence" (Hewett with Forness, 1977). Along the way the terms used for some levels were changed, and one level was deleted altogether. The evolution of this concept, while interesting, will not add appreciably to our present discussion. Although the concept was based on a translation of psychodynamic principles into terms associated with learning, it does not represent a theory of anything. It is a pragmatically derived statement that has proven useful to the authors (and to others over the years) in conceptualizing the educational meaning of emotional disturbance and in formulating relevant educational curricula.

However, there is an obvious developmental logic to the sequence of levels. At birth the child first notices and hears things (attention). He or she begins simultaneously to respond, first motorically and vocally, and later verbally (response). Routines of eating, sleeping, and eventually toileting are encountered (order). From the very beginning, the child is learning about the environment through looking, listening, touching, tasting, and smelling; and people, objects, and experiences become familiar (exploratory). Also from the beginning, the child is intimately involved with others. They are essential for keeping him or her alive at first; later gaining their approval and avoiding their disapproval becomes important (social). Finally, with entrance into school, the child begins a long period of learning the tasks that hopefully will lead to the eventual assumption of an independent role in society (mastery). The levels do not constitute a hierarchy, but rather an overlapping sequence of behaviors, most of which are being learned simultaneously.

Normal children arrive at school ready to pay attention, to look at and listen to what is presented. They are ready responders, eagerly participating in class activities. They adapt easily to the routines of the school: coming on time, hanging up one's coat, waiting one's turn, raising one's hand, finishing assignments, etc. They are hungry explorers of the environment, eager to look, listen, touch, taste, and smell. They want to know the names of colors, the rhythms of songs, the names of animals and flowers, the experiences of sliding down a slide or climbing a tree. They are anxious to make friends and play with others, and they learn the "give and take" of successful relationships. And all the while they are becoming more knowledgeable and independent and are learning to read, write, spell, and do arithmetic. Such children are a delight to teach. Many of these levels of competence are readily visible during a visit to a kindergarten classroom. Alertness, eagerness, cooperation, enthusiasm, joy, fun, sharing, and learning are very exciting to see on display.

Unfortunately, the uniqueness of emotionally disturbed children derives from their failure to have acquired one or more of these levels of learning competence prior to school or their failure to acquire them once in school. Disturbed children often do not pay attention, instead preferring to daydream or focus on the irrelevant. They may not care to participate in learning at all, refusing to join in activities or answer questions. They may range from being overly conforming and compulsive to wildly acting out and being destructive in an attempt to set their own rules by breaking rules imposed on them by others. Some will explore their environments only tentatively or not at all because of fearfulness. Others will "plunge into anything" or "tear up the place" at any opportunity. Some will be hopelessly dependent on help from the teacher and whine and cry when left alone. Others "won't give a hoot" what anybody thinks of them and seemingly go out of their way to alienate everybody. Finally, some will not learn to read or write or to function independently in their environment. Or they will fall far behind their classmates and necessitate either part-time special educational assistance or a full-time placement in a special class because of the severity of their problems.

We will use the concept of six levels of learning competence as the basis for our development of a functional-descriptive approach to emotional disturbance. In Chapter 1 we introduced several classification schemes that have been used to describe children who are disturbed (see page 37). One spoke of "conduct disturbance," "neurotic traits," and "psychotic disorders" (Watson, 1959). Another utilized ten categories to describe various types of problem behaviors such as "developmental deviates" and "personality disorders" and provided behavioral examples of each (GAP, 1966). Still another spoke of "conduct problems," "personality problems," and "inadequacy-immaturity" and described clusters of problem behaviors based on terms professionals had used to describe emotionally disturbed children (Quay, 1972). The problem with these schemes is that they all stop short of bridging the gap between classification and practice. To varying degrees, all are no more helpful to the classroom teacher than Donald's horrendous diagnostic label of "catatonic schizophrenia with severe psychomotor retardation." Why not reference the disturbed child to the six levels of learning competence and convert "disturbance" to "lack of competence on one or more levels." This lack of competence, when specifically stated, becomes the educational definition of emotional disturbance for the child and provides a direct link to the setting of curriculum goals. When the NPI School staff took a long, hard, "educational" look at Donald, we discovered that he lacked competence on the response level. While this may have been implicit in the psychiatric diagnosis of "severe psychomotor retardation," as far as we were concerned, it was too vague and cloudy to have direct educational relevance.

When we look at the various descriptions of problem behavior associated with emotional disturbance that accompany the classification schemes proposed in Chapter 1, we find that many of them can be organized as negative variants of the six levels of learning competence. Thus, "excessive daydreaming" is a negative variant of attention, "self-stimulation" is of response, "disruptiveness" of order, "bizarre interests" of exploratory, "fighting" of social, and "blunted unevenness in fragmented intellectual development" of mastery.

We will be discussing common behavioral characteristics of disturbed children as negative variants of the levels of learning competence. In doing so, we will be using a bi-polar approach. This bi-polar approach reflects various classification schemes that have been proposed for emotional disturbance since the early 1940s. These schemes often end up describing two extremes of behavior. Hewitt and Jenkins (1946) have correlated traits associated with emotional disturbance and behavior disorders, and they found two major factors: *anxiety factor* (anxious, timid, nervous) and *rebellion factor* (aggressive, destructive, oppositional). Achenbach (1966) also found a bi-polar principle factor in his analysis of 600 child psychiatric patients. He put *internalizing* (anxious, phobic, compulsive, somatic, withdrawn) at one end of the spectrum and *externalizing* (aggressive, delinquent, social) at the other.

Thus, behavior disorders and emotional disturbance appear to involve problem behaviors associated with withdrawal on the one hand and aggression on the other. While there are many "shades of gray" represented by the descriptive terms used in the various classification schemes, it is clear what is being described are two general types of coping attempts on the part of children—one involving a tendency toward isolation and the other toward striking out.

In Table 3–1 we have attempted to present many behavioral characteristics of disturbed children as negative variants of the six levels of learning competence.* As can be seen, too much or too little of a good thing is

*The authors are indebted to the following colleagues for their assistance in developing this framework: Paul Amuchie, Susan Aumann, Yvonne Chan, Barbara Gruen, Med Mosher, Nora Slaff, Douglas Smith, and Emy Lu Weller.

Table 3–1. Common characteristics of disturbed children viewed as negative variants of six levels of learning competence.

Too Little		Optimal		Too Much
Disturbances in sensory perception (sed)	Excessive daydreaming (ii) Poor memory (a) Short attention span (ii) In a world all his or her own (ii)	Attention	Selective attention (a)	Fixation on particular stimuli (a)
Immobilization (a)	Sluggishness (ii) Passivity (ii) Drowsiness (ii) Clumsiness Depression (pp)	Response (motor)	Hyperactivity (cp) Restlessness (cp)	Self-stimulation (sed)
Failure to develop speech (sed)	Failure to use language for communication (sed)	Response (verbal)	Extremely talkative (a)	Uses profanity (cp) Verbally abusive (a)
Self-injurious (sed) Lawlessness (a) Destructiveness (cp)	Disruptiveness (cp) Attention seeking (cp) Irresponsibility (cp) Disobedience (cp)	Order	Overly conforming (a)	Resistance to change (sed) Compulsive (a)
Bizarre or stereotyped behavior (sed) Bizarre interests (sed)	Anxiety (pp) Preoccupation (pp) Doesn't know how to have fun (pp) Behaves like adult (pp) Shyness (pp)	Exploratory	Plunges into activities (a)	Tries to do everything at once (a)

Social	Preoccupation with inanimate objects (sed) Extreme self-isolation (sed) Inability to relate to people (sed)	Social withdrawal (pp) Alienates others (a) Aloofness (pp) Prefers younger playmates (ii) Acts bossy (cp) Secretiveness (pp) Fighting (cp) Temper tantrums (cp)	Hypersensitivity (pp) Jealousy (cp) Overly dependent (a)	Inability to function alone (a)
Mastery	Blunted, uneven or fragmented intellectual development (sed)	Lacks self-care skills (a) Lacks basic school skills (a) Laziness in school (ii) Dislike for school (cp) Lacks vocational skills (a)	Preoccupation with academics (a)	Overintellectualizing (a)

KEY: cp   conduct problem (Quay, 1972)
      ii   inadequacy-immaturity (Quay, 1972)
      pp   personality problem (Quay, 1972)
      sed   severely emotionally disturbed (GAP, 1966; Eisenberg & Kanner, 1956)
      a   authors

maladaptive. A child can pay no attention at all because of distractability or perceptual-motor problems, or he or she can narrowly fixate attention on a specific stimulus. A child can remain immobilized as Donald did, or he or she can be a hyperactive responder. Too little order behavior may result in lawlessness, but too much may result in over-conformity or obsessive-compulsive rituals. The child who resists exploring the environment because of fearfulness or inhibition is no better off than the child who explores it in a free-wheeling and random fashion. Too little concern for social relationships can lead to alienating others or withdrawal, but too much concern can result in an extreme dependency or an inability to separate from mother. Finally, it is a serious problem if a child lacks the ability to learn and the skills necessary to care for himself or herself, but if a child's world is confined to the academic and cognitive and overly intellectual, he or she can hardly be described as behaving in an adaptive fashion.

The attempt to encompass the vast array of problem behaviors associated with emotional disturbance in Table 3–1 is far from perfect, and there is a conceptual unevenness to the chart. We have used behaviors derived from the classification scheme of the Group for the Advancement of Psychiatry (GAP, 1966), the Behavior Problem Checklist (Quay, 1972), and descriptive terms related to autism used by Eisenberg and Kanner (1956). In addition, we have liberally added descriptive terms ourselves. The major contribution of this descriptive scheme is that it establishes emotional disturbance as consisting of negative variants of adaptive behaviors necessary for learning. There is nothing more mysterious to it than that. Our goal is to move the disturbed child toward one or more of these adaptive behaviors. In the process, we are firmly establishing each and every emotionally disturbed child first and foremost as a learner who we must help "unlearn" his or her negative variant of adaptive behavior and "learn" the adaptive behavior itself.

We have by no means solved the classification dilemma with our too-little-too-much approach, but, hopefully, this framework will help in conceptualizing disturbed children within an educationally relevant context. Achenbach lends some support to this idea:

> Since classification is not an end in itself, how to classify should be dictated by the goals of the classifier. The similarities sought out among clients should be those that will best guide an effective course of action (1974, p. 543).

So far we have moved away from relying on traditional labels such as *autistic* for describing disturbed children. We have also moved away from describing disturbed children in terms of general behavioral characteristics such as engaging in self-stimulation or resisting change. Our too-much-too-little scheme has allowed us to conceptualize these general characteristics in an educational or "needs to learn" framework. Self-stimulation has become needing to learn appropriate motor responding, and resistance to change has become needing to learn to follow directions and routines.

But we are still a ways from permitting the teacher to *directly* translate "what we call the child" into "exactly what we need to do to help the child." In Chapter 5 we will present an approach we have developed in an effort to move toward this goal. This approach, "The ABC's of the IEP," is designed to meet the requirement of the most important legislative act ever conceived and implemented for the handicapped—The Education for All the Handicapped Act of 1975, Public Law 94–142.

Public Law 94–142

The Education for All the Handicapped Act stipulates that all handicapped children must have access to a free and appropriate public education with special education and related services available as needed. In the preamble to the act, it was estimated that of the eight million handicapped children in the United States, four million were receiving an inadequate education, and one million were excluded entirely from the public school system. It was shortly after the Civil War that the United States began to put into practice the principle that education should be available and free to all, but this principle seldom applied to the handicapped. It took well over one hundred years for a law to be enacted that guaranteed handicapped children the same educational rights as the nonhandicapped.

In order to obtain congressional support for the law, the case was made that without a free and appropriate education available, handicapped children were being denied their basic constitutional rights. The fifth and fourteenth constitutional amendments were cited. The fifth amendment guarantees that no person shall be deprived of life, liberty, or property without due process of law. The fourteenth amendment states that no state may deny the equal protection of the law to any person.

There are six major provisions of the law:

1. *Zero Reject.* No handicapped individual is to be denied an education. Such denial is seen as a violation of the fifth amendment, since without an education no individual could hope to learn the skills and knowledge to enable him or her to acquire property.

2. *Nondiscriminatory Classification.* Methods used for purposes of evaluating and classifying handicapped, or possible handicapped individuals, must not be discriminating and penalize such individuals because of their range or nature of previous experience. Misuse and misinterpretation of IQ tests standardized on white, middle-class children is of particular concern in this provision.

3. *Individualized and Appropriate Education.* It is not enough just to provide the handicapped with educational opportunities. These opportunities must be individualized for each child and appropriately meet his or her learning needs. Central to this provision is the Individual Education Program (IEP) which must be prepared for each child and include the following:

a) A statement of the child's present level of educational performance;
b) A statement of annual goals, including short term instructional objectives;
c) A statement of the specific special education and related services to be provided to the child and the extent to which the child will be able to participate in regular educational programs;
d) The projected dates for initiation of services and the anticipated duration of the services; and
e) Appropriate objective criteria and evaluation procedures and schedule for determining, on at least an annual basis, whether the short term instructional objectives are being achieved.
(Federal Register, Vol. 42, No. 163, p. 42491).

Parents must be provided access to the written program and to records of the child's progress. The IEP must be written so that both teachers and parents understand what the school is going to do. Describing the child's present level of educational performance with such phrases as "autistic withdrawal" or "dyslexic" will not be acceptable. Goals and short-term objectives will have to be more specific than "provide successful experiences" or "help improve in reading." Chapter 5 will present our approach for writing an Individual Education Program.

4. *Least Restrictive Placement.* This provision states that every effort will be made to remove the handicapped child only as far away from the normal or mainstream educational program as necessary. One of the requirements of the IEP is the specification of the extent to which the child will be able to be in a regular classroom. Thus, self-contained special education classes, while not out of the picture, will not constitute the "automatic option" when a child is identified as needing more than the regular class program can provide.

5. *Right of Parents to Participate.* Gone are the days when parents might learn that their child had been removed from the regular classroom program, had been given an IQ test, had obtained a score in the mentally retarded range, and had been placed in a special day class without parental permission. Under this provision parents must be consulted from the outset and give their permission for the child to even be considered for special education placement. One of the requirements of the IEP is that the parents sign a document acknowledging their approval of the program and giving permission for it to be implemented.

6. *Right to Protest.* Public Law 94–142 makes it very clear that not only must the parent be involved in the formulation of the child's IEP, but that should disagreement arise between the parents and the school with respect to the provision of that program, the parents have the right to a court hearing to consider the matter. Again, the rights of parents of handicapped children are as major a consideration as are the rights of their children.

Public Law 94–142 is not a half-hearted effort to improve educational opportunities for the handicapped. It is a bold mandate that does not merely suggest we turn our attention to the long overdue problem of better preparing the handicapped for a more satisfying and productive future; it demands that we do and holds us accountable every step of the way.

This chapter concludes the introductory section of the book. Now that we have conceptualized emotional disturbance within a learning and educational frame of reference and disturbed children as students waiting to be taught rather than patients waiting to be treated, we can get on with the business of teaching them. In the next chapter we will present our basic teaching philosophy—the orchestration of success.

chapter 4

The Orchestration of Success

In this chapter we are going to move into the classroom and discuss a strategy for teaching disturbed children the "somethings" that they need to learn, are ready to learn, and can successfully learn. Basic to our strategy is the idea that there are three critical ingredients in any learning situation. These ingredients can be conceived of as the sides of a triangle (*see* Figure 4–1): *curriculum, conditions,* and *consequences.* It is the selection of and provision for each of these sides that is central to the orchestration of success. We will first discuss each side of the learning triangle and then consider the part each side plays in orchestrating success in the classroom. Finally, we will turn to several research studies that illustrate what our strategy is attempting to convey. Our focus and examples will apply most directly to elementary-aged children. However, in Chapters 8 and 9, we will apply our strategy to the secondary level.

The Learning Triangle

Curriculum

Curriculum can be defined as any activity, lesson, or assignment given to the child which is directed toward assisting him or her in achieving competence on one or more of the six levels of learning competence—attention, response, order, exploratory, social, and mastery.

Many disturbed children exasperate teachers who throw up their hands in disgust and exclaim: "I've done all I can. Johnny could learn if he wanted to, but he *won't!*" Coaladarci (1967) studied the comments made by teachers next to failing or near-failing grades on the report cards of several thousand elementary-aged children in regular classrooms. He found that the majority of such comments tended to explain the poor grades on the basis of "child failure," and a very small percentage suggested that perhaps the problem might be the result of a "teaching failure."

While not denying the fact that some children seem to defy even herculean efforts on the part of the teacher to change their behavior and help them learn, if we are truly individually oriented, there is no child who cannot learn something. In the past, many educators might have described one of their goals with disturbed children as "to help them develop good citizenship." That goal is in line with "bucketful thinking" and is so vague that it is virtually meaningless. What we are suggesting here is "thimbleful thinking" that will specify turn waiting, seat sitting, or even mouth closing as the components of good citizenship that teachers can do something about. When we fail with any child, the explanation often relates to a bucketful orientation. With a thimbleful orientation, no child-failures can exist. Every child—disturbed and normal—is at all times ready to learn something. If the child learns nothing, it is clearly the result of a teaching failure.

In Chapter 3 we introduced Donald, the eleven-year-old child de-

Figure 4–1. The learning triangle.

scribed as in a "catatonic, schizophrenic stupor with severe psychomotor retardation." The educational program developed for him at the NPI school provides a good example of thimbleful thinking. As we stated earlier, Donald was almost completely immobilized, refusing to speak, eat, walk, care for himself, or move any part of his body. However, his eyes moved from time to time, usually to check the classroom clock on the wall. By conceptualizing Donald as a response problem, we decided upon a suitable curriculum task. A box with a lever in the middle was placed on his lap. The lever activated a slide projector. The projector was focused on a frosted glass screen set up on a table directly in front of the boy. A slight push of the lever to the right turned the projector on, a slight push to the left turned it off. The curriculum task was to get Donald to move the lever from right to left in order to activate the projector.

With this curriculum task of lever pushing, we had settled on the first ingredient in Donald's educational program. The other ingredients will be discussed shortly. Because Donald was such a severely disturbed boy, the curriculum task we selected had to be quite simple and specific. Less severely disturbed children will be candidates for tasks on several levels of competence at the same time.

Conditions

The conditions of learning which are important to consider to maximize the child's chances for success include the following: when, where, how, how long, how much, and how well.

When. Most regular elementary classrooms operate on a daily schedule that is adhered to consistently with changes occurring to accommodate special events in the school. The same can be said for special education classrooms. Helping disturbed children get used to a routine daily schedule is important if they are to return to a regular school program. In addition, predictability in general is a vital component of a successful classroom program for disturbed children, although an occasional "surprise" change in schedule or introduction of a "fun" activity is by no means ruled out.

Perhaps the condition of when is most important to consider on an individual child basis. The child who arrives in tears after a fight on the school bus or who rushes in hot and sweaty after recess may not be the best candidate for a reading lesson even though the schedule says it is time. We may find Friday afternoon a poor time for concentrated academics. The post-lunch period may better involve the teacher reading aloud for twenty minutes than arithmetic drill. Thus, an important determiner of whether a given child or group of children will be successful is "when" we choose to teach them.

Where. Most regular classrooms assign each child a particular desk or seat at a table which constitutes a kind of home-base working area "where" tasks are done. In addition, there may be centers and other areas in the room to which children move during the school day. Again, it is important for disturbed children to have a home base established in the classroom. We will discuss specific aspects of this home base in Chapter 7.

More important than the desk itself is its location. Some children will be easily distracted seated near certain classmates. Some children will pay greater attention seated near the front of the room. Some children may work very poorly when seated at a table with other children but will work more successfully at a separate desk.

In addition to specific seating arrangements, "where" the child is when we try to teach him or her is important. This relates to the setting variable. In a regular classroom, instruction is delivered when children are seated in a group of thirty, when they are in groups of five or ten, and occasionally on a one-to-one basis. Disturbed children may be ineffectively taught in a large class or even in a small group. We may have to provide individual tutoring. But a continuing goal will be to help the child profit from working in groups of increasing size.

One eleven-year-old disturbed boy who entered the NPI School went straight to a study booth that was enclosed on three sides. He promptly moved a portable chalkboard closing off the open side and established this as his working area. The teacher went along with this because any attempt to get him to join the class group was met with great resistance. She would slip assignments through a crack between the chalkboard and the booth, and the boy would slip them out when he was done. One day he brought an assignment out himself, and he was invited to look at the class rabbit. Over time he spent longer and longer periods outside his classroom fortress and eventually he joined the other children "where" they worked.

How. The condition of how relates to the actual means the child uses to accomplish a task. Stories can be written with pencils or pens or even felt-tip markers. They can also be dictated to the teacher, to another child, or into a tape recorder. They can be typed or written in longhand. They can be copied from a book or from the chalkboard. Arithmetic problems can be done with numbers, poker chips, plastic soldiers, fingers, or flash cards. Reading can be done from a teaching machine, from a textbook, or from a film. It can be done silently or aloud. Answers on a test can be circled or written in by the child.

Learning in school involves a variety of modalities and methods. We have found that taking "how" disturbed children do tasks into consideration may increase our chances of being successful with them. The child who balks at story writing and grows increasingly restless may get right to work using a felt-tip pen or a typewriter or even a rubber stamp set. We have found crayons used when pencils were not, arithmetic problems attempted with plastic scuba divers but not with poker chips, and reading readily done silently but not aloud. There are many examples. The main idea is to take "how" a child does a task into consideration in efforts to promote the child's success.

How Long. A work period in a regular classroom may be forty or fifty minutes long; in a special education classroom, a work period may be fifteen or twenty minutes long. There are some children in both situations who work for five or ten minutes and who mark time the rest of the work period. There are those who work for five minutes, mark time for ten, then work for five more minutes. The point we are trying to make is this: it is very important to determine how long each child can profitably be expected to work on assigned tasks. We have found three fifteen-minute work periods each hour to be effective with disturbed children; although, for some children, we have had to assign three different five-minute activities during each of those periods. We should try not to fail with a child because we expected him or her to work too long.

How Much. Related to "how long" is "how much" we expect a child to do. There may be a weekly spelling list of twenty words in a regular classroom, a daily arithmetic drill with thirty problems, and nightly homework assignments of two chapters of science and one of history. Just as children differ with respect to how long they can profitably work on given assignments, they differ with respect to how much they can realistically be expected to do. A child staring blankly at the arithmetic drill sheet on his or her desk overwhelmed with its four rows of problems may get right to work if we move in, crease the paper, tear off a single row, and place it back on the desk. We should not fail with any child because we expect "too much."

How Well. Finally, we arrive at the condition of how well. If a child gets 80 percent of the problems correct, we give him or her a B; 50 percent correct and we give an F. The problems may be correct, but the smudges all over the paper earn a "next time be more neat" notation. "How well" relates to putting one's name on the paper above the date, putting a margin on the left side of the paper, indenting the first word of a story, using capitals and correct punctuation, answering the questions at the end of the chapter, lining up appropriately for recess, and taking good care of textbooks. And this has only scratched the surface with respect to all the times children are judged according to how well they meet the expectations of the school and the teacher.

Disturbed children are often experts at letting others down. Their lives have been an accumulation of instances when they have failed to measure up to the expectations of others. The job of a teacher of disturbed children is to prevent those children from being involved in situations where they let anyone down (including themselves). One way to do this is to greatly alter traditional standards of "how well." Trying rather than completing, completing rather than being perfect, a step in the right direction rather than the finished product, a thimbleful rather than a bucketful: these are the considerations of the orchestration of success.

Consequences

As we discussed in Chapter 1, what happens following a child's efforts is of particular importance to the behavioral point of view. In providing consequences in the classroom, there are four possibilities: (1) giving children something they want, (2) taking away something children don't want, (3) taking away something children want, or (4) giving children something they don't want. Teachers use all four possibilities throughout the class day as they attempt to motivate and control individual children and keep the class on an even keel. Looks of praise and comments such as "Good for you, Charlie," are common. Promising to let the class go home early or see a movie instead of doing arithmetic drill if everyone behaves may also occur. The reversal of this or keeping individual children or the entire class in from recess because of misbehavior is also possible. Finally, slaps on the wrist, whacks on the buttocks, critical comments, and ridicule have not disappeared from American classrooms.

It is interesting to note that while each of the examples just cited may be readily classified by most of us as "positive" or "negative," until we consider them from the individual child's perspective, we can be fooled. Being singled out by the teacher and praised would seem to be desirable to all children, but some may view such attention as negative if it sets them apart from their peers and leads to teasing as "teacher's pet" or outright ostracism. Emotionally disturbed children may also be made uncomfortable or anxious because of their previous unhappy relationships when a teacher attempts to get "too close" or to become too friendly. Letting the class go home early and shortening the school day may be a punishment to some children who fear they will be harassed by a school bully on the playground for even a longer time than usual. Seeing a movie instead of doing arithmetic drill may be very disappointing to the child whose first love is academics and who delights in being the best student in the class in arithmetic. Keeping children in from recess may seem an obvious punishment, but to the child who is teased and abused on the playground, it may be a blessing to be allowed to remain in the sanctuary of the classroom. And strange as it may seem, "getting the teacher's goat" and being criticized in front of the class may actually be positively reinforcing to the child who is seldom a candidate for attention from the teacher except for misbehavior. Thus, one child's reward may be another child's punishment, and it is important to keep this in mind when considering the provision of consequences in any educational program. Schwitzgebel (1965) has speculated that the idiosyncratic nature of what is rewarding in learning for one individual as compared to others is probably a guarantee that a society of conditioned human automatons will never develop.

In our discussion we will first consider positive consequences and then review the issue of punishment in educational programs for disturbed children.

Positive Consequences

What actually constitutes a positive consequence that can be provided in the classroom? Six types of positive consequences have been identified (Hewett with Forness, 1977):

1. Acquisition of knowledge and skill
2. Knowledge of results
3. Social approval
4. Multisensory stimulation and activity
5. Task completion
6. Tangible rewards

Acquisition of Knowledge and Skill. Children find it satisfying to acquire facts, knowledge, and skills that they can use to impress others or to expand their competence and independence in relation to the environment. Some disturbed children are very motivated by acquiring knowledge, but, unfortunately, some have narrow ranges of interest and fixate on very specific topics and subjects. It may actually be rather idealistic to consider this type of consequence effective with most children with learning and behavior problems. The negative experiences they have in school often preclude their being "turned on" by learning itself.

Knowledge of Results. It is a well-established fact that knowing how you stand in relation to some criterion measure can be highly motivating. Grades constitute "knowledge of results" since they tell you how well, in the teacher's judgment, you have performed in relation to his or her expectations. But there are other examples. Who is the fastest runner in the class? The second fastest? Which row will win the spelling bee? While disturbed children may enjoy games and activities in which they have a chance to "win, place, or show," many of them will not be motivated to work for grades since they have received far more D's and F's than A's or B's.

Social Approval. The classroom is a social arena into which the child enters early in life and engages in daily give-and-take interactions with peers and adults. These interactions are both positive and negative, pleasurable and painful, and feared and eagerly anticipated. In American society, what others think has perhaps become too important. Nevertheless, when normal children are asked to select the type of rewarding consequence they most prefer in school, they often choose social approval, particularly teacher approval.* This probably does not hold for some disturbed children who have had continual negative interactions with parents and others in their lives, but it certainly does hold for many disturbed individuals. The warm, accepting teacher who makes a "big deal" out of small successes and patiently and gently deals with minor infractions is probably performing the most important "therapy" that can be provided in school.

The importance of both teacher approval and disapproval is well illustrated in this example provided by Martin and Stendler (1959):

> Consider Miss A, a third-grade teacher. Miss A's class is writing letters to Tony, who is ill at home. Miss A walks up and down the aisles, supervising the children's work. She stops at Pete's desk and picks up his paper.
>
> "Boys and girls," she says to get the attention of the group. "May I have your attention? That means you too, Matilda.
>
> "This is Pete's paper. I want you to notice how carefully Pete has followed my directions. See? He has left margins at both sides and has written the heading exactly right. See how neat and clean his paper is, too?"
>
> Miss A returns Pete's paper with a beam of approval and goes on. She stops at Raymond's desk. Raymond does not fare so well.
>
> "Boys and girls!" Again the heads go up. "Look at Raymond's paper. Raymond needs some help. See the smudges and spots on his paper? What can we tell Raymond to help him improve?"
>
> "He should wash his hands before he starts and not erase," say the children.
>
> The teacher returns the paper to Raymond with a look of disapproval. "It will have to be done over, Raymond, and that's wasting paper, you know."
>
> Some of the children finish their letters and must wait for the others to finish. Several sit and do nothing. Miss A comments to the class.
>
> "I like the way some people are finding jobs to do when they finish. I saw two children studying spelling and one boy doing his workbook. That's using time wisely, isn't it, boys and girls? You'll have five more minutes to finish and I expect all of you to be done, if you haven't been dawdling."
>
> Miss A did not distribute gold stars as rewards or spankings as punishments. Yet she made certain ways of behaving pleasurable to the children and other ways painful by her approval and disapproval of their actions. In the short space of five minutes, she indicated her liking for children who obeyed her requests for attention, followed her directions, did neat, clean work, kept obviously busy, did not

---

*Dunn-Rankin, P. Personal communication, 1967.

waste supplies, and finished work on time. The children in Miss A's class did not learn obedience, respect for authority, neatness and cleanliness, avoidance of waste, and the importance of time in this one lesson, but when day after day, school year after school year, teacher after teacher, the same kinds of actions are rewarded and punished, these responses become reinforced in the child.†

Multisensory Stimulation and Activity. Children are "turned on" by the sights, sounds, textures, shapes, tastes, and smells that surround them. The term *sensory reinforcement* has been used to describe the increase in the probability that certain behaviors will occur when these behaviors are followed by sensory experiences. There is strong support for this idea in the research literature (Rincover & Koegel, 1977).

Learning comes about as the result of the impingement on our senses of the stimuli around us and through our movement and activity in the environment. Emphasis on multisensory experience and activity in the classroom is probably given more importance in preschool, kindergarten, and the early grades than it is at the later-elementary or secondary levels. That is unfortunate since we know how motivating such experiences can be to all children.

Systematic provision of multisensory stimulation and activities contingent on task accomplishment is the basis of the Premack Principle (Premack, 1959). Simply stated, this principle involves using behaviors that normally occur with high frequency (e.g., watching TV) as rewards for increasing behaviors that normally occur with low frequency (e.g., making one's bed, taking out the trash). The parent who only allows the TV set to be switched on "after" the bed is made and the trash is taken out is utilizing this principle. In the classroom, the teacher may observe the child for a period of time to determine his or her interests (e.g., model building, playing with a rabbit). By setting up a plan whereby a certain amount of low-frequency behavior such as reading must be accomplished before the child may engage in the more desired activity, a considerable increase in the low frequency behavior may occur.

Task Completion. It is motivating simply to complete a task or activity. This statement derives support from the classic work of Zeigarnik in the 1930s. Zeigarnik (1938) found that tasks that were not completed were recalled almost twice as often as completed tasks. This was explained by means of Gestalt psychology. According to the Gestalt conception of motivation, if an individual is motivated toward success in a task, a specific tension system is aroused which persists during the time the individual is undertaking the task and is only resolved by its completion.

Providing the experiences of task completion in the classroom often involves setting aside concern for such conditions as "how long" or "how

†From *Child Behavior and Development,* Revised Edition by William E. Martin and Celia Burns Stendler, pages 349–350. © 1959 by Harcourt Brace Jovanovich, Inc. Reprinted by permission of the publisher.

well." The child who tries to write a story and waits beaming for the teacher to praise him or her even though there are spelling errors and the handwriting is atrocious may be experiencing the motivation of task completion. The sensitive teacher who reinforces the child on the task completion level and who ignores the errors or who carefully calls attention to "something I want to help you improve in" is allowing this reward to have its effect. All too often a red pencil descends and vividly calls attention to the spelling errors, and a critical voice exclaims: "You also forgot to draw a margin on your paper and to indent the first word of your opening sentence. There are no capital letters or proper punctuation and your handwriting is unacceptable." Consider the task completion motivational potential destroyed.

Tangible Rewards. When the first edition of this book was published (1968), it was still a big deal to use candy, food, trinkets, and other tangible rewards to increase management and instructional effectiveness with exceptional learners. And, it was probably quite a novelty for the children themselves. Nowadays the use of tangible rewards is fairly common particularly with severely handicapped individuals. The novelty among exceptional learners has probably diminished and been replaced by the wide-eyed wonder of nonexceptional children in regular classrooms when they discover that a mainstreamed exceptional child also participates in a resource or special day class program where M & M's are passed out!

We have witnessed public declarations by educators, both regular and special, to the effect that "I want it to be known that I have *never* used a tangible reward in any classroom with any child." Despite more general acceptance, the use of tangible or extrinsic rewards is still controversial. Consider this quotation:

> Materialistic rewards are to behaviorism what opening a can of beans is to the culinary art—the lowest possible form. (Hunter, 1978, pp. 192–193).

Adelman (1978) has urged consideration of intrinsic rather than extrinsic motivation. From an intrinsic orientation, people act on their environments rather than being passively controlled by reinforcers and contingencies. Thoughts and feelings play a primary role in determining behavior. Activities in which children seek out stimulation and conquer challenges on their own lead to development, maintenance, and even enhancement of intrinsic motivation. Activities in which rewards and/or punishments are meted out by the teacher in order to motivate children interfere with learning because they make learning dependent on obtaining a reward or avoiding punishment rather than on meaningful personal involvement (Deci, 1975).

As far as we're concerned, the tangible reward issue ultimately becomes a "straw man." It's been shown (and our experience agrees) that the use of tangible rewards in educational programs for most exceptional learners in only necessary on a temporary basis (Haring & Phillips, 1972; Forness, 1970). Once the child begins to experience success, other reinforcers such as task accomplishment and social praise become effective. Indeed, intrinsic motivation may develop—and more power to it if it does!

The initial use of tangible rewards with children with whom they are more effective than other traditional consequences can be justified on two counts. First, it is foolish to overlook any approach that may increase a teacher's effectiveness with disturbed or other exceptional children. (It is also foolish to use tangible rewards when they are not effective or necessary with any child.) Second, the use of tangible rewards has a basic logic to it that is inherent in the instructional process. The teacher who discovers that a child cannot add 2 + 2 because he or she does not understand their numerical value or the concept of addition will most likely reduce the task to the concrete level and, by means of counters, demonstrate that *two things* added to *two things* equals *four* things. In a similar fashion when it is discovered that a child is not rewarded by grades, praise, or more symbolic and abstract reinforcers, the temporary use of concrete rewards makes good educational sense. Children given concrete arithmetic lessons do not have to carry around sacks of counters to solve addition problems for the rest of their lives; they will soon learn to deal with numbers symbolically. The child given candy or tangible reinforcers will not become addicted to them but will eventually respond to more traditional incentives in the classroom. It is foolish for teachers to fail for foolish reasons. A flexible, open-minded, pragmatic approach to selecting curriculum, conditions, and consequences is one of the distinguishing characteristics of successful regular and special educators who work with disturbed and other exceptional children.

Positive consequences are, of course, the consequences of choice in educational programs for all children—exceptional and nonexceptional. But what if none of the possibilities we have just considered proves effective? Aren't there times when children should be given responsibility for their behavior and "suffer" the consequences when they are very clearly out of line? In short, are we justified in using punishment in the schools?

Punishment

Interestingly, the United States is one of the few countries which has not federally banned the use of corporal punishment in the schools. The Soviet Union has taken a strong position forbidding it, as have the eastern European countries. In western Europe, only Great Britain, Ireland, Switzerland, and Germany permit corporal punishment (Hyman, 1977). Along with the United States other former English colonies are prominent among countries still permitting corporal punishment. These include Canada, Australia, New Zealand, and South Africa (Newell, 1972).

In 1977, the U.S. Supreme Court was asked to rule on the constitutionality of a severe paddling a junior high school student had received in Florida *(Ingraham* v. *Wright)*. The bruises that resulted from the paddling required medical attention and kept the boy out of school for eleven days. Since the Eighth and Fourteenth Amendments forbid "cruel and unusual punishments" in prisons, advocates for the abolishment of corporal punishment in the schools argued that school children should also be so protected. But the court ruled five to four that the boy in Florida had not had his constitutional rights violated. The majority of the justices decided that the use of corporal punishment in prisons is unconstitutional because they are "closed" institutions. But schools are considered "open" institutions that can be monitored by the community and corporal punishment in them is therefore justifiable. According to one justice writing a majority opinion, "It can hardly be said that the use of moderate paddlings in the discipline of children is inconsistent with the country's evolving standards of decency" *(Ingraham* v. *Wright,* 1977, pp. 684–685).

In Chapter 9 we will discuss the use of corporal punishment, including electric shock, with severely disturbed children. With respect to noncorporal punishment, Rutherford has concluded, "The bulk of the current empirical evidence on punishment in the classroom supports the effectiveness of this procedure in suppressing the inappropriate behavior of children and youth" (1978, p. 57). However, "suppressing the inappropriate behavior" has an ominously incomplete ring to it and leaves us with unanswered questions. How does the child feel? How long will the behavior remain suppressed? Will it be suppressed in all situations with all individuals? These questions have not been answered to everyone's satisfaction. Rather than review specific research studies, we will briefly discuss the major types of punishment commonly used in school programs for disturbed children: response cost, time-out, and overcorrection.

Response Cost. Response cost is a term referring to removal of an opportunity to participate in a desired activity or withdrawal of a quantity of previously acquired reinforcers. Parents often rely on loss of television watching privileges as a response cost procedure following misconduct. Teachers may use this procedure in the context of a token system. Tokens or points previously awarded may be taken away for misbehavior. There is a considerable body of research literature that shows the effectiveness of response cost procedures (Rutherford, 1978), although there appears to be increased effectiveness if the child is also being given rewards. But like all techniques we may use with disturbed children, implementation of response cost may backfire on us. Children may withdraw from responding or they may aggressively react toward the individual taking something away from them.

Although we have not systematically studied response cost in the program to be described in Chapter 7, we have found that teachers who warn children in advance that they will not earn a full quota of points because of some problem behavior or teachers who actually take away previously earned points for misbehavior seem to create an uneasy classroom climate.

Classroom climates are extremely important. Positive climates are probably much more apt to develop as the result of a success orientation rather than a "one false move and we've got you" approach.

Time-out. Theoretically, the use of time-out procedures is supposed to involve "losing something you want" (i.e., lack of opportunity to receive positive reinforcement in the classroom). In practice, this may not always be the case. If removal from a classroom that is boring and negative occurs, it may actually constitute positive reinforcement. But the research literature supports the use of time-out procedures as generally effective with various types of disturbed children at various age levels. In reviewing the literature, MacDonough and Forehand (1973) have concluded the following:

1. Explaining to a child the reason for time-out does not appear to increase the technique's effectiveness.

2. The effectiveness of prior warnings or the use of physical force to remove the child has received little systematic study.

3. Isolation time-out appears more effective than keeping the child in the classroom area.

4. Short duration time-outs (e.g., 1–15 minutes) are as effective as time-outs of longer duration (e.g., 30 minutes to 3 hours).

5. Terminating time-out should be contingent on the child's manifesting some specific desirable behavior during the time-out period.

A school district one of us visited had constructed a special classroom for disturbed children in a regular elementary school. The room had a built-in time-out room with a self-locking door. If a time-out was felt appropriate for a given child, he or she would be told to go into the room. It had no windows and was lit by a single light bulb in the center of the ceiling. If children assigned a time-out refused to go into the room, they would be dragged, often kicking and screaming, and were locked in the room for varying periods of time. Thus, "time out" had really become "solitary confinement" with physical force thrown in for good measure.

One episode of the use of "time out" in this classroom made local newspaper headlines and TV newscasts. A new student had arrived and had been placed in a regular classroom. In twenty minutes he had kicked the teacher twice and was removed to the special classroom for disturbed children. In less than another twenty minutes, he went after the teacher in this classroom. Dragged kicking and screaming, he was forced inside the darkened time-out room (a previous occupant had smashed the light bulb) and was locked up for two hours. He emerged with bleeding fingers from scratching on the door.

It is our opinion that the practice of physically forcing a child into a time-out area is a losing proposition from the start. The message, "We must have you leave the classroom for a time because you are not behaving as a student," is simply overshadowed by the message, "We are bigger and stronger than you, and we will punish you when we think you are bad." This latter message completely violates the principle of time-out as a constructive "lack of opportunity to receive positive reinforcement." In cases where children refuse to go to a time-out area, they should probably be sent to the principal's office with whatever force necessary applied by someone other than the classroom teacher (i.e., PE coach, custodian, principal). Physical confrontations or "show downs" between teacher and student in the classroom, in full view of the other children, are not likely to have positive consequences for anyone.

Overcorrection. Overcorrection procedures have been utilized with disturbed children, particularly with the severely disturbed. Overcorrection may involve restitution and positive practice. Negative practice also has been considered an overcorrection procedure by some. Restitution has not been systematically studied, but we are reminded of an example of its use with a mildly disturbed boy. The boy was a bully and often destroyed school property. One day he ripped an expensive upholstered chair with a knife. The principal confronted him and explained that the chair cost fifty dollars which the boy would have to pay. However, an alternative was available. For each day the boy did not physically abuse another child, one dollar credit would be subtracted. This meant that the agreement would be in effect for ten weeks of school. The effect was remarkable. The boy never came close to touching anyone else and improved his general behavior in the classroom. But the Monday morning of the eleventh week was something else. On the playground before school he "beat up" four smaller children. Escorted into the principal's office and confronted with what he had done, the boy replied with a puzzled look, "But I already paid you back for the chair!" One would have hoped that his improved behavior would have brought him enough positive reinforcement to result in a maintenance effect. Sad to say, it had not.

Positive practice involves the child practicing a positive behavior following the exhibition of a negative behavior (Sulzer-Azaroff & Mayer, 1977). The Dejarnette Center for Human Development in Staunton, Virginia, systematically applied this approach by means of a "fix-it shop." Children who exceeded classroom limits were sent to a special area supervised by a full-time teacher. Here the negative behavior (e.g., leaving your seat without permission) was discussed and its counterpart was practiced (e.g., raising your hand and asking permission). The fix-it shop was not a punitive environment but rather a relatively positive-reinforcement-free setting within which the child's attention was directed toward specific behaviors that needed to be improved. While this approach (as is true with *any* approach in special education) does not work with all children, it has proven to be a useful "alerting" and training tool with many.

Negative practice (or getting the child to engage in negative behavior) has been used with severely disturbed children in an effort to reduce self-stimulatory behavior. We are aware of three instances in which a negative practice approach was applied. In each instance a ten-minute practice period was imposed as follows:

1. An eight-year-old girl was continuously annoying her family by switching the living room light on and off in rapid fashion. Her mother forced her to turn the switch on and off by holding the girl's hand on the switch and pushing it up and down.

2. A seven-year-old boy was constantly crawling on the floor and rubbing his nose on the carpet. The teacher held his head down and forced the boy to rub his nose.

3. A nine-year-old boy was given to "flicking" tufts of hair on his temples in a repetitive fashion. The teacher held his wrists and forced him to perform the behavior.

The use of physical force to promote negative practice is not viewed by all as an overcorrection procedure. Rather, verbal or physical prompting (e.g., telling the child what to do or guiding his or her hands) is utilized. In the instances cited above the negative practicer told us that the technique "worked." However, in the cases of the seven- and nine-year-old practicees, the ten-minute period ended with a skin-scraped nose and red wrist welts, respectively. While there has been some research (some pro, some con) for positive practice, negative practice has not been systematically studied. If the approach worked with the two boys, and their self-stimulatory behavior was actually reduced, isn't a scraped nose and reddened wrist actually a small price to pay for such improvement? This question, as is the case with all questions regarding what constitutes too great a price to pay with respect to the sometimes beneficial effect of punishing consequences, must be answered strictly on an individual basis. From our experience, the following questions are relevant in deciding whether punishment is appropriate in an individual case:

1. Is it absolutely necessary? Have all nonpunishing avenues been explored?

2. Is there any possibility of physical harm being suffered as the result of the punishment? With what degree of certainty can you answer this question in the negative?

3. Is the administration of the punishment a well-understood procedure on the child's part? Does the child not only understand what is likely to happen when he or she behaves in a particular manner, but also why the punishing consequence is applied?

4. Is the administration of the punishment a well-understood procedure on the parents' part? In the case of physical punishment, have the parents been given an actual demonstration and have they signed a statement giving their permission for its use?

5. Is the administration of the punishment a well-understood procedure on the punisher's part? Does the punisher know precisely why the punishment is being applied, and is his or her value system entirely at peace in the punishing situation?

This latter question has been of particular concern to one of us. During a speech-training program with an eleven-year-old, nonverbal, autistic boy, the author was invited to use an experimental room which had an electric grid on the floor. A mildly painful electric shock could be delivered by the experimenter to anyone standing barefoot in the room. The author and the boy removed their shoes and entered the room. The author was attempting to get the boy to elicit a particular sound on cue. When the boy failed to respond appropriately after three prompts, the shock was turned on. After two trials the author terminated the session. The effect of the shock on the boy, the look of terror on his face, and the sickening discomfort felt by the author all combined to lead to the termination. Whether we like it or not, we are what we are. Use of the electric grid room might be both disputed and supported on a number of grounds. But before we consult the research literature or the experts, we must consult ourselves. In short, the use of any approach in special education that we cannot wholeheartedly endorse and feel entirely comfortable using is highly unprofessional. With respect to behavior modification techniques questioned by some teachers as too mechanistic for their teaching style, we have often made the following point:

> Behavior modification techniques are to help you be yourself more effectively and efficiently. If you cannot be yourself using them, forget it. They probably won't work for you anyway.

What about the use of punishment in classrooms for disturbed children? Does it belong? Unfortunately, we have not answered these questions and will not by the end of this book. All we can answer with respect to the questions is: "It all depends."

The Orchestration of Success

The process of assigning a task the child needs to learn, is ready to learn, and can be successful learning; selecting conditions which are appropriate; and providing meaningful consequences can be conceived of as the orchestration of success leading to harmony in the classroom. The concepts of "orchestration" and "harmony" closely relate to the idea of critical eclecticism discussed in Chapter 2. Orchestrating success implies a concern for a broad perspective regarding the disturbed child. It implies concern for cognitive and affective variables. Yet, the concept of the orchestration of success also implies an orderliness and a systematic approach which we view as fundamental to any educational program for disturbed children. Harmony is not achieved through inconsistency, randomness, or lack of knowledge of expectations. It is accomplished through structure.

Haring and Phillips have defined structure as "the clarification of the relationship between behavior and its consequences" (1962, p. 9). We have previously defined it as consisting of "teacher expectations associated with the task assigned the child which determine the conditions under which a reward will be provided" (Hewett, 1968, p. 62).

Among the considerations Haring and Phillips took into account in developing their structured educational program for disturbed children were the following:

1. Maintaining a definite and dependable classroom routine

2. Starting with specific and limited tasks and extending these when the child is ready

3. Maintaining consistency on the part of the teacher

4. Forwarding the impression to children that they are at school for work

Gallagher (1979) has developed a structured program along these same lines but has expanded the Haring and Phillips definition to include clarification of the relationship between behavior and stimuli such as curriculum materials, teacher instruction, and room furnishings.

We are in general agreement with these definitions of structure. Our definition is, however, "the orchestration of success." This orchestration is concerned with all three sides of the learning triangle. We do not only need a curriculum task that is harmonious with the child's level of functioning or a set of conditions that produce a harmonious working situation for the child or consequences harmonious with what is meaningful and motivating to the child, we need total harmony among all three. The potentially effective task presented under inappropriate conditions leads to disharmony. The ideal working conditions are of little effectiveness if a disharmonious task is involved.

Harmony. You can tell when it is there in a classroom. Things are in tune. Tasks, working conditions, and consequences are synchronized with the children. The teacher conducts. Everyone is playing their part. You can also recognize disharmony in the classroom. Things are out of tune. Tasks, working conditions, and consequences are not synchronized with the children. The teacher may be trying to conduct, but the results are off key.

We will now illustrate two important principles related to the orchestration of success by presenting examples of the basic types of conditioning associated with learning theory—operant and respondant. The first principle is *shaping,* and it is associated with operant conditioning. The second is *desensitization,* and it is associated with respondant conditioning.

Shaping

Operant conditioning is concerned with voluntary behavior learned as the result of certain responses being followed by reinforcement or punishment. Children learn to come to school, take their seats, salute the flag, get out their readers, and follow the teacher's directions for a variety of reasons, some positive, some negative. For a certain number of children, school holds the promise of positive reinforcement, of the good feeling that comes when you get a high grade or are praised by the teacher. Some children attend school, however, largely to escape the punishment of their parents and a community that requires each child go to school. And for some, escaping one type of punishment leads to experiencing another type in the confusion and misery of the classroom.

Several times in this book we have spoken of the importance of considering every disturbed child first and foremost as a learner, ready at all times to learn something. And we have spoken of the importance of selecting the somethings they are ready to learn and need to learn. One of the principles of operant conditioning is *shaping*. The following example of shaping will serve as a model for how we can both individualize instruction and guarantee success with disturbed children.

A classic study with institutionalized, severely emotionally disturbed individuals was done by Allyon and Haughton (1962). In most mental hospitals there are patients who present serious eating problems. They may refuse to eat at all, they may have to be coaxed to eat at every meal, or they may actually have to be spoonfed by an attendant. Naturally, this presents complicated problems and is time-consuming. It is also an example of how we may unwittingly reward individuals for maladaptive behavior such as immobilization, overdependency, and helplessness. If an attendant will devote his or her time solely to you during mealtime and feed you mouthful by mouthful, why bother to feed yourself?

But what alternatives are there? Surely we don't want to let any individual starve to death. Unfortunately, in many institutions for the mentally ill and mentally retarded, it has traditionally been easier to dress, feed, toilet, and shower individuals who lack self-care skills than to teach them these skills. This reinforcement of helplessness is perhaps the most tragic and destructive aspect of institutionalization.

In Allyon and Haughton's study, it was decided that many of the spoon-fed patients were actually capable of feeding themselves. They were not physically incapacitated. With the cooperation and participation of the institution's medical staff, thirty-two female patients with no physical impairments that would preclude their feeding themselves were selected for an experiment. Seven of these were severe eating problems. The patients were placed on a special ward with a specially trained staff. Once they had moved to the ward, a simple message went out—all patients had to enter the ward dining room at mealtimes. There were to be no exceptions.

At first, some patients did not respond. But gradually they all made it to the dining room and began to feed themselves. Thus, an important change had been brought about in the lives of these seriously disturbed individuals. We can liken this accomplishment to finally getting a disturbed child who greatly fears leaving home and going to school actually in the classroom. The steps that were followed by Allyon and Haughton in increasing the demands made upon the patients provide us with an excellent example of an approach to follow with such a child by altering curriculum, conditions, and consequences.

The first step had involved the curriculum or task of going to the dining room to eat; the conditions imposed were where you had to go and how long you had to go there; and the consequences consisted of the food itself. Initially the condition of a half-hour time period following the announcement that the dining room was open was imposed. For the disturbed child who has finally come to school, we could let him or her do pretty much what he or she wants in the classroom but expect arrival at school on time. And we would hope that our acceptance and praise, interesting tasks and activities, or even candy rewards would be effective consequences.

Step two of the study required entrance into the dining room during shorter and shorter periods of time following the announcement regarding mealtime—twenty minutes, then fifteen minutes, and finally five minutes. The condition of how long was systematically altered during this step while the task and consequences remained the same. We could liken this to perhaps setting some limit on the disturbed child in the classroom such as how long he or she could pursue a self-selected activity.

During step three in the study, the patients were required to drop a penny in a can at the door to the dining room in order to gain admittance. The pennies were distributed by a nurse outside the dining room. Thus, the task had been made more complex while the conditions (e.g., five-minute interval following the mealtime announcement) and the consequences were held constant. For our disturbed child, we might restrict the number of choices of activities available to two or three, thus gradually establishing a teacher-directed school routine.

The fourth step required that a specific routine be followed in order to obtain the penny. A table with one doorbell button at each end and a red light and buzzer in the middle was brought into the ward. When the two buttons were simultaneously pushed, the buzzer sounded and the light came on. The nurse would then give each patient pushing a button a penny. Since the table was seven and one-half feet long, a single patient could not push both buttons at once. As a result, each individual had to request the assistance of a fellow patient in order to get the mealtime pennies. This often involved verbal and social behavior that had not been evidenced by these severely disturbed patients in years. We could liken this step to pairing the disturbed child with a classmate and introducing a cooperative task (e.g., taking turns putting a puzzle together).

By this point in the study, a truly remarkable change had come about in the behavior of the patients. Instead of lying in their beds waiting to be fed, those who had previously evidenced severe eating problems were going to the dining room, watching the clock to meet the five-minute interval, conversing among themselves to locate a button-pushing buddy, and engaging in a cooperative task with another person. These were "thimbleful" accomplishments when the complexities of normal social behavior are considered, but they were vitally important first steps in what, hopefully, would be a training program to continuously improve their functioning level. By similarly increasing our "thimbleful" expectations with the disturbed child in our classroom, we would now have a child who was coming to school, involved in a schedule and routines, and beginning to relate to a classmate instead of remaining isolated at home.

Operant conditioning provides a helpful set of principles for teaching the disturbed child more adaptive behavior. Respondant conditioning provides some useful principles for understanding and changing fears and negative attitudes toward learning and school through desensitization.

Desensitization

In respondant or classical conditioning a previously neutral stimulus (the conditioned stimulus or bell in Pavlov's famous experiments) acquires properties for automatically eliciting a response (salivation) that formerly was only elicited by an unconditioned stimulus (food). This is done through repeated pairing of the conditioned stimulus with the unconditioned stimulus. In other words, the bell comes to eventually signal the coming of the food. Two little boys, Albert and Peter, who participated in experiments of classical conditioning, provide us with excellent examples of how fears and negative attitudes may be learned and how they may be unlearned.

The Case of Albert*

Albert was a normal, eleven-month-old infant whom we introduced in Chapter 1. He was reported to be particularly calm and nonfearful. Motion picture records were taken to show that he was not upset by being presented such objects as a white rat, a rabbit, a dog, or a monkey. A white rat was selected for the experiment which was designed to show how a fear of a previously nonfeared object might be acquired. As Albert reached for the rat, a steel bar was loudly struck with a hammer directly behind him. Albert

*Watson & Rayner, 1920.

immediately jumped and fell forward, evidencing considerable fear. After a number of pairings of the white rat and the loud bar-striking, Albert drew away from the rat and evidenced a marked fear of it even though the bar-striking no longer occurred. Albert had acquired a "fear" that he previously had not had. In addition, this fear was reported to have generalized to a rabbit, a dog, a fur coat, cotton, and a Santa Claus mask—all things with some white and furry attributes like the rat. The fear was also reported to be quite "attribute specific" meaning it did not generalize to objects such as blocks.

Unfortunately, a careful analysis of this so-called classic study has revealed a number of problems in methodology as well as in interpretation (Harris, 1979). Despite these inadequacies, we can use this experiment to illustrate how children may come to fear and hate school. The concept of school may be quite positive to children as they prepare to enter it following their fifth birthdays. They have heard about it from brothers, sisters, or playmates and have learned that it is a place all children go on a regular basis throughout much of their pre-adult lives. Thus, they may arrive at school with a fairly positive attitude toward it and only minor trepidations regarding its unknowns.

Before entering school, all children have experienced the pain of criticism, rejection, and failure. Very early in life we communicate our displeasure to children when they fail to meet our expectations or follow rules and routines we consider important. The pain of failure is a very real pain and most children learn early to try to avoid it. For whatever reason, many disturbed children are unable to avoid it and a classical conditioning paradigm occurs.

As children attend school and participate in classroom activities, they may be initially engaged in a positive or neutral situation. But as their involvement in school, in lessons, in taking tests, in meeting teacher expectations, and in competing with others is frequently followed by the already established "pain of failure," they are in the process of being conditioned to fear and hate school. And the process of generalization most certainly occurs. It isn't only the first teacher who was critical, the first lesson that was misunderstood, or the first negative relationship with a classmate that is feared. It may be all aspects of "schoolness" including teachers, tests, books, rules, classmates, etc. Indeed, school and learning may become equivalents of the white rat and all white, furry objects that Albert came to fear.

The Case of Peter†

Peter was a boy almost three years old. Unlike Albert, he had already acquired the fear of a white furry object—a rabbit—before the study began.

† Jones, 1924.

He was also fearful of other white furry objects, but not of blocks. The experiment he participated in was to examine ways of decreasing these fears. A series of forty-five training sessions was held. Initially, Peter was exposed to other children who liked and petted the rabbit, but this approach was interrupted by a two-month illness and a severe fright Peter received from a large dog that jumped at him on the street. Once he was again available to participate in the study a new approach was tried—desensitization. While seated in a high chair, Peter was given food that he liked while the experimenter gradually brought the rabbit closer and closer over the course of the training session. At no time, however, was the rabbit brought so close that it disrupted Peter's eating.

By the forty-fifth session Peter would let the rabbit nibble on his finger; he was heard to say, "I like the rabbit"; and he evidenced a total absence of fear of cotton or fur coats. There were seventeen steps in the direct conditioning program for Peter. They were as follows:

a) Rabbit anywhere in a room in a cage causes fear reaction

b) Rabbit 12 feet away in cage tolerated

c) Rabbit 4 feet away in cage tolerated

d) Rabbit 3 feet away in cage tolerated

e) Rabbit closed in cage tolerated

f) Rabbit free in room tolerated

g) Rabbit touched when experimenter holds it

h) Rabbit touched when free in room

i) Rabbit defied by spitting at it, throwing things at it, imitating it

j) Rabbit allowed on tray of high chair

k) Squats in defenseless position beside rabbit

l) Helps experimenter to carry rabbit to its cage

m) Holds rabbit on lap

n) Stays alone in room with rabbit

o) Allows rabbit in playpen with him

p) Fondles rabbit affectionately

q) Lets rabbit nibble his fingers

(Jones, 1924, pp. 310–311).

The desensitization approach provides an excellent model for dealing with the fears and negative attitudes toward learning and school that are found among many disturbed children. We need to do the equivalent of giving Peter his favorite food while gradually bringing the feared rabbit closer and closer. For us the ingredients of the conditioning process are much more nebulous and complex. In place of food we are concerned with giving the child as positive and successful an experience as possible in the classroom. We need to capitalize on the child's interests, ask no more than he or she can comfortably do, and provide meaningful positive consequences for the child's efforts. Gradually, we may be able to move the aversive "white rabbit of schoolness" with its demands for conformity, rules, competition, and complexity closer and closer until the child is functioning in a normal manner in school.

We have found it valuable to emphasize with teachers of disturbed children that when problems with a child occur in the classroom, the first question to ask is, "Is the white rabbit of schoolness too close?" That is, is there something in the learning situation that has triggered off a negative reaction in the child based on his or her previous experience? Disturbed children seldom consciously contemplate misbehavior in a plotting, conspiratorial manner (although this certainly can occur). Many of the tantrums, the striking-out episodes, the angry outbursts, the refusals, the tears, and the incidents of running away are the results of negative conditioning in the past and the white rabbit of schoolness coming too close.

In the case of Peter, if the experimenters got "too close" with the rabbit and saw Peter begin to be upset, favorite food or not, the implications were clear—*move the rabbit back.* That is precisely what we need to consider when working with disturbed children. The orchestration-of-success concept depends greatly on the sensitivity of the teacher in deciding how close the rabbit can comfortably be with each child and being prepared to quickly and creatively move it back whatever distance is necessary. Moving the white rabbit of schoolness back and forth may seem a somewhat farfetched analogy to some readers. But it can be translated into classroom reality. For example, reducing the length of an assignment, reassigning the child a more interesting or challenging task, or providing individual tutoring may result in getting a child back on the learning track when he or she has strayed.

Success. What a necessary and important phenomenon it is in all of our lives. And what a powerful positive reinforcement. Consider this quotation:

> The human organism fortunately for us all, is reinforced just by being successful. Consequently, if material is designed to facilitate correct responses, the resulting frequent success is enough reinforcement for most persons. Not only will the child's behavior change as he learns to do things he could not do before, but he will become highly motivated, his morale will improve, and his attitude toward teachers will change. (1972, p. 11).

This statement was made by B. F. Skinner, the acknowledged founder of the contemporary behavior modification movement. It may surprise some, who associate behavior modification with purely external events and a cold, impersonal approach toward children, to hear its founder talk about improving motivation and morale and changing attitudes by means of the experience of success.

Both shaping and desensitization are central to the orchestration of success. The first achieves harmony by whittling down complex tasks into manageable sizes and gradually increasing task demands at a pace which is reasonable for the child. The second achieves harmony by establishing a healthy learning climate of success for children whose psychological well-beings may have been jeopardized in the past by unhealthy climates of fear, mistrust, anxiety, and failure. Setting aside theoretical considerations, the processes of shaping and desensitization are, in many respects, synony-mous: children undertaking curriculum tasks which involve positive consequences, while the conditions of when, where, how, how much, how long, and how well are varied to promote and maintain success. That is the definition of the orchestration of success.

chapter 5

The ABC's of the IEP

In this chapter we are going to consider meeting the requirement of Public Law 94–142 that an Individual Education Program (IEP) be formulated for each handicapped child. Our plan is derived from the functional-descriptive approach presented in Chapter 3 that was concerned with six levels of learning competence or adaptive behaviors.

The plan to be described in this chapter involves a progressive sharpening of focus moving from the six levels of learning competence down through three stages—A, B, and C.* Each stage brings us closer to a functional description of the child that will serve as a basis for selecting specific curriculum tasks. The six levels of learning competence establish conceptual "ball parks" within which to focus on the child. But they are broad and general. The A-B-C stages progressively move us toward more specific locations in the ball park. The A stage, or skill areas, gets us into center field. The B stage, or skill subcomponents, gets us on base. Finally, the C stage, or short-term objectives, gets us on home plate where, hopefully, we have the IEP ingredients with which to work. The six levels are first divided into several A headings that broadly define the skill areas associated with the levels. Thus, Level I, attention, is more specifically defined as involving vision and visual perceptual skills, hearing and auditory perceptual skills, and task attention skills. The subdivision of the six levels of learning competence into A headings is as follows:

I. ATTENTION LEVEL

A. Vision and Visual Perceptual Skills

A. Hearing and Auditory Perceptual Skills

A. Task Attention Skills

II. RESPONSE LEVEL

A. Motor Coordination Skills

A. Verbal Language Skills

A. Nonverbal Language Skills

A. Task Response Skills

III. ORDER LEVEL

A. Direction-following Skills

A. School Adjustment Skills

*The authors are indebted to Karen Clark, Anita Johnson, and Mike Soloway for their assistance in formulating the ABC's of the IEP.

IV. EXPLORATORY LEVEL

A. **Degree of Active Participation**

A. **Knowledge of Environment**

V. SOCIAL LEVEL

A. **Relationships with Others**

A. **Self-concept**

VI. MASTERY LEVEL

A. **Self-help Skills**

A. **Health and Hygiene Skills**

A. **Reading Skills**

A. **Written Language Skills**

A. **Computation Skills**

A. **Vocational and Career Development Skills**

For each of the A headings under the levels of learning competence, we have established B headings that further delineate subcomponents of the skill areas. These are as follows:

I. ATTENTION LEVEL

A. **Vision and Visual Perceptual Skills**
   B. *Vision*
   B. *Visual Discrimination Skills*
   B. *Visual Memory Skills*

A. **Hearing and Auditory Perceptual Skills**
   B. *Hearing*
   B. *Auditory Discrimination Skills*
   B. *Auditory Memory Skills*

A. **Task Attention Skills**
   B. *Task Attention Skills (visual)*
   B. *Task Attention Skills (auditory)*
   B. *Retention*

II. RESPONSE LEVEL

A. Motor Coordination Skills
  B. *Basic Motor Skills*
  B. *Coordination Skills*
  B. *Hand–Eye Coordination Skills*

A. Verbal Language Skills
  B. *Articulation Skills*
  B. *Language Comprehension Skills*
  B. *Language Usage Skills*

A. Nonverbal Language Skills
  B. *Nonverbal Communication Skills*

A. Task Response Skills
  B. *Task Response Skills (motor)*
  B. *Task Response Skills (verbal)*

III. ORDER LEVEL

A. Direction-following Skills
  B. *Direction/Position Skills*
  B. *Copying Skills*
  B. *Task Order Skills*

A. School Adjustment Skills
  B. *Classroom Behavior Skills*

IV. EXPLORATORY LEVEL

A. Degree of Active Participation
  B. *Curiosity*
  B. *Mobility*

A. Knowledge of Environment
  B. *Objects, Events, and Experiences*
  B. *Direction and Location Skills*
  B. *Beliefs*

V. SOCIAL LEVEL

A. Relationships with Others
  B. *Relationships with Others Outside School*

B. *Relationships with Peers*
B. *Relationships with Teachers and Others in School*

A. Self-concept
B. *Degree of Self-confidence*
B. *Reaction to Frustration*
B. *Emotional Mood*

VI. MASTERY LEVEL

A. Self-help Skills
B. *Eating and Drinking Skills*
B. *Toileting Skills*
B. *Grooming Skills*
B. *Dressing Skills*

A. Health and Hygiene Skills
B. *Knowledge and Understanding*
B. *Health and Hygiene Habits*

A. Reading Skills
B. *Prereading Skills*
B. *Word-analysis Skills*
B. *Vocabulary Skills*
B. *Comprehension Skills*
B. *Study Skills*

A. Written Language Skills
B. *Handwriting Skills*
B. *Spelling Skills*
B. *Story-writing Skills*
B. *Mechanics of English and Grammar Skills*

A. Computation Skills
B. *Precomputation Skills*
B. *Number Operations Skills*
B. *Money Measurement Skills*
B. *Linear and Liquid Measurement Skills*
B. *Clock and Calendar Skills*

A. Vocational and Career Development Skills
B. *Preparation*
B. *Seeking Employment Skills*
B. *Conduct on the Job*

The A headings presented so far have all concerned themselves with the curriculum side of the learning triangle. What about conditions and consequences? We will treat each of these other sides of the triangle as A headings and develop B and C headings that allow us to consider skill areas related to them.

A. Conditions
  B. Setting Behavior Skills

A. Consequences
  B. Responsiveness to Consequences

One final progression is in order. Let's subdivide each B heading into very specific C headings that, hopefully, will serve as references for our short-term objectives on the IEP. The C headings are as follows:

I. ATTENTION LEVEL

A. Vision and Visual Perceptual Skills
  B. Vision
    C1.   Able to identify familiar objects
    C2.   Able to move safely in an unfamiliar environment with aid of dog, cane, or sighted person
    C3.   Able to move safely in an unfamiliar environment without aid of dog, cane, or sighted person
    C4.   Able to read or write with the aid of optical or other visual enlarging devices
    C5.   Able to read or write without the aid of optical or other visual enlarging devices
    C6.   Other_____

  B. Visual Discrimination Skills
    C1.   Follows moving object with eyes
    C2.   Matches like objects
    C3.   Matches three primary colors—red, blue, yellow
    C4.   Matches long and short objects
    C5.   Matches big and little objects
    C6.   Matches shapes (circle, square, triangle, diamond)
    C7.   Matches and recognizes colors—red, blue, green, yellow, orange, purple, brown, black
    C8.   Discriminates object from group of different objects
    C9.   Discriminates object from group of similar objects
    C10.   Identifies missing or incongruous elements in picture
    C11.   Identifies look-alike words
    C12.   Other_____

  B. Visual Memory Skills
    C1.   Select, match, and reproduce previously viewed shapes, designs, letters, and numbers from memory
    C2.   Other_____

A. Hearing and Auditory Perceptual Skills

B. *Hearing*

C1. Able to hear only noise-type sensations
C2. Able to hear some sounds with amplification
C3. Able to hear most sounds with amplification
C4. Able to hear at a distance with amplification
C5. Able to hear most sounds without amplification
C6. Other_____

B. *Auditory Discrimination Skills*

C1. Matches environmental sounds
C2. Identifies direction of sound (far/near, up/down)
C3. Identifies loud/soft and high/low sounds
C4. Identifies and categorizes sounds (e.g., animal noises)
C5. Identifies differences in speech sounds
C6. Identifies initial, final, and medial sounds of words
C7. Identifies consonant sounds of spoken words
C8. Identifies vowel sounds of spoken words
C9. Identifies consonant blends of separate letters (e.g., b+l=bl)
C10. Identifies number and order of sounds in words
C11. Identifies fine differences in words (e.g., *bat* versus *bad*)
C12. Identifies and forms words that rhyme
C13. Other_____

B. *Auditory Memory Skills*

C1. Chooses from group of sounds the one previously presented
C2. Repeats numbers, letters, or words
C3. Repeats tapped rhythms
C4. Repeats recently told story or poem maintaining original logic and sequence
C5. Recalls story or poem recited in past
C6. Repeats numbers, letters, or words backwards
C7. Other_____

A. Task Attention Skills

B. *Task Attention Skills (visual)*

C1. Makes eye contact with task
C2. Makes eye contact with teacher
C3. Maintains eye contact with task
C4. Maintains eye contact with teacher
C5. Not distracted by irrelevant visual stimuli
C6. Pays attention to relevant details of task
C7. Other_____

B. *Task Attention Skills (auditory)*

C1. Listens to teacher

C2. Not distracted by irrelevant auditory stimuli
C3. Profits from instruction delivered verbally by teacher
C4. Other_____

B. *Retention*
C1. Has immediate accurate recall for what was presented in lesson
C2. Can accurately recall what was presented in lesson over varying periods of time (e.g., several days, one week, etc.)
C3. Other_____

II. RESPONSE LEVEL

A. Motor Coordination Skills
B. *Basic Motor Skills*
C1. Lifts head while lying on stomach
C2. Creeps while lying on stomach
C3. Turns from side to back
C4. Turns over by self
C5. Sits if supported by pillow, chair, etc.
C6. Pulls self to sitting position and sits alone
C7. Creeps
C8. Crawls
C9. Pulls self to standing position and stands alone
C10. Walks with aid from adult
C11. Walks forward alone
C12. Walks up and down stairs
C13. Runs
C14. Climbs ladder
C15. Jumps
C16. Balances on one foot
C17. Skips
C18. Hops
C19. Hangs from bar
C20. Other_____

B. *Coordination Skills*
C1. Rolls a large ball while seated on floor
C2. Opens and closes doors
C3. Tosses large ball with both hands
C4. Kicks a large ball
C5. Bends over and picks up objects
C6. Catches a large ball
C7. Tosses large ball and catches it
C8. Bounces large ball and catches it
C9. Performs somersault

C10. Maintains momentum on swing
C11. Rides tricycle
C12. Runs avoiding obstacles
C13. Walks twelve feet on four-inch wide beam without falling off
C14. Propels, rides, and steers a wagon
C15. Rides bicycle with training wheels
C16. Strikes ball with bat (differing size balls thrown from differing distances)
C17. Runs to and kicks large moving ball
C18. Jumps or skips rope
C19. Jumps over objects
C20. Rides standard bicycle
C21. Participates actively in team sports
C22. Other_____

B. *Hand–Eye Coordination Skills*
C1. Grasps objects with hands
C2. Builds block towers (from two to nine blocks)
C3. Strings large beads
C4. Rolls clay into snake shape
C5. Unscrews lids
C6. Puts together form boards
C7. Puts together simple puzzles
C8. Paints with large brush
C9. Cuts paper with scissors
C10. Rolls clay into ball
C11. Strings small beads
C12. Places pegs in pegboard
C13. Cuts pictures following shape
C14. Other_____

A. Verbal Language Skills
B. *Articulation Skills*
C1. Demonstrates pre-articulation skills (e.g., blows, opens/closes mouth, controls saliva, purses lips, moves tongue, vocalizes, babbles)
C2. Imitates sounds or words
C3. Says an intelligible word
C4. Uses all consonant and vowel sounds in phrases and sentences
C5. Uses all consonant and vowel sounds in spontaneous speech with 100 percent intelligibility
C6. Other_____

B. *Language Comprehension Skills*
C1. Stops actively upon simple command (e.g., "No," "Stop that")

C2. Responds to name
C3. Points to parts of the body as instructed
C4. Points to members of family or familiar objects on request
C5. Follows verbal commands of varying complexity (e.g., "Come here")
C6. Performs appropriate actions when self-pronouns, me, my, mine, am, and I, are used
C7. Performs appropriate actions when the pronouns, he, she, and it, are used
C8. Performs appropriate actions when the pronouns, him, her, you, and they, are used
C9. Performs appropriate actions when the pronouns, his, hers, yours, and theirs, are used
C10. Points to objects according to function (e.g., something to sleep on = bed)
C11. Points to objects according to location (e.g., on top, under, beside, etc.)
C12. Points to persons and objects connected with school, neighborhood, or community on request
C13. Answers specific questions based on spoken material
C14. Chooses main ideas from spoken material
C15. Understands standard English as used in school
C16. Other_____

B. *Language Usage Skills*
C1. Vocalizes feelings of pleasure or pain
C2. Does not manifest echolalic speech
C3. Uses one word for many related things
C4. Refers to self by first name
C5. Names familiar objects, people, places, body parts
C6. Imitates phrases and whole sentences spontaneously
C7. Uses pronouns appropriately (me, my, mine, I, him, he, his, her, hers, you, yours, their, their's)
C8. Combines pronouns and verbs to make complete sentence
C9. Uses negatives, contractions, conjunctions, plurals, possessives, articles in sentences
C10. Carries on and initiates a conversation
C11. Answers questions such as "Do you want?" or "Can you?" with appropriate yes or no
C12. Asks for things needed or wanted
C13. Tells about feelings and ideas with verbal language
C14. Answers "who" and "where" questions
C15. Describes action in a picture
C16. Describes events of past and future experience in logical, sequential order
C17. Can give personal data verbally (age, address, phone num-

ber, birthday, brothers and sisters, parents' names, occupations)

C18. Uses appropriate standard English when speaking
C19. Other_____

A. Nonverbal Language Skills

B. *Nonverbal Communication Skills*
C1. Communicates by pulling another to show object, person, or situation
C2. Gestures appropriately to verbal commands
C3. Communicates by pointing to object, person, or situation desired
C4. Can communicate using signing
C5. Can communicate using finger spelling
C6. Can communicate by means of lip reading
C7. Other_____

A. Task Response Skills

B. *Task Response Skills (motor)*
C1. Attends school regularly
C2. Is a willing participant in activities
C3. Does not engage in self-stimulation
C4. Demonstrates vitality and eagerness when participating in activities
C5. Starts assignments on own
C6. Readily volunteers to participate in activities
C7. Other_____

B. *Task Response Skills (verbal)*
C1. Is not verbally abusive toward others
C2. Does not use profanity
C3. Is a willing participant in discussions with one person
C4. Is a willing participant in class discussions
C5. Answers questions when called upon
C6. Readily volunteers to participate in class discussions
C7. Other_____

III. ORDER LEVEL

A. Direction-following Skills

B. *Direction/Position Skills*
C1. Locates up/down, in/on/out, under/over, top/bottom, by/beside, before/after, above/below, etc.
C2. Identifies right/left direction, right hand and foot, left hand and foot
C3. Other_____

B. *Copying Skills*
- C1. Strings beads reproducing color and shape sequence
- C2. Copies model to reproduce number, pattern, and color of pegboard design
- C3. Copies model to reproduce block design
- C4. Copies a given shape (circle, square, cross, triangle, diamond)
- C5. Can draw a human figure
- C6. Puts together complex puzzles
- C7. Other_____

B. *Task Order Skills*
- C1. Follows one, two, three task directions in sequence
- C2. Follows task directions independently
- C3. Readily understands directions associated with a task or lesson
- C4. Completes tasks if given extra time
- C5. Completes tasks on time
- C6. Regularly does homework assignment
- C7. Turns in work that is neat and legible
- C8. Other_____

A. School Adjustment Skills

B. *Classroom Behavior Skills*
- C1. Comes to class on time
- C2. Follows class rules without being reminded
- C3. Is not disruptive in class
- C4. Exhibits disapproval when others are disruptive
- C5. Is dependable when given duties in the class (e.g., paper monitor)
- C6. Other_____

IV. EXPLORATORY LEVEL

A. Degree of Active Participation

B. *Curiosity*
- C1. Demonstrates curiosity regarding new objects (e.g., toys)
- C2. Demonstrates curiosity in new situation (e.g., first visit to zoo)
- C3. Independently seeks new objects to explore
- C4. Independently seeks new situations to explore
- C5. Has a variety of interests (specify_____)
- C6. Has a favorite toy or toys (specify _____)

C7. Has a hobby or hobbies (specify _____)
C8. Has a pet (specify _____)
C9. Has developed a talent (e.g., music, art, drama, athletics, crafts, etc.) (specify _____)
C10. Has a favorite television program (specify _____)
C11. Has a favorite game that he or she can play well (specify _____)
C12. Other _____

B. *Mobility*

C1. Can travel independently
C2. Seeks to travel independently
C3. Knows how to use public transportation facilities
C4. Knows how to find way home from any place in community
C5. Knows rules of conduct in community (e.g., waiting in line)
C6. Can make purchases in store
C7. Knows how to use post office
C8. Can avoid hazards in community including approaches by strangers
C9. Crosses streets in pedestrian zones or when appropriate at intersections
C10. Obeys laws and ordinances that exist in the community
C11. Knows how to use leisure time and engages in variety of leisure-time activities
C12. Drives a car safely obeying traffic laws
C13. Other _____

A. Knowledge of Environment

B. *Objects, Events, and Experiences*

C1. Familiar with wide range of objects (e.g., animals, flowers, transportational vehicles, furniture, etc.)
C2. Knows physical characteristics of wide range of objects (e.g., color, shape, size, weight, texture, taste, smell, etc.)
C3. Understands function of wide range of objects (e.g., sit in chairs, ride in cars, etc.)
C4. Understands groupings or classes objects are placed in (e.g., chairs, sofa, table = furniture)
C5. Has had a wide range of experiences (e.g., visits to zoo and circus, camping trips, airplane travel, trips away from home and community, etc.)
C6. Has learned independent living skills (e.g., consumerism, money management, home management, parent responsibilities, etc.)
C7. Other _____

B. *Direction and Location Skills*
  C1. Can locate north, south, east, west
  C2. Is aware of major streets and can locate them by direction
  C3. Is aware of significant places in the local community (e.g., library, police station)
  C4. Other_____
B. *Beliefs*
  C1. Maintains contact with reality
  C2. Prefers reality to fantasy
  C3. Has accurate beliefs (e.g., natural phenomena, bodily functions, motivation of others)
  C4. Other_____

V. SOCIAL LEVEL

A. Relationships with Others
B. *Relationships with Others Outside School*
  C1. Relates positively with members of family
  C2. Is accepted by others in community (e.g., postman, grocery clerk, etc.)
  C3. Relates positively with others in community
  C4. Has playmates when playing at home
  C5. Has one close friend
  C6. Has a number of close friends
  C7. Assumes responsibilities at home and follows through with them independently
  C8. Understands how people live together in family units
  C9. Other_____
B. *Relationships with Peers*
  C1. Readily seeks out peers in school
  C2. Readily seeks to participate in group activities
  C3. Is accepted by peers in school
  C4. Relates positively with peers in school
  C5. Respects the rights of others
  C6. Does not bully others or physically abuse them
  C7. Participates cooperatively in group activities
  C8. Willingly waits turn
  C9. Does not lie to others
  C10. Readily shares with others
  C11. Has one close friend in school
  C12. Has a number of close friends in school
  C13. Is popular with most other children
  C14. Exhibits leadership abilities
  C15. Is turned to by other children for leadership

C16. Readily accepts praise from peers
C17. Other_____

B. *Relationships with Teachers and Others in School*
 C1. Is accepted by the teacher and other school staff
 C2. Relates positively with teacher and other school staff
 C3. Seeks contact with teacher
 C4. Does not demand excessive attention or time from teacher
 C5. Respects teacher's authority
 C6. Readily follows teacher's requests
 C7. Does not lie to teacher
 C8. Appears to want to please teacher
 C9. Readily accepts praise from teacher
 C10. Other_____

A. Self-concept

B. *Degree of Self-confidence*
 C1. Enters into activities even when unsure of what is expected
 C2. Enters into activities that are competitive
 C3. Will respond without constant reassurance
 C4. Recognizes school problems but demonstrates confidence that he or she can learn
 C5. Realistic with respect to expectations for own achievement
 C6. Other_____

B. *Reaction to Frustration*
 C1. Adjusts easily to changes in routines or activities
 C2. Takes responsibility for own problems
 C3. Communicates positive attitude toward school
 C4. Communicates positive attitudes toward work that is assigned
 C5. Other_____

B. *Emotional Mood*
 C1. Facial expression communicates lack of fear or sadness
 C2. Body position communicates lack of tension (e.g., not slouching in chair or hiding face)
 C3. Other_____

VI. MASTERY LEVEL

A. Self-help Skills

B. *Eating and Drinking Skills*
 C1. Retains all semi-solid and semi-liquid food from spoon without spitting, drooling
 C2. Drinks from cup
 C3. Holds finger foods

C4. Bites off appropriately sized pieces of finger foods using teeth
C5. Chews and swallows food appropriately
C6. Eats with spoon
C7. Eats with fork
C8. Serves self at table
C9. Spreads with knife (e.g., butter)
C10. Cuts with knife
C11. Cuts with knife and fork
C12. Prepares food for eating (e.g., peels banana)
C13. Opens food containers (e.g., jars, lunch pail)
C14. Serves self in cafeteria
C15. Sets or prepares table
C16. Uses napkin to wipe hands and mouth
C17. Eats and drinks without supervision
C18. Eats and drinks in manner appropriate for home, school, restaurant, cafeteria, friend's house
C19. Other_____

B. *Toileting Skills*
C1. Maintains dry diaper/pants for at least two hours
C2. Indicates when wet and/or soiled
C3. Sits on toilet when placed and supervised
C4. Sits on toilet when left alone
C5. Indicates when needs to go to toilet
C6. Goes to toilet independently
C7. Goes to toilet properly by self with no accidents
C8. Adjusts clothing before leaving bathroom (e.g., zippers, buttons)
C9. Asks location of bathroom in unfamiliar situation
C10. Other_____

B. *Grooming Skills*
C1. Goes to sink when requested to or on own
C2. Washes hands and face properly (e.g., uses soap, water, towels appropriately)
C3. Washes hands and face and dries them without having to be reminded or checked
C4. Can take bath or shower appropriately
C5. Combs hair
C6. Grooms and takes care of hair properly
C7. Cleans fingernails
C8. Files and cuts own nails (hands and feet)
C9. Shaves self
C10. Other_____

B. *Dressing Skills*
C1. Cooperates passively when being dressed or undressed
C2. Identifies own clothing

C3. Puts on pull-over clothing (e.g., t-shirt, dress)
C4. Closes snaps, buttons, zippers
C5. Puts on pants
C6. Puts on front-opened clothing
C7. Puts on socks
C8. Puts on shoes
C9. Ties shoelaces or closes other fasteners on shoes
C10. Puts on all clothing when told to do so
C11. Selects appropriate clothing for various occasions
C12. Takes off pull-over clothing
C13. Opens snaps, buttons, zippers
C14. Takes off pants
C15. Takes off front-opened clothing
C16. Takes off socks and shoes
C17. Takes off all clothing when told to do so
C18. Hangs clothing on hook
C19. Folds clean clothing and puts in storage area
C20. Other_____

A. Health and Hygiene Skills

B. Knowledge and Understanding
C1. Understands bodily functions (e.g., digestive, reproductive)
C2. Understands normal body development and growth
C3. Understands importance of personal hygiene
C4. Understands importance of proper nutrition
C5. Understands causes of health problems
C6. Understands safety procedures
C7. Understands effects of drugs, tobacco, and other artificial stimulants and depressants
C8. Other_____

B. Health and Hygiene Habits
C1. Blows nose independently when necessary
C2. Uses toothbrush appropriately
C3. Cares for personal hygiene needs during menstrual cycle
C4. Uses routine habits necessary to maintain good health (e.g., exercise, rest, sleep, nutrition)
C5. Avoids hazards (e.g., poisonous substances, broken glass, dangerous situations)
C6. Other_____

A. Reading Skills

B. Prereading Skills
C1. Matches objects by color/size/shape
C2. Reproduces pegboard designs in terms of number, color, pattern

C3. Places five pictures in logical sequence left to right
C4. Visually matches identical words in group of grossly different words
C5. Visually matches identical words in group of similar words
C6. Other_____

B. *Word-analysis Skills*
C1. Names capital and lower-case consonants when shown printed letters
C2. Names capital and lower-case vowels when shown printed letters
C3. Says what sounds capital and lower-case consonants make when shown printed letters
C4. Says what sounds capital and lower-case vowels make when shown printed letters
C5. Recognizes and says how consonant blends sound
C6. Recognizes and says how consonant digraphs sound
C7. Recognizes and says how consonant trigraphs sound
C8. Recognizes and says how vowel diphthongs sound
C9. Scans letters of word left to right
C10. Blends letter sounds to say word as unit
C11. Uses phonic skills to read unfamiliar words
C12. Other_____

B. *Vocabulary Skills*
C1. Can adequately read vocabulary words at_____
(insert preprimer to twelfth grade) level
C2. Can read_____
percent words correctly from_____
standard basic sight vocabulary list
C3. Can read common sign words (first aid, danger, hands off, fire alarm, don't walk, no running, wet paint, no admittance, emergency exit, fire escape, do not enter, high voltage, beware of dog, watch your step, employees only, hot, wait, walk, stop, police, poison, warning, ladies, women, toilet, keep out, gentlemen, men, telephone, restroom, bus stop)
C4. Other_____

B. *Comprehension Skills*
C1. Can adequately comprehend reading material at_____
(insert preprimer to twelfth grade) level
C2. Can select and tell main idea in sentence, paragraph, or story
C3. Can predict outcomes, draw conclusions, make inferences, and make interpretations from material read
C4. Reads with appropriate expression
C5. Other_____

B. *Study Skills*
- C1. Understands and uses charts, maps, tables, and index to locate specific information
- C2. Reads and uses basic reference materials (dictionaries, encyclopedias, etc.) for specific purposes
- C3. Reads at an adequate rate of speed
- C4. Understands and uses the facilities of a library (e.g., locate books, use card file, check out books)
- C5. Other_____

A. Written Language Skills

B. *Handwriting Skills*
- C1. Traces and reproduces circles and horizontal and vertical lines
- C2. Holds pencil correctly
- C3. Holds paper with free hand
- C4. Joins two dots with straight line starting and stopping at appropriate points
- C5. Traces name
- C6. Prints own name with model
- C7. Prints own name without model
- C8. Prints all upper- and lower-case letters of alphabet
- C9. Copies letters and words from chalkboard in manuscript form
- C10. Writes all upper- and lower-case letters of alphabet in cursive form
- C11. Copies letters and words from chalkboard in cursive form
- C12. Writes own name in cursive form with model
- C13. Writes own name in cursive form without model
- C14. Other_____

B. *Spelling Skills*
- C1. Writes letters when name is spoken
- C2. Writes letters when sound is spoken
- C3. Writes blends when sound is spoken
- C4. Writes diphthongs when sound is spoken
- C5. Writes simple words without model
- C6. Decodes multisyllabic words by breaking them up into meaningful units
- C7. Uses knowledge of phonics to spell new words
- C8. Studies and learns to correctly spell words used in story writing
- C9. Studies and learns to correctly spell words from basic spelling lists
- C10. Uses dictionary to look up unfamiliar words
- C11. Other_____

B. *Story-Writing Skills*
   C1.   Prints/writes title for picture drawn
   C2.   Copies sentence from model on paper or chalkboard
   C3.   Dictates story and later reads it back
   C4.   Participates in group dictation of story
   C5.   Copies paragraph from chalkboard
   C6.   Writes story independently
   C7.   Other_____

B. *Mechanics of English and Grammar Skills*
   C1.   Uses capitals for first word in sentence, names, days, months, special days, streets, cities, states, countries, titles, special groups
   C2.   Uses periods at end of sentences and after abbreviations and initials
   C3.   Uses other punctuation marks correctly (question mark, exclamation point, comma, semicolon, colon)
   C4.   Identifies and correctly uses parts of speech (noun, pronoun, adjective, adverb, conjunction, preposition, interjection)
   C5.   Understands and uses prefixes and suffixes
   C6.   Other_____

A. Computation Skills

B. *Precomputation Skills*
   C1.   Sorts according to shape, size, and length; arranges from smallest to largest
   C2.   Determines more, less, many, few, big, bigger, biggest, and small, smaller, and smallest
   C3.   Locates first, middle, and last in group of objects
   C4.   Constructs sets of objects from one object to ten objects
   C5.   Counts orally to ten
   C6.   Locates object of given number in group of ten (e.g., fourth object)
   C7.   Matches groups having equal number of objects up to ten
   C8.   Reads and writes numbers 0–9, 10–19, 20–49, 50–100, over 100
   C9.   Counts orally to 19, 20–49, 50–100, over 100
   C10.   Counts backward from ten
   C11.   Performs simple addition facts with objects
   C12.   Performs simple subtraction facts with objects
   C13.   Constructs set of one hundred objects
   C14.   Can read number words (e.g., *one, two, three,* etc.)
   C15.   Can count by 2's, 5's, 10's, 3's, 4's, 6's, 7's, 8's, and 9's
   C16.   Can read Roman numerals
   C17.   Can name fractional parts of circle cut into pie-shaped pieces
   C18.   Other_____

B. Number Operations Skills

C1. Performs basic addition facts with counters/without counters

C2. Performs basic subtraction facts with counters/without counters

C3. Regroups in addition

C4. Regroups in subtraction

C5. Solves practical word problems requiring addition and subtraction

C6. Performs multiplication combinations

C7. Performs division facts

C8. Regroups in multiplication and division

C9. Solves practical word problems requiring multiplication and division

C10. Equates fractional and decimal notations (e.g., $\frac{3}{4} = .75$)

C11. Can convert fractions

C12. Adds and subtracts fractions and decimal quantities

C13. Multiplies and divides fractions and decimals

C14. Computes simple percentages

C15. Does advanced basic math beyond sixth grade level

C16. Does algebra

C17. Does geometry

C18. Other_____

B. Money Measurement Skills

C1. Matches coins (e.g., quarter to quarter, dime to dime)

C2. Names and selects coins

C3. Compares values of coins (e.g., dime is worth more than nickel)

C4. Names bill denominations and compares values (e.g., $1, $5, $10)

C5. Combines coins to equal larger one (e.g., 2 nickels = 1 dime)

C6. Combines coins to equal an odd total (e.g., 24¢)

C7. Counts out correct change up to one quarter, half-dollar, one dollar, over one dollar

C8. Matches coins and/or bills to decimal and symbol (e.g., dime = $.10)

C9. Selects items for purchase whose total price is under amount possessed and then figures change to be received

C10. Other_____

B. Linear and Liquid Measurement Skills

C1. Uses evenly spaced markings on tool to measure a line shorter than the tool

C2. Measures liquid to capacity of container, to marked line on container

C3. Tells measurement facts (e.g., 12 eggs = 1 dozen, 12 inches = 1 foot)

C4. Adds items to attain a requested weight on a numbered scale of weights
C5. Tells weight of item to nearest pound and ounce on scale
C6. Measures using inch, foot, yard
C7. Uses measurement facts (e.g., 16 oz. = 1 lb.) to compute weight
C8. Reads thermometer
C9. Uses metric measures
C10. Other_____

B. *Clock and Calendar Skills*

C1. Reads numerals on clock face and associates hand placement with routine activities
C2. Uses morning, afternoon, night to describe the parts of the day
C3. Tells time at the hour, half hour, and quarter hour
C4. Tells time to five-minute intervals
C5. Names days of week in succession
C6. Relates today, tomorrow, yesterday to days of the week
C7. Locates day of week and date (number and day) on calendar
C8. Names months in succession and current month; locates month on calendar; locates special holidays
C9. Other_____

A. Vocational and Career Development Skills

B. *Preparation*

C1. Knows that people work at many different types of jobs
C2. Knows that different skills and knowledge are required to perform different jobs
C3. Identifies personal skills possessed and relates these to vocational opportunities
C4. Determines job area interests after testing, counseling, or experience in training settings
C5. Enters training program to learn specific job skills
C6. Other_____

B. *Seeking Employment Skills*

C1. Reads newspaper to locate jobs or training
C2. Knows community agencies that will help locate jobs or training (e.g., Department of Human Resources)
C3. Can role-play job interview
C4. Can fill out job application
C5. Determines job related information (e.g., hours, location, pay, pay periods, working conditions, job benefits)
C6. Can participate in actual job interview
C7. Other_____

B. *Conduct on the Job*

C1. Arrives at work on time

C2. Follows daily work schedule including breaks and lunch
C3. Calculates wages for hours worked
C4. Accepts criticism and attempts to implement suggestions
C5. Stops work on project when mistake is identified
C6. Asks for advice after identifying mistake
C7. Accepts and follows directions
C8. Participates in group projects
C9. Maintains tools and equipment with and without supervision
C10. Does not waste materials
C11. Works steadily at reasonable speed to get job done
C12. Evaluates own performance based on company or supervisor standards
C13. Other_____

A. Conditions*
  ### B. *Setting Behavior Skills*
  C1. Works well one-to-one
  C2. Works well in small group activities (two to six students)
  C3. Works well in total class activities (e.g., when lessons presented by teacher from front of room)
  C4. Works well independently
  C5. Gets along well on the playground
  C6. Gets along well in the cafeteria
  C7. Gets along well on the school bus
  C8. Gets along well on field trips
  C9. Gets along well during recess or lunch time
  C10. Other_____

A. Consequences
  ### B. *Responsiveness to Consequences*
  C1. Responds well for tangible rewards (e.g., food)
  C2. Responds well for teacher praise
  C3. Responds well for check marks (or other token rewards)
  C4. Responds well for free-choice time
  C5. Responds well for grades
  C6. Responds well on a self-motivated basis
  C7. Is disciplined effectively by loss of privileges
  C8. Is disciplined effectively by being sent out of room for a brief period
  C9. Is disciplined effectively by being sent to the principal's office
  C10. Is disciplined effectively by being sent home
  C11. Other_____

---

*As noted earlier, the conditions and consequences sides of the learning triangle are considered as separate A headings.

We have introduced this A-B-C approach in a general fashion, but we need a much more specific means of meeting the requirements of PL 94–142 with respect to the Individual Education Plan. Remember, in Chapter 3 we quoted from the law that the following questions must be answered:

1. What is the child's present level of educational performance?

2. What are your long-term and short-term instructional objectives?

3. What are the specific services to be offered the child?

4. To what extent can the child participate in regular education programs?

5. When will these services begin, and how long will they be provided?

6. How are you going to determine if your short-term instructional objectives have been accomplished?

In response to this need, we have developed a format for reporting the IEP. The format is presented in Figure 5–1.* Permission is granted by the publisher to reproduce Figure 5–1 in conjunction with the use of *The Emotionally Disturbed Child in the Classroom: The Orchestration of Success,* Second Edition, by Frank M. Hewett and Frank D. Taylor.

Filling Out the IEP Format

1. With the A-B-C framework as a reference, we turn to the Individual Education Program cover sheet. After filling in identifying data, we consider the skill areas which consist of our original A headings. We will derive our long-term objectives from them. First, however, we rate each of the A headings with respect to the child's actual functioning level. The scale on the lower right corner allows us to rate both strengths and weaknesses. We must always keep in mind the importance of identifying children's strengths, not just areas in which they are handicapped. The A heading, "degree of active participation," covers children's interests and can often be rated as a strength providing clues for motivation in later formulation of the IEP.

Once the skill areas are rated, we select those which are most critical and which we would like to set as long-term objectives. How many we check will depend on the type of child and educational program. For some, every skill area could be rated 4. For others, a single area (e.g., school adjustment skills) will reflect the primary problem that has led to a child's referral for special education.

The bottom two A headings, "conditions" and "consequences," are not checked as they will be taken into consideration later for each child.

(Text continues on pg. 161.)

*The authors are indebted to Yvonne Chan whose suggestions for the format reported here are greatly appreciated.

Name	Birth Date	School

SKILL AREAS (A Headings)	Long-term Objectives (✓)					
	Date:		Date:		Date:	
Curriculum (Vision & visual perceptual skills)						
Curriculum (Hearing & auditory perceptual skills)						
Curriculum (Task attention skills)						
Curriculum (Motor coordination skills)						
Curriculum (Verbal language skills)						
Curriculum (Nonverbal language skills)						
Curriculum (Task response skills)						
Curriculum (Direction-following skills)						
Curriculum (School adjustment skills)						
Curriculum (Degree of active participation)						
Curriculum (Knowledge of environment)						
Curriculum (Relationships with others)						
Curriculum (Self-concept)						
Curriculum (Self-help skills)						
Curriculum (Health & hygiene skills)						
Curriculum (Reading skills)						
Curriculum (Written language skills)						
Curriculum (Computation skills)						
Curriculum (Vocational & career development skills)						
Conditions (Rate for each student)	Rating Key					
Consequences (Rate for each student)	0 Does not apply / 1 Strength / 2 Average / 3 Moderate problem / 4 Severe problem					

Figure 5–1. A format for reporting the Individual Education Program.

SKILL SUBCOMPONENTS
(B Headings)

Skill Subcomponents	Strengths	Weaknesses

Figure 5–1 (continued).

Conditions (A)	Strengths	Weaknesses
Setting behavior skills (B)		
Consequences (A)	Strengths	Weaknesses
Responsiveness to consequences (B)		

Figure 5–1 (continued).

Copyright © 1980 by Allyn and Bacon, Inc. Reproduction of this material is restricted to use with *The Emotionally Disturbed Child in the Classroom: The Orchestration of Success,* Second Edition, by Frank M. Hewitt and Frank D. Taylor.

SHORT-TERM OBJECTIVES
(C Headings)

Objectives	Curriculum	Conditions	Consequences	Evaluation	Results
Baseline:				Criteria: Time period: Method:	Date: Comments:
Baseline:				Criteria: Time period: Method:	Date: Comments:
Baseline:				Criteria: Time period: Method:	Date: Comments:
Baseline:				Criteria: Time period: Method:	Date: Comments:

Figure 5–1 (continued).

```
Services to be provided:




Extent of participation in regular education program:




Date of program initiation and expected duration:






Authorization signatures:


_____        (parent) _____


_____                 _____


_____                 _____


Date signed              _____
```

Figure 5–1 (continued).

2. The second part of the IEP consists of a form on which we may abstract B headings from the A heading long-term objectives checked on the cover sheet. First, we write in the pertinent B headings. Next, we turn to the C headings related to these B headings for descriptions that identify either the child's strengths or weaknesses. (*See* the outline listed earlier in this chapter for B headings and C headings.) Sometimes a given B heading will provide C headings describing both strengths and weaknesses, and these should be so noted.

Throughout this book, we have attempted to reject claims of certainty and convey the importance of using information and knowledge in an open-minded and flexible manner. The C headings listed in our A-B-C approach are *only suggestions*. They have not been handed down from some mountaintop and do not include every skill and behavior possible to consider in preparing an IEP. They are intended to touch base with certain critical socialization and educational behaviors, but they do not in any way describe the total universe of such behaviors. The writer of the IEP should add headings, reword headings, and break the C headings down into smaller D or even E behaviors.

The C heading, "engages cooperatively in group activities," may have to be further broken down into a D heading, "works cooperatively with one other student," or even further into an E heading, "accepts invitation to participate in game with another student." It will be noted that the C headings are stated in the positive (e.g., the child possesses the skill or does not have the problem). We keep the positive statement when recording a strength on the form, but restate it in the negative when reporting a weakness. Teachers of children with handicapping conditions such as hearing or visual impairment will have to freely create other C headings. The same is true for teachers working at the secondary level.

3. The final two skill areas on the cover sheet are "conditions" and "consequences." These are not to be considered long-term objectives. When we identify the curriculum areas, we have zeroed in on one side of the learning triangle. The next part of the IEP allows us to do the same for the other two sides. As we did for the curriculum areas, we draw upon the relevant C headings under "setting behavior skills" and "responsiveness to consequences."

4. Once the B headings have been broken down into C headings, we are ready to conceive the heart of the IEP—the short-term objectives along with instructional strategies and evaluation procedures. This is done in the next part of the IEP. Depending on how many short-term objectives we can realistically hope to attain, we write in the rated C headings we consider most important. We can use as many additional short-term objective forms as needed to do this. In addition, we note the child's baseline behavior related to the objective. For example, if the C heading is "arrives late to school," the baseline statement might read, "tardy 2 to 3 times a week."

5. We next consider the specific instructional components of the IEP—curriculum, conditions, and consequences. Capitalizing on strengths and bolstering weaknesses will be our orientation as we develop teaching strategies. The curriculum statement will cover the specific approach or task and materials we will use to teach the child. Conditions will state the setting in which we will work and consideration of how long or how much and when. The conditions of how well will be considered under the evaluation component of *criteria*. The statement under consequences will reflect what is apt to be motivating for the child or effective in accomplishing the short-term objective.

6. The evaluation box requires three types of information:

Criteria. Exactly how proficient will the child become as a result of our instructional efforts? If we are concerned about tardiness, how much do we expect the child's on-time record to improve? If we are concerned about reading vocabulary, precisely how many words do we expect the child to learn or what grade level progress do we expect?

Time Period. What span of time are we talking about? Do we expect to accomplish objectives in a week, half-semester, semester, or year?

Method. How are we going to know if we have accomplished our objective? What evidence can we present to the parents or others to inform them of the child's accomplishments? This is often difficult to specify, and the more objective and quantitative our evidence, the better. However, if we are concerned with the child's self-concept and the fact that he never smiles, we may set up a short-term objective of "increase number of smiles." Our method may be to observe the child and report at the end of our time period. "He never smiled during the first part of the semester, but now I can joke with him, and he smiles readily." We will not always be able to present reliable, observational data, frequency counts, or test scores for every short-term objective.

7. In the comment column, we are going to state whether or not our objective was accomplished within the specified time period and any brief comments pertinent to why we did or did not accomplish the objective.

8. Depending on the child's progress or other instructional considerations, we may wish to up-date the IEP or review it periodically. This can be done by rerating the long-term and short-term objectives, adding new objectives, discarding old objectives. The long-term objective skill areas provide for three ratings. We can thus retain this portion of the IEP. The B heading and short-term objective forms will have to be done over to reflect the child's progress or lack of it and our new goals and approaches.

9. The final part of the IEP provides the additional information regarding the child's program required by PL 94–142. The signatures of all concerned, including the parents, complete the IEP.

In Chapter 3 we introduced Donald, the severely disturbed boy who was classified by the psychiatrist as a catatonic schizophrenic and by the teacher as a response problem. Figure 5–2 presents the Individual Education Program devised for him. As can be seen, Donald was a candidate for a variety of *4's* for severe problems and several *1's* for strengths. The teacher selected two of the *4*-rated skill areas for focus. Attention was also paid to the skill areas, "knowledge of environment" and "computational skills" when entering the B headings in the next part.

On the B-heading form, the teacher has entered the more specific skill-area problems and described them with C headings under weaknesses. Two strengths are noted using B and C headings. The conditions and consequences form reveals Donald's severe isolation and the fact that he has previously been highly motivated by academics. Under short-term objectives, the teacher described two response level tasks that were used in the

(Text continues on pg. 168.)

Name DONALD HUBER Birth Date 11-19 School NPI

Long-term Objectives (✓)

SKILL AREAS (A Headings)	Date: 4-16		Date:		Date:	
Curriculum (Vision & visual perceptual skills)	2					
Curriculum (Hearing & auditory perceptual skills)	2					
Curriculum (Task attention skills)	4	✓				
Curriculum (Motor coordination skills)	4					
Curriculum (Verbal language skills)	4					
Curriculum (Nonverbal language skills)	0					
Curriculum (Task response skills)	4	✓				
Curriculum (Direction-following skills)	4					
Curriculum (School adjustment skills)	4					
Curriculum (Degree of active participation)	4					
Curriculum (Knowledge of environment)	1					
Curriculum (Relationships with others)	4					
Curriculum (Self-concept)	4					
Curriculum (Self-help skills)	2					
Curriculum (Health & hygiene skills)	4					
Curriculum (Reading skills)	1					
Curriculum (Written language skills)	1					
Curriculum (Computation skills)	1					
Curriculum (Vocational & career development skills)	0					
Conditions (Rate for each student)						
Consequences (Rate for each student)						

Rating Key
0 Does not apply
1 Strength
2 Average
3 Moderate problem
4 Severe problem

Figure 5–2. Donald's Individual Education Program.

Skill Subcomponents	Strengths	Weaknesses
Task attention skills (visual)		No eye contact with teacher; does not pay attention to any task
Task response skills (motor)	Eyes have been seen to look at clock; otherwise stares blankly ahead	Does not move at all
Task response skills (verbal)		Stopped speaking 6 months ago
Curiosity	Extreme interest in prehistoric life	
Number operation skills	Three years advanced in arithmetic. Previous teacher says it is his favorite subject	

Figure 5–2 (continued).

Conditions (A)	Strengths	Weaknesses
Setting behavior skills (B)		Appears unaware of surroundings; even one-on-one is not effective
Consequences (A)	Strengths	Weaknesses
Responsiveness to consequences (B)	Previous teacher reports he is highly motivated by reading encyclopedia and doing arithmetic	Will not respond for any reward

Figure 5–2 (continued).

SHORT-TERM OBJECTIVES
(C Headings)

Objectives	Curriculum	Conditions	Consequences	Evaluation	Results
Get to pay attention to task Baseline: No indication of attention at present	Set up slide projector in back of frosted glass/screen. Place box with lever to turn on projector on his lap. Put dinosaur slides in projector. Task is to turn lever on & off.	One-on-one. Give as much time as necessary Keep no longer than 10-20 minutes at first	Opportunity to view dinosaur slides Teacher praise	Criteria: Will push lever on & off from 3 to 20 times in 20 minutes Time period: 2 weeks Method: Count of lever pushes	Date: 4-16 Comments: At end of 2 weeks was pushing lever 25 times in 20 minutes
Get him to move Baseline: No movement at all	Same	One-on-one. Do not attempt to get him to speak. Talk with him but do not ask questions.	Same	Criteria: Same Time period: Method:	Date: Comments:
Introduce arithmetic assignment Baseline: Three years above grade level	Prepare 3x5 cards with basic number facts on them. For each have 3 answers, one of which is correct. He must move finger across desk and stop under correct answer.	One-on-one. Give as much time as possible. Move on to this objective only after lever pushing objective met.	Satisfaction from task Teacher praise	Criteria: Will move finger across desk from 5-15 times in 20 minutes Time period: 2 weeks Method: Count finger movements	Date: 5-20 Comments: At end of 3 weeks, this objective was met.
Baseline:				Criteria: Time period: Method:	Date: Comments:

Figure 5–2 (continued).

Services to be provided:

Daily 20-minute tutoring sessions

Extent of participation in regular education program:

No participation

Date of program initiation and expected duration:

April 16. Will continue and be modified
as long as Donald is in the NPI.

Authorization signatures:

Margaret Huber   (parent) *Thomas V Martin PhD*

Mary Smith

Samuel Hopkins

Date signed   4-16

Figure 5–2 (continued).

initial educational program with Donald. Finally, the participation and duration form signed by Donald's mother, teacher, social worker, and psychologist completes the IEP form. Donald's case is unusually unique. More typical of the types of problems dealt with in the public schools are those exhibited by Bobby Myron, the behavior disordered celebrity who has been referred to several times in this text. His hypothetical IEP is reproduced in Figure 5–3.

In Bobby's case, four severe-problem skill-areas were selected by the teacher. These are all behavioral (as compared to academic) since Bobby only had moderate difficulties in basic school subjects. We also note Bobby's strengths in the response, motor, and exploratory areas. The B and C headings further delineate Bobby's behavioral difficulties as well as his

(Text continues on pg. 173.)

Name BOBBY MYRON   Birth Date JULY 6 School WOODSIDE

SKILL AREAS (A Headings)	Long-term Objectives (√)					
	Date: 10-2		Date:		Date:	
Curriculum (Vision & visual perceptual skills)	2					
Curriculum (Hearing & auditory perceptual skills)	2					
Curriculum (Task attention skills)	4	√				
Curriculum (Motor coordination skills)	1					
Curriculum (Verbal language skills)	2					
Curriculum (Nonverbal language skills)	0					
Curriculum (Task response skills)	2					
Curriculum (Direction-following skills)	4	√				
Curriculum (School adjustment skills)	4	√				
Curriculum (Degree of active participation)	1					
Curriculum (Knowledge of environment)	1					
Curriculum (Relationships with others)	4	√				
Curriculum (Self-concept)	3					
Curriculum (Self-help skills)	2					
Curriculum (Health & hygiene skills)	2					
Curriculum (Reading skills)	3					
Curriculum (Written language skills)	3					
Curriculum (Computation skills)	3					
Curriculum (Vocational & career development skills)	0					
Conditions (Rate for each student)						
Consequences (Rate for each student)						

Rating Key
0 Does not apply
1 Strength
2 Average
3 Moderate problem
4 Severe problem

Figure 5–3. Bobby's Individual Education Program.

SKILL SUBCOMPONENTS
(B Headings)

Skill Subcomponents	Strengths	Weaknesses
Task attention skills (visual)		Easily distracted
Task attention skills (auditory)		Seldom listens to teacher
Coordination skills	A good athlete, very well-coordinated	
Task order skills		Seldom completes class work. Papers are done sloppily
Classroom behavior skills		Seldom follows class rules. Often disruptive in class
Curiosity	Plays sports well. Great passion for surfing and skateboarding	
Relationships with peers	Appears to want peer praise	Bullies others; no respect for their rights or property; won't wait turn; physically abusive
Relationship with teacher	Appears to want teacher praise	Does not have a positive relationship with teacher

Figure 5–3 (continued).

Conditions (A)	Strengths	Weaknesses
Setting behavior skills (B)	Works well one-on-one	Works poorly in total class setting
Consequences (A)	Strengths	Weaknesses
Responsiveness to consequences (B)	Responds well to praise and opportunities to play sports	Taking privileges away provokes much anger

Figure 5–3 (continued).

SHORT-TERM OBJECTIVES
(C Headings)

Objectives	Curriculum	Conditions	Consequences	Evaluation	Results
Easily distracted Baseline: Looks up from work at least 10 times an hour	All academic work	Assign to study booth	Praise for work accomplished	Criteria: Will not look up from work more than 5 times per hour Time period: 10 weeks Method: Teacher observation	Date: Comments:
Seldom listens to teacher Baseline: Seldom remembers directions given	All class lessons. Stop by his desk and have him repeat directions given	Next to his desk	Praise for correctly repeating assignment. Give 5 check marks for free time	Criteria: Will be able to repeat correct directions for all assignments Time period: 10 weeks Method: Count number of check marks	Date: Comments:
Seldom completes class work; papers are sloppily done Baseline: Continual problems with all assignments	All academic work	Shorten assignments	Give possible 5 checkmarks for finishing and neatness. Use "F's" and "N's" instead of checkmarks	Criteria: Will complete all assignments and earn 4-5 F's & N's on average Time period: 10 weeks Method: Count F's & N's	Date: Comments:
Seldom follows class rules Baseline: Out of seat. Often talks out. Bullies others	Give him card with three rules: 1. Stay in seat 2. Don't talk out without raising hand 3. No fighting or hitting Put card with one side red, one side green, on desk. When following rules green side is up. When not, red side up.*	At his desk for entire day	For every 15 minutes green side is up, give praise. Every hour with green side up earns 5 minutes of looking at surfing magazine	Criteria: Card will not be red side up more than 4 times a day Time period: 10 weeks Method: Teacher observation	Date: Comments:

Figure 5-3 (continued).

*The red–green card technique is from *The acting-out child: Coping with classroom disruption* by H. M. Walker. Boston: Allyn and Bacon, 1979.

Services to be provided:

Assign Bobby to resource specialist program two hours a day where short-term objectives will be introduced. Begin to use them in regular classroom, also.

Extent of participation in regular education program:

Bobby will be in regular classroom program for P.E., reading, arithmetic, and language arts.

Date of program initiation and expected duration:

Begin program on October 15. Reassess at mid-semester and consider placing Bobby back full-time in regular classes.

Authorization signatures:

Helen Myron   (parent) _____

Robert Arthur   _Michael Bloom Ph.D._

Sue Billings   _____

Date signed   10-10

Figure 5–3 (continued).

strengths. The conditions and consequences form also gives a picture of both strengths and weaknesses. Short-term objectives are all aimed at getting Bobby to be less distractible and more conforming to class expectations. We learn from the participation and duration form that Bobby was referred to part-time special education in a resource room and that the assignment will be reassessed at mid-semester.

The approach to writing an Individual Education Program presented in this chapter is only one of dozens that have been, and are being, developed throughout the field. There is no way any single plan will satisfy the needs of all individuals in all situations. We hope that the A-B-C orientation toward selecting long-term and short-term objectives and the concept of the learning triangle—curriculum, conditions, and consequences—will prove useful to those charged with writing IEP's regardless of the specific format followed.

chapter 6

Increasing the Disturbed Child's
Level of Learning Competence

I n this chapter we will review ideas, activities, and tasks that have been found to be useful for increasing disturbed children's competence in paying attention, responding, following directions, exploring the environment, and gaining social approval. Some of our suggestions will be quite general; others will be quite specific. For each level of learning competence, we will first present task characteristics that apply and then describe specific activities or tasks.

Attention Tasks

Task characteristics that are useful in getting the disturbed child to pay attention in learning fall into at least four categories:

1. Removal of distracting stimuli
2. Presentation of small, discrete units of work
3. Heightening the vividness and impact of stimuli
4. Use of concrete, rather than abstract, tasks

Removal of Stimuli and Presentation of Small Work Units

Some disturbed children may be easily distracted in classrooms: (1) where a high degree of visual and auditory stimulation is produced by the movements and noise level of other students, (2) where assignments are complex, and (3) where teacher demands frequently shift. As we discussed in Chapter 2, careful control of distracting stimuli for neurologically impaired and hyperactive children is recommended (Strauss & Lehtinen, 1947; Cruickshank, 1975) to help them pay attention for longer periods of time. Just how far the teacher should go to reduce such stimuli is debatable, however, particularly with disturbed children who may be given to more fantasy and self-stimulation when placed in drab, sterile surroundings. But helping disturbed children pay attention to specific tasks may well involve clearing their desks of clutter, providing a quiet work area when needed, and presenting them with clearly defined units of work.

Vague, open-ended assignments often overwhelm disturbed children who cannot focus their attention on a whole page of problems at one time. For some children, presentation of a single problem on a page may be necessary so that "the end is in sight." For others, pages may have to be torn out of workbooks one by one, rather than assigning the entire book and expecting the child to work systematically through it.

Teaching machines and programmed instructional materials are often very useful with inattentive children. Single units of work are presented frame by frame, and no long-range demands are made for accomplishment. Provision for immediate knowledge of results and a gradual increase in level of difficulty are also advantages offered by programmed instruction.

Heightening Vividness

Increasing the vividness and impact of instructional materials is generally seen as an aid to increasing attention and retention. Riggs (1956) investigated the learning of nouns associated with violence. He found that increasing the configural emphasis of these words during learning trials (from arsenic to *arsenic* to *arsenic!*) increased the efficiency of recall. Bousfield, Esterson, and Whitmarsh (1957) presented similar evidence for the addition of pictures to stimulus words. They observed that words accompanied by descriptive uncolored pictures were recalled more efficiently than words presented alone and that words accompanied by descriptive colored pictures were recalled best of all. This should come as no surprise to educators because of the common practice of enhancing the content of basal readers with colored illustrations. A great number of such illustrations with their prominent page after page displays, however, may actually provide a source of distraction for children with attention problems.

The nature of the pictorial context within which words appear had a highly significant effect upon rate of learning and immediate recall in one study (Hewett, 1961). Underachieving adolescent boys learned a phrase such as *swallow this gradually* far more efficiently when it was accompanied by a picture of a bottle of poison complete with skull and crossbones than when it was accompanied by a picture of a tempting ice cream soda. Several examples of the phrase-picture combinations used in this study are found in Figure 6–1. In each case, the violent, more vivid pictorial context enhanced learning rate and immediate recall.

For normal children, and some mildly disturbed students, assignments emphasizing fantasy are highly motivating, but these should be avoided with children who have difficulty discriminating what is unreal from what is real. In story-writing activities, teachers may successfully stimulate normal children's creative thinking by asking them to finish sentences such as "If I were on the moon and a two-headed green monster came after me, I would _____" and then write a story. For children preoccupied with fantasy, however, story topics should focus on the here and now. They might include "If I were going on a camping trip, the five most important things I would need to take with me would be _____."

Extremely disoriented and delusional adolescent students have been successfully engaged in simple labeling and coloring activities with drawings of fish and cars. First assignments involve copying a single label for an entire drawing, and then gradually spaces are drawn by the teacher alongside individual parts. At this point the student is directed to label each part

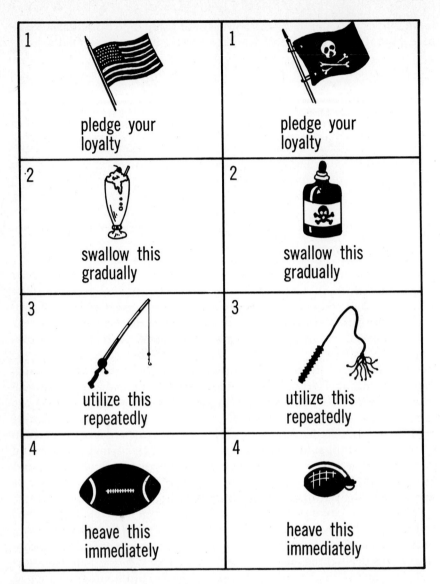

Figure 6–1. Phrase-picture combinations.

with the aid of reference materials. Map copying, coloring, and labeling also provide a type of activity where attention can be directed toward specific reality tasks.

Younger children enjoy sorting actual objects into categories of "real" and "not real." Objects including flying horses and space creatures may be mixed in with toy cars and furniture and a child asked to sort them out.

Activities such as having the children close their eyes and try to describe as many objects in the room as they can in terms of location, size, color, and use also help develop an awareness of the real environment.

Concrete Experiences

With many emotionally disturbed children, concrete experiences are superior to assignments that rely on abstract symbols and a high degree of verbal instruction by the teacher. Early learning in school is accompanied by many concrete experiences in language and number development. By the upper elementary grades, however, children are expected to function on a much more symbolic level through reading, discussion, and listening. The disturbed child may find it difficult to pay attention when primarily presented with symbolic assignments. Teachers should investigate the use of concrete aids normally emphasized only in the primary grades with these students.

Tachistoscopic Activities

A useful device for preparing the child for paying attention in learning is the tachistoscope. Tachistoscopes are available as overhead projectors for group presentation or as individual units. They provide controlled exposures of geometric designs, pictures, digits, words, and phrases. Exposures may vary from a full second to 1/100 of a second. The simplest targets are line drawings of familiar objects which the child is asked to recognize as they are flashed before him or her for a fraction of a second. Later, these objects may be shown in an incomplete form (e.g., table without a leg, clock without hands), and the child is given the task of locating the missing part. Various symbols may also be flashed in pairs; in this case, the child is expected to determine if the two symbols are the same (□ △), are facing the same direction (⌐ ⌐), or are the same size (o 0).

Digits varying in length from three to ten numbers are conventionally used as targets on tachistoscopes to foster widening of eye span and accuracy of visual perception. Words and phrases can also be flashed, although these defeat the purpose of increasing attention level if reading is difficult for the child.

If a tachistoscope is not available, a substitute activity that has been used successfully by Jensen* with children with attention problems may be prepared with numbers and words as follows:

687	786	867	687
495	459	495	549
821	821	812	182
saw	was	saw	aws
girl	gril	gilr	girl
smile	smile	simle	smeli

The child is instructed to look at the number or word in the left-hand column and then cross out the identical number or word in the right-hand columns. Sheets of these tests can be mimeographed and then inserted in plastic covers. The child can then use a black crayola to make a mark on the

*Jensen, C. Personal communication, 1966.

plastic cover which can be wiped off following use. In actual practice, the sheets might contain a series of three-digit numbers followed by a series of longer digits and words. The same sheet may be used several times with a given child and a record kept of the time it takes the child to complete it, as well as the number of errors made. Self-timing and competition with one's own record in activities such as this are often appealing to children who balk at time pressure for academic accomplishments.

General Attention-Getting Tasks and Activities

"What's missing?" work sheets and games which present the child with incomplete drawings of animals, people, and objects such as cars and trains are also useful for getting children to pay attention, identify the missing part, and possibly draw it in themselves.

A flashlight which has been extended by a roll of cardboard tubing to provide a sharp, circular area of light is useful to get young children to attend to objects in the classroom. The lights in the room are turned off and the teacher flashes the light around the room, stopping at various places (e.g., the clock, the flag, pictures); the children are then asked to identify the objects aloud.

Older children and adolescents can be encouraged to pay attention to directions given by the teacher when these are prerecorded on tape and imbedded in a popular musical sequence. The music starts playing and at various times the volume diminishes and the teacher's directions are given (e.g., "Take out your math books"). Later directions, such as specific page references to individual students, may also be given. This approach has been effective in getting students to settle down and get to work the first thing in the morning or after recess.

Children who lean back in their chairs; rock back and forth; drum their fingers on their desks; make constant trips to the bathroom, pencil sharpener, or nurse's office; start their work over and over because the paper is smudged or because they have made a mistake often fail to pay attention in learning because of constant interference. Problems of pencil sharpening may be quickly resolved by providing a constant source of sharpened pencils for exchange. Chair tipping may be prevented by bolting the chair and desk to the floor. Such anticipatory actions on the teacher's part may reduce the frequency of interfering behaviors, but others are more difficult to eliminate.

Constant trips to the bathroom and drinking fountain by some disturbed children have been controlled by use of a pass system. The child is given a number of passes to keep at the desk. Each time he or she needs to go to the bathroom, the child stops by the teacher's desk and deposits a pass. The number of passes initially given the child may equal the number of trips usually made; over a period of time, fewer and fewer passes are given with the understanding that the child can only go to the bathroom or drinking fountain the number of times equal to the number of passes possessed. It is obvious that this procedure is not appropriate unless the teacher is certain there is no organic basis for the child's bathroom or drinking fountain needs.

An emotionally disturbed second-grader who almost always tore up his work after encountering the least bit of frustration was effectively helped by his teacher to reduce and finally eliminate this behavior. A stuffed toy tiger which sat on the teacher's desk was a great favorite of the children in the class. Whenever the teacher observed this boy appropriately starting an assignment, she would place the tiger on his desk without saying a word. When he "blew up," the tiger was removed with nothing said. In a short while the boy "got the idea" that his behavior while working controlled the presence or absence of the tiger, and without any verbal instruction his behavior greatly improved.

Getting disturbed children to look at the teacher and pay attention to verbal directions in a classroom is often a difficult task. Teachers have found that speaking softly and using simple terms and phrases often increase the degree of attention they can elicit from their children. (Experimental evidence for this was cited in Chapter 2.) Excessive verbalization and the use of vague or complex terminology are best avoided when teaching all children, particularly the disturbed.

Younger children have increased their degree of visual and auditory attention to the teacher through participation in various games and activities. One teacher used a colored stick which had been established as the "attention wand." Whenever she used it to point to an object in the room or to written work on the chalkboard, the children were expected to give their full attention.

An "attention mask" may also be useful in getting severely disturbed or very young children to establish eye contact with the teacher. The teacher puts on a rectangular mask cut from construction paper which provides a one-inch wide frame around his or her eyes. The children may also be given similar masks to put on. While teacher and pupils are wearing these "attention masks," the task is for the children to look directly at the teacher's face while the teacher looks directly at each of them in turn. Candy, or other tangible rewards, may be distributed to those children who look at the teacher for periods of ten seconds or more.

Teachers have also successfully used a "drum echo" procedure to help children pay attention. This procedure requires that children tap out the same number of beats or rhythm patterns on a drum at their desks that the teacher taps out on a drum at the front of the room. An alternative is to have the children tap directly on their desk tops.

Young children who do not pay attention to the teacher's directions may also initially be reached with a hand puppet which the teacher controls and which "speaks" to them, giving them their assignments. The teacher may also pantomime group instructions with no verbal explanation and obtain more attention from the class.

Older, elementary-aged children can be given mirrors at their desks which they hold up in front of them to view the teacher standing in the back of the room. The teacher displays various familiar objects which they must identify during this unique teacher-attention activity.

Rolled paper telescopes may also be given to students with instructions to keep the teacher in view when directions are being given.

Having the teacher draw objects on the blackboard, work simple arithmetic problems, or spell basic words making obvious errors in the process which the children must "catch" have also been found to elicit attention from children with problems in this area.

One teacher of adolescents found that kicking over the wastebasket and sending it noisily across the floor quickly drew his class to attention during times when it was difficult to get them to settle down. He also found dropping coins one at a time in a jar on his desk was effective in getting his class to pay attention since few individuals fail to respond to the sound of clinking money.

Another teacher used a loud ticking clock for the same purpose. When she wanted to get the attention of her students, she started the clock ticking and waited quietly until all eyes were on her desk.

Tasks and Activities for Aiding Retention

Task repetition aids children with retention problems, but such repetition must be varied in order to maintain the child's interest. Frequent checks for recall also may have to be made, rather than relying on weekly or monthly tests. Teachers of disturbed children who observe a given child's failure to grasp a concept or to retain a fact or process must quickly move back and review previous material. This technique is one of the advantages of programmed instruction on teaching machines where "branching" from the regular program is often provided to give slower learners a chance to "brush up" before continuing on.

An activity in the classroom which has been found to appeal to disturbed children with attention problems is the familiar "memory for objects" game. The teacher exposes a picture of various items, or an actual assortment of objects on a tray, for a brief period of time and the children are instructed to try to remember as many items as possible. For younger children, such an activity may use animals and toys. For adolescents, car parts; Army, Navy, and Marine insignia; radio and television components; or jewelry and make-up may be utilized. Variations include the teacher removing an object behind a screen and then asking students to identify what is missing.

A variation on the old "shell game" has proven useful with disturbed children who will not pay attention or who have difficulty retaining information. The teacher hides a piece of candy or a penny under a paper cup which is one of three in front of the child. As the cups are interchanged a varying number of times, the child is instructed to watch carefully. After the teacher stops, the child is supposed to point to the cup covering the desired object, and if it is the correct choice, the object is given to the child. For children with extreme attention and retention problems, the cups may be different colors. The desired object is then always put under the cup of a specific color, and after the interchange, the child has the color cue to aid in the selection.

Attention tasks should invite the child's ready participation. They will inevitably involve some type of responding (which we will discuss next), but the emphasis in on "capturing" the child's interest and awareness and "getting one's foot in the door" in respect to the learning process.

Response Tasks

Characteristics of attention tasks are equally applicable to response tasks. Reducing distraction, heightening vividness, presenting limited assignments, and emphasizing concrete rather than abstract approaches all increase the probability that the disturbed child will do something, as well as notice something, in learning. Therefore, some of the following examples overlap with those presented earlier. Actually this overlap will exist throughout our discussion of the first four levels of learning competence. The characteristics of tasks at each level will be applicable to all other levels.

Two characteristics deserve particular emphasis with respect to response tasks:

1. Reduction of the criteria for correctness
2. Guaranteeing the child success in learning

The Problem of Grades

While removal of the pressure of grades is often a source of relief for many disturbed children, it can create problems for others. Some consider school without grades no school at all and become frustrated and unhappy when each unit of work they accomplish is not graded in a conventional manner. Often this seems related to the child's awareness of the parents' academic aspiration level for him or her. The teacher, therefore, is faced with a dilemma: no grade at all makes the child unhappy; a letter grade truly reflecting accomplishments according to chronological grade-level expectation may be a devaluating F for failure; a complimentary A given on the basis of individual effort and progress may set up a false standard of accomplishment that will be entirely unrealistic when the child returns to a regular classroom.

Despite such problems with disturbed children and their parents who may also demand a report card with "genuine grades," we have found that "satisfactory—needs to improve" grading is the most successful. Its use often entails individual conferences for both the child and the parent in order to explain the purpose of the special classroom—helping the child "catch up" as quickly as possible. The teacher points out that since each child in the classroom has unique learning problems and is progressing at an individual rate, he or she really represents a separate class. Therefore, traditional grades are meaningless. In actual practice, most disturbed children who have failed in regular classrooms are helped to respond and to become involved in learning by the removal of grades, although some type of progress reporting is important.

Public school teachers who have two or three children with emotional problems in their regular classroom are often forced to assign these children letter grades based on group and grade-level expectations. The futility of this practice is seen in the report card of David, a grossly psychotic boy of eleven, who sat in a regular classroom in a compliant and passive manner, seldom interacting with the teacher or the other children, and who daydreamed his way through most of the fifth grade. A copy of David's report card is seen in Figure 6–2. Although he was rated as doing very poorly in most academic subjects, the teacher awarded him an *A* for behavior. It can be argued that David really should have been given an *F* for behavior and more individualized grades for academic accomplishments, but in the framework of a traditional grading system, the teacher had little choice. The emphasis on compliancy and passivity, even to the obviously unhealthy degree seen in this case, may be found in some public school classrooms and is reflected in David's *A* for behavior.

Don't Stifle Communication or Success

In addition to removing letter grades, teachers wishing to encourage children to respond in learning can reduce emphasis on such skills as handwriting, mechanics of English, grammar, and spelling. For children who do not respond in school, who are constricted, and who readily withdraw, the crucial task is to establish contact with them and start them functioning. For that reason, getting such children to express themselves in writing may be a highly significant event, although their writing is barely legible, their sentences run together, and their spelling is extremely poor. Allowing children to initially copy compositions or encouraging them to dictate stories aloud to the teacher who writes them down also promotes response to written assignments.

We have observed programs for mentally retarded and disturbed children that placed great emphasis on handwriting perfection. Long periods of tedious drill in making letter forms were imposed on the children in what seemed to be an activity designed to stifle response and communication.

A - Markedly Above Average

B - Above Average D - Below Average
C - Average F - Markedly Below Average

In the subheadings, a check (✓) indicates an area where improvement is needed.

PUPIL'S NAME _____ David J.

	First Quarter	Second Quarter	Third Quarter	Fourth Quarter
READING 2nd reading group				B-
Interest				
Understanding				
Development of Skills				
ARITHMETIC				F
Number Skills				✓
Measurement				✓
Problem Solving				B-
ENGLISH				
Oral Expression				
Written Expression				
SPELLING				B-
Assigned Words				✓
Accuracy in Written Work				
HANDWRITING				C-
Neatness				
Legibility				
SOCIAL STUDIES (History, Geography) and SCIENCE				B
Participation				✓
Use of Information				✓
ART				B
Participation				
Development of Skills				
MUSIC				C
Participation				✓
Development of Skills				
INSTRUMENTAL MUSIC				
PHYSICAL EDUCATION				F
Sportsmanship				
Participation				✓
Development of Skills				
Health Practices				

	First Quarter	Second Quarter	Third Quarter	Fourth Quarter
BEHAVIOR AND ATTITUDE				A
Self-control				
Cooperation				
Courtesy				
Dependability				
Respect for Property				
Respect for Rights of Others				B
WORK AND STUDY HABITS				
Initiative				
Listening Habits				
Response to Directions				
Use of Time				
Neatness				
Safety Practices				
Independent Work Habits				
Acceptance of Suggestions				

4/19 P.E. Will not participate in any games.

Figure 6-2. David's report card.

185

intriguing approach for guaranteeing success is found in "errorless
which was pioneered by Terrace (1963) and by Moore and Gol-
(1964). Moore and Goldiamond presented normal preschool
children with a difficult discrimination task that involved matching triangles on the basis of degree of rotation. For example, a rotated triangle
would be presented and then withdrawn. The child was then shown three
triangles, only one of which matched the original sample. Most of the children could not correctly select the previously shown sample from the three
rotated triangles. But by initially illuminating the correct choice with a
light, the child was "given the answer" and engaged in a sequence in which
few if any errors were made. Gradually, the illumination of the light under
the correct choice was decreased and finally deleted, and it was found that
the children could then discriminate accurately on the basis of degree of
rotation alone.

Acker (1966) utilized the prompt-of-size difference in teaching color
and form discrimination to young normal and autistic children. His subjects learned to respond to the "smaller" of two color plates or letter pairs
and eventually to respond to color and letter form alone when the size
differences were gradually eliminated. Learning under such errorless conditions was superior to learning during more conventional training when
subjects were rewarded for making correct choices and nonrewarded for
making errors. In our discussion of approaches for teaching reading in
Chapter 10, we will describe a program based on errorless training.

The elimination of letter grades and the reduction of a demand for
perfection in certain skills such as handwriting, mechanics of English and
grammar, and spelling are aids to getting the disturbed child to respond in
school. When it becomes necessary to confront the child with an error,
one teacher (Douglas, 1961) of disturbed children found elimination of
red pencil marks useful, since such red pencil "correcting" of schoolwork
may be associated with previous failure.

Use of question marks next to incorrect answers or actual erasing of
incorrect answers are seen as aids in communicating to the child the ac-
ceptability of making errors yet the importance of checking over work.
With children who have continually failed in school and who may resist
responding because of fear of further failure, considerable reassurance
may be necessary to establish the point that making mistakes is essential if
areas for remedial help are to be uncovered.

General Response-Facilitating Approaches

Giving children assignments that draw on information they have readily available and that capitalize on their major interests also helps initiate
responding. Work sheets asking no more than a list of three or more street
addresses and the titles of a few recently seen television programs or movies

have been used successfully with disturbed children. Providing surfing enthusiasts with a series of surfing pictures to caption or describe or a story title such as "My Biggest Wave" may start them writing in the class.

Younger children may be engaged in simple social imitation activities involving handclapping or touching parts of their bodies in response to the teacher's cue. A year-long individual training program was undertaken with Eddie, a nonverbal, four-and-one-half-year-old autistic boy (Hewett, 1965). The program was designed to initiate speech, but the first activities were simple, hand imitation games. Following each imitation (e.g., touching an ear in imitation of the teacher), Eddie was rewarded by a spin in a revolving chair or a short sequence of a color cartoon movie. Each time he touched the teacher's face as directed, music was provided from a children's record and continued as long as Eddie maintained physical contact with the teacher. From these attention and response tasks, Eddie went on to learn to follow more complex directions (e.g., assemble simple puzzles), approximate the teacher's vocalizations, and later to imitate actual words. Many of these more complex tasks used social praise alone (e.g., "Good boy!" said by the teacher) without any other form of reward. The complete speech program with Eddie will be described in Chapter 10.

Musical games in which the child scribbles continuously in a circular motion on a piece of paper as long as music from a record player continues also may be used for young disturbed children. Whenever the teacher stops the music, the child is to stop scribbling.

Children who will seldom attempt more than an absolute minimum assignment (e.g., one problem on a page, a one-sentence story) can be helped to increase their responding by means of several of the approaches already discussed. In addition, the introduction of a personal work record in the form of a graph may be useful. This work record may be kept on the basis of time or on the basis of units of work. For some children who resist doing assignments altogether, setting goals such as "See how quickly you can do two problems" or "See how many problems you can do in five minutes" may increase their response rate. They may later graph the time or number of problems completed on a chart and compare records day by day. With such a procedure, it is important that the teacher accurately time the child (or possibly have him or her use a timer on the desk) and that the selected problems are well within the capability of the child.

Helping the Child Who Won't Come to School

Despite individualized assignments and lack of pressure to participate as a member of a group, some disturbed children are too upset to even set foot in the classroom. With these children, individual tutoring at home or out of the classroom in the school may have to take place initially. Home teaching is provided in many school districts for children who are too disruptive to be tolerated in a classroom or who are so frightened of attending school that they refuse to leave home. While it may be necessary at the very beginning, teaching children in their homes when they are physically able to work elsewhere is probably undesirable. Parents are seldom able to remove themselves completely from such an arrangement, and it requires an objective and firm teacher to deal with the barrage of questions, complaints, and bits of advice which some parents may offer. The home setting is also not conducive to a work orientation on the part of the child. Distractions, interruptions, and attempts at manipulating assignments are all too frequent. For these reasons, getting the child to come to school, even if only to work in a separate room with a home teacher, is more effective. More positive results are apt to ensue when teacher and child interact in school and parental influence is removed from the teaching situation.

Once out of home, *systematic inclusion* is the next natural step to get a disturbed child into a classroom. In contrast to systematic exclusion which involves removing the child for periods of time because of misbehavior, this procedure involves gradually introducing a child into the class for increasing periods of time until he or she can tolerate a full day.

Spencer was an eight-year-old, emotionally disturbed boy whose lack of control in public school had made home teaching necessary for one year. With the cooperation of the teacher, an attempt was made to systematically include him in a special class for disturbed children which used a checkmark system to acknowledge appropriate behavior and accomplishments. The check marks were given on a card, and the filled cards could be exchanged for tangible rewards of toys and candy. This system was introduced by the home teacher for several days while Spencer worked at home. For the next several days he worked with his home teacher in the classroom after the regular group had been dismissed. Use of the check marks was continued, and finally he was brought into the classroom with the home teacher for fifteen minutes each day while the regular class was present. During this time he was tutored individually in the back of the room. The length of time Spencer spent in the class was gradually increased, and eventually the home teacher withdrew altogether. At this point, Spencer became part of the regular group.

Although this procedure was ultimately successful in getting Spencer back into a regular classroom, it would have proceeded more smoothly had the home teacher not worked with him in the room while the other class members were present. It appeared that introduction of a new boy and his own special teacher at the same time drew undue attention to Spencer, and some resentment was expressed by the other children.

Response tasks should emphasize involvement and "trying" rather than accuracy and quality. The effort itself is the focal point, not the quality of the behavior or product.

Order Tasks

Order tasks aim at helping children learn to adapt to routines, follow directions, complete assignments, and control their behavior. Order task characteristics include:

Defining a specific starting point and a series of steps leading to a conclusion which is scorable as complete or incomplete.

Helping the Child Learn to Follow Directions

Order tasks should minimize conflict and confusion and maximize follow-through and completion. While it is difficult, if not impossible, to separate the concepts of completion and accuracy, order tasks aim at helping children finish what they start. Emphasis is on following through with the steps necessary for completion without unduly stressing the quality of the results.

The ideal order task is one that is simple enough to do so that when completed it is also accurate. Picture puzzles are used as order tasks and it is obvious that a complete puzzle with all the pieces in place is also an accurate one. For students who are uncritical and uncontrolled in learning, it is extremely important to assign tasks that have a high probability of successful execution and that involve a satisfying and novel activity. If this is done, the concepts of completion and accuracy are practically synonymous.

In this book, our position is that perceptual-motor training techniques such as those developed by Strauss and Lehtinen (1947), Cruickshank (1975), Kephart (1971), and Frostig and Horne (1964) for children with learning disabilities are often very useful as order tasks for disturbed children.

The direction box assists disturbed children in following both written and spoken directions. It is based on an activity developed by Birnbrauer, Bijou, Wolf, and Kidder (1965) for use with institutionalized retarded children. Each direction box is filled with familiar objects such as model cars, airplanes of various colors, miniature animals, toy soldiers, small plastic scuba divers, and colored poker chips. Accompanying each direction box is a 6 x 16 inch card with three numbered squares (each 4 x 4 inches) printed on it. For the box of cars, the squares are labeled *Lot,* for the airplanes, *Airport,* for the animals, *Corral,* for the soldiers, *Fort,* for the divers, *Tank,* and for the poker chips, *Box.* A series of direction cards accompanies each direction box. The cards are graduated in difficulty starting with Step I (e.g., "Put two red cars in Lot 1; put 6 blue cars in Lot 2; put 4 yellow cars in Lot 3."). This step is illustrated in Figure 6–3 along with the direction box and cars.

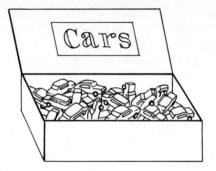

Figure 6–3. The direction box.

At Step I, the child's task is merely to put the assigned number of cars in the designated boxes. Later steps involve moving the cars from box to box (e.g., "Put one red car from Lot 1 in Lot 3; put 4 blue cars from Lot 2 in Lot 1; put 2 yellow cars from Lot 3 in Lot 2"). These tasks are scored by use of answer cards given to the student. The answer card states the exact number of cars which should be in each box at the completion of the task. The sequence used in the construction of steps for the activity is as follows:

Step I	Place a designated number of objects in each box
Step II	Same as Step I with the addition of a single transfer of objects from one box to another
Step III	Same as Step II but add an additional transfer of objects
Step IV	Same as Step III with one additional transfer

The steps can be increased in difficulty indefinitely, but one to five steps have been found most suitable for elementary-aged children. Adolescents can be given different objects such as electrical and radio parts, military insignia (e.g., "Put four corporal stripes in Box 1."), or pieces of costume jewelry.

In the creation of this direction box material a very simple reading vocabulary was used. With some children, however, reading introduces such resistance that the activity is unsuccessful. For these children, the directions can be tape-recorded on Language Master cards. A strip of recording tape affixed to the bottom of the direction card records each step, and as these are played back on the Language Master, the child arranges the objects as directed. Visual cues can also be utilized by having drawings of the exact number of objects to be put in each box on a card.

We have found it useful to stress that the materials (e.g., model cars) in the direction boxes are to be used only for the assigned order task and not for free play.

Secret code writing has a fascination for most children and adolescents and, like the direction box, it can be used to foster direction following. A code that has been used successfully with emotionally disturbed children is illustrated in Figure 6–4. The teacher may have the child first write his or her own name in the code and then the names of other children in the class. Longer coding assignments can be given in a variety of ways and the teacher can write messages to the child in code which the child must decipher. Older students may be given messages written in other codes without a deciphering key and assigned the task of "breaking" the code.

The International Signal Flag Code System can also be used. The child is provided with a key with the twenty-six colored flags used to send messages between ships printed on it. Several masts are mimeographed on a sheet of paper with four or more blank flags suspended from each mast. At the bottom of the paper spaces are provided for a simple message (e.g., "SEND US FOOD"). The child must refer to the key and translate the message by coloring the blank flags with the appropriate colored insignia. An example of a colored-in sheet is shown in Figure 6–5. Since "coloring" may be tedious or distasteful to some children because of association with primary-grade activities, flags can be printed on cards in advance and sorted into boxes or envelopes according to the letters they represent. The

(A) >	(H) +	(O)]	(V) ⌐
(B) +	(I) <	(P) ⊖	(W) →
(C) ⊖	(J) ⊢	(Q) ⤙	(X) □
(D) ⌐	(K) ⊂	(R) +	(Y) ⌐
(E) ∧	(L) ⊣	(S) ⊕	(Z) △
(F) +	(M) ⊕	(T) =	
(G) ⌐	(N) ∟	(U) ∏	

Figure 6–4. The symbol code.

Message: Send _____ us _____ food _____

Figure 6–5. The International Signal Flag Code activity.

child's task is to select the appropriate flags and arrange them properly in order to put the message into code.

Direction-following tasks which involve reading should only be used with students who are well able to read at the level required. Some examples of order tasks that require reading are paragraph puzzles, ordering of events in a paragraph into a logical sequence, and spotting obvious errors in written material.

Paragraph puzzles engage the child in following printed directions, step by step. An example of a paragraph puzzle is as follows:

> Read this entire paragraph carefully. Put a red line under all four and five letter words. Next draw a blue circle around all words ending with "e." Write your name in each blank space on the paper._____. Cross out all words that start with the same letter as the first letter in your name.

This activity can be shortened or lengthened, simplified or increased in difficulty, according to the attention span and reading level of individual students.

Simple stories may be typed on cardboard and cut up so that one line of the story is on each of several cardboard strips. The story should involve a clearly understandable sequence of events such as the following:

John's Day
John got up in the morning.
He ate his breakfast.
In school he learned a new song.
On the way home from school he met Tom.
John and Tom played until it was time for supper.

The child is given the cardboard strips, each with a sentence of the story on it, in random order. The task is to organize them one under another, so that the story makes sense. Again, length and level of complexity are subject to change. For adolescents a more suitable theme would obviously have to be chosen.

Inserting errors (e.g., illogical statements) in reading paragraphs and assigning the child the job of locating them has also been used by Jensen (1966) with institutionalized delinquent boys.

Simple direction-following tasks that do not involve reading are provided by sorting activities. Sorting objects (e.g., skeins of yarn and commercial paint chips) on the basis of color alone is perhaps one of the simplest order tasks. Classifying such items as geometric cutouts or nuts and bolts according to form and size is a related activity.

Stan, an adolescent boy in the NPI School, frequently became extremely restless and distractible in the classroom. He often had to be removed from class because he could not be engaged in any activity. One day the teacher brought a large box of assorted nuts, bolts, and washers to school and gave Stan the job of sorting them into different piles according to size. The boy quickly settled down and began sorting. Although he tired of this after a while, he was then able to respond to another assignment. After that first day, the box of nuts and bolts was used regularly by the teacher to help Stan "settle down" during periods of distractibility.

Pencil and art activities also foster direction following without involving reading. Dot-to-dot number-connecting pictures are useful since most children are motivated to work until a recognizable picture emerges. Painting-by-number art kits requiring that the child paint a specific color in a specific area in order to complete an oil painting are readily available. Although these are too complex and tedious for many disturbed children, they have been useful with some.

Treasure maps that require simple following of arrows, reading of directions, or computations of arithmetic problems in order to locate the

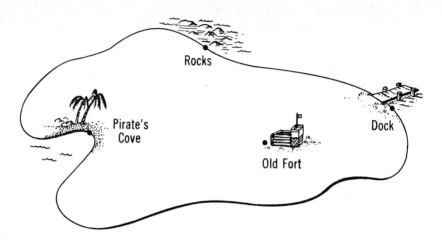

Figure 6–6. A sample treasure map direction-following activity.

"treasure" are intriguing to children. The complexity of the map assigned again depends on the functioning level of the individual. A sample map (not to scale) that was used with one child is seen in Figure 6–6. The child was given a special ruler with ¼ inch spaces marked off on it. The scale on the ruler read "Each mark is equal to ten paces." The directions accompanying the map read as follows:

Mark off 50 paces from Pirate's Cove toward the Old Fort.

Now mark off 70 paces toward the Rocks.

From this point mark off 100 paces toward the Dock.

You have just found the treasure. Mark the spot where you think the treasure is located.

This is only an example and many variations are possible. Once the child has "searched" for the treasure, the teacher checks his or her calculations. If they are correct, the child is allowed to choose a reward from a "treasure chest" kept in the teacher's desk for such purposes. Rewards may include a pass for twenty minutes of free time or a cracker or a cookie. Such assignments cannot produce miracles or guarantee the child will never leave an assignment incomplete again, but they can be helpful in initiating an interest in pursuing tasks to completion in school. Obviously the teacher's skill and ingenuity will have to be relied on to round out an educational program for a student with order problems.

Model-copying tasks which do not depend on academic ability but rather on hand-eye coordination and attention to detail have been successful in encouraging children with order problems to complete assignments. Toy construction kits are readily available commercially and can be utilized to make such objects as small rocking chairs, toy trucks, and miniature buildings by assembling wood and plastic units according to pictorial diagrams. The teacher can mount each diagram on a card and assign the child the task of building the object illustrated from an assemblage of parts. Once the model is copied, the parts can be dismantled for future use.

Car, airplane, and ship models can be permanently constructed with commercial kits but are more difficult and often frustrating for the child who is not adept at fine motor tasks. However, these can be used effectively in the classroom with some children.

Pegboard designs can also be copied by children who insert colored wood or plastic pegs into a board in order to match a model design given them by the teachers. Similar model copying can be done with colored beads, blocks, and plastic units available commercially. The teacher can also assemble several painted washers and nuts on a bolt and give it to the child as a model. The child's task is to assemble as many similar units as possible from a supply of painted washers, nuts, and bolts.

Some children who have difficulty completing assignments are highly motivated if timed records are kept of their work. The child is given an individual timer and a page of arithmetic problems to do. The timer, which may be one commonly used in the kitchen, is set by the teacher when the child starts; the child is given the responsibility for stopping it when finished. Of course, such time pressure may create frustration and an uncritical approach to the assignment with some disturbed children; therefore it has to be used advisedly.

Record keeping, mentioned earlier in the discussion of response tasks, may also contribute to the child's desire to complete his or her assignment. A daily or weekly schedule written down by the teacher, with a box opposite each assignment to be checked off following completion, may serve as an incentive. Graphs recording number of problems done, pages read, or spelling words reviewed are also useful with some children.

An on-going class jigsaw puzzle provides an excellent order task which all children can participate in collectively. The puzzle may be started by the teacher and then added to by individual children or pairs of children throughout the day as they have extra time. Order tasks often calm fidgeting or upset children. One of us was interested to find an on-going jigsaw puzzle in the waiting room of a hospital coronary intensive care unit. It appeared that the staff sensed how anxious and uneasy family members and friends might be when waiting to see a patient, and an "order" task was provided to help momentarily divert their concern.

Attention, response, and order tasks involve a great deal of overlap. Noticing, doing, and following directions occur simultaneously, and most of the tasks described in the previous three sections involve all three characteristics. We separate the three by our emphasis on a particular aspect and our differential reinforcement of that aspect (e.g., "Great, you were looking right at me!" or "I really liked the way you tried to do it." or "Good, you followed all three steps and completed your assignment.").

Exploratory Tasks

There are three major characteristics of exploratory tasks:

1. A wide range of multisensory experiences
2. An emphasis on reality
3. Predictable outcomes

Multisensory Experiences

Children learn about the world in which they live through looking, listening, touching, moving, tasting, and smelling. The stove may be labeled *hot* by a parent, but it is often the experience of touching the hot stove that teaches the meaningful lesson. Children can be encouraged to visually explore their environments through periods of observation outdoors. Trees, plants, flowers, and other objects can be described in terms of color, size, shape, and location. Drawings can be made during such observations or material can be gathered for later story writing. Art work may be preferable for some children because it offers a more direct exploratory experience and does not involve translation of a description into words.

Some disturbed children may constantly engage in drawing the same object to the complete exclusion of anything else. We observed Tom, a deaf, eight-year-old boy with severe order, exploratory, and social problems, who, if left alone, would draw one fluorescent light tube after another. If not interrupted, Tom covered sheet after sheet of drawing paper with carefully drawn and spaced fluorescent tubes. Because he was generally disruptive in school, but remarkably calm and controlled while drawing fluorescent lights, the teacher encouraged him to sit and draw for much of each day. His most prized possession was a fluorescent desk lamp which his mother had purchased for him. Tom was a real exploratory challenge, but unfortunately the teacher did not attempt to get him involved in other types of art activity. Such activities might at first have focused on different kinds of light fixtures such as neon signs. Later they could have focused on the variety of shapes (geometric designs, letters, and finally human forms) which are often made with neon tubing.

One teacher in a state hospital school who worked with a boy who would only draw airplanes was successful in getting him to begin drawing the pilots who flew the airplanes, paying particular attention to the insignia they wore in different countries and the branches of service which they represented.

Some disturbed children appear to have no clear-cut interests and activities of their own. Others may have only a greatly reduced number. Still others may always adopt the role of the "follower" and only select what someone else has selected first. Teachers have encouraged such children to express themselves through forced-choice situations. Such children may be asked to select a task, book, or activity from one of two or three possibilities. These possibilities are clearly presented to the child who is told to make a choice.

In the area of reading, teachers may make a mistake by taking dependent children to the school library and directing them to "find a book" they like. Confronted with all the possible selections available on the shelves, such children may balk, pick a book similar to one a classmate has chosen, or randomly pick up the first one seen. In such cases, if the teacher will take the time to study interests which the child overtly or covertly expresses, preselect two or three books in these areas, present them to the child, and state that the child must choose from these, some degree of independent choice may be fostered.

We have observed tutors working with emotionally disturbed children who sat down with a child and, in an attempt to establish rapport, a non-threatening atmosphere, and some degree of self-expression on the part of the child, cheerfully exclaimed, "Well, what shall we do today?" Often, in such open-ended situations, children become confused and change their minds again and again. As a result, a great deal of time is wasted. If the teacher feels the child should be encouraged, it is usually wise at first to set definite limits within which a choice must be made.

In the classroom, when it is appropriate for children to select their own activities for a period, dependent children may be given first choice so that they do not merely fall in line with their classmates. Of course, the advisability of putting the child "on the spot" has to be weighed carefully beforehand by the teacher.

Mail-order catalogs have been utilized in an interesting exploratory activity designed to encourage some independent selection on the part of children. The child is told that he or she has a certain amount to spend (e.g., $500) and is shown a section of the catalog which displays a specific type of merchandise (e.g., camping equipment). The task is to "spend" the money to prepare for a camping expedition, keeping in mind all of the requirements of a trip to a familiar camping area in the locale. This activity also lends itself to the building of addition, subtraction, and decimal skills.

Mixing food coloring in glasses of water to provide an assortment of hues also provides an interesting visual exploratory task. Tempera paints, when mixed to match color samples, can be the basis for teaching the child about primary colors and the combinations involved in creating the full range of colors for art work. Older children may by intrigued with the principles of mixing colored transparent filters to obtain different shades and colors of light.

An auditory exploratory task that has proven appealing to children involves tapping glasses filled with varying amounts of water and listening for the differences in pitch. Rubber bands stretched with different degrees of tightness across the open top of a cigar box can similarly be plucked and compared for sound.

A "mystery box" has been used successfully by some teachers. Each week a closed shoebox is presented to the children. An object (e.g., pencil, eraser, tennis ball) has previously been placed inside. Members of the class attempt to "solve the mystery" by shaking the contents of the box and listening for clues that might disclose the object's identity.

Tactile exploratory tasks include a familiar guessing game that involves reaching in a paper bag containing such objects as a piece of fur, a sponge, and buttons and attempting to identify these objects from touch alone. One teacher has given students the task of matching adjectives describing tactile qualities of objects with which the child is familiar. A list of words such as *hot, warm, cold, freezing, gooey, sticky, slimy, slippery, slick, smooth, hard, brittle, soft, taut, slack,* and *wet* may be printed on a work sheet. The child's task is to write the names of objects with each characteristic.

Experiences of tasting and smelling can also be offered to children to increase their awareness and knowledge of the environment. Substances that are sweet, sour, and bitter can be sampled and described. Containers of familiar household substances such as vinegar, perfume, and iodine can be smelled and described and the nature of their contents identified.

Art, music, dance, and dramatic play provide additional exploratory activities for the disturbed child. Painting, clay modeling, drawing, crafts, and creative activities associated with music, dance, and drama offer opportunities for self-directed exploration by the child and can be a useful part of the educational program.

Science as Exploratory Curriculum. The curriculum area of science holds excellent promise for successfully engaging the disturbed child in multisensory exploration of the environment. It also incorporates the other characteristics of exploratory tasks by providing emphasis on reality and experiences with predictable outcomes.

As children undertake simple science experiments with air, heat, light, sound, magnetism, color, and various chemicals, they are exposed to a multitude of sensory stimuli. Exploratory tasks aim at getting children involved in learning with their hands, eyes, ears, nostrils, and taste buds, not necessarily in focusing on underlying scientific principles or theories. This does not mean that simple explanations of science activities should not be given, but rather that they should not become tedious or overdrawn.

A fascinating, simple science experiment that appeals to children involves a demonstration of air pressure by utilizing a milk bottle, a peeled, hard-boiled egg, and a burning piece of paper. The egg will not go through the neck of the bottle initially, but when the burning paper is placed in the bottle using up the air inside, the egg "pops" through the neck as a result of external air pressure. One teacher of the disturbed using this experiment and attempting to strictly adhere to the exploratory emphasis just mentioned avoided any discussion of the reason for the egg's descent into the bottle. One boy decided on his own that the neck of the bottle had "stretched," and the teacher let his comment go unchallenged because of her conviction that the purpose of the experiment was only to get the child involved in a multisensory experience and not to teach a formal science lesson. Such literalness is undesirable and a simple explanation that the fire used up the air inside the bottle so that the air outside pushed harder on the egg is most appropriate.

A long and complicated verbal explanation of the properties of air would also have been inappropriate, however. In this regard, we are reminded of the story of a little boy who saw a penguin for the first time at the zoo. When he got home he described it to his father and asked what it was. The father, obviously delighted at his son's inquisitiveness, took out the encyclopedia and obtained several reference books from the library. After a lengthy lecture on penguins the father noticed the troubled look on his son's face. "What's the matter," he asked, "didn't you want to learn about penguins?" His son looked up and said slowly, "Yes, but not that much." The goal of exploratory tasks is to maintain children's interest and provide them with intriguing information and experiences through exploration of the environment, not to overwhelm them with in-depth information.

What About Animals in the Classroom? The presence of animals in the classroom provides many opportunities for exploration through physical contact, feeding, care, and cleaning of cages. Over a period of years, we have observed with interest the kinds of animals best suited for inclusion in classrooms for emotionally disturbed children. The indestructible turtle is ideal for younger children, and large rabbits can be fed and petted with few problems. Tame white rats have been particularly popular with older elementary-aged children and appear to be more appropriate than hamsters. Guinea pigs have also been housed with few problems. Snakes and lizards have been successfully kept, although how appropriate they are in the classroom may well depend on the teacher's comfort in handling them. A fish tank provides children with a constant source of changing movement and color. Caged birds such as parakeets, canaries, and pigeons have been less successful due to the fact that they can seldom be handled.

Just what constitutes an "attractive nuisance" or "genuine hazard" in classrooms for disturbed children is by no means an easy question to answer. While exposure to fragile animals is in many cases best avoided, allowing disturbed children to use gas burners, delicate scientific instruments, and sharp objects in science experiments has never proven to be a problem in either the NPI School or public school programs with which we have been associated. One important point must be made, however. In all cases, the classrooms where these activities took place were well-structured with clearly stated expectations for all of the children.

Emphasizing Reality

In addition to a variety of multisensory experiences, the area of science offers a distinct emphasis on reality. For this reason it was important for the teacher who demonstrated the egg-in-the-bottle experiment to call attention to the causal factors involved. This was an opportunity to emphasize the real existence of air and the fact that it takes up space and has weight.

Disturbed children may have superstitions and fears that inhibit their exploration of the environment. Susan, an eight-year-old child in the NPI School, who had severe attention, response, exploratory, and social problems, entered the classroom for the first time and screamed with terror at the sight of a caged white rat. She immediately sat down on the floor by the door, curled up, and covered her eyes. The teacher calmly stated that the rat was a part of the classroom, that it would remain in the cage, and that it would not bother her at all. Susan was not about to take the teacher's word for this at first and remained huddled on the floor. She was allowed to stay in the room, as the teacher immediately recognized her attention and response problems and decided it would be inappropriate to expect more from her initially. For several days Susan would enter the classroom, see the rat, and huddle on the floor, while the rest of the children went to their desks and began work. Not a great deal of attention was paid to her; the teacher only briefly explained that the rat would not harm her and pointed out that a desk was waiting when she was ready to take her place with the other children. There was not a great deal of verbalization on the teacher's part, and she purposely avoided rewarding Susan's inappropriate behavior with attention. Her message to Susan was simply: "That's just the way it is in this classroom. The rat belongs here. But you do not have to go near it if you do not wish."

It was not long before Susan voluntarily went to her desk where she readily undertook academic assignments. She was a bright and capable learner, functioning well in all academic areas. Problems with Susan and the rat were not over by any means. She screamed loudly when any of the other children went to play with the animal and took it out of the cage. Again, this behavior was largely ignored, and it soon diminished. After several weeks Susan was observed to be quietly watching the other children when they picked the rat up, fondled it, and let it crawl on their shoulders. Susan never progressed to the stage where she joined them, but watching her classmates from a distance provided an important "reality" lesson regarding rats.

The controlled use of fire in simple science experiments demonstrating the properties of heat can provide valuable reality experiences for disturbed children. One teacher devised a unit demonstrating the three essential requirements for fire—heat, oxygen, and fuel—consisting of a number of clever experiments that the children could replicate on their own. Snipping off the wick of a burning candle illustrated the importance of a source of heat, and covering the candle with a glass provided an example of the necessity for oxygen. A simple fire extinguisher which could be used to put out the flame was constructed using vinegar and baking soda. While children may be trained "never to play with matches," they do need to know something about fire, why it occurs, and how it can be controlled in order to function adequately in their environments.

Both science and art activities are useful for getting disturbed children to freely explore with their hands. Some disturbed children display discomfort in "making a mess" or "getting dirty." Whatever the basis for this aversion, such children can be aided in becoming more complete explorers through participation in activities involving touch and manipulation. Cleaning a fish tank; feeding animals and cleaning their cages; tending a garden; working with clay, papier-mache, or plaster of Paris; and finger painting are examples of tasks that promote manual exploration of the real world.

Predictable Outcomes

The predictability associated with science demonstrations and experiments is very valuable for disturbed children. For many of them, what they have experienced in their lives has been anything but predictable. As a consequence, every effort should be made to select activities that are simple yet intriguing to children and that have a high probability of success when undertaken in the classroom.

Some science demonstrations can involve complex preparation and exacting maneuvers before they "work." When they do not work, it is both frustrating and disappointing. We recall a craft and science project we utilized in a classroom with disturbed adolescent boys. The task was to construct tin-can submarines which operated on calcium carbide. The submarines filled with water and sank when placed in the tub. The water eventually overflowed into a container of the chemical inside the submarine and a gaseous reaction occurred. This reaction was supposed to close several intricate valves in the submarine and force the water out through a propulsion tube thereby moving the submarine through the water and eventually raising it to the surface. At least, that was the intention. But the sad truth was that after several months of cutting metal and shaping and soldering various parts of the submarine, not one functioned according to plan. While the entire project was an interesting exploratory activity in itself, it was somewhat defeated by the letdown experienced when the submarines failed to operate.

Other such examples we can recall involved constructing metal pinwheels which were supposed to rotate when held over a flame, but which could not be balanced with precision so that they would turn, and a candle-making project which resulted in disaster because the wicks could not be centered during the process. Suffice to say that teachers are advised to try out exploratory activities before presenting them to their students so that frustrating failures like these can be avoided for all.

When an exploratory activity really works, it can be highly motivating for all children. Sanford was a fifteen-year-old boy in the NPI School who spent long hours designing mathematical formulas, computers, and elaborate electronic devices which were based more on fantasy than on fact. He refused to participate with the class in simple science experiments because he felt they were too elementary. His resourceful teacher, however, gradually got him interested in constructing a simple buzzer which operated on a dry cell battery. Despite Sanford's preoccupation with electronic wizardry, he was led patiently through the buzzer-making project and actually finished it. When a loud buzz ensued on the day of completion, the boy was obviously delighted. He displayed the buzzer with pride to his classmates and later confided to the teacher, "Do you know that this is the first thing I ever planned and made that actually worked!"

Exploratory tasks are designed to engage children in a variety of multisensory experiences, put them in maximal contact with reality, and guarantee them a predictable outcome. Science is particularly useful at the exploratory level, although a variety of other activities that involve the child in visual, auditory, and tactile exploration of the environment are also valuable.

Social Tasks

The goal of social tasks is to help the child learn to obtain the approval of others and to avoid their disapproval. Toward this end, characteristics of social tasks emphasize:

1. Communicating with the teacher or one or more peers
2. Maintaining appropriate social behavior
3. Tolerating periods of delay, during which time children must cooperate and "wait their turns"

All social tasks given to disturbed children in a classroom should be communication-oriented. Getting children to listen to others, to appropriately express themselves, and to contribute as members of a group toward attainment of a mutual goal are prerequisites if they are to receive social approval and avoid disapproval.

Listening Tasks

Perhaps the most fundamental communication task that can be given to the child is listening. In both the NPI School and in public school classrooms for the disturbed, we have observed the obvious satisfaction children derive from listening to the teacher read aloud. Such a group-listening period can be incorporated into the daily schedule of the class and a portion of a book read each day by the teacher. In this way, several books may be read to the class over the course of the school year. While "far out" science fiction tales may be too stimulating for children with tendencies to dwell on fantasy, real-life adventure stories from both fiction and nonfiction have been used with marked success.

A social task similar to listening to teacher-read stories as a member of the class group is listening to a story record with one or more classmates at a listening post (e.g., record player with headsets). Placing the child in such a situation with other classmates is a simple social communication activity. In fact, any of the exploratory activities described earlier can be used as social tasks by assigning two or more children to work together on them.

Social Communication Tasks

Code activities, which were described as order tasks when pursued by the child alone, are intriguing social communication tasks when undertaken by children in pairs. The Morse Code is intriguing to many children. Two telegraph keys which utilize flashing lights can be arranged as shown in Figure 6–7. One child sits on each side of the screen in order to send and receive messages. The teacher may provide a word or simple phrase to be sent at first; later, the children may devise their own messages. The symbol

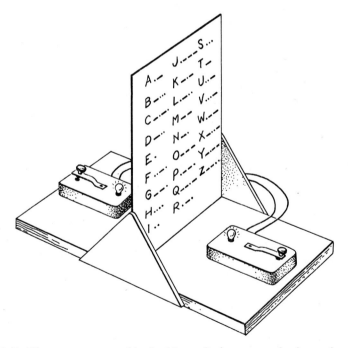

Figure 6–7. The apparatus used in the Morse Code communication task.

code task and International Flag Code task discussed earlier may also be used in a similar manner.

Inexpensive walkie-talkies are available commercially. These sending and receiving sets permit children to be separated across the room or even across some distance outside the class. The children may not only engage in spontaneous conversation but also work on assigned tasks. One such task involves direction-following. A simple street map of the immediate area around the school may be given to both children. One child's map is blank, but the other has a route drawn on it that covers several blocks. The children are separated and each given a walkie-talkie. The child given the map with the route drawn on it "sends" the other child the directions (e.g., "Start at the corner of Maple and Elm Streets, go north three blocks to Main Street, turn left, and go four blocks left to city hall."). The child receiving the directions attempts to duplicate the route on his or her map. Later the two maps are compared. The treasure-map order activity described earlier may also be varied to be utilized in this manner.

In addition to promoting communication between children, social tasks should encourage appropriate social behavior, including waiting one's turn. Many commercial games can be used toward this end. However, those that are quite elaborate with complicated directions and rules and which require long periods of time to complete should probably be avoided. Disturbed children are often easily frustrated when they do not clearly understand what to do and when they cannot finish playing a game. We observed one teacher of institutionalized severely disturbed children who presented such a game to two children with order and social problems. In a very short time one child was in tears, loudly accusing the other of cheating. The other child then began tearing up the game materials in an angry outburst.

Simple paper and pencil games like "Battleship" are more successful. In this game, children draw a fleet of ships on a paper among printed coordinates without letting their game partners see the position of their fleet. The children take turns naming coordinates to see if they can score a "hit" on the other child's ships. Despite the competitive aspects of this game, we have observed its success with many disturbed children.

In selecting games which minimize competition for use as social tasks, we have observed that those depending more on luck (e.g., "Battleship") than skill (e.g., checkers or chess) are viewed by children as less competitive. Selection of more skill-oriented and competitive social tasks will not prove difficult for the teacher because of the large number of commercial games available. In summary, games assigned two or more children should involve the level of competition which each child can handle comfortably, and while the reality of competition should be recognized by the teacher its pitfalls must also be appreciated.

Group Projects

Working on a class project with disturbed children, in which each child must assume independent responsibility for the project's successful completion, may be viewed with trepidation by the teacher. While group projects are admittedly a great deal of work and involve careful preparation and supervision, they often provide excellent opportunities for emphasizing the goals of social tasks—communication, appropriate social behavior, and learning to take turns.

One Christmas season the teacher of ten junior high students in the NPI School decided he would attempt a class drama project, using a radio script version of Dickens' *A Christmas Carol.* The story was read to the class and they expressed varying degrees of interest in the project. Two students with serious response problems claimed they would have no part in it since they would have to perform in front of an audience, but these were the only strong dissenters. The teacher was particularly concerned about one child who had a serious reading problem and who was unable to read the script. This boy, he decided, could work on sound effects, where accurate reading would not be necessary. One of the reluctant response problems was assigned as "engineer" to control the volume on the loudspeaker. He was assured he could perform his duties off stage, away from the audience. The other response-problem child loved to play the piano. She finally agreed to play a few bars of Christmas music at the opening and closing of the program, although in situations of stress she frequently fainted. The other children were assigned parts in the play which they practiced, and the whole class was "standing by" when the show went "on the air" in an auditorium filled with doctors, nurses, and other staff members of the NPI. The performance was flawless. Nobody fainted, ran away, made serious mistakes, or for that matter, displayed much stage fright. The class had functioned as any group of junior high children in a public school setting might have been expected to.

The success of this project was largely due to the enthusiasm and extreme patience of the teacher, as well as his skill in viewing each child as a candidate for "doing something" and in making wholly individual assignments based on the child's readiness for participation on the social task level. Radio plays offer ideal group experiences for disturbed children. There is no memorization of lines to worry about and no fussing with costumes or scenery. Radio plays can be of any length and can be obtained from the library or written by the teacher or students. The variety of jobs available ranges from the nonverbal (e.g., engineer, sound effects, musician) to the highly verbal (e.g., actor, director, announcer). As a result, even children with the most serious attention and response problems can usually do something (e.g., putting a record on the turntable).

The NPI School version of *A Christmas Carol* was tape-recorded and played back several times not only for the class but for other people. The group satisfaction and cohesiveness, which was promoted by this project, was readily recognizable and a Radio Club was formed.

Helping the Child Adjust to the "Socialness" of the Classroom

The social nature of the classroom is upsetting to the disturbed child who is not comfortable functioning as a member of a group. Removal of competition with other children, including in some cases individual tutoring, is a helpful first step with such a child. Once such children are assured that they are only competing with their own records and will not be graded or judged in comparison to others, the special or regular classroom becomes a safer environment. All recitation and forced participation in group activities should be avoided at first.

Assigning a socially withdrawn yet academically strong child responsibility for tutoring others less capable has been very effective in initiating social contact between students. Mayhew and Ferjo (1968) have explored the use of in-patient adolescents as teacher's assistants with in-patient elementary children in the NPI School. Their study was prompted first by the facts that the elementary children actually needed individual help with certain academic subjects and many NPI adolescent students were very competent in these subject areas; second, the role of assistant-teacher offered the adolescent a degree of prestige; third, and perhaps most significant, in the process of assuming responsibility for teaching the younger child, the adolescent might observe the younger child's problems and ways of handling them, and, perhaps, gain insight into his or her own difficulties. Adolescents selected as teacher-assistants evidenced a "nonpathological" interest in the younger group, displayed empathy in relation to the children, had scholastic ability which qualified them to assist the elementary group and, finally, manifested a degree of commonality of symptomatic behavior with the child to whom they were assigned.

Mayhew and Ferjo described two individuals in their study, Kathy and Margaret, who were severe response problems. They also contributed observations following a one-month pairing of this adolescent and elementary-aged child.

Kathy was a tall, gawky, fifteen-year-old girl whose admitting diagnosis was anorexia nervosa (a disorder involving severe conflict regarding food intake). She was alienated from her peer group by her physical looks and social ineptness. She was above average in height and far below average in weight. She was 5'9" tall and on admission to the hospital weighed 78 pounds. She further "enhanced" this emaciated, rather macabre, appearance by allowing her fingernails to grow an inch beyond her fingertips. Her peers shied away from personal contact with her, nicknamed her "Spider," and made her the ward scapegoat. Although Kathy had a frightening quality about her, it suddenly became abundantly clear that she, herself, was an extremely frightened girl.

In school, she would literally hide in her work. She would turn out reams of written work which in terms of learning were valueless. The sole purpose of her "busyness" was to hide from her peers and distance herself from her teacher. When asked to explain some fact of her studies, she would look startled, stammer, offer her notebook with the explanation— the answer was within—or look completely bland and turn mute.

Initially, she never volunteered a question or answer in class discussion and when called upon to answer, she would squirm, fidget, and shrug or say "I don't know."

Margaret was a small, thin, blonde, eight year old who never smiled, wore a permanent frown, and was extremely fearful. She was phobic about many things—animals, new people, new places. She had no friends among her peers who were either frightened by her terrified shrieks or who would tease her by saying "A rabbit will get you" to watch her hide under the desk or run to a far corner weeping. When calm at her desk she did superficial academic work and would always appear to be reading her book or writing out her assignments. When questioned about her work she showed little comprehension or would begin to cry. Margaret could not tolerate praise from the teacher, and would tear up her work if the teacher complimented her. She actively resisted all attempts by others to show friendship toward her.

Kathy was quiet and withdrawn. Margaret was frightened and shy. Both were shunned by their peers. Both hid in their academic work. After one month of being paired the following results had ensued. When Kathy was initially assigned to work with Margaret, the younger child ignored her and the teacher had to reassure timid Kathy of Margaret's fright. Then as the situation relaxed, Kathy could talk more freely to Margaret, and Margaret could respond to the interaction. Because both Kathy and Margaret were perfectionistic and showed little comprehension, it was impressed upon Kathy that Margaret could read well as long as she did not have to recall details but that this was not "true reading"; therefore, it would be necessary for Kathy to structure questions to help Margaret understand the material. In the beginning the teacher wrote out questions for Kathy to ask of Margaret. Gradually the older girl was able to develop her own questions from the academic material and discuss these with Margaret. This did not appear to generalize to Kathy in her own academics, but she gradually became more communicative and talkative in her own classroom.

Modeling, Coaching, and Role Taking

Modeling, coaching, and role taking may be effective in training disturbed and other exceptional learners to improve their social skills. Placing a disturbed child with limited social skills in close proximity to or in direct contact with a child whose behavior is exemplary, and who as a result receives positive reinforcement from the teacher, may be a means of encouraging the disturbed child to model the behavior in order to obtain the same rewards. This approach may be even more effective if the model chosen enjoys high prestige in the classroom.

A classic study done in the early 1940s demonstrates the effectiveness of coaching in improving the relationship of children who have difficulty getting along with each other (Chittenden, 1942). Two puppet dolls were introduced to the children. The puppets were then engaged in a skit concerning how two individuals who wanted to play with the same toy might resolve their problems. Sometimes the puppets were unsuccessful and a fight erupted. Other times the puppets were successful and took turns, shared, or played cooperatively. Over eleven sessions the purpose was to teach the children to discriminate unhappy outcomes such as fighting and anger, from happy outcomes such as having a good time. Later, the children were asked to verbalize to the puppets how they could play together more successfully. Observation of the children who had interpersonal conflicts in follow-up, real-life play situations revealed a significant decrease in dominating behavior and an increase (although not statistically significant) in cooperative behavior. A group of control children receiving no training showed little change in their behavior.

In another study, a group of low-accepted third- and fourth-graders was coached on "how to have the most fun" playing a game with a classmate (Oden & Asher, 1975). The suggestions given to the children included such things as participating fully, cooperating, communicating, and showing interest in the classmates. After five weeks of training, the coached children were found to be receiving higher acceptance ratings from their classmates than noncoached low-accepted children. Unfortunately, while the children were rated more highly, there was little change in their actual behavior (e.g., they did not begin to initiate interactions).

A problem found among many disturbed children including delinquents is an inability to "put themselves in someone else's shoes" and view situations from other perspectives. The ability to do this is called *role taking* and training disturbed children to better understand the problems they face from two sides, rather than only one, has been found to improve their social relationships (Chandler, 1973; Chandler, Greenspan, & Barenboim, 1974). In one training program, the children were engaged in creating skits that were later videotaped. The training involved one two- to three-hour session each week for ten weeks. The skits were brief and concerned individuals the same age as the subjects. In the skits, the players acted out problems familiar to the group such as being "put down" by an authority figure. The children took turns playing all parts (e.g., the "put downer" and the "put-downee"). Follow-up results indicated that there were improvements in social adjustment among the participants, as rated by the adults who worked with them.

Another study involved disturbed preschool children who were extremely limited in social and language development (Strain & Wiegerink, in press). The teacher read familiar children's stories such as "The Three Bears" and prompted the children to assume the role of a character in the story by performing certain verbal or motor behavior typical of the character. For example, the teacher might say "Lift your feet high, like you're climbing steps," or "Say *soup*." Following the story time, the children were given a free play period. As the story sessions progressed, the amount of spontaneous play observed among the children significantly increased.

A comprehensive effort to develop a formalized curriculum for teaching children social skills is represented by the Social Learning Curriculum, or SLC (Goldstein, 1974). It is designed to build the child's potential for critical thought and independent action. Among the ten components of the program are "recognizing and reacting to emotions," "communicating with others," and "getting along with others." Each component has fifteen to twenty lessons that involve games, work sheets, group discussions, and other activities. Some seventy-two 11 x 14 photographs depicting events and problems associated with each component are used to stimulate student discussion.

Planned Positive Peer Interaction

Project 3PI (Planned Positive Peer Interaction) was a project funded by the Bureau of Education for the Handicapped. It aimed at introducing to-be-mainstreamed disturbed children to their regular classroom peers by means of an indispensability curriculum (Hewett, Hoffman, Kahn, Lahti, Peck, Reynard, Weller, & Zoeller, 1979). An indispensability curriculum task is one that requires two children to communicate and cooperate in a reciprocal fashion in order to achieve a mutually desirable reward. Each individual, then, is indispensable to the other.

The basic setting within which the curriculum tasks were undertaken consisted of a table with two chairs on opposite sides. In the center of the table, there was a divider. This divider could be a solid panel of wood or a framed curtain with one or two openings for a child to put his or her arms through. In addition, there were two small boxes with lids, one to each side of each child. The following are examples of activities that could be undertaken in this setting:

1. *Pan Sorting.* The solid screen is placed on the table. Three pans (red, yellow, blue) are placed on each side of the screen along with a selection of objects (e.g., blocks, miniature animals, toy cars, etc.). Two children are seated opposite one another. One serves as "dispatcher" and proceeds to place the objects one at a time into the three pans. The dispatcher describes what he or she is doing, and the child on the other side of the screen attempts to place identical objects into identical pans (e.g., "I am putting a red block into the yellow pan."). When all of the

objects are distributed, the screen is lifted, and the children check to see if the pans and objects have been matched correctly. If they have, the children open their boxes and see what is inside. Each child has two of the same items (e.g., two colored stickers, two small cups of juice, two cookies). The children give each other one of what they have.

The stickers, depicting animals or birds, are pasted on a card that will be kept by the child. For each activity undertaken, a new sticker is provided. Another reward may consist of missing puzzle pieces. Each child has an incomplete puzzle on his or her side of the screen. Each child also has the missing pieces to the other child's puzzle which will be exchanged, one at a time, after each trial.

2. *Maze Guiding.* In place of the wooden screen used in pan sorting, a screen with a curtain in it is used here. The curtain has an elastic rimmed hole large enough for a child's arm to go through it. On the dispatcher's side is a raised wooden maze and a napkin ring with a steel ball bearing in it. The dispatchee puts his or her arm through the hole and is guided to the beginning of the maze where the napkin ring is grasped. The dispatcher then begins to verbally guide the other child in an effort to move the ring and ball bearing through the maze without having the ball bearing slip off the maze. If the children are successful, a reward exchange follows as in pan sorting.

3. *Map Following.* Various maps are used such as a treasure map, a map of the community, and a map of the school buildings and grounds. The dispatcher traces a trail to various points on the map describing what he or she is doing. The dispatchee tries to follow an identical path. Rewards are then exchanged if the maps are identical.

4. *Matching Sounds.* A frame with two arm holes is used here. One child places both arms through the holes. The other child then provides a Montessori-type cylinder which when shaken provides a distinct sound pattern. The dispatchee shakes the cylinder and determines the sound. The dispatcher then gives the dispatchee another sound cylinder which is shaken to see if it is identical with the first cylinder. If it is not, additional cylinders are provided until the correct match is identified. Rewards are exchanged after a given number of cylinders are matched.

5. *Matching Weights.* Wooden tablets of identical shape and thickness, but of differing weights, are given the child until ten tablets of the same weight are identified.

6. *Matching Textures.* Materials of various textures are provided with the task being to match those that are the same.

7. *Matching Thicknesses.* Materials of various thicknesses are presented, and the child attempts to identify identical pairs.

8. *Dress Up.* Two children sit in chairs close together but facing in opposite directions. A table is set up in front of each chair. On the table are various costume articles such as a fake nose and glasses, large ears,

moustache, monster hands and feet, eye patch, crown, rings and other jewelry, and a straw hat. Articles of clothing may also be used. Each child has the same articles on his or her table. The to-be-mainstreamed child has been trained to teach the other child the game. He or she begins by saying: "I am going to put on some of the things that are on my table. As I do, I will tell you what I am doing. You put on the same things from your table. When I am through, we will stand up, turn around, and look at each other to see if we both have the same things on." This activity usually ends with much merriment when the children look at each other. Two full-length mirrors also add to the fun of "Dress Up."

Tasks 4–7 have a more instructional than indispensability focus to them, but they have been found to be motivating and to engage children in positive interactions. In practice, a to-be-mainstreamed child in a special day class is coached until he or she has thoroughly mastered both the dispatcher and dispatchee roles of the curriculum tasks. Then, up to one third of the children in the regular class to which the child will be assigned, come, one at a time, into the special day class to meet the child and be taught by him or her how to participate in the tasks and later to share the rewards.

Children in resource-room settings who are already part-time in a regular classroom can also profit from 3PI. Even though they are known to the other children, an opportunity to interact in a unique activity in which the disturbed child is placed in a positive and favorable light may increase the acceptance of such a child in the regular classroom program. Of course, the interaction must be positive if it is to contribute to the probability of increased acceptance of the disturbed child. Children who cannot communicate appropriately or who cannot thoroughly master the task may only decrease their chances of acceptance.

This brings to a close our review of various activities and considerations related to increasing the disturbed child's competence on the first five levels. Our discussion of the mastery level has particular relevance to the severely disturbed child. We will, therefore, present it in Chapter 10.

chapter 7

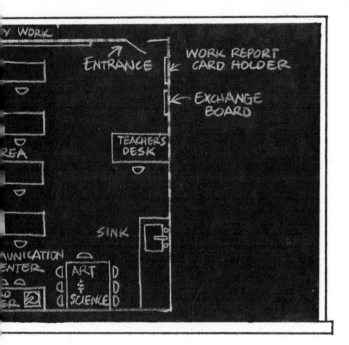

A Classroom Design
for Disturbed Children

I n this chapter we will review a basic classroom design or model which we developed for the orchestration of success. The application of this design at elementary and secondary levels as a special day class or as a resource room will be discussed in Chapters 8 and 9.

In developing an educational program or a classroom design for disturbed children, one must be concerned with two factors: (1) the "climate" or "learning atmosphere" one wishes to establish, and (2) the "procedures" including room arrangement, furnishings, activities, and scheduling. The first of these is an intangible and consists of variables such as feelings and attitudes on the part of both teachers and children. The second is more tangible and can be conveyed from developer to teachers by means of lists, charts, directions, and diagrams. In the discussion that follows, we will consider both the establishment of a harmonious learning climate and general classroom procedures.

The Establishment of a Harmonious Learning Climate

How do you go about creating a climate or learning environment that is conducive to positive relationships between children and their teachers, a climate that motivates children to try to learn, and one that readily provides for the three sides of the learning triangle? The answer to this question represents the fundamental philosophy underlying all of our efforts to develop innovative institutional and public school programs for children with learning and behavior problems. We have already provided this answer in part in previous chapters, but we will restate it here.

1. *Every Child Is a Learner.* Despite the seeming unreadiness of some children to learn, there is never a child who is not ready to learn something. Children who learn nothing in school are clearly teaching failures, not child-failures.

2. *Give the Child the Dignity of Being Expected to Learn.* If all children are learners, we must expect them to learn. Allowing them to continuously wallow in the confusion of self-directed learning is a questionable approach. How many disturbed children are going to "discover their way" out of their learning and behavior problems without our careful and thoughtful guidance?

3. *Don't Ask if the Child Is Ready to Learn, Ask if the Classroom Is Ready to Teach.* The classroom environment should be ready to spring to life at a moment's notice in order to engage the child in a successful learning experience. Don't rummage through cupboards and drawers to find

alternative tasks when problems arise, have an instant intervention-oriented classroom set up well in advance.

4. *Recognize that Time Is Often Our Enemy.* While some disturbed children "grow out" of their problems during the elementary years, a substantial number do not. Autistic children who have not acquired communicative speech by age five usually never learn to talk. The second grade hellion who never settles down to learn to read is in serious trouble in the upper elementary grades and a disaster in junior high school if we aren't effective in teaching him or her.

5. *Think Thimblefuls.* We may fail with children if we conceive of learning in bucketful amounts. No task is too small to be considered legitimate if it moves the child even slightly ahead on the learning track. Try to have a specific set of A-B-C goals with each child. If we don't plan our strategy in advance and prioritize, we may miss our chance to truly help the child.

6. *Think Sequentially.* There is a building-block logic in the use of shaping techniques. Identify the bottom block and build your learning tower step by step. Be willing to use smaller or even larger blocks if it seems appropriate. Be prepared to back up and dismantle your tower block by block if necessary. But start building again as soon as possible.

7. *Consider Conditions.* Don't let children fail because they are asked to work too long or to do too much in the wrong place or at the wrong time. And don't let concern for correctness or accuracy eliminate the child as a candidate for some level of success. Be flexible. Move quickly to alter when, where, how, how long, how much, or how well.

8. *Consider Consequences.* Don't be squeamish about rewards. They are a fact of life. Be sure there is something that makes it worth the child's while to try in the program. Don't use candy if the child is rewarded by praise or multisensory stimulation and activities. But don't not use candy if it offers a quick and efficient means of rewarding the child. Punishment is a risky business. While it may be effective at times, exhaust all positive possibilities before considering it. Withholding rewards is probably the most appropriate negative consequence for use in the classroom.

9. *Keep the White Rabbit of Schoolness Moving.* Try to establish each child's tolerance level for handling demands, schedules, competition, rules, tests, assignments, and directions. Expect the child to function toward his or her highest tolerance level by moving the rabbit closer. But when bad news develops, gracefully and imaginatively move the rabbit back until a reassignment or alteration reduces the child's discomfort.

These nine points constitute the big ideas inherent in the classroom design to be discussed in this chapter.

General Classroom Procedures

In this chapter we will use the concept of the learning triangle—curriculum, conditions, and consequences—to discuss general classroom procedures that are applicable to both a special day class and a resource room program. In Chapters 8 and 9, we will expand on these procedures and more specifically apply them to the special day class and the resource room at both the elementary and secondary levels.

Curriculum

Our framework for selecting curriculum tasks, which we introduced in Chapter 3, consisted of six levels of learning competence—attention, response, order, exploratory, social, and mastery. Let's begin our discussion here by asking the question: How does the classroom design make provision for these levels?

The answer can best be begun by referring to the floorplans depicted in Figures 7–1 and 7–2. These depict elementary and secondary classrooms respectively.

At the elementary level, the room is arranged so that specific areas are available for work on the six levels of learning competence (*See* Figure

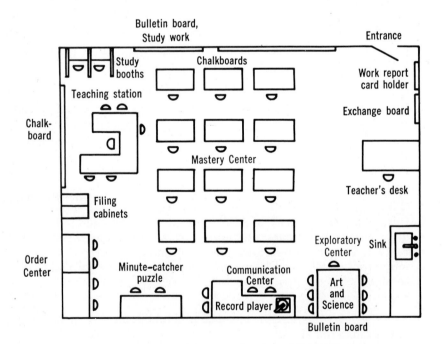

Figure 7–1. The floorplan of an elementary level special day classroom.

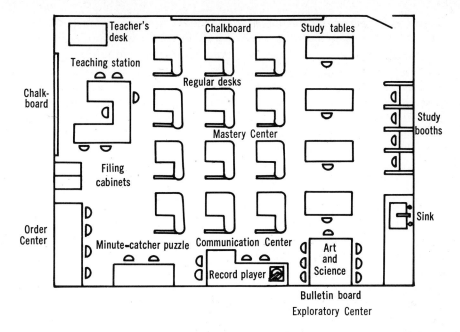

Figure 7–2. The floorplan of a secondary level special day classroom.

7–1). The Mastery Center consists of the student desk area, a teaching station, and two study booths. Academic assignments are normally done at this center. Social competence is fostered at the Communication Center where two or more children engage in cooperative tasks. The Exploratory Center provides art and science activities. Order Center tasks emphasize paying attention, responding, and following directions.

All student desks in the room are tables providing a desk top working area 2 x 4 or 2 x 3 feet in size. We have found that such tables have at least three advantages:

1. The child is separated from the other students by virtue of the size of the desk; physical and verbal contact with others is more difficult to initiate.

2. The student is provided with a large surface on which to spread out materials and work.

3. A large desk permits the teacher to sit down next to the child at a respectful distance and work with him or her in a businesslike manner. It is difficult to work with children who are seated at small desks without "closing in" or "hovering" over them. Such hovering may be awkward for the teacher or troubling for the disturbed child who is not comfortable with physical closeness or contact.

According to this floorplan, the class consists of twelve students. We have found this to be an appropriate number for a special day class, while as many as eighteen may be taught in a resource room program at any one time. A teacher's aide is important in both types of programs.

The teacher's aide need not be a credentialed individual; PTA volunteers, parents (usually of children not assigned to a particular class, although success has been reported by some teachers with parents of children in their classrooms), college and high school students, and even mature children from slightly older grade levels have all adequately fulfilled the role. Of course, the advantages of a salaried individual, who maintains a regular schedule, who is dependable, and who accepts a defined responsibility cannot be ignored. The presence of an aide in the classroom increases the probability that a child's request for assistance will be met in a far shorter time than is normally possible when only the teacher is available. Provision for such "instant" assistance when needed may greatly reduce the incidence of maladaptive behavior and frustration commonly seen when disturbed children are subjected to long waiting periods.

The Mastery Center includes two study booths. These are for use with children who are distractible at certain times or with certain assignments. They are for "interventions" and are not included in the design because of any conviction on our part that all disturbed children are so stimulus-prone that they must be kept isolated full-time in drab, sterile surroundings. The booths are very useful, however, when a degree of stimulus control will help a disturbed child pay attention and get an assignment done. The use of the teaching station will be discussed later.

The Communication Center features activities and games that minimize competition, encourage waiting one's turn, and are based more on luck than skill. A record player is part of a listening post where one or two children may listen to musical or story records with earphones. Activities aimed at increasing the child's social competence may also be undertaken here. Such activities were discussed in Chapter 5.

The Exploratory Center offers art and science activities. A variety of art materials such as paints, colored paper, crayons, clay, and other materials for creating art projects are located here. There may also be a variety of science materials for performing simple experiments, microscopes for looking at tiny organisms, small telescopes for looking out the windows at birds or other objects of interest, and kaleidoscopes for exploring a myriad of colors and forms. A projector for viewing color slides and a collection of magazines such as *National Geographic* provide additional visual experiences. A shortwave radio provides fascinating experiences for children as they hear programs from all over the world, keep track of the locations picked up, and perhaps plot these on a map.

One simple exploratory activity involves placing carrot tops and avocado seeds in water. These can be watched day by day until they begin to grow. A class garden in a window box, or perhaps in a plot of ground outside, provides many tactile exploratory experiences. A terrarium in which exotic and unusual plants will grow is also of special interest to children. Carnivorous plants such as Venus's-flytraps are particularly fascinating.

An interesting science exploratory activity that can be done with older elementary- and secondary-aged children is a weather station. Commercial kits are available with inexpensive devices for measuring wind speed and direction. Thermometers, hydrometers, and barometers can also be obtained from science supply houses. Reference materials describing types of cloud formations, their scientific labels, and their relation to various weather conditions are also readily available. A large weather chart can be maintained in the classroom, and the children can be given various responsibilities for taking readings describing each day's weather conditions, noting them on the chart, and attempting to predict the following day's weather.

Small incubators for poultry eggs are also available commercially or can be constructed as a class project. Maintaining the appropriate degree of temperature, taking periodic readings of the temperature inside the incubator, and keeping track of the time it takes for the eggs to hatch are intriguing exploratory activities. Of course, watching the baby chicks emerge from their shells provides the highlight for children. We have observed that this activity is even very popular with children who live in rural areas where eggs and chickens are commonplace.

One teacher made a large chart divided into two sections. One was labeled *Bird of the Day,* and the other, *Animal of the Day.* Each day a different bird or animal picture was placed in each section. The children were either given the name of the bird or animal, or they were asked to identify it from various reference sources. In this way the exploratory or mastery emphasis of the activity could be manipulated.

Invisible ink made with milk or lemon juice seldom fails to be of interest to children of all ages. Messages can be prepared in advance by the teacher and given to children who "discover" what they are by holding them over an electric light bulb or candle flame. Children can also write their own messages and exchange them with their classmates. Other exploratory activities were described in Chapter 5.

The Order Center is the fourth major defined area in the classroom. It includes two tables and a storage cabinet set up in a corner of the room so as not to be distracting to students working in the Mastery Center. The purpose of this center is to provide activities for the child emphasizing active participation, direction following, and task completion. This area is referred to as the Order Center in the classroom even though attention and response activities take place there.

The minute-catcher puzzle is an ongoing jigsaw puzzle which the class is putting together collectively. Students can be assigned there alone or in pairs whenever they have a minute or so of extra time. Examples of other activities offered at the Order Center were given in Chapter 5.

At the secondary level, the basic floorplan is retained, but there is an increased emphasis on the mastery level (*See* Figure 7–2). Twelve students have home-base student armchairs, identical to the armchairs found in all regular classes in the school. Rather than working there during all academic assignments, however, they rotate every fifteen minutes to two other settings. While four students remain at the armchairs, four go to individual study booths, and four go to large study tables. This results in each child working for fifteen minutes each hour in each setting. (The remaining fifteen minutes in the hour are taken up by the giving of check marks—five minutes after each work period.) We have found that frequent changes in body position and working area increase the alertness of disturbed children. Some teachers have used drafting tables with high stools or even work counters at which students stand while doing assignments.

The Communication Center is similar to that at the elementary level. Age- and interest-appropriate games and records quickly make this center relevant for teenagers. The same principle applies to the other two centers. Art and science projects at the Exploratory Center are geared to the secondary students' interest level as are the tasks available at the Order Center.

Conditions

In order to maintain a successful and harmonious relationship between the child and the learning environment, a great deal of flexibility is often necessary. What do you do, for example, when discord strikes and the child becomes upset at an assigned task or at the teacher or at another child? We have answered this question before: *You move the white rabbit of schoolness away temporarily.*

This movement involves altering the conditions of when, where, how, and how well. An additional condition of what is also important to consider. This has not been presented as a condition before since it actually refers to the curriculum, not the conditions, side of the learning triangle. In this section, however, we will treat it as a major condition. Each of these conditions is alterable and can effectively help establish harmony between the child and the learning environment. As a means of illustrating this, we have devised nine interventions that involve both moving from the highest level of learning competence to the most basic level and alteration of the conditions side of the learning triangle.

Before presenting the interventions, it is important to discuss the concept of the *student role*. We have found it very useful to stress to disturbed children that they are expected to be students when in the classroom. Essentially, this means:

1. A respect for the working rights of others

2. A respect for limits associated with time, working space, and assigned tasks

3. A respect for classroom rules

Thus, "being a student" is emphasized throughout the day.

The interventions will be discussed one by one. In actual practice, the teacher may try them one at a time in sequential order or, more likely, select the one that appears to be most appropriate for a given child at a given time. The ideal time for initiation of an intervention is in anticipation of the actual problem or very shortly after the first sign of inability or unwillingness to do an assigned task. The first seven interventions are considered "student interventions" because they involve continuation of the earning of check marks by the child at all times. Interventions 8 and 9 are "nonstudent interventions" and do not enable the child to continue earning check marks.

Student Interventions

1. *Send Student to Study Booth (Mastery Level).* The first intervention involves sending the child to work on an assigned mastery task in one of the study booths or "offices." These booths are presented to the children in a positive manner; as a result, they are desirable working areas. Merely allowing the child to change position and move around in the room often effectively interrupts a period of boredom or resistance.

2. *Modify Assignment (Mastery Level).* The next intervention is to change the mastery task given to the child, making it easier, different, or perhaps more difficult in an effort to get him or her involved. Sending the student to the study booth with modified assignment may also be used at this time.

3. *Restructure Verbally (Social Level).* When the mastery interventions just described are not successful or appear inappropriate, an intervention at the social level should be considered next. This intervention involves verbal restructuring on the part of the teacher, using social approval or disapproval as leverage. The child is reminded of the teacher's expectations in relation to the assigned task and behavior. The interactions between teacher and child may initially be largely task-oriented because of the poor relationships with adults previously experienced by many disturbed children. Nevertheless, with some students a reminder by the teacher regarding what is expected may be all that is necessary to help them improve their behavior. This intervention is perhaps most often used by teachers in regular classrooms with children who display problem behavior. It often reinforces the child's negative concept of school and teachers. Therefore, it should be used only after careful consideration, and it is often left out of the intervention process.

4. *Send Student to Exploratory Center (Exploratory Level).* The next intervention reassigns the child to another task center in the room. The teacher selects a previously demonstrated science, art, or craft task and assigns it to the child, making sure all the materials are available and that the child understands what to do. Assignments at the Exploratory Center are always teacher-selected. In practice, the teacher should always have one or two exploratory tasks set up in advance for instant use as interventions.

5. *Send Student to Order Center (Order Level).* Since the Exploratory Center involves a high degree of stimulation, it may not be as appropriate for some disturbed children at a given time as the Order Center. At this center, the child is given a simple direction-following task such as making a puzzle, copying a pegboard design, stringing beads, deciphering a secret code with the aid of a key, or constructing a model of plastic or metal components.

6. *Take Student Outside Classroom and Agree on a Task (Response Level).* In an effort to maintain contact with the student, an intervention at the response level may be undertaken outside the room. Both student and teacher (or aide) go out of the classroom and agree on some task the child will undertake, such as turning somersaults on the lawn, swinging on a swing for fifteen minutes, punching a punching bag, or even resting in the nurse's office for a period of time. Following a response intervention, the teacher attempts to select some assignment in the classroom to ensure the student's success.

7. *Provide Individual Tutoring (Attention Level).* The intervention corresponding to the lowest level of learning competence involves the teacher or aide devoting full time to individual instruction with the student. Such individual tutoring is not always possible for extended periods of time because of the needs of the other students, but it is the next logical step to take in order to help the child.

Nonstudent Interventions
8. *Send Student Outside Classroom for Specified Time-out.*
9. *Send Student Home.*

The first seven interventions are generally positive in nature. The idea is to use the resources of the classroom in any way possible to get the child back on the learning track at some level. Actually, there is nothing that new about what is being suggested in the first seven interventions. Teachers have been doing such things in one form or another for many years. But perhaps not so common about these interventions are the following:

1. *The anticipation of possible discord* between the child and the learning environment by creating a room ready to spring into action at a moment's notice. Order or exploratory tasks are not searched for on the spur of the moment. They are ready at all times.

2. *The immediacy in handling problems of discordance.* As in so many aspects of our work with disturbed children, time is not our friend. When reassigning a child a task, seconds count. If you want to send the child to listen to a record with earphones, have the record on the player, turn the player on, adjust the volume, and have the earphones handy. In this way you may have the child in a new setting, participating in a new task in five seconds, well before the "lid really comes off."

3. *The conceptualization of a logical sequence of interventions* rather than reaching into thin air for something at the last minute.

One question which arises out of the use of these interventions in the manner described is: What about children who are far more rewarded by exploratory and order tasks and who actively seek to create problems in the classroom so that they can be reassigned to a more attractive task? Doesn't such reassignment in effect "reward" maladaptive behavior? Viewed in the context of the operant model illustrated in the work of Ayllon and Haughton (1962), the answer is yes. But viewed in the context of the respondent model provided by Jones's study (1924) with Peter, the answer is that such a price is well worth paying if it preserves a link with learning at some level of learning competence and maintains the child as a successful student. As we have stressed, freely move the rabbit back when it gets too close. The classroom design presented here is truest to the respondent model and is more concerned with maintenance of classroom success and changing negative attitudes toward learning than with rigid adherence to the principle that rewarding maladaptive behavior may cause it to increase in frequency. This exemplifies the fact that the approach suggested here uses behavior modification methodology *pragmatically.*

In actual practice, the problems created are slight. In our experience, few children persist in attempting to manipulate the teacher into assigning them to a different work area. In cases where this does occur, a time-out period is used directly as a negative consequence. We will discuss the use of time-out procedures shortly. Most children in classrooms we have supervised "get the idea" very quickly that the class is set up to help them, and they relax and fit comfortably into the routine. In addition, most disturbed children, despite their avoidant behavior in relation to mastery activities, really want very much to learn to read and to improve in arithmetic and other skills. It is when we place them in a truly supportive learning environment and devise individual programs for them according to the learning triangle that their motivation for succeeding can be fully exploited.

What if none of the first seven interventions is appropriate? Or what if none of them work? As with all our efforts to think positively and guarantee success, sometimes we can't win. This is where consideration of "nonstudent interventions" may be necessary. By nonstudent, we mean the child can no longer remain in the classroom and be a student. One of these interventions involves a time-out procedure; the other involves sending the child home.

In Chapter 2 we discussed how having the child leave the room for a specified period has been shown to be effective, particularly if being out of the room really means a time-out from positive consequences for the child. If the child really prefers to be alone, or if the time-out procedure involves being sent to the principal's office where the school clerks enlist the child's help in stapling bulletins or where the child can watch the fascinating parade of office visitors, time-out is a losing proposition. A lecture by the principal may work with some children, but for others it is "old hat" and ineffective. Rather than relying on a time-out procedure as a first resort when discordance occurs, the teacher should rely heavily on making the classroom program so attractive, the activities so inviting, and success so enjoyable that, indeed, the worst thing that could happen to children from their point of view is to be denied the opportunity to remain in the classroom. That is ideal.

In an in-patient hospital school for disturbed children, one of us attempted to do just that. A great deal of effort was expended in finding outstanding teachers who had a wide variety of interests and who knew how to put real "fun" into learning. Most of the children soon really wanted to come to school and they appeared to be genuinely disappointed when they were sent out of the classroom for misbehavior. This ideal is difficult to attain, but we should strive toward it at all times. How much better it would be for teachers and schools in this country to go on the offensive with the message, "What we have to offer you is so interesting and exciting you cannot afford to miss out!" rather than the defensive, "You're going to come to school whether you like it or not, and we have ways of making you conform if you get out of line."

If this ideal has been attained, it doesn't make much difference which type of physical setting is used for a time-out. Outside in the hall, on the stairs, or in an adjoining room may all be effective. The principal's office may also be effective provided that the school staff takes steps to make it a nonrewarding situation. The following considerations are important when using a time-out procedure:

1. It should occur only after the child's behavior has exceeded the limits that have been clearly stated previously and after consideration or trial of one or more of the student interventions.

2. It should occur with emotional control on the part of the teacher rather than exasperation.

3. It should be presented to the child as a constructive aid to learning rather than as an arbitrary punishment. ("It seems as though you cannot function as a student right now in the classroom. I hope you will be able to after a time-out period.")

4. It should involve a specific period of time ("You are on a five-minute time-out") rather than an open-ended exclusion ("You may come back when you think you can behave").

5. Once the time-out period has passed, the child should immediately return to class without any lecturing or attempts to get him or her to "promise to be good from now on."

6. When the child returns, every effort should be made to select a task that has a high probability of interest and success for him or her.

Some teachers may read these suggestions and react with "They are all well and good, but what if the child refuses to leave the room?" We have

found that most mildly disturbed children in public-school special education programs seldom resist. When they do, the teacher may have to request that the principal, custodian, coach, or another teacher come in and physically remove the child. This is probably preferable to the teacher and child engaging in a physical struggle right there in the classroom. While some teachers might easily drag an obstinate student out of the room, this pitting of teacher strength versus child strength and the witnessing of the whole event by the rest of the class can lead to undesirable side effects.

When a time-out procedure is not appropriate due to the severity of the child's problem behavior or if it simply does not work, it can be effective to send the child home. This is no easy matter with working parents who have no one at home to supervise the child. When it is the only alternative, the child may have to spend the entire remainder of the school day in the office. In sending the child home, consideration of all of the suggestions presented earlier with respect to time-out are applicable. But these additional points are important:

1. Be sure the child's parents have been told in advance of the possibility that the child may be sent home. Be sure they understand that the purpose is to reinforce the message: Only students stay in the classroom. Nonstudents may have to go home.

2. Try to get the parents to adopt a nonpunitive approach and not to punish the child on their own. We recall a child sent home whose parents locked him in a closet for two days as additional punishment.

3. Where both parents work and it seems important to have the send-home option available, see if a neighbor or relative could take the child in. (This would involve a signed parental permission to send the child someplace other than home.)

4. In the event the child is displaying continual daily behavior problems at school and is not responsive to any school-based intervention, the parent may have to be contacted and a plan set up whereby the child can be sent home on a given day when the parent is available. This does not mean planning to send the child home at the parent's convenience regardless of what the child's behavior is like. This is only done when the problem is so chronic that it almost certainly warrants a send home on any day.

Sending a child home in a firm yet nonemotional manner can have dramatic effects if the parents and school are in close communication and total agreement as to what it is supposed to accomplish. We have seen a single send home turn a child around for an entire semester. Among the messages conveyed to the child may be the following:

1. We want you in school, but you must share some responsibility and meet us at least part of half way.

2. School is for students. We will provide you with schooling (e.g., home tutoring) but we must expect you to assume the student role in order to stay in school.

3. We hold no grudges and want very much to never have to send you home again.

An important aspect of the seven student interventions and the two nonstudent interventions is that they convey to the disturbed child a sense of preparedness on the part of the school program. It is our conviction that most disturbed children are helped more by programs that have a predictability about them than by programs that fluctuate with respect to procedures and limits on a day-to-day basis. When an approach is ready at a moment's notice to alter the learning environment in a systematic manner in order to help the child succeed, the child is getting a powerful message. And if nonstudent interventions are necessary, and if they occur in a predictable and eminently fair manner, another powerful message is provided. The key words in this paragraph are *systematic, predictable, and fair*. These ingredients may well express the essence of the philosophy and program being described here.

Consequences

The third side of the learning triangle, consequences, is largely provided by the check mark system. The check mark system is a temporary extension of the traditional system of acknowledgements used in regular classrooms. It is designed to guarantee that even the most disinterested and resistant learners will be rewarded for their efforts. It is also designed to create a wholly unique system of immediate consequences consistent with the nature of the classroom design under discussion by removing the white rabbitness of grades for the moment.

Each morning as the children enter the door, they pick up a work record card from the work record card holder. A sample work record card which has been partially filled with check marks is shown in Figure 7–3. The bulletin board area utilized for the holder is illustrated in Figure 7–4.

As the child goes through the day, he or she is given check marks reflecting task accomplishments and classroom functioning. Cards filled with check marks can later be exchanged for rewards. (This will be discussed later.) The original criteria for receipt of check marks are presented on the work record card holder. Usually a possible ten check marks are given by either the teacher or the teacher's aide following each fifteen-minute work period in the classroom. During the time devoted to giving check marks (usually five minutes), all work done within the preceding work period is corrected and the new assignment for the next fifteen minutes is given. This allows three fifteen-minute work periods and three five-minute check-mark-giving periods during each class hour.

According to one approach, two check marks are given if the child started the task, three if the child followed through on an assignment, and five bonus check marks are possible for "being a student." The phrase,

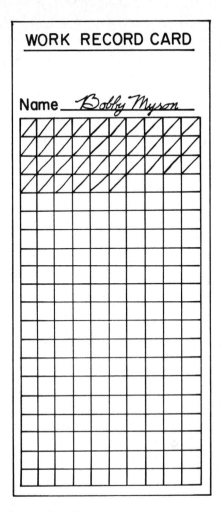

Figure 7–3. The work record card.

being a student, refers basically to the student role described earlier. That is, it refers to how well the child respects the working rights of others, the limits of time, space, and activity, and the classroom rules. For the student with no problems on the order level, the five bonus check marks can reflect functioning on the levels most critical to his or her learning needs. For some extremely inattentive children, the bonus check marks may be given "because you put your name on the paper and paid attention to your work"—even though no actual work was accomplished. For those children with response problems, the five check marks may be given "because you tried to do the assignment"—regardless of the number of problems correct. Children with exploratory problems may receive their five bonus check marks for "trying to do more of the assignment than usual." The

Figure 7–4. The work record card holder.

child who is functioning well at the attention, response, order, and exploratory levels, but who has trouble getting along with others, may be given check marks largely for social behavior. "These can be given because you worked well without bothering anybody else" or "because you worked well with Johnny" on a cooperative task or "because you did the assignment just as I [the teacher] wanted you to." The mastery learner may receive bonus check marks as letter grade equivalents and be told, "You earned five bonus check marks for getting all the problems correct."

In giving check marks, the teacher or aide takes time to explain why the child is either receiving or not receiving the possible ten. Thus transaction between child and adult is quite significant and is not brushed over mechanically or carelessly. The check marks must reflect what the child has actually earned in terms of the teacher's expectations according to the child's level of learning competence. Selection of suitable educational tasks aimed at attaining these goals is vitally important.

Another approach to the giving of check marks involves using letters instead of slashes on the work record card. Five letters are given in each of two categories: task behavioral and setting behavioral. The task behavioral category is concerned with how well the child did with the task. The following letters may be used for this category: A–attention, S–starting, W–working, T–taking part (oral participation or making contributions to the class), F–following directions, R–being right, N–being neat. The setting behavioral category concerns "being a student." The following letters are used:

B–being a student, D–doing what you are told, G–getting along with others. Letters, like check marks, are given every fifteen minutes.

The check mark system can be used to evaluate whether or not short-term objectives on the child's IEP are being met. For example, if getting a child to participate orally in group discussions is a goal, the teacher can be sure to award T's to the child whenever this occurs and then count these at the end of the semester as a record. If slash marks are being used, the teacher can use a different colored pen to administer check marks for a particular accomplishment that is related to an IEP objective.

If the tasks chosen are truly on the child's level, each child should be receiving the majority of the ten possible check marks each fifteen minutes. When the child has not earned these, the teacher needs to reconsider the type of task assigned. If, however, in the teacher's judgment, the task is appropriate and the child needs reminding of the expectations, reduction of the number of check marks given is essential. This is not done punitively, but in a matter of fact manner. "Here are your two check marks for starting and three for working and following through, but you have only earned two bonus check marks because you did not . . . . Next time you can earn them all by . . . ."

Those who might view the check-mark-giving responsibility of the teacher as "technicians' duty which anybody, including a robot, could carry out" should reflect on the considerable degree of awareness of the appropriate educational goals for each child which is necessary in order to truly individualize the check-mark-giving transaction. The fifteen-minute, fixed-interval basis for awarding the check marks may also seem mechanistic, but its very regularity guarantees that all the children will be visited by either teacher or aide at least three times each hour, have their work corrected, and find out where they stand. This routine is in marked contrast to the inconsistent and often infrequent teacher-pupil contact, reliance on group-directed teaching, and the long delay in receiving grades or teacher appraisal of work accomplishments in the regular classroom. Here again we have a unique aspect designed to reorient the child more positively toward school and to help him or her learn more efficiently. There is no magic in the fifteen-minute interval. In line with reducing emphasis on rigid engineering, the teacher should select the interval most appropriate for the individual group of students and the situation.

The role of the teacher during the check-mark-giving process may also be unique. Words may be used sparingly. Verbal contact with students may be largely restricted to individual conversations during the correcting of assignments, the giving of check marks, and the assigning of tasks during the five-minute check-mark-giving periods. Of course, verbal contact is also established whenever the student asks for help during a work period. This verbally limited role has been found to be useful with some types of disturbed children. The rationale for a controlled amount of verbalization and a "task oriented" relationship, rather than a highly verbal "interpersonal" relationship, stems from recognition of the negative associations many disturbed children have with adults who "talk too much." This is not a harsh criticism, it is a simple statement of fact. Parents and teachers who are confronted with resistant, noncooperative, and seemingly inaccessible children often remind, lecture, and resort to long-winded verbal discourses in an attempt to "bring such children into line." Without dwelling on why this occurs, the fact remains that such verbal excess is probably one of the most prominent characteristics of schools and classrooms that negatively orient children toward learning. Temporary removal of this characteristic may be yet another move in the direction of creating a unique classroom environment for the child. However, degree of verbalization must ultimately be determined by the teacher and the type of children in the class.

In the classroom design being described here, the teacher attempts to establish a working relationship with each child. An effort is made to convey the notion that the teacher "works" in the classroom too, and his or her job is assigning tasks that the child needs to learn, is ready to learn, and can be successful in learning. Part of the teacher's job is also administering check marks which the child has earned as a result of task accomplishments. In this regard, the teacher may be viewed as a "working partner" who credits workers for actual accomplishments and yet is also a worker in the school setting. Check marks are presented as objective consequences of the child's efforts and, literally, as part of a reality system in the classroom over which the teacher has little subjective control. The teacher's message to the child is, in essence: "That's just the way it is. I work here, too." The check mark system, then, can serve as a neutral, nonconflictual meeting ground for teacher and student that is devoid of the connotation that acknowledgement of the child's accomplishments is based on the fact that the teacher is a powerful adult who is bigger and smarter than the child.

Viewing emotionally disturbed children as workers who are paid what they have earned, rather than as helpless individuals who are to be pitied, is valuable in giving such children self-respect. By placing definite responsibility, which the child can assume, on the child's shoulders and by providing predictable consequences for appropriate behavior, it is the child's strengths that are being appealed to rather than his or her weaknesses.

Despite the "work" and "task" orientation of such a teacher-pupil relationship, very definite interpersonal aspects are present. The fair and predictable administration of check marks establishes the teacher as a classroom ally who has the child's best interests at heart, who accepts the child as he or she is, and who wants more than anything else to assist the child in learning and achieving success. This is done without always having to tell the child: "I like you. You did exactly what I asked" or "I want to help you."

In classrooms where the check mark system has been abruptly removed and the more traditional rewards of teacher attention, praise, and grades thereafter relied on, there has been little noticeable change in the children's cooperation and learning efficiency. Teachers in these rooms apparently had become far more than mere purveyors of check marks.

They had acquired secondary reward value of their own through association with the more primary check mark reward system. However, when teachers have been given the opportunity to discontinue the system because the children were working for more traditional rewards, most opted to maintain it. They liked the way it guarantees that they will have a regular, evaluative contact with each child during each class hour.

It is our contention that attempting to guarantee children's success through assigning tasks they need to learn and are ready to learn, and then providing fair, predictable, and systematic consequences related to their accomplishments is the greatest expression of teacher love which can be given in the classroom. Despite the seemingly mechanical routine involved in the giving of check marks, most teachers who have utilized the check mark system are warm and personal in their manner, although expression of these attributes does not necessarily occur verbally. The use of the check mark system can enhance the good teaching qualities of any teacher through providing regular contact with pupils and constant assessment of progress. There is still plenty of room for teachers to be themselves and to create and innovate despite the structured nature of the overall classroom design.

It should be emphasized at this point that the program being described here is only effective if the teacher believes in it and takes such routines as the check-mark-giving process seriously. We have observed teachers who in a mechanical fashion approach each child and quickly repeat "You've earned five for working and five for being a student," apparently just to get the boring business over with as quickly as possible. This "broken record" syndrome quickly defeats the meaningfulness of the system. Some teachers have even drawn horizontal lines through ten boxes on the work record card making the transaction even less meaningful. Check marks should be given personally with eye contact between teacher and child. For children who can be related to on a social and verbal level, a private, personal conversation should occur for a few moments. The child should know that the check marks are a "big deal" to the teacher. It is equally important that the child understand the importance of the check marks and precisely why he or she is or is not getting the full complement. Children are very adept at seeing through insincerity and phoniness. Any teacher who considers the check mark system more trouble than it is worth should never use it. Used in a mechanical, ritualistic fashion, it probably will be a waste of time.

In the Santa Monica, California schools, where we developed this classroom design, a special procedure is sometimes used to introduce children to the program. On the first day of school, the children are greeted outside the room by the teacher. They are lined up and each is handed a work record card with his or her name on it. With no more explanation than "This is going to be a different classroom from any you've ever been in before," the teacher instructs them to go inside the room and sit down at the desk with their name on it. Immediately after they are seated at that desk, the teacher and aide circulate and give each child ten check marks— "Five because you were on time, and five because you found your desk and are ready to go to work." In addition, a candy unit is placed on top of each check mark to establish the card and checks as important and rewarding. The children are told that they can eat the candy whenever they wish, and the first assignment is also given to the child during this initial check-mark-giving period. Questions inevitably arise regarding children who have dental problems, who are allergic to chocolate, or who have diabetes. In this regard, sunflower seeds, popcorn, raisins, and peanuts have proven just as effective as candy. In addition, when it appears that the candy motivation is unnecessary, the procedure can involve the giving of check marks only. However, the surprise factor associated with the appearance of a tangible reward may be important in the launching stage of the program. But there are no hard and fast rules. Make the design fit the teacher, children, and setting.

For the first two hours of the first day, some teachers have found it useful to place a candy unit over each check mark given. Following this the children are told that the check mark card is valuable but that they will not get any more candy on top of their check marks. Instead they will have to wait until the card is filled with check marks, at which time they may turn it in for any of the exchanges shown on a bulletin board in the classroom.

In the Santa Monica program, children may either exchange completed work record cards as soon as they are filled or in some classes teachers set certain days and times for the exchange. While candy was utilized almost exclusively as an exchange item originally, teachers in the district have found that most children are now satiated on it. The children now usually prefer either a twenty-minute free-time period during which they can choose a friend to play a game with or "take-a-chance." If the child chooses a free-time period, an activity card such as that shown in Figure 7–5 is given to him or her. When the child chooses to "spend" the time, the teacher draws in the hands on the clock face indicating when the twenty-minute period will be over.

The take-a-chance exchange consists of allowing the child to reach into a sack or box and draw out a card. On the card is written a special privilege to which the child is entitled such as:

Be first in line at recess for 2 days.

Go home five minutes early.

Be ball monitor for 2 days.

Be first in the cafeteria line for 1 day.

Have lunch with the teacher.

In addition to these exchanges, the child may elect to have the teacher write a note home to his or her parents commenting on good work done in the classroom.

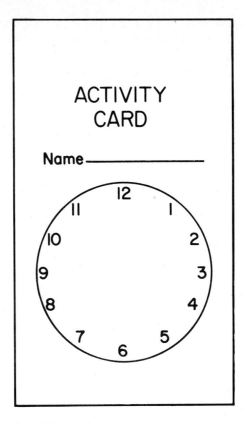

ACTIVITY
CARD

Name _____

Figure 7–5. A sample activity card.

As with the giving of check marks, teachers need to make a "big deal" out of the exchange transaction. Teacher belief is absolutely essential to make the program being discussed here work. With the take-a-chance exchange, the child keeps the card with the privilege on it at his or her desk for the time specified, showing it to the teacher to claim the privilege at the appropriate time. However, it is much more powerful for the teacher to anticipate the privilege and give the child the added reward of special attention by calling him or her to the front of the line, etc.

The process of having children exchange their completed work record cards for tangible rewards can become unnecessarily elaborate. We visited one classroom in which the teacher allowed each child ten minutes to "shop" from five tables covered with items available for one, two, or three completed cards. In another program, exchange items lined the walls of the hall leading to the classroom. The items ranged in value from fifty cents to ten dollars and involved a complicated exchange procedure. In still another classroom, each completed work record card was worth $1.50 and parents of the students in the class objected because their "problem" children brought home costly toys which they displayed with pride before their "nonproblem" siblings, creating a somewhat confusing situation regarding rewards, learning, and school.

The cost and nature of an exchange item is generally unimportant, particularly with elementary-aged children. What does matter, however, is the reward was "earned" in school. Children with enough money in their pockets to buy the equivalent of the teacher's entire supply of exchange items at a local store display delight with a five-cent item earned with check marks. One teacher who used miniature candy bars as exchange items had one student who would bring a regular-sized bar to trade with a classmate for a more valued "school" candy bar that was used as an exchange item.

Neither *what* you give the child in exchange for check marks, *how much* you give, nor the *monetary value* of the reward is the crucial determiner of its real worth. These considerations constitute the "small ideas" inherent in the check mark system. The "big idea" is that children's accomplishments are being acknowledged in a systematic fashion and that the children come to recognize that their behavior controls certain consequences.

An exception to this general guideline may occur when working with severely deprived youngsters. We observed a class for inner city youths that was dominated by Tommy, a thirteen-year-old with a record of several felonies and attempted rape. He would come to school late every day, fling open the door so it smashed against the wall, look around the room with an expression that would have befitted Caesar entering the Forum, go to the back of the room, take out a checkerboard, set it up, and then beckon to one of his classmates to come be his partner. Although most of the other boys wanted to complete their work so that they could earn check marks, nonacceptance of Tommy's bidding would most certainly lead to a bloody nose or a twisted arm at recess.

Tommy had been doing this for a semester. He never did any class work but played checkers and left school when he felt like it. The teacher was trying to patiently work with him because even coming to school for checker-playing was better than having Tommy roam the streets and commit a crime. But he was bright and had obvious leadership ability. He was also an outstanding athlete. A plan was devised whereby Tommy could earn a twenty-five dollar football for accumulating a certain number of check marks. To this deprived young man the prospect of owning such a valued object was extremely motivating. He began to work and conform to all class rules (e.g., coming on time earned extra check marks). It took Tommy the better part of a semester to earn the football. Once it was his, he continued to work and cooperate in class, although not at the same level as when he was trying to earn the football. The teacher then introduced records as long-term exchange items, and Tommy was hooked again.

The withholding of check marks for purposes of alerting the child that a problem has occurred in the classroom has been generally effective with disturbed children with whom we have worked. However, in at least one program, the holding back of check marks created havoc. The boys in the program were in their early teens and were extremely hostile toward authority figures, including the teacher. No sooner would the teacher start to say "I can only give you three of your five checkmarks because . . ." than the check mark receiver would angrily grab the card, tear it up, sometimes turn over his desk, and sometimes charge out of the room. It seemed that holding back check marks was viewed as a confrontation between the boys and an authority figure who was exercising power to keep them from getting something they wanted.

In an effort to retain the check mark system (which the boys really liked) and yet remove the confrontational circumstances surrounding the withholding of check marks, the teacher decided on a unique plan. Instead of holding back check marks, the teacher began to give every boy his full ten. But if a problem had arisen, the teacher would draw extra boxes on the margin of the card saying, for example, "Because you didn't come to class on time, I am adding three extra boxes which will have to be filled before you can exchange your card." No negative reactions came from the class. It seemed as though adding boxes was a challenge, while holding back check marks was a confrontation. Whatever the reason, it worked and while technically constituting a punishment, it was palatable to these authority-sensitive boys.

Another example of the effectiveness of adding boxes versus holding back check marks occurred in a class for deaf youngsters. One ten-year-old girl simply never understood what it meant when the teacher held back check marks and tried to explain why. The girl would become upset and look away. However, when the teacher began adding boxes the girl understood it would take longer to fill the card and exchange it. In a dramatic turnaround, the girl's behavior improved in one day and the box-adding approach became unnecessary after a few days. In general, alternatives to the regular check mark system have been very rarely needed.

In addition to giving check marks after work periods, the teacher may use a "surprise" bonus when children are displaying some behavior close to one of the teacher's goals for them (e.g., keeping all four legs of the chair on the floor, not disturbing others, raising their hands to request assistance). The child may be "surprised" and be given five or ten extra check marks on the spot. At other times, when the class is having difficulty settling down, the teacher may announce, "Each student who is ready to work and who has followed my directions will receive five extra check marks." These are then immediately given out to those students who have fulfilled the teacher's expectations, and no additional comment is made about the children who were "not ready" and who did not receive bonus check marks. In addition, when a particular child is getting disruptive, the teacher may circulate among nearby children and give them bonus checks for "working and not paying attention to Johnny." Another approach using the check mark system in this situation is to loudly award attentive students for the very behavior not being shown by the problem student. "I like the way you are working quietly and not disturbing anyone around you!"

In addition to the fifteen-minute intervals and surprise situations, check marks are usually given first thing in the morning following the flag salute, after recess, and after the nutrition and physical education periods.

In Chapter 2 we discussed the use of self-management techniques by which the child can determine the actual number of check marks he or she had earned. We have found this to be an effective extension of the check mark system for children who are able to handle this responsibility. Three stages of the self-administration of check marks are illustrated in Figure 7–6.

Looking at Figure 7–6, the shaded boxes indicate the times the child actually decides how many of the possible ten checks are deserved. As can be seen, by Stage 3 the teacher is only giving fifty of the possible two hundred checks. We feel it is important to have the teacher participate in the check mark process even at Stage 3 to maintain the working-partnership relationship with the child.

This self-administration approach is particularly successful when the children come in from recess. Recess and free-play times on the playground are typically "bad news" for many disturbed children. Some teachers award ten checks at the close of recess as the children enter the room. Each child is asked what he or she did during recess and how many checks are deserved—five possible for the type of activity and five possible for not having any problems on the playground. We have been amazed as to how seriously most children take this responsibility. Instead of cheating or arrogantly claiming "I earned them all," they sincerely want to be fair and deny themselves checks if problems have occurred. Of course, some disturbed children are in no way candidates for this level of responsibility, and teacher discretion is essential so that it does not become a meaningless farce.

With respect to children's sense of fairness and honesty, one of us watched an interesting example of a type of behavioral therapy. The subject was a hard-core delinquent, a twelve year old who had refused to talk to any of the psychiatrists in the hospital setting into which he had been placed. A behavioral psychologist sat across the table from him. The psychologist started by saying, "I am interested in how kids think, and I'm willing to pay you to find out." He then proceeded to take out a dollar bill and put it on the table saying to the boy, "Give me a dollar's worth of how a kid thinks." While the frustrated psychiatrist who had never reached the boy looked on in dismay, the boy began to open up, revealing many of his private feelings and conflicts. After a half hour, he asked the psychologist in all seriousness, "Did I give you a dollar's worth?" The psychologist replied, "What do you think?" whereby the boy continued talking for another twenty minutes and then picked up the dollar bill and put it in his pocket. We may sell many children—disturbed and nondisturbed—short in terms of basic fairness, honesty, and integrity.

At the close of the day, each child may total up all earned check marks

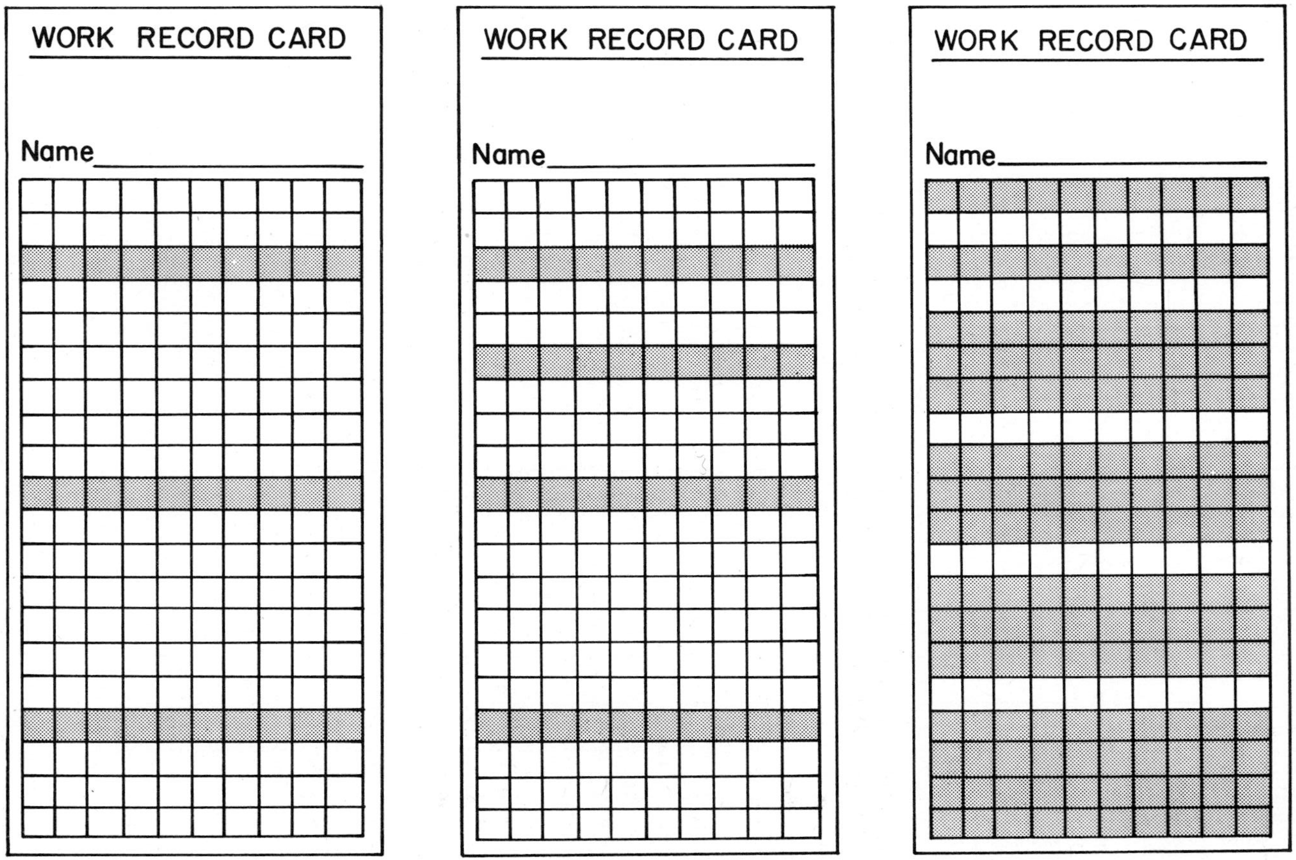

(Stage 1) (Stage 2) (Stage 3)

Figure 7–6. Three stages of the self-administration of check marks.

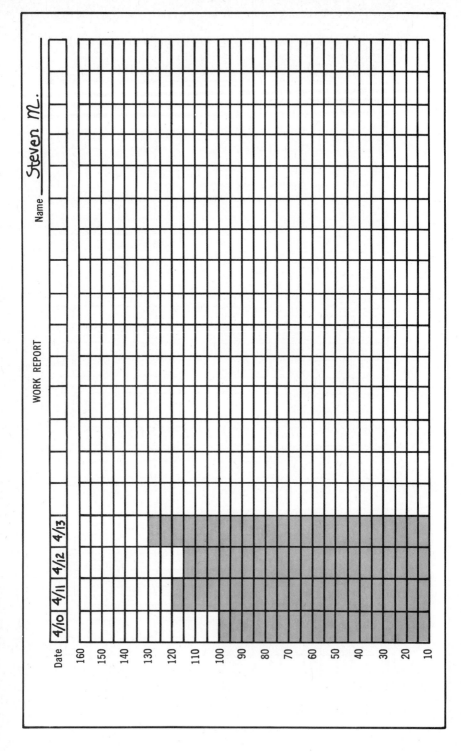

Figure 7-7. The work report.

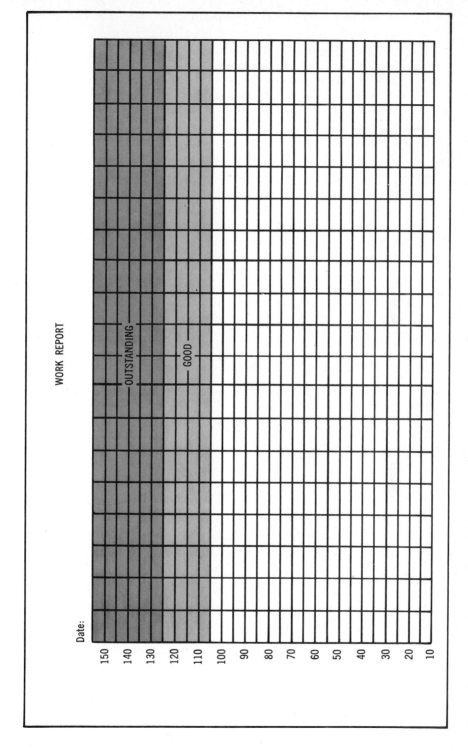

Figure 7–8. An alternate version of the work report.

and graph these on a work report fixed on his or her desk. This technique, which is illustrated in Figure 7–7, allows the child to compare his or her individual progress day by day. Another version of the work report is illustrated in Figure 7–8. The child fills in the total number of check marks earned and sees if they reach the "good" or "outstanding" levels. Teachers need to adjust the levels to the actual number of check marks a child has the opportunity to earn in a given program.

Some children may become preoccupied with the number of check marks given their classmates and become competitive regarding comparisons. But it has been found that a reminder causes such behavior to rapidly diminish (e.g., "In this room all students receive check marks for doing what they need to do. Since all of you are working at your own level, check marks are given to different children for different reasons."). In Chapter 9 we will present another version of the check mark system. That one is designed to fit a resource room model.

The classroom design discussed in this chapter has been put into practice in a number of school districts in California and elsewhere. Whenever we visit some of these classes, we are struck with the individuality of the rooms. Teachers put themselves into the design, drawing what fits for them, and adding their own creative contributions. That is how it should be. We are suggesting some ideas that have worked for many teachers over the past decade or so. Hopefully, this individualization of the design to fit teachers, children, and settings will continue in the future.

chapter 8

The Special Day Class
at Elementary
and Secondary Levels

D espite the fact that current literature refers increasingly to main-streaming, least restrictive alternative, and the resource specialist, the special day class is still very much alive and healthy. There always will be some disturbed children who need to spend the majority of the school day in a self-contained environment. For some disturbed children, the period of time may only be a matter of weeks or months as they learn the basic skills of attending, responding, and following directions that will prepare them for a resource room or a regular classroom. For others, the more severely disturbed, the stay may be longer, extending through the majority of their school years.

In this chapter, we will review the daily schedule and curriculum of a special day class based on the design presented in the last chapter. We have found this design to be equally effective at the primary, elementary, and secondary levels.

How Long?

Increasingly, it is a requirement that programs for the handicapped be available for the same length of time as programs for regular students. In the past, a special day class program for handicapped children might have run from 8:00 AM to 12:30 PM with the students being dismissed before lunch. Now it is the responsibility of the school to make available a full day without imposing it on every handicapped child.

The Individual Education Program will specify the length of school day as well as the long-term goals and performance objectives for each child. Selecting the appropriate school day length for the elementary or secondary child is just as critical as selecting the correct grade level work in reading or arithmetic. While some handicapped children may remain potential winners from 8:30 AM to 3:00 PM, many will not. If the latter are forced to stay a full day, they often end up in trouble of some sort and leave school as losers. When we are able to correctly specify how long an appropriate school day should be for each child, we are making an important contribution to the orchestration of success. Thus, parents, administrators, teachers, and other professionals who participate in the conference that plans the IEP need to consider very carefully whether the child is a one-, two-, three-, four-, five-, or possibly even a six-hour attender.

A typical daily schedule for an elementary special day classroom and a typical daily schedule for a secondary special day classroom are shown in Figure 8–1 (*see* pages 246–247).

Entering the Room

In our experience, the orchestration of success depends greatly on teachers paying careful attention to small, even minute, details in the class-room program. Such careful attention can avoid confrontation and antici-pate possible problems. For example, some elementary teachers have found it very helpful to have lines drawn approximately eighteen inches apart in an assembly area or outside the door for children to line up on after the bell rings and before entering the classroom. While the teacher supervises the lining up, the aide is inside ready to give check marks to each student because "you entered in a quiet, orderly manner, picked up your work record card, and sat down ready to begin school."

At the same time the aide is giving out the check marks, he or she hands the student an order task. An example is shown in Figure 8–2 (*see* page 248). Starting the day with an order task has been found useful since it helps create a work-like atmosphere with a minimum of talking/sharing or distraction. The teacher enters the room with the last two or three students and quietly gives them their check marks and order tasks. The entire class may be given the same task or different tasks may be given to certain children.

This procedure establishes a business-like climate first thing in the morning and has been found to be more effective than the sometimes traditional:

"We are waiting for Jimmy to line up."

"I like the way Carl is standing."

"Sam, please stop pushing and go to the end of the line."

"We will have to wait until May is ready before we can go into the classroom."

In situations where such comments are necessary, the children are actually in limited control. One student can arbitrarily delay the orderly beginning of the school day for the entire class. In several instances, we have seen a teacher lean casually against the door or sit on the side of a desk as the students enter the room on their own, and wander aimlessly around amidst casual conversation or a scuffle or two. While this approach may appear more relaxed, the lack of order and direction can often actually produce tension.

Many traditional, regular classrooms start the day with a "sharing" period. We have found that in the special day class such a period is best held toward the close of the day during the exploratory period (to be discussed later) or just before students are dismissed from the classroom. We do not allow students to enter the room and browse among the centers, working or playing with the materials. The centers should be reserved for assigned tasks, earned-time activities, interventions, or "minute-catchers" when a child finishes a task at his or her desk a few minutes early and is assigned for a brief time to a center (e.g., to continue putting the class jigsaw puzzle together). Even during inclement weather when recesses or passing time must be spent in the room, it is better to bring center materials to the student's desk or the teaching station rather than to allow students to "play" at the centers themselves. This orientation toward the classroom activity centers as "assigned working areas" rather than play areas is important in creating and maintaining a business-like atmosphere in the classroom.

Elementary Daily Schedule

	Mon/Weds/Fri		Tues/Thurs	
8:45	Order task			
9:00	Individual reading		Motivation for story writing	Story
	Word study	Reading	Story writing	writing
	Skill development		Sharing	
10:10	Recess			
10:25	Practice in basic facts			
	Arithmetic instruction	Arithmetic		
	Skill development			
11:25	Language instruction (phonics, spelling, handwriting, language development)			
11:50	Lunch			
12:40	Listening (teacher reads to class)			
1:00	Art tasks			
	Science tasks			
	Communication tasks	Exploratory		
	Order tasks			

(Two exploratory tasks are selected daily. The students are divided into two groups, the teacher supervising one, the aide, the other. Both groups spend 25 minutes on each task.)

1:50	Recess
2:00	Physical education
2:20	Group and individual activities (music, current events, sharing, group discussion, individual tutoring)
3:00	End of school day

Figure 8–1. Typical daily schedules for elementary and secondary special day classrooms.

The Order Period

Devoting the first period of the day to an order activity has been found to be successful at both elementary and secondary levels. Order tasks may be simple pencil and paper activities such as maze tracing, dot connecting, perceptual-motor training exercises, locating hidden pictures, or coloring by number. With younger children and with children who have problems working with a pencil, the teacher can bring material from the Order Center for use during the order period. These should be concrete, manipulative materials (e.g., pegboard) that will serve the function of settling the child down and engaging him or her in a direction-following activity. Even with children who can successfully undertake paper and pencil order tasks, the use of a manipulative order task on occasion may introduce variety into the order period and thereby be motivational.

Order tasks may consist of commercially available work sheets or readiness ditto-type materials. Many teachers, however, prefer to develop their own materials. These are often ingenious and creative. Furthermore, they have the advantage of being conceived and prepared for a particular classroom or particular type of children. No commercial materials can achieve such individualization or personalness. Whatever the material, it is impor-

Secondary Daily Schedule

	Mon/Weds/Fri		Tues/Thurs	
8:30	Order task			
8:45	Individual reading	} Reading	Motivation for story writing	} Story writing
	Word study		Story writing	
	Skill development		Sharing	
9:25	Break			
9:30	Practice in basic facts	} Arithmetic		
	Arithmetic instruction			
	Skill development			
10:25	Break			
10:30	Spelling	} Language		
	Handwriting			
	Language development			
	Phonics			
	Grammar			

(Teacher decides on two or three activities depending on time available and students' needs. Students are grouped and rotated through them.)

11:25	Lunch	
12:15	Art tasks	} Exploratory
	Science tasks	
	Communication tasks	
	Order tasks	

(Two exploratory tasks are selected daily. The students are divided into two groups, the teacher supervising one, the aide, the other. Both groups spend 25 minutes on each task.)

1:05   Physical Education
(Students are enrolled in specialized or regular PE classes. Some students may stay in the classroom for individual tutoring.)

2:00   Electives
(Students are enrolled in appropriate electives or receive individual tutoring in the classroom. Students who cannot profit from a full day go home.)

Figure 8–1 (continued).

tant not to use tasks that require a lengthy verbal orientation by the teacher from the front of the classroom. The task should speak for itself and any instruction needed should be given by the teacher or aide at the child's desk. During such instructions, it is important for the teacher to maintain eye contact with the child and demonstrate a genuine personal interest.

As described earlier, an order task is any task that has a specific starting point and a series of intermediate steps which leads to a conclusion. Use of exercises that require a great deal of coloring or dot-to-dot connecting should be used sparingly, particularly if they are viewed as "babyish" by older students.

Depending on the child's ability, order tasks at the secondary level can become considerably more mastery-oriented. Some teachers have introduced tasks requiring the use of:

Protractors to measure angles or triangles

Compasses to construct geometric figures

Order Task   No. 6

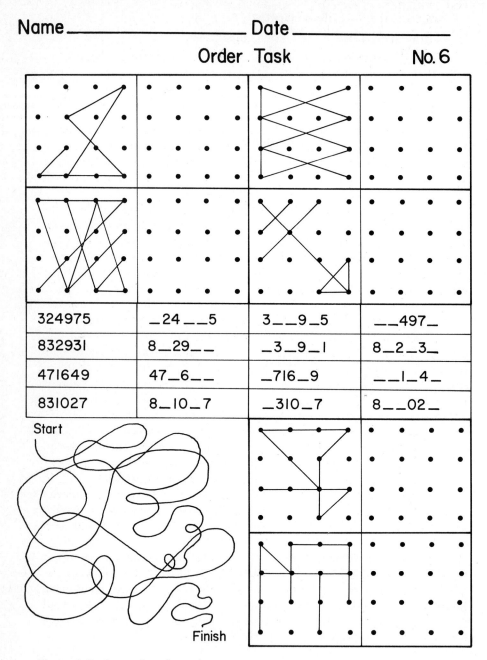

324975	_24 _ _5	3 _ _9 _5	_ _497_
832931	8_29_ _	_3_9_1	8_2_3_
471649	47_6_ _	_716_9	_ _1_4_
831027	8_10_7	_310_7	8_ _02_

Figure 8–2. A sample order task.

Rulers to measure distances

Dictionaries to use in reference-skill tasks

Telephone books to look up numbers in the regular or classified sections

Catalogues, encyclopedias, and reference books to complete simple direction-following tasks

The order period is intended as a launching learning experience. While tasks used during this period are designated as order tasks, they also provide emphasis on the attention and response levels. Thus, the first three levels of learning competence, those most basic to guaranteeing the child's success, receive initial focus at the start of each day.

To those who interpret this emphasis on guaranteeing success as indulgent and an example of babying the student, we take definite exception. The bedrock upon which we must build our program of remediating the problems of disturbed children is an attitude on the child's part of "I can," "I will," "I did." Such an attitude will not develop unless we go out of our way to keep the child successful, particularly in the early stages of our work. There will be plenty of time for challenging the child in later stages. Initially, the responsibility is ours, not the child's, for orchestrating success.

As the order period or any other work period during the day draws to a close, the teacher and aide prepare to give check marks. In so doing the teacher first gives a preliminary signal to the class that "it is almost time to stop." Notice that the term *stop* is used rather than *to be finished*. This avoids confronting and frustrating the child who simply is not going to be able to complete the assignment on time. In a minute or so the teacher says, "It's time to put down our pencils and get ready for check marks."

It is important for the teacher or aide to be near the one or two students that are not going to be able to finish and to lean over and quietly say, "I made a mistake and this assignment was a little too long to complete in the time available" or "I didn't explain this carefully enough, and it is my fault you cannot quite finish today." This is the teacher's responsibility since, as stated earlier, the teacher and aide must initially guarantee each child's success.

After the class has been alerted to "get ready for check marks" and before they are actually given the next task assignment, directions for the next activity are given. This technique of initiating the next assignment before or while giving check marks for the previous assignment helps avoid "sitting and waiting time" when students with behavior problems often get into trouble.

The Reading Period

On Monday, Wednesday, and Friday, the class is divided into three separate groups. Even though the reading program is individualized, it is helpful if the students are seated in rows somewhat by ability. There are three fifteen-to-twenty-minute assignments during the reading period. These are kept track of by a reading assignment wheel. Figure 8–3 depicts the reading wheel and the three assignments—individual reading, word study, and skill development. The inner wheel is rotated by one-third turns so that each of the rows can be assigned each of the reading activities.

To begin, the teacher calls attention to the row assignments while pointing to the wheel: "Row one, get ready for individual reading. Row two, get ready for word study. Row three, get ready for skill reading." Following this announcement, the teacher and aide administer the order-period check marks while at the same time individually introducing each student to his or her first reading activity.

Individual Reading

The individual reading activity begins with all of the students in a given row moving from their desks to the teaching station (*See* floorplans in Figures 7–1 and 7–2 in the previous chapter). By having all the students from the row come to this small-group area, situated near a chalkboard and adjacent to the study booths, it is possible for the teacher not only to conduct the individualized reading with each child in turn but to encourage the remaining two or three children to get ready for their turns by prereading in their books. It is also possible to teach some skills to the entire group, play some word games, have flash card vocabulary drills, develop some group stories, and, on occasion if appropriate, have some competitive reading in the individual work readers of each student. In addition, since there are two nearby study booths, the teacher can supervise any child in the other two reading groups who requires a mastery intervention (change of task and/or assignment to a study booth).

Each student brings his or her "work reader" to the teaching station for individual reading along with the work record card. The work reader may be a basal reading text or a remedial reader written at the student's level. In general, we have found that when students miss more than four or five words on a page of text, the grade level of the book should be lowered. However, each case must be considered individually. For some students, the teacher may initially want the child to be familiar with every word so that no errors occur. For others, the teacher may select a more challenging book in order to identify basic vocabulary words the student needs to learn more quickly.

Ideally, the students in the row assigned to individual reading should move quietly to the teaching station when the teacher directs them during the administration of the order period check marks. This will involve some sitting and waiting time on the part of the students while the teacher and aide complete the giving of check marks and assignments to the other two rows. The students assigned to individual reading have been told to begin

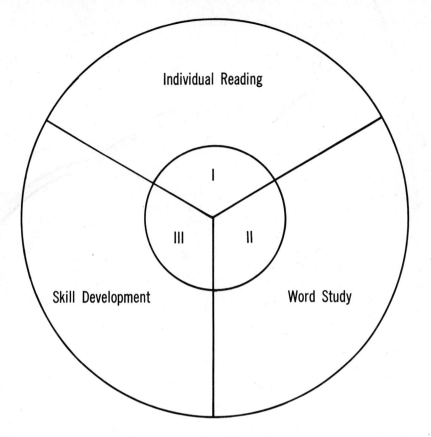

Figure 8–3. The reading wheel.

to silently practice in their work readers until the teacher arrives. For those students who follow these directions, the teacher may award bonus check marks.

Once the teacher is seated at the teaching station, the children may be engaged in a short group-activity to stimulate interest and enthusiasm, use flash cards denoting common community streets or names, or launch directly into individual reading. When starting individual reading, the first student is given a three-minute egg timer to turn over as soon as he or she is ready to begin. Once the egg timer is activated and the child begins to read, the teacher acknowledges each line of reading material read aloud correctly in one of the following ways:

1. Drops a candy (or other edible) unit in paper cup
2. Drops a plastic chip in paper cup to be counted and recorded
3. Records one check mark on a special reading work record card,

good as an exchange for fifteen minutes of free time when filled (*see* Figure 8–4)

4. Keeps a tally of all lines read correctly for later graphing on a chart

The teacher selects the acknowledgment technique that appears most suitable for the individual student. For some students the candy units are very motivating, and they "practice" diligently in order to receive them. For others, mere record-keeping is all that is necessary. Some may view the candy or chip dropping and the use of an egg timer as distracting and pressuring on the student. However, in our experience, this has seldom been the case. These two aspects of the individual reading period appear to alert the student and increase his or her level of effort.

When words are miscalled the teacher immediately corrects the student who is instructed to repeat the word aloud and then go on reading. Any word the student cannot read is provided at once. There is no sounding out of words or phonic instruction during this period. As the student is reading, the teacher keeps a record of the words missed on the reading record card shown in Figure 8–5. Notation is also made of the number of lines read correctly during the three-minute period.

Once the sand in the timer has run through, the student stops reading and is asked several comprehension questions about what was read. Then the student is given 3 x 5 inch cards with the words missed during individual reading on them. If the student has missed more words than can be comfortably handled, the teacher selects the most basic vocabulary words to be practiced later during word study.

The other students at the teaching station then take their turns. The teacher may wish to work first with the student who has the most difficulty waiting. This student can read aloud, be reinforced, and then be assigned to one of the centers in the room for the remainder of the individual reading period. This may prevent lost time at the teaching station attempting to deal with disruptive behavior. However, over time the teacher may let such a student read in second and later third place, reinforcing "turn waiting" behavior with bonus check marks and comments such as "You did a fine job waiting for your turn."

Another way to deal with students who have difficulty waiting or working independently is to use two egg timers during individual reading. The problem student reads first but only until the sand in the egg timer has run half through. At this point, the timer is turned on its side, the student is encouraged to practice the next few lines silently, and the second egg timer is used to give another student a turn. At the conclusion of the second student's turn, the problem student can stand up his or her egg timer and continue reading aloud until the remainder of the sand has run through. Thus, the student gets two short turns rather than one turn during individual reading. Once students have completed individual reading, they may be encouraged to silently read ahead in anticipation of the next day's ses-

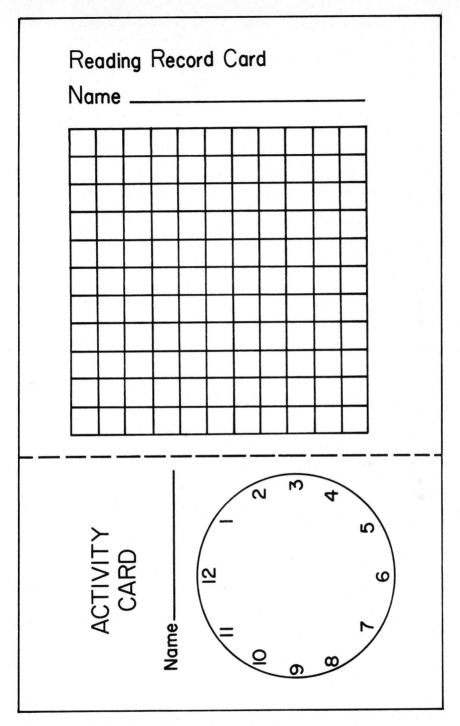

Figure 8–4. The special reading work record card.

READING RECORD

Name _____

TITLE OF BOOK	DATE	PAGES READ	LINES READ IN 3 MIN.	STUDY WORDS

Figure 8–5. The reading record card.

sion or be sent to a center until the next turn of the wheel and a new assignment.

Another approach to individual reading is to have the students read competitively in a rotation system. This is only appropriate when each student is reading in a book well within his or her reading ability and when limited competition will not threaten any student's self-confidence. Using the rotation system, each student is allowed to read and earn a reward unit for each line read correctly until a word is missed. The teacher then prints the word on a 3 x 5 file card and turns to the next student who reads aloud and earns rewards until a word is missed. This approach is often highly motivating to "waiting" students who diligently practice reading ahead so that they will not miss a word. The rotation system continues throughout individual reading with each student getting three or four turns. At the close of the period, the teacher spends a minute or two reviewing the word cards given to each student. As a result of such an approach, students may carefully count and compare the number of reward units they have earned. This comparison and competitive situation is rarely upsetting to any student provided the teacher has selected reading material for all students that is well within their ability range.

The individual reading period can also be used to teach skills necessary to use independent reading materials such as the Science Research Association (SRA) Reading Labs or the Sullivan Series. In addition, the teacher may occasionally have the students play a game such as "Word Lotto" or "Word Bingo."

While the teacher is working with the students at the teaching station, the aide is answering questions and assisting the other two rows with word study and skill development. Students who finish early or who need an intervention can be assigned to an appropriate center. As the end of the first segment of the reading period approaches, the teacher alerts the class by saying, "It is almost time to stop." Then in a minute or so, "Please put down your pencils and get ready for check marks." Following this, the teacher goes to the front of the room and turns the reading assignment wheel so that each row has a new reading activity. The teacher and aide circulate, giving check marks for the first portion of the reading period, and then they individually lead the students into the next activity.

Normally, the teacher gives check marks to those students who have had individual reading, and the aide gives check marks to those with whom he or she has worked during the period. Throughout the day, the teacher and aide try to give check marks to those children with whom they have worked during a particular period. This is especially important when problems have arisen with a given student during a work period. The person most familiar with what the student has actually done should be the one to evaluate the work and administer the check marks.

The question often arises regarding how the students perceive the teacher and aide. Will they try to pit teacher against aide, or vise versa, and complain, "She always gives me more check marks than you, so I want her to give me my check marks this time." If this occurs there is no verbal defense put forth by either teacher or aide. Both are "teachers" in the room, both are concerned about assigning the children tasks that they are ready for, need, and can be successful doing, and both are part of a working team devoted to giving each child exactly what has been earned. If such a comment is made by the student, the teacher or aide should quietly point out that "these are the check marks which you have *earned*" and quietly move on to the next student.

In general, this problem arises infrequently and is easily handled in the manner described. Of course, the importance of a close and positive working relationship between teacher and aide cannot be overemphasized. Both must be mature and objective enough not to attempt to win certain children's approval and loyalty through check mark generosity.

Word Study

The word study segment of the reading period involves review of the word cards the student has been given during individual reading. Spelling words acquired during story writing (to be discussed later) are also reviewed at this time. The aide circulates among the students, flashing the word cards in a recognition drill and dictating the spelling words. As each word is read or spelled correctly, the teacher puts a plus on it, and after three consecutive pluses, the card is filed away alphabetically in a small file box on the student's desk and no longer reviewed. It may be recalled that in the case of students who are very poor readers, the teacher does not compulsively write every word missed on a card but selects the most basic words. Similarly, during word study, the aide may not hold such a student responsible for every reading or spelling word but may select those that are most basic.

Some teachers have found the word card useful for increasing the child's vocabulary skills in other ways. For example, the following directions may be written on the reverse side of the word card:

1. Write several words that begin with the same letter.

2. Using your work reader, find and write three words with the same number of letters.

3. Look around the room and find three things that start with the same letter.

4. Using your work reader, find three words that have the same vowel sounds.

5. Write two sentences using the word.

6. Find another word in your work reader that means the same thing or about the same thing.

7. Find three words that end with the same letter.

Some teachers have found it helpful to have a separate list of very common words written prominently on the chalkboard or on separate flash cards. These words can be the days of the week or month, parts of the body, streets in the town, etc. The aide can then play some flash games or drill with these "Words of the Week" with each student.

In some cases, assignments that are open-ended and applicable to almost any word can be written on the chalkboard. These can be very similar to the word tasks written on the back of the 3 x 5 file cards. Two examples are:

Write 5 words that have the same number of letters as one of your words.

Write one of your words vertically. Find a word in your book that starts with the letters in your word.

h	have
o	our
m	many
e	ear

The purpose of all the word study tasks is to increase the vocabulary of the students. Any kind of word task which increases the students' use of words or increases their encountering new words in a success situation is a valuable experience.

As students complete their word study turn or their tasks during word study, the aide either directs them to continue studying the words independently or assigns them to one of the centers in the room.

Skill Development

During skill development, each student is given an independent vocabulary and comprehension reading assignment. A wide variety of commercial materials, including programmed units, can be used. Typical materials might be: Sullivan Readers, SRA Reading Labs or Reading for Understanding Kits, Barnell Loft materials, as well as commercial or teacher-made ditto materials. Since one of the purposes of the special day class is to prepare students for the regular class, it may be advisable to occasionally use follow-up materials that are similar to those used by the regular teachers. The significant factor to constantly keep in mind is promoting student success. The aide directs the activities, answers questions, and modifies assignments or sends students to centers if necessary during this time.

We have found that in general these three activities—individual reading, word study, and skill development—constitute a workable and effective reading program. However, they can be assigned in a more flexible manner. For example, individual reading or skill development may be assigned for two time segments rather than one if this would better meet the needs of the class. Speed reading, reference skills, or study skills can be taught during individual reading to secondary or more advanced students. For beginning readers, the individual reading period may focus on group reading readiness activities. In fact, group activities related to reading and spelling at any level are appropriate to engage in during this period. Of course, any student who is not ready to participate in any type of reading activity may be assigned to a center.

The Story-Writing Period

The reading period usually occurs three times weekly on Monday, Wednesday, and Friday. Twice a week, on Tuesday and Thursday, story writing is focused on during this period. The use of the first major period of the day for reading and written language work has been found more successful than waiting until late morning or afternoon when students may be tired and restless in school. Since these mastery areas are often difficult for children with learning problems and are the ones they have had the most discomfort with in the past, taking advantage of the early part of the day when students are apt to be fresher and more alert is only logical.

Story writing is done by the entire class rather than by rows as was the case with reading. Usually the teacher takes fifteen minutes to present a short motivation lesson in some area of interest to the class (e.g., knighthood, deep-sea life, the circus, or some current event). Filmstrips, movies, and the sharing of experiences by the children, themselves, are utilized. This is one period when the class is dealt with as a group in a manner similar to a regular classroom. Check marks are given at the close of the fifteen-minute motivation segment, and each student is given a sheet of composition paper to write on. Depending on the level of the student, story writing may consist of the writing of a single sentence, a caption placed under a picture the child has drawn, or the dictation of a story to the teacher or aide.

A story-writing sequence gradually increasing in complexity that has been successfully used with disturbed children is as follows:

1. Child draws picture, teacher prints title below it.

2. Child draws picture and copies title from teacher's model.

3. Child draws picture and dictates one-sentence description which teacher prints (then two-, three-sentence, etc.).

4. Child copies story from chalkboard and illustrates.

5. Child dictates story to teacher who types or prints it.

6. Child dictates story and writes in any words he or she can spell.

7. Child and teacher alternate writing sentences. Teacher writes any word not known by child.

8. Child writes story and teacher provides words on 3 x 5 cards which child studies, says aloud, and writes on back of card while saying aloud. Child then puts word in story.*

It is often very motivating to let students draw a picture related to the story they are writing on the top, side, or bottom of the page. For students that have difficulty drawing, it is helpful to have old mailorder or department store catalogues or magazines available to cut pictures from to glue on the story page. Regardless of the level of the child, an attempt is made to get some writing from each student. As they write, the students are assured that any word they need will be given to them by the teacher.

Toward the end of the story-writing period, the teacher may select several of the stories that have been written to read them to the class. In some cases, the teacher may encourage selected students to read their stories and show their pictures to the class.

---

*This technique (number 8) is similar to Stage 2 of the Fernald (1947) method. Kinesthetic tracing, or Stage 1 of that method, involves presenting the child with needed words that have been written in large cursive form on 4 x 10 inch newsprint slips.

Students who cannot write for more than a few minutes may be given reading activity sheets when they finish their stories, or they may be sent to one of the centers in the room. At the end of the period, the class gets ready for recess. A set routine is usually followed at this time. The students are dismissed by rows, they put their work record cards back in the holder, then they line up by the door or go directly outside.

Depending on the type of behavior problems the students exhibit, it may be necessary for either the aide or the teacher to take the elementary level students to the playground area and provide "in the general area" supervision. At the secondary level, students who are integrated part-time in the regular school program and who can function appropriately are dismissed to do whatever they wish for the passing-time period. At both the elementary and secondary levels, students who cannot function successfully during recess or passing time are provided activities within the room. These can consist of playing games, reading magazines, or having discussions at the teaching station with either the teacher or aide. Supervising a student in this manner should not be viewed as punitive since it really is an effort to provide a place where the student can be successful and not have to experience failure in the halls or on the playground. As soon as these individually supervised students and the teachers believe that the students can be successful on their own, they should be dismissed with the rest of the class and given encouragement through bonus check marks and appropriate comments. Of course, the teacher and aide will obviously need to make arrangements to be sure each of them has time for appropriate breaks during the day.

At this point in the discussion, some may wonder if placing children in a more open playground situation after holding them to the planned routine of the classroom design discussed here will produce a "cork out of the bottle" effect. Will old maladaptive behavior patterns erupt with fury because of demands for conformity in the classroom? This has not been found to occur. Although Lewin, Lippitt, and White (1939) found that "authoritarian" climates produced eruptions of misbehavior whenever the authoritarian adult left children unsupervised, the inclusion of a degree of child-centered structure and the "working partner" role of the teacher in the classroom itself can preclude this from occurring. Structured, yes; rigidly authoritarian, no.

When the bell rings at the end of recess or passing time between classes, or at the end of lunch, the students return to the room and either line up or enter and pick up their work record cards. The teacher and aide immediately circulate around the room and give check marks based on observed behavior during recess or passing time. Since the teacher or aide may wish to stand in or near the doorway and observe the students as they enter and leave, comments and check marks may also focus on this behavior. As check marks are given, the next task can be passed out along with such typical comments as:

George, you earned five check marks because you entered and left the classroom quietly and five bonus check marks because you have your pencil and are ready to go to work. You are doing a fine job at recess time. Here is your next task. [Quickly explain the task.] Please raise your hand if you need help.

Carl, you only earned three of your five check marks because you started to run when you left the classroom. Next time, you can earn all five check marks if you walk in and out. You did do a good job sitting down quietly and taking out your pencil and you have earned all five bonus check marks. Here is your next task. [Quickly explain the task.] Please raise your hand if you need help.

The Arithmetic Period

As the teacher and aide are giving check marks, and during the time they are quickly explaining the first arithmetic task, they may refer to the arithmetic wheel (*see* Figure 8–6). Three colors—blue, red, and green— are used as a basis for grouping children who are functioning at similar levels in arithmetic. In our experience, even in classrooms with students ranging in ability from first through sixth grades or in classrooms with secondary-level students ranging over three or four grades, these individual differences can be dealt with by three groupings or by three groupings with a subgrouping in one or more of them.

Once the teacher has grouped children at similar levels, he or she gives them a small piece of construction paper in the color corresponding to their grouping assignment (or a geometric figure or some other symbol for secondary students). This is taped to their desks, and they are informed that during the arithmetic period they will participate in the activity on the outer wheel that is paired with the same color or symbol on the inner wheel. Of the ten to twelve students in the special day class, it is not unusual to have three or four students in the red (low) group, five or six students in the green (middle) group, and two or three students in the blue (high) group. As students make progress in arithmetic, it is a simple matter to change them from one group to another by changing the color of the construction paper taped on their desks.

The fifteen-to-twenty-minute arithmetic activities are listed on the three segments of the outer wheel. These are: arithmetic instruction, skill development, and practice in basic facts.

Arithmetic Instruction

This group joins the teacher at the teaching station. In this setting, which is near a chalkboard, the teacher presents an instructional lesson.

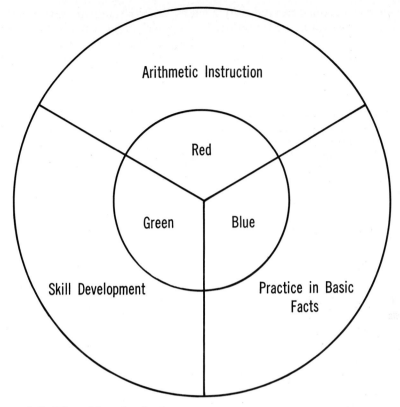

Figure 8–6. The arithmetic wheel.

Teachers are encouraged to use a variety of methods and materials including manipulatives, chalkboard exercises, magic slates, work sheets, inexpensive electronic calculators, commercial materials, kits, textbooks, and teacher-made lessons and materials.

Many teachers have found that it is advisable to begin the arithmetic period with the low group at arithmetic instruction first since students at this level may have only limited recall of the previous day's lesson. Such lack of recall presents a problem if these students start with follow-up or basic drill which are related to the previous day's lesson. However, if the lesson is presented first with the related follow-up and drill coming during the succeeding periods, the problem with recall is not encountered.

Skill Development

This segment involves students working independently at their desks on a lesson that reinforces or provides practice for the lesson taught by the teacher either that day or the day before. Experience suggests that teachers start the high group here since they will be doing an assignment based on the previous day's "working with teacher" lesson. Again, many commercial (e.g., SRA Computational Math Kits, Singer Math Kits) and teacher-made materials can be used for this follow-up assignment, which provides reinforcing practice for the instruction provided during "working with the teacher."

Practice in Basic Facts

During this segment the students practice the basic combinations. For elementary students, this may involve practice on addition, subtraction, multiplication, or division facts. For example:

$$\begin{array}{cccc} 3 & 4 & 6 & 5\overline{)25} \\ +2 & -1 & \times 3 \end{array}$$

Many students who have not mastered such basic facts have spent endless hours practicing them in this form. For this reason, it is often a good idea to "camouflage" the form by using a little imagination and creativity. Upper-elementary and secondary students can learn some basic fractions while practicing those tiresome but important combinations. For example:

$$\frac{1}{3} \times \frac{3}{4} = \qquad \frac{3}{4} \times \frac{1}{3} = \qquad \frac{3}{5} \times \frac{1}{8} = \qquad \frac{2}{5} \times \frac{1}{4} =$$

$$\begin{array}{ccc} \dfrac{3}{14} & \dfrac{13}{20} & \dfrac{5}{30} \\ + & + & + \\ \dfrac{2}{14} & \dfrac{3}{20} & \dfrac{10}{30} \end{array}$$

The actual operations involved here are identical to the more traditional $\frac{4}{\times 3}$ and $\frac{3}{+2}$ but involve a novel and more interesting format.

Open-ended work sheets such as shown in Figure 8–7 are also useful in breaking down the monotony of practicing basic arithmetic combinations. For some students, numbers under 10 such as 3 and 5 may be put in the centers of the circles with the instruction to multiply that number by each of the numbers in the middle ring and then to put the answer in the outer ring. For students needing practice in a different skill, numbers (e.g., 38, 247, 412, to give some random examples) may be put in the center circle with the instruction to add them to the numbers in the middle ring. There are many ways this format can be used, and teachers can adapt it to the level of any student. Interestingly enough, this individualized system for basic arithmetic drill first appeared in a math book published in 1889.

Several hypothetical lessons that might be given during the arithmetic period for several levels of students are as follows:

Name_____Date_____

Arithmetic Circles No. 15
+ X — ÷

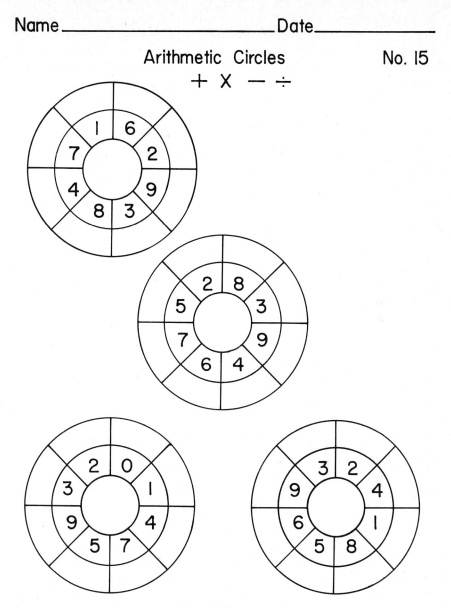

Figure 8–7. A sample open-ended work sheet.

For the Primary Student

Arithmetic Instruction
1. Actually make paper clocks and work on learning to tell time.
2. Use Cusinairre rods and work on the concept of subtraction.
3. Match concrete objects with numbers.

Skill Development
1. Practice drawing "hands" on ditto clock faces for various times during the day.
2. Independently use Cusinairre rods to do subtraction problems.
3. Compile a ditto page of matching objects and numbers and color the pictures.
Practice in Basic Facts
1. Practice basic addition facts using beads, and record answers on a teacher-prepared ditto.

For the Elementary Student

Arithmetic Instruction
1. Learn to measure with a ruler.
2. Cut up various pieces of paper and learn about fractions.
3. Learn a new skill in multiplication.
Skill Development
1. Practice measuring lines or parts of the desk.
2. Practice identifying pictures with fractions.
3. Practice some problems similar to those taught during arithmetic instruction.
Practice in Basic Facts
1. Practice in basic multiplication or division.

For the Secondary Student

Arithmetic Instruction
1. Learn to use a protractor.
2. Learn to use a simple slide rule.
3. Learn to use a simple calculator.
Skill Development
1. Practice measuring angles on triangles.
2. Practice doing simple slide-rule problems.
3. Practice using the calculator to do simple or complex problems.
Practice in Basic Facts
1. Practice some simple fraction combinations that reinforce multiplication tables.

As each segment of the arithmetic period draws to a close, the aide who has been working with students doing skill development assignments and practice in basic facts signals the teacher that "it is almost time to stop." The segments are usually fifteen to twenty minutes in length, but if the skill development or basic practice is extra easy on a given day the segment can be shortened. This may be preferable to holding on for a longer time and having to send all the students to various centers because they have finished too early.

Following the third fifteen-minute arithmetic segment, the children receive check marks and are provided with a second recess or a recess/nutrition period. Snacks may be brought from home or they may be obtained from the school cafeteria; these are eaten in the room. Children are normally free to move about and talk informally together. However, they are not permitted to "play" with the materials at the centers. Some teachers have provided a separate "free time" shelf with magazines, games, and activities not utilized at the centers to be used by students during the times they must spend recess, nutrition, or lunch in the room.

The Language Period

Check marks are given following the recess/nutrition period and students are instructed to get ready for the language period (language development, grammar, handwriting, spelling, etc.). The only significant difference between the elementary and secondary programs is that at the secondary level, language probably constitutes a forty-five-to-fifty-minute period in itself, while at the elementary level, it takes up a shorter part of the morning program.

A wide variety of activities, depending on the ages and skill of the students, have been used during the language period. Some of these activities are:

1. Peabody Language Development Kits which give easily understood, specific directions for each lesson. Many of these lessons can be adapted for the secondary level.

2. Phonics lessons, exercises, and activities. These have been equally effective in improving word attack skills, spelling, and minor speech articulation problems. The authors and many of the teachers working with us have found the Phono-Visual, Bethena Maryland, and Anita Johnson systems to be particularly effective. The materials are multi-level (kindergarten–high school) and have teachers' manuals requiring virtually no teacher preparation time.

3. Formalized spelling, with actual spelling books selected at appropriate grade levels, has been effective for more skillful upper-secondary students.

4. Formal grammar lessons, including punctuation and capitalization, are often included for the more skillful upper-elementary and secondary students.

5. We have introduced speech and debate during this time for secondary students. The *Toastmasters International Beginners Speech Manual* has interesting ideas that can be a resource for the creative teacher. One adaptation, which has been very successful, is to have each student think of several topics for a speech and write each on a separate slip of paper. These are then placed in a hat and each student walks to the front of the room, draws a topic, and then speaks on it for three minutes. This can be embellished by having rating sheets for quality and a small trophy that the winner can keep until the next speech-giving day.

6. Many teachers have introduced classroom discussions during this time. These can be patterned after Glasser's "Classroom Discussion," Pelmaro's "Classroom Circle," or Shaftels's "Unfinished Story" concept. These discussions can be very effective in getting students to express feelings and concerns and basic conceptions about the world in which they live.

7. Many of the materials designed for English as a Second Language (ESL) are excellent. They provide activities that teach the concepts that many of the handicapped in special day classes need to practice.

At both the elementary and secondary levels, the language period should be divided into fifteen-to-twenty-minute segments with changing assignments or activities. Students can be given check marks between the activities as well as at the end of the period before being dismissed for lunch.

In practice, we have found that most special education students can be taken to the school cafeteria or lunch area to eat lunch with the rest of the students. After a fifteen-to-twenty-minute lunch eating period, all students are generally dismissed to a play area for a twenty-to-thirty-minute period.

Several modifications may be necessary if some students cannot function in the relatively unstructured lunch-time setting:

1. The students may take their work record cards with them to lunch and receive check marks for: (1) walking to the lunch area, (2) their behavior during the eating period, (3) their conduct going to the play area, and (4) the nature of their interactions with other students during the play period. This means that the aide or teacher must accompany the students during lunch. However, it has been found that this can be phased out after a few weeks for the majority of students.

2. Students who have great difficulty in any unstructured situation may eat in the classroom and then engage in some activity during the play period. Of course, this is subject to the availability of supervision. We are not suggesting that teachers never have breaks or private lunch hours. We are merely suggesting options that can be considered. As mentioned earlier with respect to keeping children in from recess, this should not be considered a punishment but rather a special effort to help the student avoid failure experiences on the playground. As such a student makes progress, he or she can be given short free-play periods on the playground. Gradually, these time periods can be extended. Check marks with appropriate comments can be used to reinforce improved playground behavior at the end of the lunch period.

The Listening Period

Students may not always readily settle down to work after returning to the room from lunch. In order to gradually reintroduce them back into a learning environment, a short, ten-to-twenty-minute listening period is held immediately after the students enter the room and receive check marks.

The value of listening activities in general, and reading aloud to disturbed children in particular, has been discussed earlier. The teacher may select a children's classic with high interest value to the students and read a portion of a chapter each day. With younger children, teachers have often selected short books with pictures that can be read in fifteen to twenty minutes. The book can then be put in a center for students to browse through, or it can be made available to students to check out.

Secondary students may develop a continuing interest in longer stories and follow the events, characters, and suspense of the story. Many teachers have developed the technique of teaching listening skills and increasing comprehension during the listening period. Using one effective technique, the teacher pauses occasionally and asks a question about what has been read.

Several skills are being taught or reinforced during the listening period:

1. Learning to listen
2. Increasing recall ability of events heard several minutes before
3. Increasing comprehension skills
4. Learning to raise one's hand when one wants to talk
5. Learning to enjoy books

Check marks are given for the listening period as they are for all of the periods of the day. While checks are being given, the exploratory period is introduced.

The Exploratory Period

The exploratory period is the next period of the day. It is designed to engage students in highly stimulating and interesting activities below the mastery level and to provide a full range of rewards, including social attention, task completion, multisensory experience, and social approval, as well as routine check marks. Students have opportunities to work together, take turns, share, and learn to be a good winner or loser.

This period is divided into two segments of about twenty to twenty-five minutes each. Half the students are engaged in an activity with the aide while the other half are working with the teacher. Typical activities are science, art, and communication activities which are centered around card games, Monopoly, Bingo, Chutes and Ladders, or other commercial games that emphasize rules, taking turns, and sharing.

In practice, half the students may go to the Exploratory Center to work on an art task with the aide. This task may be finger painting, working with clay, drawing with crayons, or a craft project. The aide explains the task, passes out materials that are needed, and helps the students for the twenty-to-twenty-five-minute time segment. At the same time the other students are with the teacher learning to play a card game or a game like "Monopoly." The emphasis here is on taking turns and sportsmanship. Teachers often use the teaching station discussed earlier in the arithmetic and reading sections for this exploratory activity. This area provides a setting in which five or six students can work with the teacher while the other five or six students are in the Exploratory Center. The teacher and aide should work in the area where they have the greatest expertise and not make any one activity strictly the teacher's or the aide's domain.

Prior to the end of the first time segment, students should be alerted that they will be stopping in about one minute. This notice is given by either the teacher or the aide depending on the type of activities in progress. Students then clean up the two areas and return to their desks for check marks.

The students that were with the aide now go to the alternate activity with the teacher, while the students that were with the teacher now go with the aide. It is important to have the students return to their desks and not just move from one center to the other. This provides practice in passing in close quarters, gives the teacher and aide a chance to do some very quick "getting ready for the next group," and avoids a roadblock in case one or more students take an extra minute or two leaving the work area.

When students delay leaving a center and have to be reminded over and over, problems can arise. If students are not expected to return to their desks, there may be a head-on collision with new students coming for their second exploratory period. If it takes a minute or two to get one or more students away from an exploratory area, the teacher may have another listening period. While that is being conducted, the problem student can be ushered to his or her seat by the aide. After such a listening period, the students move to their next assigned area as already described. This procedure of shifting to an alternate group-type activity led by the teacher or aide while the other solves an immediate problem can be used at any time during the day if necessary. Some other holding activities that have been used in this type of problem situation are: "Simon Says"; "Thumbs-up, Seven-up"; "Bingo,"; "Clap Echo" (teacher claps a rhythm and a student is asked to replicate it).

At the conclusion of the second exploratory segment, students are first alerted and then asked to return to their desks for check marks. They are then dismissed for recess at the elementary level or passing to the next class (physical education in the gym) at the secondary level. At the secondary level, students can go directly to a physical education class, while at the elementary level students return to the room following recess.

The Physical Education Period

Once the elementary students are at their desks, check marks are given and the students are instructed to get ready for physical education. They are then dismissed by rows and line up at the door. Sometimes it is useful to have the students take their work record cards with them to the playground so that they may be given check marks in the actual setting where physical education takes place. Once the students are on the playground, the work record cards are picked up by the aide, checks are given for "leaving the room," and play is initiated under the supervision of a PE teacher. In addition to lining up and going to the play area as a group supervised by teacher and/or aide, some students who have demonstrated appropriate school adjustment skills may be allowed to go to the area and return on their own.

During physical education, the students may engage in a single game such as four-square, handball, volleyball, or kickball, or divide into smaller groups for more individualized recreational activities. Since some disturbed students possess limited sports skills, are poor team members, and are easily upset by competition and particularly by the threat of losing, the teacher or aide attempts to get them involved in the game or activity which they enjoy and can handle successfully.

Once the physical education period is over, the students line up and are given their work record cards. Check marks for "being a student" during the period are administered, and the group returns to the classroom after opportunities for going to the drinking fountain and the restroom are provided. Once in the room and at their desks, the students receive additional check marks for "returning and being ready to work." With some students, it has been found useful to have the PE teacher give check marks in the play area or send notes praising a particularly "good day" during the physical education period.

Special, adaptive, physical education classes may be necessary for some students. Here highly individualized approaches are used. For others, physical education game participation may be delayed until appropriate behavior skills are acquired. This can be specified in the IEP and is another illustration of making every effort to ensure success.

At the elementary level, the physical education period usually lasts twenty to twenty-five minutes. At the secondary level, it often includes a shower and lasts forty-five to fifty-five minutes. Thus, time for additional activities to round out the school day is left for the elementary students. These may include: current events and sharing, music, or individual tutoring.

The teacher and aide administer the final check marks for the day following any additional activity. All that remains to be done is the totaling of all check marks received for the day and the entering of these on the work report, the 8½ x 11 inch histogram depicted in Figures 7–7 and 7–8 in the last chapter. The teacher or aide and the student quickly add up the day's total and draw a line at the appropriate point on the graph. The students fill in the column below the line and compare their functioning that day with previous days.

The teacher then dismisses the class by rows, and as the students leave the room, they return their work record cards to the work record holder. In general, no homework assignments are given students in the special day class. The small class size, individualization of instruction, and work orientation of the program allows for much more work to be accomplished than would take place with these students in a regular classroom. Hence, there is seldom a need for outside assignments. However, as students approach the point of return to a regular classroom, homework may be introduced as a transition aid. Homework is so often a source of conflict and anxiety for disturbed children with learning problems and their parents. Its removal, at least initially, in a special class program is often useful.

This chapter and the last have introduced a classroom design, including operations, schedule, and curriculum. The design represents an attempt to translate the concept of the orchestration of success into actual classroom practice. Despite an emphasis on structure and routine, it provides opportunities for teacher flexibility and creativity and is essentially a framework within which "good teaching" may take place on a highly individualized basis rather than being a rigid and arbitrary system. As has been stated earlier, the personality, previous experience, sense of timing, and specialized teaching skills of the teachers will create unique classroom environments which will make classes following this model different, one from the other.

In the next chapter we will examine an extension of the orchestration-of-success concept to a resource specialist program.

chapter 9

The Resource Specialist Program at Elementary and Secondary Levels

The special day class concept has been giving way to the concept of a resource room or resource specialist program for a number of years. In this chapter we will discuss this resource-type of program which aims at maintaining the disturbed child at least part-time in a regular classroom. A resource specialist program goes beyond the idea of a special resource room in the school to which students come for part-time, individual, or small-group instruction. It encompasses the concept of the itinerant, special education teacher who may call out students for instruction or who may go into regular classrooms and work individually or on a small-group basis with students. The resource specialist program may also include several teachers and aides who work in a variety of settings with students who have special learning needs.

A distinguishing factor in the emerging resource specialist concept is the movement away from labeling and traditional compartmentalization in providing special education services. Part of the rationale behind the rigid special day class approach is not difficult to understand. It was felt that if handicapped children were protected from competing with their more able peers, provided with a more appropriate curriculum in smaller classes, and taught by specially trained teachers, they would attain their highest potential. However, the research literature has not validated this rationale (Bruininks & Rynders, 1971). In the late 1960s, many parents and educators began to question the desirability of traditional self-contained classrooms for mildly handicapped children. Labeling, damage to self-concept, compartmentalization, concerns by minority groups, and loss of stimulating opportunities became matters of increasing concern. Also, as identification of various types of exceptionalities increased, each of which needed a special classroom and a specially trained teacher, it became more difficult for smaller school districts to offer a full range of special classes.

The Role of the Resource Specialist

There are many versions of resource specialist programs in operation across the nation. We will not attempt to review all of them; instead we will describe such a program developed in the state of California in the Santa Monica schools.

Some of the state of California's regulations governing the operation of the resource specialist program illustrate the role of the resource specialist.

ARTICLE 3, SECTION 3321, (b) Role and caseload of the resource specialist shall include:

1. Only pupils whose needs are identified in a written instructional plan, who are assigned to regular classroom teachers for a majority of the school day, and who are provided either instruction or services or both by the resource specialist.

a. Instruction is working with pupils individually or in small groups for regularly scheduled periods of time on goals and objectives described in the written instructional plan. This instruction shall be *given by the resource specialist in any appropriate setting* [italics added], including the regular classroom.
b. Service is assistance given a pupil on a regularly scheduled basis *through the resource specialist aide* [italics added] or the regular classroom teacher under the direction of the resource specialist.

2. The caseload of the resource specialist shall not exceed 24 pupils.

3. The resource specialist may also provide, in addition to the caseload in (b) (2), *coordinative and consultative services* [italics added]. Coordinative and consultative services are:
a. *Coordinating the recommendations* [italics added] of the SAT* with the staff and parents.
b. Providing *consultative services, resource information, and materials* [italics added] regarding individuals with exceptional needs to staff and parents.
c. Coordination of educational *services and guidance for individuals with exceptional needs and their parents* [italics added]. (California Administrative Code, TITLE V, ARTICLE 3, SECTION 3321, D–124).

The italicized sections in the code section suggest the wide range of activities that are required in the resource specialist program and further emphasize a "program" as opposed to a "teacher" concept of services. The program as originally funded and designed was to be implemented with 1 resource specialist for every 600 regular students, anticipating that about 4 percent of the population, or 24 students, would need services. However, the actual number of children served has varied up and down with 28 students appearing to be the upper limit if the services described are going to be provided. Because of these variations in numbers served and the sizes of schools and school districts, different models have emerged in California.

Some Common Resource Specialist Program Models

One Resource Specialist Program in One School

By far, the most common model is one resource specialist program which is responsible to the students, parents, and staff of one elementary

---

*This is the School Appraisal Team—the local school level assessment and planning committee that develops and monitors the student's Individual Education Program.

or secondary school. This occurs when the overall student population varies from 500 to 700. In this model, the actual resource specialist does not have to contend with traveling, being off-campus, or working with more than one group of students, parents, teachers, and administrators. It is much easier to arrange a schedule that is convenient for the teachers and to have opportunities before school, at recess, at lunch time, or after school for casual conversations with teachers or more formal conferences with parents. The resource specialist can also observe students during activities in their regular classrooms and perhaps work with them in that setting.

One Resource Specialist Operating a Program in Several Schools

When one resource specialist is serving more than one elementary or secondary school, an already demanding job is compounded. Various types of half- or part-time assignments have been tried. In some cases, the resource specialist goes to one school in the morning and to another in the afternoon. While this has the advantage of daily contact with students, time is lost traveling each day and there is virtually no opportunity for casual teacher conversation which does much to build a team-type rapport. It also limits the resource specialist's ability to plan the best time during the day to help the student and limits the time available for parent conferences or appraisal team meetings.

In situations where the resource specialist goes to one school on Monday, Wednesday, and Friday and to another school on Tuesday and Thursday, other problems occur. For some teachers in Monday–Wednesday–Friday schools, Tuesday and Thursday may be better days for releasing children to the resource specialist and vice versa. In addition, maintaining a fixed schedule may interfere with special school and classroom events that can be worked around when there is a full-time resource specialist in each school. One possible solution to this problem is to have a full-time aide at each school. The aide can maintain a flexible schedule when necessary, thus covering the resource specialist who must maintain a more rigid schedule.

Multiple Resource Specialists Operating a Program in One School

In larger elementary or secondary schools, it is often necessary to have two, three, or four resource specialists. Several different staffing models have emerged in an effort to provide less duplication and a wider range of services.

1. The resource specialists are assigned to a particular grade level but have the same basic duties and responsibilities.

2. One resource specialist has a limited instructional caseload and is responsible for the testing and assessment of all the students in the program. The responsibility also includes attending all assessment team meetings, holding parent conferences, and completing all forms. The other resource specialists are primarily involved in instruction.

3. Each resource specialist has his or her own basic caseload but develops a specialized skill such as vocational/career education, comprehensive IEP development, or work experience supervision.

4. Each resource specialist responds to the referrals as they are submitted and is responsible for the full range of duties typical of a one-specialist school. This is probably the most common practice since schools usually start with one or two specialists and then additional specialists are added as more students are identified.

Instructional Aides

It is relatively common for the resource specialist program to utilize instructional aides. The instructional aide may actually do a great deal of instruction, particularly when the resource specialist is covering more than one school or has a large number of students to evaluate for appraisal team meetings. Depending on the local school district policy, instructional aides may work with students without the resource specialist being present as long as such work is deemed to be under the direction of the specialist.

In addition to instruction, aides may be asked to score papers, report grades, prepare instructional materials, and schedule the calendar for monitoring the student's progress in the regular classroom. Students are sometimes able to relate better on a personal basis to nonteachers. Even though we earlier stressed presenting the aide as a "teacher," the children are very aware of who the real teacher is. They may view the aide as someone with whom they can share their problems and concerns. In a similar way, aides may be seen as less of a professional rival to the regular classroom teacher. The resource specialist can assign an aide to a regular class in which there are several students who are eligible for special education services. The teacher in the classroom then decides on the aide's specific duties. Placing aides in regular classrooms to work with disturbed students has been done with great success and has benefited the students by giving them more support, but in a less restrictive environment.

Several factors to consider when recruiting and training instructional aides are:

1. Attempt to select people who can be objective, who do not have a "rescue fantasy" expecting to "save" any child with whom they work, and who have had some educational or work experience that has given them a good self-concept.

2. Attempt to make all student Individual Education Programs avail-

able so there will be an understanding of long- and short-term objectives.

3. Encourage participation in the appraisal team meetings or other staff discussions, whenever appropriate, to build the feeling of being an involved team member.

4. Provide initial and on-going in-service meetings to increase academic, behavior management, and interpersonal skills.

The whole concept of a resource specialist program is relatively new, and the duties and responsibilities of the aide are still somewhat undefined. This lack of definition, however, may be positive since it offers real opportunities to be innovative in developing ways to utilize this additional resource person. Should the aide be one person who works six hours each day, or a combination of several people who work two or three hours each? Should the aide take over all of the resource specialist's clerical duties? In studying the cost effectiveness of the funds allocated for the aide, is it better for the program and economically feasible to have one full-time aide for whom fringe benefits must be paid by the district or to have several part-time aides who do not qualify for such benefits?

Services Provided by the Resource Specialist Program

Many resource specialist programs in various parts of the country have caseloads varying from twenty to thirty students who actively receive instruction or services on a regular basis. In addition, the resource specialist is responsible for the testing, evaluation, and development of an Individual Education Program; participation in the appraisal team meeting; and coordination of the school day for each of his or her students. This requires a carefully planned schedule allowing time for both instruction and administrative duties. The typical daily schedule for the elementary and secondary resource specialists in the Santa Moncia schools allows about half the time for instruction and half for administration. At the elementary level, morning and afternoon recesses and lunch time delineate four general blocks of time. At the secondary level, the typical six-period day allows three periods for instruction and three periods for administrative duties.

Resource specialists are encouraged to divide their time in the manner that best serves their school. This will vary from school to school and from grade level to grade level. Even though it is often tempting to serve a few students needing instruction during the time set aside for administration, particularly if pressure is exerted to do so by the principal and other teachers, this should be avoided. The successful resource specialist must use the administration time to test, observe, formulate IEP's, participate in appraisal team meetings, hold conferences with parents and teachers, and fulfill the necessary record-keeping duties.

Typical daily schedules for elementary and secondary resource specialist programs are shown in Figure 9–1.

The actual instructional techniques and materials used in the resource specialist program in Santa Monica are not markedly different from those described in our discussion of the special day class in Chapter 8. The teacher and aide continue to approach each student as a "learner" and to focus on improving readiness for regular classroom functioning as well as on academic skills.

This readiness concept grew out of the Madison School Plan (Hewett with Forness, 1977) and is concerned with four basic behaviors or abilities that all students must have in order to function successfully in the regular classroom:

1. The first set of behaviors includes the ability to pay attention, respond, follow directions, take part verbally, and follow reasonable classroom rules.

2. The second set of behaviors includes the academic abilities of being neat, being correct, and developing increased ability to read, spell, write, and do arithmetic.

3. The third set of behaviors requires that the child must be able to function in the different instructional settings that occur in the regular classroom— when the teacher is giving directions from the front of the room, when the child is working in a small group, and when the child is working independently. Differing kinds of concentration or atten-

Elementary Daily Schedule		Secondary Daily Schedule	
8:45	Instruction	8:30	
10:00	Recess	Period 1	Instruction
			Passing
10:15	Administration	Period 2	Instruction
			Passing
11:45	Lunch	Period 3	Administration
			Lunch
12:34	Instruction	Period 4	Instruction
			Passing
1:50	Recess	Period 5	Administration
			Passing
2:00	Administration	Period 6	Administration
3:00	End of day	3:15	End of day

Figure 9–1. Typical daily schedules for elementary and secondary resource specialist programs.

tion are required when the entire class is reading silently for information as opposed to when the teacher is explaining a new concept at the chalkboard.

4. The fourth area is related to the student's susceptibility to regular classroom consequences. While some children are motivated by report card grades, others are encouraged by a smile or a word of praise from the teacher. Some are eager to learn because of the satisfaction they receive when they acquire knowledge or skill.

During the instruction time, the resource specialist focuses on these four basic sets of behaviors or abilities necessary for success in the regular classroom. In order to help maintain a continuous assessment of each student's progress, the check mark system described earlier is continued in a modified form. The title of the card itself is changed from work record card to recognition card and the number of spaces are reduced since the student never spends more than half a day in the program. An example is seen in Figure 9–2.

In general, completed cards can be exchanged for fifteen minutes of free time or a "take-a-chance" card as in the special day class program. Candy and other edibles may be used in individual cases, but they rarely seem necessary. Check marks are given in two categories: (1) a possible five are given for the student's performance with the instructional tasks (reading, history, arithmetic, spelling, English, etc.), and (2) an additional five bonus check marks are possible for behavior or "being a student."

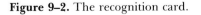

Figure 9–2. The recognition card.

The specialist or aide in the resource specialist program might have one of the following interactions with an elementary or secondary student during the administration of check marks:

Carl, you have earned five check marks because your paper is much neater, and all your math problems are completed. You have earned your five bonus check marks because you listened carefully when I was giving directions from the front of the room.

Mary, you have earned five check marks because you read today with fewer mistakes, and you have earned all five bonus check marks because you paid attention, followed directions, and worked very well by yourself. Students need to learn these skills if you are going to be successful in the regular classroom.

Frank, you earned five check marks because your spelling paper was much neater. You put the date and your name on the top. You earned three of your five bonus check marks because you worked better in a large group today. Next time you can earn all your bonus check marks if you listen more carefully and do not raise your hand so many times for help. Teachers do not have time to give each spelling word over and over again so we must learn to listen carefully.

These examples emphasize the importance of providing students with meaningful feedback if we expect them to improve their skills for regular classroom adjustment. As stated before, one of the real advantages of the check mark system is that it forces the teacher or resource specialist to interact with each individual student every fifteen to twenty minutes in a meaningful way that gives the student specific information regarding what is expected. This interaction between student and aide or student and specialist is very similar to the interaction described with respect to the special day class. The most significant difference in a resource specialist program is that the interchange is more mastery-oriented. The focus is on the kinds of behaviors and skills regular teachers expect (e.g., following group directions, working in a large group, listening carefully to a presentation by the teacher or to a group discussion, avoiding interruptions, or keeping questions until the end of discussion period). The specialist and aide should still use objective statements about the student's actual work and accomplishments but should also use social praise more frequently (e.g., "I am really pleased with the way you did this assignment.").

It is also still important to have centers in the resource room and to use them for interventions for promoting success with a student whenever necessary. The whole intervention strategy as discussed earlier should still be utilized when appropriate. It is not unusual for the resource specialist to use one or more of these interventions when giving directions or lecturing from the front of the room. For example, the resource specialist may be giving a lecture from the front of the room to provide practice in this junior and senior high school type of activity. If a student's attention seems to wander, the specialist can implement one of these alternatives:

1. The specialist can casually walk back nearer the student.

2. If it is prearranged, the aide can walk over and quietly whisper, "Students are expected to listen carefully during a discussion."

3. The specialist or aide can give a bonus check mark to each student who is listening carefully and say: "You are doing a good job listening. Students must learn to listen if they are going to be successful in the regular classroom."

From these examples of resource specialist–student interactions, it should be apparent that instruction in a resource room must include more than academics alone. The resource specialist and aide must continually be alert to the basic behaviors and abilities that seem to contribute to a readiness for regular classroom functioning. A sound instructional program is still a must, of course. Materials that are both the same and different from those used in the regular classroom are important elements. But the actual instruction in the resource specialist program is very similar to that provided in the special day class. This includes a sensitivity to ensuring each student's success; a willingness to change assignments in line with a student's needs of the moment; appropriate use of centers; and knowledge of four or five ways to teach reading, spelling, or arithmetic, and of when to "nudge" and when to give a little. No system can replace the good judgment of a skillful teacher.

An important part of the instruction time may be devoted to offering students help with tests assigned by their regular classroom teachers. Resource teachers for the blind and deaf have done this for many years. Help may be provided by administering a test orally or by modifying the reading level without actually interfering with the content of the test. Since this kind of help has been provided for blind and deaf students in the past, many regular teachers will agree to such an arrangement once they are sure that the credibility of the test or the class will not be compromised.

It is also valuable for the resource specialist to occasionally prepare and administer various kinds of tests to teach test-taking skills to the students. A variety of different techniques may be used:

1. Present a short, factual lecture and have the child take a test related to the contents of the lecture.

2. Prepare and pass out some written material with specific factual information and follow this with a test.

3. Assign a few pages of textbook material at the student's level and later give a test.

4. Administer different kinds of tests with multiple choice questions, true-false questions, matching questions with names and dates, and essay questions.

In using such activities, every effort should be made to promote success, even to the point of avoiding grading the tests the first few times. The resource specialist may let each student correct his or her own paper or pass out answer keys. Sometimes a class discussion on how to take a test is helpful. Topics for discussion might include:

What should you do if you don't know the answers?

When should you guess?

How can the resource specialist help?

Learning how to take a test is a skill just like learning to read or write, and many students need help with this skill.

Additional Responsibilities of the Resource Specialist

Working with Regular Teachers

Maintaining ongoing communication with regular teachers and administrators can be an almost full-time job. Therefore, adequate time must be allowed for this in the resource specialist's schedule. Communication and coordination of services is a vital part of the program. This can be difficult at the elementary level where each student has only one regular teacher and very difficult at the secondary level where each student has several teachers. However, it is only by achieving communication and coordination that the resource specialist can maintain a successful program.

The establishment of cooperative relationships with regular education personnel by the resource specialist is essential if students with exceptional needs are to be accepted in the regular program. In order to foster this cooperation, the resource specialist needs to possess many special, personal qualities as well as professional skills. No amount of special legislation or specific rules and regulations will mandate the cooperative acceptance of handicapped students into the regular classroom. The successful resource specialist must "sell" himself or herself as a skillful teacher and willing assistant ready to help the regular classroom teacher when the need arises.

Among the competencies that appear important for a resource specialist are:

1. Consultation Skills
   a. Ability to enable students, teachers, and parents to gain greater understanding of and to utilize resources in meeting a student's needs
   b. Ability to demonstrate effective communication skills
   c. Ability to demonstrate conferencing and interviewing skills
   d. Ability to inform and advise students, teachers, and parents on

the characteristics and identification of individuals with exceptional needs

e. Ability to inform and advise students, teachers, and parents on how to refer individuals with exceptional needs for services

f. Ability to inform and provide school staff with resources on formal and informal assessment procedures and instruments

g. Ability to work with students, teachers, and parents to interpret educational findings, develop an appropriate personalized instructional plan, implement the instructional plan, and evaluate and modify the instructional plan

h. Ability to inform students, teachers, and parents of services and resources within the school district and community

2. Coordination

a. Ability to coordinate the identification referral, assessment, instructional planning, and instructional review process for individuals with exceptional needs

(1) Contacting other personnel for needed information

(2) Obtaining assessment and planning information prior to appraisal team meeting.

(3) Collaborating with students, teachers, parents, and others in assessment, writing, and reviewing the Individual Education Program

The resource specialist must enjoy working with people and be able to tolerate frustration while continuously being engaged in a "soft sell approach" to gain the acceptance of the resource student and the program by the regular teacher. At Santa Monica High School, the school cafeteria charges 15¢ for each cup of coffee purchased by the school staff before school starts in the morning. Since the resource room is rather centrally located, the two resource specialists in the school began preparing a large urn of coffee each morning and charged 5¢ per cup with free refills. Before long twenty-five to thirty regular teachers began to drop in each morning for coffee and chatted for a few minutes with each other. The resource specialists soon became involved in these casual conversations and became much more visible among school personnel. Occasionally a resource student's name would come up, and the concerns or problems would usually be quickly solved over a cup of coffee. This is only one example of how the resource specialist can open informal as well as formal lines of communication. The lawmakers will never be able to legislate willing and cheerful cooperation between regular education and special education—only thoughtful people will make that come to pass.

In-Service Training

Another responsibility of the resource specialist is to arrange for and conduct in-service meetings for teachers, parents, and administrators, and for regular as well as disturbed students. These in-service discussions and workshops, both formal and informal, can often become additional cornerstones on which the program can build over the years. Since there are so many unanswered questions with respect to mainstreaming and how to make it work, frequent meetings with all the parties involved can aid in identifying these problems and working toward solutions.

There are at least two important types of meetings the resource specialist may want to consider:

1. *Awareness or Orientation Level Meetings.* The purpose of these meetings is to have the participants gain a greater awareness of the resource specialist program or some problem area associated with it (e.g., how students might feel about being assigned to the resource program). Such awareness level meetings can do much to change negative attitudes and improve acceptance of both students and program. The resource specialist can use a slide presentation to show the resource program in operation. Regular classroom teachers can share some positive experiences they have had working with resource students. A panel of resource students might discuss their concerns or offer suggestions to improve the program. Awareness level meetings are perhaps less threatening to parents and regular teachers since they can be rather casual and easy to plan and to hold.

The resource specialist should also consider the value of one-to-one awareness level activities such as casual conversations in the lunch room or an invitation to a regular teacher to "come and visit my room for a few minutes." Every effort should be made to capitalize on all opportunities possible for increasing awareness and acceptance of the program.

2. *Knowledge or Skill Training Meetings.* This type of meeting is designed to actually increase the participants' skill in implementing or using a particular practice or technique. A topic of interest to the special teacher might be "How to Write an Individual Education Program." For the regular teacher, it might be "Ways to Implement the Individual Education Program in the Regular Classroom" or "The Regular Teacher's Role in the Appraisal Team Meeting." It is much easier and more productive to hold the skill training meetings after one or more awareness level meetings have established the problem or need and have presented the "big picture."

There are many other ways the resource specialist can provide in-service education for students, parents, and school staff. These include: inviting regular staff members to attend a special education conference with the specialist, showing films, circulating written materials, notifying about relevant television shows, making PTA meeting presentations, leading discussions during faculty meetings, and even swapping teaching assignments for a day with a regular teacher.

Involvement during the appraisal team meeting can provide a valuable in-service training experience for regular teachers. Witnessing a group of professionals working with a parent to find ways to help a particular student can leave a lasting impression. Also, the fact that the student being discussed is that regular teacher's own student makes it all the more meaningful.

Organization of the Room

The facilities for the resource specialist program may consist of a classroom, an office in the administrative wing, a trailer at the far end of the campus, or possibly even a storeroom or closet for storing supplies with actual instruction being given to students in the regular classroom or hallway. The closer the resource specialist's room is to the hub of the school, the more integrated the resource program and the regular school program will be. Also, the closer the room is to the center of school activity, the less the stigmatization associated with the room and resource students. The following additional factors may also need to be considered when planning the physical facilities for the resource specialist's room:

1. The number of students seen at one time. (Twelve students are the maximum number that may be in a full-sized room at a given time in the Santa Monica program.)

2. The number of adults working in the room and their schedules and responsibilities (e.g., one resource specialist and one aide).

3. The number of different activities that can go on in the room at one time (e.g., testing, conferencing, instruction).

4. Flexibility of furniture arrangement.

5. Traffic flow, providing space for getting in and around the room.

6. Emphasis of the resource specialist program (e.g., instruction versus assessment services).

7. Acoustics both inside and outside the room

8. Lighting and windows in the room.

9. The number of electric outlets in the room. This is important when using tape recorders and record players.

There seem to be two different approaches for setting up the resource specialist's room. One is making the room a colorful—almost like an "oasis"—and relaxed place for learning to occur. The other approach looks at preparing the learner for success in the regular classroom. Hence the room looks and is set up very much like a regular classroom. There are pros and cons for both philosophies. We have used a combination of both in programs we have devised. In general, the resource rooms in Santa Monica are very similar to the special day classrooms (*see* Figures 7–1 and 7–2), except that the student desks in the center of the room are arranged much closer together in a manner that encourages student interaction. Since students are coming and going all day, each desk must also serve two or more students. Thus, there is a minimum of desk storage space for individual student materials.

Perhaps the most important point we have attempted to make in this chapter is that a working partnership between the regular and the special educator is essential if the concepts of least restrictive environment or mainstreaming are to have any positive meaning for disturbed and other exceptional children. We will make this same point with respect to the school and the parent in Chapter 11. The resource specialist program provides an important middle link between the regular classroom and the special day class, between regular education and special education.

chapter 10

The Severely Disturbed Child

In Chapter 3 we functionally defined emotional disturbance as consisting of behaviors that were negative variants of six levels of learning competence—attention, response, order, exploratory, social, and mastery. In this chapter we are going to review educational efforts with severely disturbed children utilizing the six levels of learning competence as a framework for our discussion.

But first let's consider the types of children we are talking about when we use the term *severely disturbed child*. Terms such as *childhood psychosis*, *childhood schizophrenia* (Potter, 1933; Bradley & Bowen, 1941; Bender, 1942), *autism* (Kanner, 1943; Rimland, 1964), *atypical child* (Rank, 1949), and *symbiotic psychosis* (Mahler, 1952, 1965; Mahler & Furer, 1972) have often been used interchangeably (Achenbach, 1974). However, at the present time, two types of severe emotional disturbance are generally thought to exist (Werry, 1979). Whether these disorders comprise separate homogeneous classes, whether they are related causally, or whether they are related to the development of adult psychosis are unknown.

1. *Schizophrenic Disorders.* Evidenced by a regression or arrest in development after a period of relatively healthy development. In addition, schizophrenic children have some useful language and are able to relate at some level to others. (Onset 5–12 years of age.)

2. *Early Infantile Autism.* Evidenced by two primary symptoms— extreme self-isolation and an obsessive insistence on sameness. A secondary symptom consists of speech and language disorders which range from mutism to echolalia. (Onset 0–2½ years of age.)

With respect to the educational orientation or role perspective of individuals working with severely disturbed children, we can say at the outset that the trainer-diagnostician, therapist, and behavior modifier roles we discussed in Chapter 2 have all been influential. Of these orientations, behavioral approaches have been studied the most extensively. Such studies have demonstrated that severely disturbed children can develop more adaptive behavior, although the progress may be extremely slow. Rather than attempt to separately discuss the schizophrenic child and the autistic child, we will refer generally to severely disturbed children. Since children considered afflicted with one of these types of disorders often manifest similar behaviors, it is doubtful that educational procedures by type will ever be developed. The question is: How can we get the severely disturbed child to pay attention? The question is not: What specific approaches aid autistic children in learning to pay attention as compared to schizophrenic children? However, more research into ways to teach autistic children has been done than into ways to teach schizophrenic children. Many of the studies to be cited here have used autistic children as subjects.

Attention Level

At the attention level, variants in behavior that interfere with learning include problems in perception and attention—most notably auditory perception and attention, but also visual and possibly tactile (Ornitz & Ritvo, 1968, 1976).

Autistic children may fail to adequately monitor or modulate incoming sensory input, and as a result they underreact to such stimulation or markedly overreact to it (Ornitz, 1971). Underreaction is seen in the lack of a startle response to very sudden loud noise or no visual reaction to new persons or objects in the environment. When in a state of overreaction, the autistic child may actively seek stimulation (e.g., banging objects, teeth grinding). Whirling, rocking, and head-rolling are common, as is repetitive hand-flapping.

In some cases, distress occurs as the result of exposure to routine stimuli. A siren, vacuum cleaner, or barking dog may cause the child to cover both ears in an attempt to shut out the sounds (Goldfarb, 1963). It has been demonstrated that autistic children show a preference for "proximal receptors"—touch, smell, taste—rather than "distal receptors"—hearing and seeing (Schopler, 1965).

Another related problem, *stimulus overselectivity* on the part of autistic children, often greatly interferes with efforts to teach them. In short, this term refers to the tendency of some autistic children to "lock in" on some limited aspect of the environment rather than to freely explore the range of stimuli available (Lovaas, Shreibman, Koegel, & Rehm, 1971; Stevens-Long & Lovaas, 1974). In one study, groups of autistic, retarded, and normal children were trained to press a bar when three stimuli were presented simultaneously: a red light went on, a loud noise was heard, and pressure on their arms from a blood-pressure cuff was felt (Lovaas, Schreibman, Koegel, & Rehm, 1971). Following this training, the groups were exposed to each of the stimuli separately. The normal children responded equally well to each of these. It appeared they had been paying attention to each component of the total group of stimuli. The autistic children, however, only responded to one of the three stimuli when each was presented separately. These children had been paying attention only to one of the three simultaneous stimuli; that is, they had engaged in stimulus overselectivity during the training. The retarded children fell in between the normals and autistics.

What do these findings mean in terms of educational programs for autistic children? To begin with, we may need to study each child with respect to the conditions under which either under- or over-reaction to incoming sensory stimuli occurs. This may involve identifying the "prime" sensory modality of the child and capitalizing on it in teaching. We will further discuss the importance of prime sensory stimulation when discussing the exploratory level of competence in this chapter.

It has become increasingly apparent that stimulus overselectivity may underlie much of the autistic child's failure to acquire language and social skills (Rincover & Koegel, 1977). By locking in on a single stimuli, the child learns single "treeness" but not "forestness." In many respects, autistic children live in a world of isolated trees that somehow never come together as a human and social forest. Much of the success of behavior modification with autistic children can be attributed to the molecular one-behavior-at-a-time approach. Over time and with considerable patience and perseverance, these children can build a repertoire of basic adaptive behaviors. One of us has worked with a number of autistic children from this building block point of view. First teach the child to sit near you. Next, teach eye contact. Start with single response tasks (e.g., "Hand me the ball."). Then gradually increase the complexity of the demands. This molecular approach is in marked contrast to the molar orientation of the psychodynamic school. Compare the objective of developing trust, with the objective of making eye contact.

Despite the specificity of "make eye contact" and the fact that we can see and record it when it happens rather than vaguely speculate about trusting relationships, we may never achieve anything but ladder-like learning that fails to merge into a real ladder. That is, seat sitting, eye contact, and response to commands may develop as discrete "rungs" rather than lead to an eventual relationship between teacher and child. Throughout our discussion of severely disturbed children's variant behaviors in relation to the six levels of learning competence, the problem of generalization will be relevant. What do you do if the severely disturbed child's self-injurious behavior is controlled in the experimental room but nowhere else? What if the teacher effectively suppresses the child's self-stimulatory behavior, but the parent never can? The failure of conditioned behavior to generalize across settings, situations, and individuals remains a major area for research and study in psychology and special education.

In this discussion we have raised several issues that bear directly on the types of educational programs needed by severely disturbed children. Overcoming stimulus overselectivity involves gradual introduction of increased stimuli and continual coaching and directing of the child to call attention to as many aspects of "forestness" in the situation as possible (e.g., "Where is the red block?" "Where is the blue block?" "What is that sound?" "Touch the furry rabbit." "Smell that perfume.").

With respect to generalization, one obvious approach is to provide continuity between as many aspects and settings of the child's life as possible and have the various key individuals in his or her life all participate as teachers. When one of us began teaching speech to autistic children, he originally worked strictly one-to-one in a teaching booth. But later on, when working with autistic children who were not hospitalized and came for training three times a week, he had the mother sit in the booth alongside him and gradually turned the training over to her exclusively. This worked very well and had the advantage of establishing the mother as teacher so that training sessions could be undertaken at home. Experimental teaching sessions three times a week are simply never going to make any major difference at all. Autism is a fierce and awesome adversary. We must mobilize all the forces possible to help improve the child's functioning level on a continuous basis. And we cannot afford to think of "preschool" or "elementary" school programs for the autistic child. We must think of *lifetime* programs from the very moment it becomes apparent that a child is autistic.

Response Level

In our discussion of the response level of competence, we will discuss the problems of self-stimulatory behaviors and language development.

Self-Stimulatory Behaviors

Many severely disturbed children are physically very attractive, yet they may be viewed by an individual seeing them for the first time as strange and bizarre. This reaction may be elicited by their peculiar mannerisms or self-stimulatory behaviors. These behaviors do not involve involuntary movements such as those typical of seizure patterns. The most typical self-stimulatory behavior involves the hands and arms which are usually moved in front of the face so that the child can see them. The hands may be flapped up and down with the fingers separated and the child looking at them intently. Some autistic children may "flick" their hair continuously, rock from side to side or back and forth, roll their heads back and forth, bang their heads, or engage in staccato lunging and darting movements. Toe walking and a fondness for twirling and spinning (both of themselves and of inanimate objects) is also often observed.

From a medical point of view, there is some evidence suggesting that these self-stimulatory behaviors may actually reflect central nervous system dysfunction (Ornitz, Brown, Mason, & Putnam, 1974). For example, when studied, hand-flapping has been found to occur in a given child at the same frequency over time. Groups of autistic children also have been found to flap hands at the same rate. (Ritvo, Ornitz, & La Franchi, 1968). In addition, the presence of other persons or toys does not seem to affect the child's self-stimulatory behaviors (Ornitz, Brown, Sorosky, Ritvo, & Dietrich, 1970).

Whatever their source, self-stimulating behaviors seriously interfere with efforts to teach autistic children. It is difficult to get anything across to pupils who are devoting their total time and energy to stimulating themselves. From a behavioral point of view, self-stimulation is viewed as being at least partially maintained by the visual, auditory, tactile, and vestibular consequences it provides. In one study (Rincover, Peoples, & Packard, 1976) a child was included who incessantly spun objects on a table in a stereotyped and repetitive fashion. It is often amazing to see the fine hand-eye coordination skill some autistics demonstrate which enables them to spin objects that for others would clearly be "unspinable." The investigators were interested in what aspect of the spinning was the most reinforcing and thus possibly maintained the behavior. Since spinning objects on a table top produces auditory clicking and scraping noises, the researchers controlled for these by carpeting the table top. When the child spun an object on the carpeted table top it made no noise. The spinning behavior was eliminated.

In general, the elimination of self-stimulating behaviors is very difficult to achieve (Rincover & Koegel, 1977). Distracting the child may work if something in the distraction is more interesting for the child than what's provided by the self-stimulation. This may be particularly effective if the activity involves the child using his or her hands in a particularly satisfying manner (e.g., to pet a furry, stuffed toy). Among the more negative consequences that may be applied in an effort to control self-stimulation are: having the child sit alone in the corner of the room for a period, holding the child in a chair in the corner of the room for a period, or restricting the child briefly in a time-out area away from the room (Graham, 1976). Other approaches that have been used include a loud "No!" as in "No rocking!" or penalizing an older child who understands and is motivated by a token or point system. For example, each time the child rocks and does not respond to a verbal reminder, he or she loses a given number of previously earned points.

In Chapter 4 we noted that the method of negative practice or over-correction has sometimes been utilized to control self-stimulation. The child is required to practice the behavior continuously for a period of time (e.g., ten minutes). If the child refuses, he or she is forcibly led through the self-stimulating movements by the teacher. While we have seen this technique greatly reduce the frequency of self-stimulatory behavior, it must be viewed with all the cautions and concerns expressed earlier.

One of the reasons there is continuing concern regarding methods of reducing autistic children's self-stimulation is that when a reduction occurs, the children are much more accessible and involved with their environments. Among the positive side effects that have been found to occur as the result of reducing self-stimulatory behavior are an increase in pro-social and attentional behaviors (Risley, 1968; Lovaas & Newsom, 1976), improvement in discrimination learning (Koegel & Covert, 1972), and increases in spontaneous appropriate play (Epstein, Doke, Sajwaj, Sorrell, & Rimmer, 1974; Koegel, Firestone, Kramme, & Dunlap, 1974).

From an idealistic point of view, self-stimulation might not be a problem if teaching-environment stimulation were so irresistible and motivating that autistic children readily gave up paying attention to themselves to pay attention to the teacher. In a teaching booth developed by one of us for teaching speech to autistic children, a variety of potential rewards (e.g., musical spinning chair, cartoon movie, candy) usually reduced the child's self-stimulatory behaviors during the booth training sessions. If the child began to self-stimulate and one or two verbal reminders did not work, a shutter in the booth between the teacher and child would be lowered and an "instant" time-out of several seconds would be imposed. This immediate time-out had many advantages over having to pull a resistant child to a time-out area or room. But, unfortunately, while the autistic pupils who participated in the teaching-booth speech-training program evidenced few self-stimulatory behaviors during training sessions, there was very little generalization to outside situations.

Language Development

Perhaps the most critical response skill that does not develop in approximately one half of all autistic children is verbal responding. Speech and language may never develop at all or the child may proceed to a certain level of language development and go no further (Bartak, Rutter, & Cox, 1975; Shapiro, Roberts, & Fish, 1970; Griffith & Ritvo, 1967). Echolalia is a common speech disorder. The child may articulate words very well and have a fairly sizeable vocabulary but not learn to communicate appropriately. Thus, if an echolalic child is approached and asked, "What is your name?" instead of giving an appropriate reply, we get an echo, "What is your name?" Another common speech disorder found among autistic children is the misuse of pronouns. The child may respond by calling himself or herself *he, she,* or *you* instead of *I*. When functional speech does develop, it is usually atonal and arhythmic. It lacks inflection and does not convey subtle emotion. This affectless quality in speech has been found to persist into adulthood (Churchill, 1972).

The NPI School Program

The Neuropsychiatric Institute (NPI) School has conducted research into and developed programs for teaching speech and language skills to autistic children for almost two decades. Originally beginning with a behavioral approach, the school has turned to a developmental approach. The philosophy behind the approach is that creative communicative language cannot be trained or taught but must be elicited from the child from a developmental perspective. A Developmental Scale of Language Skills (Richey, 1976) is used with this approach. It is based on the work of Bayley (1969), Menyuk (1971), and Lenneberg (1967) and contains elements of normal language from birth to thirty months. The scale is divided into both expressive and receptive components; each component is subdivided into seven levels with each level covering no more than six months.

The complete scale can be found elsewhere (Ritvo, Freeman, Ornitz, & Tanguay, 1976), but for our purposes, we will present excerpts from Levels III and VI for both the expressive and receptive components.

Development Scale of Language Skills

Expressive Skills

Level III (5–9 months)

Babbles frequently when alone or with others (5 months).
Vocalizes in response to adult voice (5 months).
Child vocalizes to his toys (6 months).
May "coo" to music (6 months).
Child utters at least four different spontaneous sounds (7 months).
Vocalizes satisfaction after obtaining desired object (7 months).
Vocalizes to get attention (8 months).
Child says "dada" or "mama" without meaning (8 months).

Level VI (18–24 months)

Vocabulary of ten to twenty words (18 months).
Uses "hello," "thank you," or other socially oriented phrases (18 months).
Names two objects (21 months).
Child uses "yes" meaningfully (21 months).

Receptive Skills

Level III (5–9 months)

Child responds to voice by turning head (5 months).
Child responds to fallen object (out of sight) by turning head (5 months).
Child looks (actively) for fallen object (6 months).
Child discriminates mother's voice from stranger's voice (6 months).

Level VI (18–24 months)

Child responds to "sit down" and "stand up" (18 months).
Child selectively looks at pictures in a book (18 months).
Child is able to point to body parts of doll (19 months).
Child is able to selectively point to one picture (19 months).
Child understands and responds to "yes" (21 months).
Child is able to selectively point to five pictures (21 months).
Child is able to find objects hidden under one of three cups (with verbal cue) (23 months).
Child is able to point to four body parts (23 months).
(Ritvo, Freeman, Ornitz, & Tanguay, 1976).

As can be seen, an attempt has been made to analyze specific aspects of language development up to two years of age. Each child with a language deficit who enters the NPI School is observed and evaluated in terms of the language or language-related behaviors he or she has attained. This is done over several sessions, each lasting approximately one-half hour. Based on the language profile that emerges from the scale on the child, a language therapy program is formulated. This program has the following characteristics:

1. There is a half-hour, daily language session for each child.

2. The relationship between teacher and child resembles as closely as possible the normal mother-child relationship.

3. The teacher treats the child in accordance with his or her language level (e.g., a three-year-old child with six-month-old language skills would be treated like a six month old).

4. No child is required to make specific verbalizations.

5. No food reinforcers are used.

6. Once the child has passed the eighteen-month expressive level, he or she may be asked to participate in object labeling activities.

7. Articulation training is not a routine part of the program, and it is only introduced once the child has expressive skills past the twenty-four-month level.

This developmental approach represents an ambitious effort to define and pin down the complex process of language development during the early years. It may be questionable to list a behavior as occurring during a particular month level. What is probably representative here are ballpark age estimates and behaviors occurring within ranges of months rather than during any specific month. Although conceived of in a nonbehavioral framework, the language and language-related behaviors presented on the Developmental Scale of Language Skills might be very useful to someone approaching the teaching of speech from a behavioral point of view.

The Los Angeles County Autism Project

This is a public-school-based program for autistic children that emphasizes the teaching of speech and language (Needles & Jamison, 1976). Although operating from a developmental orientation, the project does not attempt the elaborate analysis of a child's language level seen in the NPI School program. Rather, language tests such as the Peabody Picture Vocabulary and the Illinois Test of Psycholinguistic Ability and informal language screening surveys are used. Unfortunately, since so many autistic children have very little if any functional language, they often fall far below the lowest level on the test norms. As a result, such tests may be useful only to explore the child's level of language rather than to analyze it in any systematic fashion.

The project language program consists of three sequences of training objectives: receptive, expressive, and cognitive. In the receptive sequence, the child is taught comprehension of five nouns, five verbs, five additional nouns, five adjectives, and five prepositions. The nouns selected are "agents of action" such as mommy, daddy, baby, and man. These nouns are used in teaching verbs (e.g., mommy sleeping). Nouns such as chair and block are chosen so they can be paired with adjectives (e.g., blue block). Prepositions are then taught in relation to the nouns (e.g., block on the chair).

In the expressive sequence, the child first learns gross motor imitation (e.g., stand, sit, put arms above head). Next, less gross motor imitation is introduced (e.g., hands on shoulder, hands on head, hands on waist). Following this level, oral motor imitation is taught. This involves having the child imitate various mouth movements made by the teacher. Oral vocal motor imitation comes next with the child imitating isolated speech sounds and then speech sound sequences. For example, the child may imitate the sounds for the letters *a* and *m* and then sequence them into *mama*. At this point an actual picture of the child's mother is introduced. The program also teaches children to imitate and learn the American Sign Language system developed primarily for the deaf which is a means of communicating by use of arm and hand gestures.

The cognitive sequence involves learning to match pictures to their real-world counterparts (e.g., picture of a table with a real table) and to match identical objects. In addition to matching objects and pictures, this sequence introduces the notion of classification. The concept of "cupness" might be taught to the child by introducing cups of increasing dissimilarity while stressing that they all could be labeled as cups.

Of some twelve autistic children who entered the Los Angeles County Autism Project with no functional speech, five were reported to have acquired functional speech as a result of the language program. Three others also acquired a degree of functional speech, but their verbal responses remained dependent on cues in the training situation (e.g., a direct question from the teacher). One other child began to acquire expressive language using signing, and the remaining three progressed to the oral-vocal motor imitation stage.

Eddie

Another speech training program was undertaken by one of us with Eddie, a four-and-one-half-year-old autistic boy (Hewett, 1965). Eddie was introduced in Chapter 6. This program utilized the learning triangle concept and the levels of learning competence.

Eddie, like most autistic children, was a highly selective "attender," "responder," "direction-follower," and "explorer." He avoided eye contact, resisted efforts of others to direct his attention, and continually pursued repetitive mechanical activities such as water-pouring and tinkering with mechanical gadgets. He followed few directions given by others and was an insatiable explorer of certain features of his environment (e.g., water faucets, pencil sharpeners, cabinet hardware, and appliances). Socially, Eddie was totally aloof from concern with approval and disapproval, and he had never developed speech, although the words *da-da* and *ma-ma* appeared briefly during his first year and a half and then disappeared.

When brought for admission by his parents, Eddie entered the NPI Children's Service ward without so much as a glance back at them as they withdrew. He showed no awareness of being left by them in this new setting, although the period of hospitalization brought about his first separation from his family.

Prior to beginning speech training with Eddie, the special teaching booth illustrated in Figure 10–1 was constructed.* The booth was divided into two sections, joined by a movable shutter (2 x 2½ feet) which could be raised and lowered by the teacher. Each section of the booth was 4 feet wide, 3½ feet in length, and 7½ feet high. Eddie was seated, as shown, on one side of the booth; the teacher was seated on the other. The only source of light came from the teacher's side and was provided by two spotlights which were directed on the teacher's face. When the shutter was down, Eddie's side of the booth was dark; when it was raised, light from the teacher's side flooded through the opening and illuminated a shelf in front of Eddie. To the left of the shelf was a ball-drop device with a dim light directly above it. This device consisted of a box into which a small wooden ball could be dropped. The ball rang a bell as it dropped into the box and was held inside the box until released by the teacher. When released, the ball rolled out into a container at the bottom of the box where it could be picked up. This ball-drop device was Eddie's "key" for opening the shutter. When the ball was released into the container, he picked it up and dropped it into the box. At the sound of the bell, the teacher raised the shutter and initiated contact between the two of them.

The curriculum task of attention was presented to Eddie when the ball was released and it rolled into the container in front of him. The shutter was down, the booth was dark, and the ball-drop device was the only lighted stimulus. When Eddie picked up the ball and dropped it into the opening in the box, thereby ringing the bell, he accomplished a task at the response level. Following accomplishment of these two tasks, Eddie was rewarded by having the shutter raised, a mouthful of food provided, the teacher's face brought into view, the booth lighted, and "Good boy!" spoken by the teacher. These rewards (food, social attention, task completion, sensory stimulation, and social approval) were all provided simultaneously. The conditions in the teaching situation involved the operation of the booth itself and "how" it worked. Eddie had to attend, respond, and follow directions in the manner described before he received available rewards.

The first week of the program was devoted to introducing Eddie to the learning routine in the booth. Following this, the tasks given to Eddie were as follows over a one-year period:

*Frank Langdon made a major contribution in the design and construction of this teaching booth.

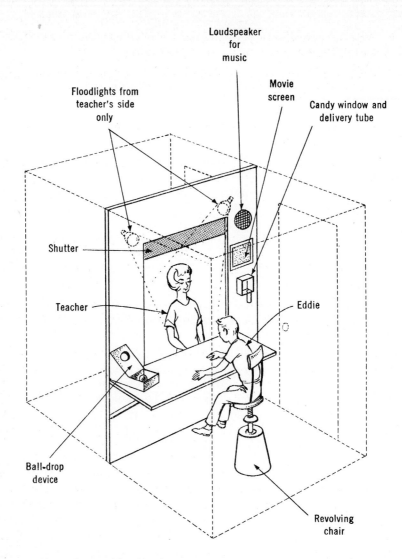

Figure 10–1. The teaching booth.

1. Eye contact with teacher expected before reward of food given.

2. Imitative hand movements involving "patty-cake," hand-clapping, and touching various parts of his body in imitation of the teacher (e.g., head, eye, ear, nose, mouth, stomach) required in order to get his motorized chair to spin one revolution and the teacher to say "Good boy!"

3. Touching the teacher's face as a means of keeping music playing.

4. Cupping his face in his hands to get a colored cartoon movie segment to show on screen.

5. Humming a few bars of a children's song in imitation of the teacher in order to obtain candy reward and "Good boy!"

6. Providing shrill, undifferentiated vowel sound (é-oo) in imitation of the teacher for candy reward and "Good boy!"

7. Giving successive approximations of the word *go* in imitation of the teacher who gradually moved from "é-oo" to "go-o-o" for candy reward and "Good boy!"

8. Using word *go* to command teacher to start spinning chair, turn on music, and open door.

9. Produce word *my* in imitation of teacher in order to get Bingo markers to place on numbered squares.

10. Use word *my* to denote possession and to obtain desired objects (e.g., puzzle pieces, toys) from teacher.

11. Produce words such as *high, see, yes, no, shoe, key, mama, daddy, water, toilet, food, eye, ear, nose, mouth, Eddie, please, juice, cracker, milk,* and *school* in response to pictures or objects held up by the teacher for reward of "Good boy!" alone.

12. Use simple phrases (*I want toilet, I want water, I want candy, I want school*) in order to have needs met by ward personnel throughout the day.

13. Practice and expand verbal repertoire with parents and siblings acting as teachers for various tangible, sensory, and social rewards.

This summary of stages in the speech training program designed for Eddie omits many details. All of the training except the transfer phase, when ward personnel and, later, parents worked with him, was undertaken in the teaching booth. During the period of booth training, the conditions and consequences sides of the learning triangle were emphasized whenever Eddie refused to obey the teacher's requests for imitative responses. Usually five seconds would be allowed following each request (when) and three separate requests would be given. If Eddie withdrew or did not comply during this time, the teacher lowered the shutter, and he was penalized with a five-second period of isolation and darkness. After this period, the ball was released by the teacher, and when Eddie dropped it through the opening in the ball-drop device, the shutter was raised, and the training continued. This punishment was rarely needed after the first few weeks.

While such limit-setting and imposition of a penalty involving isolation and darkness has alarmed some individuals because of the inferred meaning such rejection by the teacher was felt to have for the child, its use with Eddie and five other autistic children was never found to be traumatic or upsetting. Few instances of the child crying occurred after the shutter was lowered for brief periods, and most children quickly modified their behavior in order to keep the rewarding consequences of tangible rewards, social attention, light, and social approval forthcoming. It appeared they were "bored" in the stimulus-free, closed-shutter environment and were willing to "work" in order to obtain the rewards which were available when the shutter was up.

Eddie's program illustrates the use of the learning triangle and the levels of learning competence to effect learning with often inaccessible and highly resistant learners. The tasks given to Eddie were gradually increased in complexity; a variety of rewards were offered, some alone, others in combination; and a predictable learning environment and routine were established with him. When the task of vocal imitation was given to Eddie, candy was introduced for the first time. This reward was known to be the most powerful of all for Eddie and so it was reserved for the most crucial stage in the training program. It can also be seen that the higher level reward of social approval alone was eventually effective in maintaining his newly acquired behavior. This reward was paired with most other rewards given from the very beginning in an effort to establish it as a controlling consequence in its own right.

Eddie's use of speech for labeling purposes as well as for simple requests did not constitute true language. Weiss and Born (1967) have called attention to the distinction between speech acquired through operant conditioning (a series of vocal utterances) and genuine language (capability of generating and understanding novel utterances). While there can be no doubt that the level of speech development obtained experimentally was limited, the secondary gains were significant. Eddie became more aware of his social environment and was also viewed differently by others. Members of the NPI nursing staff sought him out frequently for verbal interactions, aided him in practicing his speech, and held him for verbal requests before granting his wishes.

Eddie's increased social awareness was well demonstrated when his parents would leave following a visit to the hospital. In marked contrast to his apathy and seeming unawareness when they left him upon admission to the hospital, Eddie now cried, clung to his mother, and was visibly very upset when she departed. As unpleasant as it was to see a child so distressed upon separation from his parents, the author and ward staff were delighted with this family interaction.

Goldfarb, Braenstein, and Lorge (1956) have suggested that the responses of others to the speech defects of schizophrenic children may actually reinforce such defects. Thus the nature of the relationship between nonverbal schizophrenic children and the environment may not be conducive to improved socialization. Meeting the needs of such children by responding to their primitive and often bizarre attempts at communication may merely make an unsocialized existence more rewarding. In addition, nonverbal schizophrenic children may be perceived as so atypical and difficult to reach that others develop less personal and involved means of relating with them.

Clearly, the acquisition of beginning speech skills places the child in a position to interact more favorably with his or her environment. Eddie left the hospital, was enrolled in a private nursery-kindergarten, and later a public school class for the educationally handicapped. His vocabulary grew considerably, and he quickly learned to read, write, and to master basic number concepts expected for his age.

Three years after the initial speech training program, Eddie's speech was still restricted and mechanical. He was generally echolalic (repeated exact phrases and questions spoken to him rather than giving appropriate answers) and had little understanding of pronoun references. Since almost no formal speech training was continued after Eddie's discharge from the NPI, the growth of his vocabulary and the improvements in his articulation were due to experiences he had at home and at school.

One occurrence suggested that the merging of speech and true language was occurring in Eddie's case. Following a severe spanking by his mother, he withdrew to his room and later appeared with the drawings presented in Figure 10–2. These drawings were of a "broken dryer" and a "broken washer," two of Eddie's favorite appliances in the home. He actually drew and labeled them as shown. The figure drawing was verbally labeled by him as "Eddie." Here appeared to be an attempt on quite a prim-

Figure 10–2. Eddie's drawings.

itive level to convey an emotional state of distress through written and spoken communication.

Six years after working with Eddie, one of us who had worked with him had an opportunity to see him again. Unfortunately, the meeting occurred in the children's unit of a state institution for the severely emotionally disturbed. Eddie had functioned well in the public school class for educationally handicapped children due to the heroic efforts of the teacher and to the fact that his mother went with him to supervise him during certain periods and during recess and lunchtime. He had learned to read and do arithmetic, and by age seven, he was two years ahead of his expected level. However, as Eddie got older, he got bigger and more unmanageable. While he had grown cognitively, he had not kept pace socially and would run away from home and endanger himself and others. For that reason, not that he could not be successful learning in a public school special education program, Eddie ended up in a state institution.

Although Eddie had not seen the author for six years, he smiled in an embarrassed manner when the meeting occurred. It was extremely gratifying to see this autistic boy manifest a most normal reaction to seeing an "old teacher" for the first time in years. Eddie walked over to a chalkboard and wrote his name on it—EDDIE. Then he began to write the author's name alongside (a task that had often taken place in the NPI training program). He wrote DR HE and then stopped and looked over and asked, "How do you spell your name?" It was a most touching moment. Eddie was demonstrating true language skills—a spontaneous question that was relevant to what was going on at the time and not a conditioned utterance he had been trained to say. Although Eddie still used echolalic speech on occasion, he had definitely acquired many language skills and his articulation was impressive.

Another highlight of that visit with Eddie occurred when the boy went over to a cabinet with sheet music in it. He sorted through the music and produced a copy of "When I Was a Lad" from Gilbert and Sullivan's *HMS Pinafore*. Then with perfect pitch and pronunciation, he proceeded to sing four full verses.

Eddie's speech helped him take advantage of the best the institution had to offer, and as such it was well worth all the effort that had been put into teaching him. Nonverbal, isolated autistic children are in a much less favored position. Nurses, attendants, teachers, and others sought Eddie out and interacted freely with him. The attention he received clearly was reflected in his high functioning level. But there is a sobering side to the case of Eddie. While we labored long and hard to teach him to speak, we neglected to teach him the socialization skills that are necessary to live freely in society. Respect for rules and the rights of others are learned by normal children as they grow and mature. When he was a little boy, Eddie could be "managed" by others at home, but as a budding adolescent, his freedom had to be restricted by institutional placement. The message here is clear:

while it is important to teach nonverbal disturbed children to speak as early as possible, a companion program of socialization training should be going on simultaneously. Otherwise, we may only teach speech to a child who will inevitably end up in a private, residential school or state institution.

Teaching the American Sign Language system to autistic children as a substitute for spoken language has both its critics and its advocates. Richey (1976), who works with young autistic children in the NPI School, views the teaching of sign language as limited in value since it cannot be understood by untrained individuals and tends to call attention to the child. Fulwiler and Fouts (1976), however, have found teaching sign language to a five-year-old autistic boy to be quite beneficial. After twenty hours of training (one-half hour training session twice weekly) the child began to use several signs correctly. As the use of signed speech increased, the child's vocal speech also increased in both amount and appropriateness. Fulwiler and Fouts were struck by how carefully the child attended to their facial expressions while signing. This appeared to be one of the real benefits of the signing approach as individuals using it rely on facial expression to convey the emotion of the communicator. Since gaze aversion is often found among autistic children, the teaching of signing may hold promise for teaching eye contact.

The boy who participated in the Fulwiler and Fouts study had been enrolled in a behavior modification language program that had not been successful with him. Introduced in the mid-1960s with high hopes that they would be an effective means of speech training (Lovaas, Berberich, Perloff, & Schaeffer, 1966), behavior modification techniques often involve thousands of trials to get the child to articulate the first word and many more to teach the child to use it functionally. While teaching subsequent words may require fewer trials, the "conditioned" speech does not appear to become spontaneous or to generalize beyond the training situation to any great extent (Lovaas, Koegel, Simmons, & Long, 1973). In addition, the quality of the child's verbalization may degenerate so that it is almost indistinguishable.

The approach described earlier with Eddie was a behavior modification approach that did work. This had a great deal to do with the facts that Eddie was not severely autistic and that he quickly began to verbally imitate the teacher. The same program used with Eddie was successful with a number of other autistic children, although none of them developed the speaking vocabulary that Eddie did. The program was also unsuccessful with some autistic children.

La Vigna (1977) has utilized an errorless discrimination approach in teaching three, mute autistic adolescents the expressive and receptive use of three written words: *mint, drop,* and *corn.* These words referred to candy mints, candy corn, and gum drops. Expressive training involved teaching the subject to select the word card with the correct label from the three possibilities whenever a particular type of candy was presented. Receptive training involved teaching the subject to select the correct type of candy when one of the three word cards was presented. The three autistic adolescents took from 979 to 1791 trials to learn to successfully match word with candy type and candy type with word. La Vigna speculated that learning written words as a means of communication may involve less perceptual and behavioral complexity for the autistic individual than learning verbal language and, hence, should be explored as an alternative.

Order Level

Our discussion at the order level will center around the issue of self-injurious behavior which has been found to have a high prevalence among autistic children (Green, 1967). Self-injurious behavior is particularly upsetting for parents, teachers, and others to witness. The sight of a disturbed child banging his or her head until bleeding occurs, smashing the nose against the knee over and over until it is broken, or biting into the shoulder until flesh and tissue are removed is deeply disturbing. Why autistic children engage in such behavior is poorly understood, but the fact that they do presents a serious management problem. Early efforts to control self-destructive behavior included tying the child down in bed "spread-eagled" fashion or putting a helmet on. While these lessened the probability that serious injury might occur, they accomplished little with respect to reducing or eventually eliminating self-destructive behavior.

Three approaches based on behavior modification have been utilized with children who engage in self-injurious behavior with varying degrees of success: (1) control of attention, (2) contingent application of electric shock, and (3) increase of positive reinforcement.

Paying attention to the child who engages in self-destructive behavior has been found to serve as a reinforcer for such behavior (Bucher & Lovaas, 1968; Lovaas & Simmons, 1969). Withholding attention, therefore, has been found to decrease the frequency of self-injurious behavior—but not always. To begin with, withholding attention may produce an increase in the behavior initially and waiting for it to diminish over time may expose the child to a large number of potentially dangerous self-injurious acts (Bucher & Lovaas, 1968). In addition, withholding attention may have no effect at all (Risley, 1968) or it may actually serve to increase the self-injurious behavior over time (Solnick, Rincover, & Peterson, 1977). Thus, attention in and of itself is not the only motivating factor in producing self-injurious behavior, and the exploration of other measures has been necessary.

One of the most controversial of these other measures is the application of a painful electric shock when the child moves to engage in a self-injurious act. The research literature reveals that use of electric shock usually produces a rapid and predictable suppression of self-injurious behavior (Lovaas, Schaeffer, & Simmons, 1965; Lichstein & Schreibman, 1976). However, the suppression may only be temporary and may not occur in situations outside the actual area in which the shock was delivered. We discussed earlier how the failure of training procedures to produce changes in behaviors that generalize across places and individuals has been a particularly frustrating problem for the behavior modifier. In addition, there is need for future research regarding the side effects of electric shock (Rincover & Koegel, 1977). The ethical issue with respect to the use of extremely punishing consequences with children will probably never be resolved. Never is this issue more inflammatory than when it arises concerning the use of electric shock.

A far more acceptable approach has been suggested by studies that have found self-injurious behavior to be maintained by negative reinforcement (Carr, Newsom, & Binkoff, 1976; Solnick, Rincover, & Petersen, 1977). In these studies, self-injurious acts were found to occur when the child was facing a demanding learning situation which he or she found could be terminated by engaging in these acts. They served a kind of escape function. When the teachers introduced a number of positively reinforcing activities into the learning situation (e.g., storytelling, toys, music, social interaction), even though the original task demands were maintained, the number of self-injurious acts were greatly reduced or eliminated. Unfortunately, this approach, like the others, does not work with all autistic children who manifest self-injurious behavior. In the final analysis, each child must be thoroughly studied in an effort to determine how the environment may be modified so that self-destructive behavior is brought under control. While tying children down in bed or forcing them to wear helmets may seem quite primitive, we still have a long way to go in replacing these methods with training approaches that will work with all children given to self-injurious behavior.

Exploratory Level

The self-stimulating behaviors of autistic children (e.g., rhythmic rocking, finger flapping, and object spinning) appear to provide these children with sensory stimulation that they crave. Sensory stimulation is well established as being positively reinforcing with normal children (Stevenson & Odom, 1961; Rheingold, Stanley & Doyle, 1964). Since autistic children often devote so much time to self-stimulation, using this craving for sensory experience would seem to be both logical and practical.

One study investigated the feasibility of using a variety of sensory stimuli (e.g., strobe light, music) to aid in teaching autistic children (Rincover, Newsom, Lovaas, & Koegel, 1977). The teachers of four autistic children identified the sensory stimulators they believed each child preferred. When the child's preferred stimulus was made contingent upon learning simple language skills, definite progress was noted. In testing the durability of the preferred stimuli over time, it was noted that all the children eventually satiated. However, only a small change in the sensory stimulus (e.g., changing the frequency of the strobe light) was necessary to renew its effectiveness and durability.

There is some evidence that the effect of sensory stimuli on the self-stimulatory behaviors of autistic children is related to mental age (Frankel, Ritvo, & Pardo, 1975). In one experiment, the percent of time that a number of autistic children engaged in self-stimulation was observed under two conditions. In one condition, novel stimuli such as Christmas tree lights and sound effects were provided for the children. In the other, there were few environmental stimuli. It was found that high mental-age autistic children engaged in significantly less self-stimulation during the novel stimuli conditions, while those with low mental age engaged in more such behavior. Another study showed that the magnitude of preference that autistic children showed for the higher frequencies of a flashing strobe light was highly correlated with mental age (Frankel, Chikami, Freeman, Ritvo, & Carr, 1974).

Evidence from these studies supports the idea of identifying the idiosyncratic sensory stimuli preferences of severely emotionally disturbed children for use in educational programs with them. With many such children, we may find that as we gain their attention with more stimuli provided from the outer environment, they will become less dependent on providing their own novel stimuli emanating from their inner environment.

Social Level

Disturbances in social relatedness manifested by autistic children constitute perhaps the most striking characteristic of the disorder. Research studies have revealed some interesting and surprising findings regarding the effects of social stimuli. For example, one study found that autistic children performed best on a simple marble-dropping task when a teacher was present and offering praise (Freitag, 1970). They performed less well when left alone or when the teacher was present but offering reprimands instead of praise. Thus, there seemed to be an awareness on the part of the children of the teacher's presence and the positive nature of their interaction—an awareness many might think never existed on the part of isolated, nonsocially relating autistic children.

Another study investigated the attention and eye movement patterns of autistic and retarded children of equal mental age (Hermelin &

O'Connor, 1970). The children were presented with two simultaneous stimuli, one consisting of white squares, the other of cut-up pictures of the human face against a contrasting background. Both autistic and retarded children spent more time looking at the more complex stimuli. However, the retarded children focused most of their attention on the stimuli themselves, while the autistic children focused on the background of the stimuli. The autistic children also showed fewer eye movements and spent more time fixating on a particular stimuli, while the retarded children tended to look back and forth between the two stimuli.

The problem of overselectivity found with many autistic children was discussed at the attention level. With respect to learning the identity of adults, autistic children have been found to overselect irrelevant aspects of adults rather than to attempt to discriminate them by facial or bodily features (Schreibman & Lovaas, 1973). Thus, they may not appear to readily recognize adults with whom they have had frequent contact. This lack of recognition can be particularly upsetting to individuals who invest a great deal of time and effort into attempting to teach autistic children. This reminds us of an experienced teacher taking a course to learn how to work with autistic children. She prepared elaborate curriculum materials each week for one boy and was enthusiastic and effective in her teaching. However, she came to one of us in tears after six weeks. "After all the time and effort I've spent," she cried, "he doesn't even seem to recognize who I am when I come through the door." The author reassured her by sharing similar frustrations at apparently not being recognized that often by some autistic children with whom he had worked for a year or more.

Negative reinforcement has been utilized with autistic children to build social responsiveness. In one study, electric shock was terminated as soon as the child approached a nurse (Lovaas, Schaeffer, & Simmons, 1965). This significantly decreased the frequency of self-stimulating and tantrum behavior and increased approach responses to the nurse. It was later shown that the nurse had become a secondary reinforcer since the child would work on tasks outside the shock situation just to receive her contingent attention.

Modeling procedures have also been used to establish play behavior among seriously disturbed children (Forness, 1974; Colman, Ames, & Frankel, 1975). Children who had learning disabilities but also well-developed play skills served as models for disturbed children who were seriously deficient in play skills. The presence of the high social children resulted in an increase in the cooperative and solitary play behaviors by the low social children and a decrease in the time they spent unoccupied in any play activity.

The influence of normal models on the behavior of exceptional children has become of increasing interest with the advent of mainstreaming and the placement of exceptional children more and more in programs with normal children. While many severely disturbed children may never be appropriately placed in regular classrooms, arranging opportunities for them to interact with children with good social skills would seem highly desirable at all age levels and in all types of special education programs.

Mastery Level

Jimmy

Autistic children are often quick learners of such skills as reading, arithmetic, and written language if they can be reached on the attention, response, and order levels of learning competence. An example of this is provided by a two-year reading and writing program that was undertaken by one of us at the NPI School with Jimmy, a twelve-year-old, nonverbal, autistic boy who had failed to profit from a series of earlier attempts to teach him, largely because he never paid attention to either teacher or tasks (Hewett, 1964). In this program, Jimmy's attention was initially gained through the use of a tangible reward (e.g., candy gumdrop); it was maintained through a systematic program which moved from concrete to symbolic tasks.

In the process of learning to read and write, Jimmy was first expected to hand the teacher three objects which were differentiated by shape and color: a red ball, a yellow box, and a blue cross. These objects were placed on a table, first one at a time, then paired, and later all together. Jimmy's task was to pick up the object called for by the teacher.

The next step was to get Jimmy to copy the teacher's two-dimensional drawing of a ball, box, or cross and then draw these objects on verbal command. During this stage, the concrete objects were also present.

Once this copying task was mastered, colored pictures of the objects were introduced, along with their concrete counterparts, and Jimmy had to pick up the pictures according to the teacher's instructions. Finally, these colored pictures were presented alone and word cards matched with them. To aid in this matching, the word board shown in Figure 10–3 was utilized.

First, the picture of the ball would be placed alone on the upper rail with the word card reading *ball* placed at the far left on the bottom rail. Jimmy's task was to slide the word card directly underneath the picture. Next, two picture cards were placed on the upper rail, and Jimmy had to discriminate between them when he slid the word card into place. Finally three picture cards were placed on the upper rail, and Jimmy had to correctly match word and picture. All words taught to Jimmy were introduced in this way, first with word and picture alone, then with two and later three picture cards placed on the top rail to foster visual discrimination. The position of the picture cards was regularly changed to prevent Jimmy from

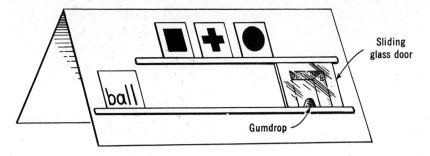

Figure 10–3. The word board used in Jimmy's reading program.

responding on the basis of card placement alone. Following each correct matching, the glass door at the far right of the board would be slid open by the teacher and a candy gumdrop which had been in plain sight all the time was made available to Jimmy. The door was then closed and another gum-drop placed in the box behind it through an opening under the word board.

Once Jimmy had mastered some seventy-five word-picture combinations presented on the word board, he had acquired characteristics of a true mastery learner. Gaining the approval of the teacher and accurately accomplishing the tasks given to him were, by and large, the only rewards he needed at this point. Therefore, a mastery program of spelling and handwriting was undertaken so that he might communicate through writing. The four phases of this program will be briefly described here.

Phase 1: Letter-by-Letter Spelling and Alphabet Mastery. A large flannel board was set up in place of the word board on Jimmy's work table. The flannel board is shown in Figure 10–4. Alphabet letters which had been printed on small squares of tagboard with flannel backing so that they would adhere to the board were affixed to the surface. A picture of an object (e.g., cow) which Jimmy had learned to label earlier was also affixed to the board. A card with the name of the object printed on it was placed below. While Jimmy watched, the teacher took the letters *c, o,* and *w* from an array of random letters also placed on the board and placed them one at a time below the picture and word in proper order. While doing this, the teacher said aloud "c-o-w." The teacher then took the three letters and randomly affixed them to the side of the board and directed Jimmy to replace them in correct order, using the word card below the picture as a model. This was not difficult for Jimmy, and he quickly responded.

The next step was to go to a regular classroom blackboard and practice one of the letters in a handwriting exercise. In the case of *cow*, the letter selected was *c* and the teacher drew a *c* on the blackboard, naming it aloud for Jimmy. Jimmy was then instructed to copy a row of *c*'s. As he did, the teacher named each letter aloud.

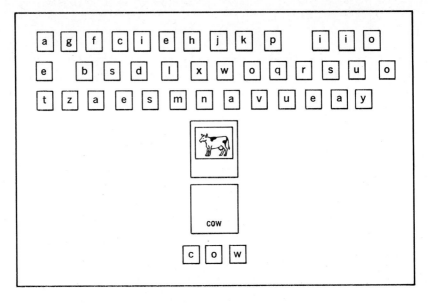

Figure 10–4. The flannel board used with Jimmy.

By referring to word-picture combinations he had learned previously in a similar manner, all twenty-six letters of the alphabet were presented to Jimmy. Candy rewards were reserved until ten to fifteen minutes had passed, and on some occasions Jimmy worked for forty-five minutes without any tangible reward. It should be pointed out that no attempt was made to foster perfect handwriting at this point. A legible manuscript alphabet was the only goal.

Phase 2: Auditory Discrimination. In this phase, Jimmy was presented with a large assortment of randomly assembled letter squares on the flannel board. On the teacher's command, he was to take off all the squares containing the particular letter (e.g., "Jimmy, give me all the *e*'s."). Since there were several duplicates for each letter, particularly for commonly used vowels, Jimmy had practice in both auditory and visual discrimination of the alphabet. This he mastered quickly and with few problems.

Phase 3: Spelling and Beginning Phrase-writing. Once Jimmy was familiar with letter names, he could spell any word dictated to him letter by letter by the teacher. Shortly thereafter, he acquired skill at reproducing complete words dictated to him without letter-by-letter spelling. Figure 10–5 presents a sample of Jimmy's writing of the word *cow* and his accompanying spontaneous drawing. At this stage a most significant communication and mastery task was introduced. Jimmy would no longer be given any candy without a written request. In one session he correctly learned to write *I want candy.* Thereafter he was only given the candy reward when he presented the teacher with such a written request. While Jimmy did not understand

Figure 10–5. An example of Jimmy's writing and drawing.

the meaning of *I* or *want* and possibly not even *candy,* he had been introduced to an appropriate means of communication which was in marked contrast to the grunting, pointing, and primitive coercion he had used previously in order to get others to satisfy his wants.

An interesting communication took place one day when Jimmy assembled all of the animal pictures used in the training program, along with the pictures of *mama* and *daddy.* Then he wrote the word *zoo.* He was describing a weekend trip to the zoo taken with his parents which he apparently enjoyed very much.

Phase 4: Phrase-writing Transfer. As Jimmy was able to write more and more words, he appeared to become fascinated with this symbolic means of referring to objects and events with which he was familiar. In a short while he was writing *I want school* in order to be allowed to accompany the teacher for his daily lessons, and *I want water, I want to eat, I want pool, I want a walk, I want toilet,* and other phrases in order to express his wants to the staff on the ward. Jimmy took great delight in offering these written communications to the ward staff and carried a pad of paper around with him for this purpose. The reciprocal reactions displayed on the part of the staff when Jimmy appropriately communicated with them through writing can be likened to those experienced when Eddie used his conditioned speech for such communication.

It would be satisfying to report that twelve-year-old Jimmy went on to expand his mastery of written communication so that he functioned on a fairly high level in relation to his environment. Unfortunately, this cannot be done. Shortly after completion of the reading and written language program, Jimmy was transferred to a private school for mentally retarded children. Although he was diagnosed as autistic, this was the only long-term residential school placement his parents could obtain for him. Despite the author's plea that the school continue the written communication program, and despite sending the school complete records of Jimmy's program along with actual materials for continuing the work, the new school decided that speech was the most essential skill to develop with Jimmy and completely neglected any continuation of the NPI School program. Three years later Jimmy was seen again.

He had been engaged in an entirely futile program of speech development which had not helped him at all. His written language skills had deteriorated almost to zero during this time, and he was again dependent on grunting and pointing in order to communicate his needs to others.

Kate*

The principles of errorless training have been applied to the teaching of reading to autistic and other severely disturbed children (Hewett, Mayhew, & Rabb, 1967). An individualized reading program using these principles was developed for use on a simple, manually operated teaching machine (Grolier Min/Max II). In addition to prompts of color and geometric form, the child was immediately rewarded for correct responses with a small bit of candy.

Kate was an eleven-year-old, autistic girl who was given the errorless training program at the NPI School because of previous failures to teach her by a more direct, programmed-instructional approach. The program designed for Kate was in three phases. It was presented frame by frame on a teaching machine with confirmations of correct choices immediately appearing after her response.

Phase 1 emphasized consistent discrimination of solid colors, solid forms, and later, color and form outlines.

Phase 1: Color and Form

a) Color only

Teacher: "Find the red box."

*Material in the following section adapted from Hewett, Mayhew, & Rabb, *American Journal of Orthopsychiatry,* 1967. Copyright 1967 by the American Orthopsychiatric Association, Inc.

b) Solid Form only

Teacher: "Find the red box."

c) Color outline only

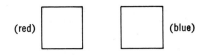

Teacher: "Find the red box."

d) Form outline only

Teacher: "Find the red box."

A similar series in which the discriminations centered around finding a blue ball was also used. Many repetitions of each item were presented and placement of correct choices alternated to control position effects.

Phase 2 presented the words *Tom* in the red box and *ride* in the blue ball and offered the color and form cues as aids in making the child's choices "errorless."

Phase 2: Two Words with Color and Form Cues

a) Matching

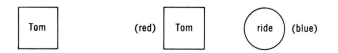

Teacher: (points to box on left) "The word in the box is *Tom*. Find the word *Tom* in the red box over here" (points to choices).

b) Directed choice

Teacher: "Find *Tom* in the red box."

The same sequence was followed for matching and choosing *ride* in the blue ball.

This series was intended to introduce the word *Tom* in association with the red box and *ride* in association with the blue ball. The teacher's color and form cues were utilized to make it virtually impossible for Kate to fail and to initially relieve her of the responsibility of any actual word discrimination or retention skills. In addition, Kate received continuous tangible reinforcement by means of tiny bits of chocolate placed in her mouth by the teacher following each correct response.

Phase 3 was the final stage in the errorless training program and involved gradual fading of the color and form cues used in Phase 2.

Phase 3: Fading of Color and Form Cues

a)

Teacher: "Find *Tom* in the red box."

b)

(red) ⋮ Tom ⋮   (ride) (blue)

Teacher: "Find *Tom* in the red box."

c)

Tom   ride

Teacher: "Find *Tom*."

Kate readily responded to the color-and-form errorless training, although she took almost two months to achieve consistent functioning on a 75 percent correct response level. While during the reading program attempted earlier she had regressed and become inattentive, she now cooperated well and appeared to thoroughly enjoy her guaranteed successes. Figure 10–6, section A, shows Kate's correct response rate during the color and form training in Phase 1. Section B of Figure 10–6 reports her rate during Phases 2 and 3 and illustrates her consistently high level of correctness which was maintained even when the color and form cues were gradually removed.

Whereas Kate initially had been unable to discriminate these words, she learned them even though color and form cues were utilized much of the time. This incidental learning of complex discrimination during errorless training is extremely interesting. Rather than merely relying on color

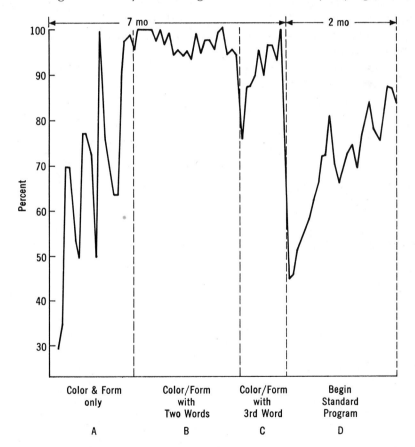

Figure 10–6. Kate's correct response rate for her errorless training and standard program. Reprinted with permission, from the *American Journal of Orthopsychiatry.* Copyright 1967 by the American Orthopsychiatric Association, Inc.

and form supports indefinitely to the exclusion of any attention to the word symbols inside, Kate and other autistic children enrolled in the NPI School program definitely acquired word discrimination skills.

Section C of Figure 10–6 represents Kate's correct response rate when a third word, *Betty*, was introduced in a cross. No color cues were utilized at this point and the form cues were quickly faded. The three errorless training phases, including the introduction of a third word, took seven months. While only forty-eight sessions are reported in Figure 10–6, and Kate was actually scheduled on a three-times-a-week basis, interruptions due to illness, teacher absence, school vacations, and the like extended these sessions over a seven-month period.

The most dramatic portion of Kate's reading program is illustrated in Section D of Figure 10–6. Following the seven months of errorless training, Kate was reintroduced to the reading program that had been unsuccessfully attempted earlier. This program presented her with six new words each week, none of which were introduced with color or form cues. While her overall correct response rate initially dropped during the program, she steadily improved and was soon efficiently learning twice as many new words each week as she had been able to acquire during the entire previous seven months.

Reading for Kate provided many opportunities for increased reality contact. Once she was able to read in a basal primer, she engaged in discussions of the pictures, names of characters, and events described. She took the book home with her and willingly read for members of her family in what was one of her first appropriate interactions with them. It was evident they were extremely impressed by her newly developed skill and the opportunities it provided for interaction and genuine praise.

The NPI School Experimental Reading Program†

A continuation of the reading program used with Kate was developed by the NPI School staff (Hewett, Mayhew, & Rabb, 1967). Of particular concern to the program were children who had failed to learn by more traditional approaches and who were often considered noneducable. This program was a modification and elaboration of one developed for institutionalized retardates by Birnbrauer, Bijou, Wolf, and Kidder (1965) at the Rainier School in Buckley, Washington.

The basic goal of the NPI School Experimental Reading Program was to get the children ready to read while they were actually learning to read. Toward this end, the following general principles were adhered to:

†Material in the following section adapted from Hewett, Mayhew, & Rabb, *American Journal of Orthopsychiatry*, 1967. Copyright 1967 by the American Orthopsychiatric Association, Inc.

1. Present the child with small increments of learning which gradually increase in difficulty based on principles of programmed instruction.

2. Initially, reward each correct response the child makes immediately; use social praise and tangible rewards and withhold these rewards for incorrect responses. Later reward the child on an intermittent basis.

3. Use systematic word review, discrimination exercises, and comprehension questions to consolidate learning.

4. Provide the child with an actual reading experience in a real book in addition to programmed learning of words on a teaching machine.

5. Freely adapt the steps, structure, and type of rewards used in the program to insure continued success for each individual child.

6. Maintain detailed records of each of the child's responses to follow progress, determine need for program modification, and provide teacher feedback.

Words to be learned in the program were taken from the 155-word basic sight vocabulary contained in the three preprimers and primer of the Ginn Basic Readers (Russell, 1957). This vocabulary was presented to the child in a series of programmed lessons involving the use of a teaching machine (Grolier Min/Max II) and the supervision of an individual teacher. While "word calling," or reading of word symbols without full comprehension of their meaning, may not be favored by some in the field of reading instruction, it was tolerated and even encouraged in the experimental program. There was no alphabet, verbal fluency, or word concept training, and no concern with handedness and laterality.

A five-part lesson based upon words introduced in each chapter of the Ginn Basic Readers was developed. This program was administered by the teacher in a one-to-one relationship. Children were given a pretest of words used in the part of the program to which they were assigned. While pretest scores varied, generally no child was enrolled in a part of the program if more than 50 percent of the pretest words were recognized. In most cases, the program took from twenty-five to thirty-five minutes a session and was offered to the child three times a week in a partially screened-off booth in a classroom.

Responses to the entire five-part program were recorded by the teacher on a data sheet, as well as the amount of time taken for completion of the session. A check mark card was also available to record for the child the number of correct responses made. For each of these correct responses, tangible rewards (e.g., candy, money) were first used on a continual, and then on a periodic, basis. These rewards were later replaced by the check marks on the card, and completed cards with 200 checks could be converted to prizes after several days' work.

Part 1 of the five-part program was an *oral reading review* of the chapter in the basic reader containing the words learned on the previous day. The child read the chapter aloud and was immediately given any unfamiliar words—without encouragement to sound them out. The teacher recorded missed words on the data sheet.

Part 2 consisted of *vocabulary building* using a systematic presentation of new words on the teaching machine controlled by the teacher. In this phase of the program, words were introduced and reviewed in the following manner:

1. *Visual Discrimination of the New Word.* To introduce new words, a simple visual-matching task was used. The new word appeared on the left enclosed in a box. It appeared again on the right with two different words which served as distractors. The child's task was to match the word in the box with the same word on the right. This was done by pointing, drawing a line under the word, or placing a marker on it, depending on the level of functioning.

Item: `Tom`   ride Tom fast
                      Tom

Teacher: "Find a word just like the one in the box."
           Immediate confirmation of the correct response was given as the machine was turned to the next frame and the correct choice appeared directly beneath it.

Confirmation: `Tom`   ride Tom fast
              Tom

Teacher: (if correct) "That's right."
           (if incorrect) "No, (points) this word is like the one in the box. Say *Tom*."

2. *Auditory Discrimination of the New Word.* The next frame presented the same word with two distracting words. The teacher verbally directed the child to find it. This task involved auditory and visual matching. The correct response was again confirmed as the machine was turned to the next frame:

Item: Tom fast ride

Teacher: "Find *Tom*."

Confirmation: Tom

Teacher: (if correct) "That's right!"
           (if incorrect) "No, (points) this word is *Tom*. Say *Tom*."

3. *Readback of the New Word.* In this frame the new word appeared alone and the subject was asked to read it. Confirmation was given verbally by the teacher.

Item:	Tom

Teacher: "What is this word?"

Confirmation: (if correct) "Yes, that word is *Tom*."
(if incorrect) "No, this word (points to Tom) is *Tom*. Say *Tom*."

4. Visual Recall of the New Word. In the next frame the new word appeared alone and the subject was asked to look at it. The machine was rolled to the following frame where the word appeared with two distractors and the subject was asked, "Find a word like the one you just saw." The subject therefore was asked to remember the word over a short time.

Item 1:	Tom

Teacher: "Look at this word."

Item 2:   fast   ride   Tom

Teacher: "Now find a word like the one you just saw."

Confirmation: Tom

Teacher: (if correct) "That's right!"
(if incorrect) "No, this word (points to Tom) is like the one you saw. The word is *Tom*. Say *Tom*."

5. Phrase Reading. Next, the new word appeared in a phrase taken from the book. This was done to promote transfer of reading skill to Part 3 of the lesson: new oral reading. The child was merely asked to read the words and the teacher immediately provided miscalled words.

Item: Ride, Tom

In the vocabulary building section of the experimental program, words were introduced into the program in the same sequence as they were introduced in the book. Review words were systematically introduced into the program along with the new words. For each new word introduced, two review words appeared as auditory discriminations. A third review word appeared as a visual recall item, and from five to ten review words appeared as readback and phrase reading items. The program thus provided for retention of words previously learned.

The actual format followed in a single lesson during the vocabulary building section was as follows:

Visual discrimination	(New word)
Auditory discrimination	(New word)
Readback	(New word)
Auditory discrimination	(Review word #1)
Readback	(Review word #1)
Auditory discrimination	(Review word #2)

Readback	(Review word #2)
Readback	(New word)
Visual recall	(New word)
Visual recall	(Review word #3)
Readback	(New word)
Readback	(Review word #4)
Readback	(Review word #5)
Phrase reading	(New words)
Phrase reading	(New and review words)
Phrase reading	(New and review words)
Phrase reading	(New and review words)
Phrase reading	(New and review words)

Part 3 of the lesson was *new oral reading*. The child was given a basic reader and asked to read a new chapter containing the words just learned during the vocabulary building section. When the child failed to read a word correctly within a five-second period, it was immediately provided by the teacher who asked that it be repeated aloud. No attempt was made to build phonic skills in this part of the program.

Part 4 consisted of a *comprehension* section involving questions about the content in the new chapter. For students using the first Primer, the student was asked to respond verbally to simple questions (e.g., "What was the boy's name?"). For those using later readers, the child was asked to read comprehension questions presented in simple multiple-choice and true/false form. This part of the program was eliminated for some of the autistic and severely disturbed children because of the confusion which existed regarding social objects and concepts. As these children became more familiar with the basic vocabulary, however, a surprising degree of comprehension of content and pictures developed.

Part 5, the *follow-up* phase of the lesson, consisted of discrimination exercises with the newly learned words. These exercises emphasized initial, medial, and final word completions and discriminations in an effort to focus attention and offer additional cues for recall.

a) Initial completion item: Tom   L   T
                              _om

The child was asked to select the missing letter and the teacher confirmed the response by writing the correct letter in the appropriate blank. Medial and final completion tasks were presented in similar fashion with middle and final letters missing.

b) Initial word discrimination item: Tom   Lom   Rom   Tom

Next the child was directed to choose the correct matching word from two distractors which varied in initial, medial, or final letters. Confirmation appeared in the next frame underneath the correct choice.

Data collection included recording the child's responses in all five parts of the lesson and calculating the percentage of correct responses. A 75 percent correct response rate was set as a criterion for moving the child ahead in the reading program since it was found that progress could be achieved with most children even though they made a 25 percent error rate. If this standard was not achieved, the program would be repeated. If a series of repetitions did not appear to move the child on to criterion performance, the errorless training sequence was introduced.

Rewards for giving correct responses (e.g., reading a single word, answering a comprehension question, selecting a missing letter) were provided on a continual basis (one correct response earned one unit of reward) for all subjects during their first three lessons. Candy, in the form of readily dissolvable (the faster the candy goes, the less it distracts the subject) fruit drops, was deposited into a small cup beside the subject each time he or she responded correctly. Older subjects were rewarded with money, and pennies were dropped into the cup rather than candy.

According to the standard procedure, after the first three lessons each subject would have to make five correct responses before having one candy or money unit placed in the cup. In addition to actual receipt of a tangible reward, the subject was given a token reward in the form of a check mark on a card ruled off with 200 squares. These check marks were always given on a 1:1 basis. Later, receipt of tangible rewards was delayed until an entire lesson was completed, although check marks were given as the child earned them. At this point the recognition of the value of the check marks increased for all subjects. Eventually a 1:200 schedule for tangible rewards was established with the child being given a choice of one five-cent prize (e.g., balloon, whistle, package of candy or gum) for each full card of check marks accumulated. These full cards could also be saved, and two could be exchanged for a ten-cent prize. The total number of possible responses varied somewhat from lesson to lesson, but it usually took two days for a subject to accumulate a full card of 200 check marks.

Subjects were moved through the different reward schedules at individual rates, and nine of the subjects had progressed from a continual schedule by the end of the first twelve lessons.

A normal subject also participating in the program was only given social rewards during her lessons which included the teacher's smiling, nodding approval, and commenting "Good girl!" The inclusion of the normal subject and the removal of tangible rewards made possible establishment of a normal developmental baseline for the first part of the reading program.

Figure 10–7 illustrates the correct response rate and learning efficiency (number of responses per minute) of the normal subject, a four-year, eleven-month-old girl, during her learning of the nineteen basic words which made up the vocabulary of the first Ginn Basic Preprimer. As is readily apparent, this subject had little difficulty reaching an almost per-

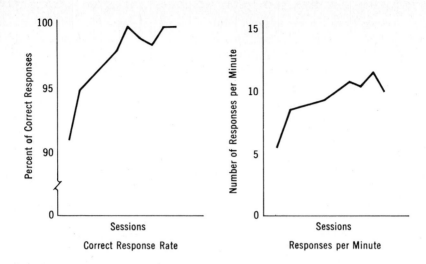

Figure 10–7. The correct response rate and responses per minute for a normal girl. (Reprinted, with permission, from the *American Journal of Orthopsychiatry.* Copyright 1967 by the American Orthopsychiatric Association, Inc.)

fect correct response level and steadily increased her learning efficiency. This type of data is what one might expect to obtain with a normal first grader of superior intelligence in a typical public school basal reading program. In such a program, it is the social reward of conformity, teacher and peer approval, and mastery of a highly valued skill which provide all the necessary rewards for learning.

Figure 10–8 shows the progress in correct response rate and learning efficiency (number of responses per minute) for a four-year, ten-month-old emotionally disturbed boy for the same portion of the program undertaken by the normal subject. This boy was highly distractible and poorly motivated in the learning situation, but the provision of candy rewards gained his attention and cooperation. He maintained a correct response rate that was lower than the normal subject's, and he also was less efficient in his rate of responding. While this boy's intelligence was estimated below that of the normal subject's, the variability he displayed may be viewed as an indicator of his emotional problem. Although there was much variability in the correct response rates and learning efficiency of the other subjects, the overall effectiveness of the experimental program was similar for all, and no subject failed to maintain progress. Because of differences in length of hospital stay and availability as outpatient participants, the range of participation in the program was from 8 to 137 sessions.

This reading program emphasized tasks at the attention, response, order, exploratory, social, and mastery levels and relied on a variety of rewards in a manner similar to that demonstrated in the speech training program with Eddie. Provision for the task and reward levels of the developmental sequence can be summarized as follows:

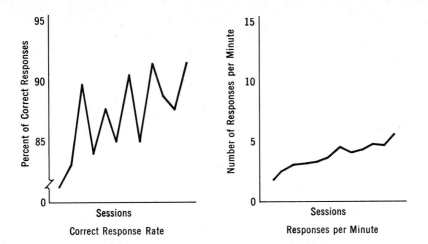

Figure 10–8. The correct response rate and responses per minute for an emotionally disturbed boy. (Reprinted, with permission, from the *American Journal of Orthopsychiatry.* Copyright 1967 by the American Orthopsychiatric Association, Inc.)

Task Level	*Reward*
1. Attention	
a) Removal of distracting stimuli (one-to-one teaching situation)	Tangible (can be money, candy, check marks)
b) Presentation of small, discrete units of work	
2. Response	
a) Active participation of learner	One-to-one teaching situation with individual attention to the child at all times
b) Guaranteeing child's success	
3. Order	
a) Program organized in small discrete steps, each providing the child an opportunity to complete a task	Task completion
b) Structured learning environment (teaching machine, controlled presentation, program systematically organized and reviewed)	
c) Specific directions must be followed in answering each item	
4. Exploratory	
a) Visual and auditory discrimination emphasized in program items	Visual-auditory stimulation
5. Social	
a) Teacher directs child in all phases of program	Gaining social approval

Task Level	Reward
6. Mastery	
a) Building a basic reading-sight vocabulary	Knowledge of results through confirmation of items and teacher comments

One of the problems in educational programs for autistic children is that they have traditionally had to rely heavily on the one-to-one teaching situation. That is, for each individual child, an individual teacher is required. At least two serious drawbacks exist with respect to this teaching situation. First, the cost of providing an individual teacher may be unrealistic and prohibitive. Second, and perhaps more important, the autistic child who is taught in a one-to-one situation still must generalize what has been learned to other individuals and other settings. The failure of such generalization to occur has been reported repeatedly here and in the research literature.

In one study (Koegel & Rincover, 1974), eight autistic children were taught a number of basic classroom skills on a one-to-one basis (e.g., paying attention to teacher, verbal and nonverbal imitation, and single receptive language skills). Following this, the children were placed in two settings that differed with respect to teacher-pupil ratio. One setting had two children per teacher, the other had eight children per teacher. Three of the autistic children had acquired a 95 percent or better correct response rate in the one-to-one setting. But in the two-to-one setting their rate dropped to 70 percent. For these same children, the eight-to-one setting produced a further drop to approximately 40 percent. Several of the other children dropped to 20 percent, and one child's rate dropped to 0 percent.

In an attempt to foster generalization of learned behavior across settings, a plan was devised whereby the children could gradually be introduced to groups of larger size. Initially the children participated in a one-to-one situation receiving a reward for each correct response. This ratio was later changed to one reward for each two correct responses. Next, two children were brought together with one teacher and two teacher's aides who alternately rewarded the children for correct responding. At first the aides prompted the children if they failed to respond, but gradually they reduced such prompting. When the two children were correctly responding at an 80 percent level, they were only given a reward following four correct responses. At this point two more children who had received identical training were brought into the group. Again, the teacher's aides prompted the children and then gradually faded the prompts until an 80 percent level was reached for all children. Now the ratio of correct responses to a reward was eight to one. These four children were then combined with the four remaining children who had received identical training and a class of eight children with one teacher was formed. It was found that not only did the basic attention and imitation skills generalize to the group of eight, but the children were able to successfully acquire new skills in eight-to-one situations. As the children became more proficient, it became necessary to individualize instruction in addition to maintaining some group activities. This was done successfully, and Koegel and Rincover saw promise for such an approach for making it possible for autistic children to participate in classrooms with normal children where they will have a variety of appropriate behavioral and language models with whom to interact.

Frankel, Tymchuk, and Simmons (1976) conducted an investigation into the contrasting effect of a one-to-one situation and a one-to-three situation with six autistic children and six mentally retarded children. According to their results, the effect of group size appears highly idiosyncratic and must be considered for individual children rather than in relation to specific types of problems. It was found that this change from one-to-one to one-to-three only affected the percent response rate of two autistic children and none of the retarded subjects. In terms of correct response rate, most autistic subjects dropped in the larger group, but one actually increased 27 percent. What this would seem to mean is that the setting variable is most important to consider in developing an educational program for autistic children. Where behaviors learned in a one-to-one situation do not generalize to larger groups, the shaping approach of Koegel and Rincover may be particularly promising. Where larger groups are actually conducive to increased response rate and correct response rates, no such shaping will be necessary. Whenever possible, every effort needs to be made to lessen reliance on one-to-one teaching with autistic children both because of cost and its potentially inhibiting effect on the generalization of learned behavior.

The Dejarnette Center for Human Development Program‡

The Dejarnette Center for Human Development is a state supported residential school for severely emotionally disturbed children. Its program is based on behavioral techniques and features a number of imaginative and innovative aspects. There are two major program components: (1) a highly individualized "forced choice" program for autistic and other severely disturbed children, and (2) an individualized day school "free choice" program allowing higher functioning children the opportunity to self-select participation in academics, arts and crafts, and movement activities.

The forced choice procedure is based on the belief that severely disturbed children often exhibit few if any self-initiating behaviors and are catered to and reinforced for such passivity by others who initiate interaction for them. Twelve children who rarely initiate contacts, who are negativistically noncompliant or passively compliant, who are loners, who gen-

‡The authors are indebted to Bill Herr, who developed this program, for permission to describe it.

erally require a one-to-one relationship at all times, and who are not hyperaggressive participate in the program at any one time.

Headquarters for the forced choice procedure is a large open area within the children's living quarters. This area is divided into a plexiglass paneled playpen approximately 10 x 20 feet in size and a surrounding activity area. The playpen is clean and bright but barren and devoid of reinforcers. The activity area is rich in objects, activities, and people likely to be sought out by the child. There is a bar with Kool Aid and cookies, toys such as Hot Wheels, wagons, and tricycles, a center with blocks and Tinker Toys, a television with cartoons playing, listening posts with multiple headphone attachments, and a number of staff members milling about.

The child's entire twenty-four-hour day is referenced in some way to the playpen area and the procedures that are used there. In the morning, the twelve children are brought to the playpen area, led through a gate, and locked in. In order to get out of the playpen and over into the activity area, each child must approach a teacher permanently assigned by the gate as "gatekeeper" and indicate on a picture menu board that depicts all the sorts of activities and individuals available outside what he or she would like to do. The children may also select a particular adult to spend time with. Once the selection is made, the outside staff is alerted and the activity made ready for the child for a five-minute period. After this period the child is returned to the playpen to make another selection. If the child fails to go to the specific activity selected, he or she is immediately returned to the playpen area. This also occurs if the child begins to engage in self-stimulatory behavior or has a tantrum.

There are six staff members assigned to the program. Their demeanor and relationships with the children while they are in the playpen or activity area are carefully structured. Children in the playpen are ignored by the gatekeeper and his or her assistant. While appearing to be indifferent to the children, they are constantly supervising them out of the corners of their eyes, and they are ready to immediately intervene if a fight or other disturbance breaks out. This indifference is a reflection of the staff's conviction that severely disturbed children should not receive noncontingent attention from them. However, once the child "makes the first move" a great deal of attention is given to him or her. In the activity area, teachers reflect the child's degree of responsiveness. If the child is enthusiastic, the teacher is enthusiastic; if the child makes a response, the teacher makes a response; if the child pauses, the teacher pauses.

When mealtimes arrive, the children must select appropriate food cards from the gatekeeper's menu board. This earns them the privilege of leaving the playpen and going to the cafeteria. If they do not select a food card, they must remain in the playpen where a meal of nonpreferred food (e.g., hominy grits) will be brought to them. Likewise, if children fail to select a bedtime card allowing them to go to their rooms at night, a cot will be brought in for them, and they will spend the night in the playpen. Similar procedures are used for toileting, washing, and brushing teeth.

Not all children enrolled in the forced choice program are equally ready to make choices, follow through on activities selected, and master the system all at once. For such children, allowances are readily made. However, the eventual goal is to place the responsibility for the child's experiences and day's activities squarely on his or her shoulders. When it is felt that the child has the behavioral repertoire necessary to assume such responsibility, the system is firmly imposed.

On Monday mornings until noon all the rewarding activities outside the playpen are made available to the children without requiring menu selection. As a result, no child enters the playpen during that time. The reason for this free play experience is to build motivation for all of the menu card activities that must be self-selected later in the day and during the remainder of the week.

The gatekeeper and his or her assistant record each child's choices, and the teachers in the activity area record the child's behavior and the intervals of time spent in the area. As a child evidences increasing ability more may be expected by the gatekeeper than just selection of a task from the menu board. For example, the child may make a selection and then be required to briefly practice speech or language skills before going outside to the activity area. Or if the child's hands are dirty, the gatekeeper may require the child to select a handwashing card and to wash his or her hands before being allowed to select an activity card. In an effort to not overwhelm a child with too many menu cards, a selected number of cards appropriate to the time of day may be placed on the board. Hence, from 7:00 to 8:00 AM only housekeeping cards may be available, and from 8:00 to 9:00 only eating and toileting cards. Another unique use of the menu board is to have pictures of the children themselves placed there and a child who wants to play a particular game may be required to select the picture of the child with whom he or she wants to play the game.

Children enrolled in the forced choice program go through two phases. A child in Phase 1 undertakes the mechanics of the playpen-activity area operation, engages in pre-menu card selection tasks imposed by the gatekeeper, travels to and from activities with only occasional assistance (e.g., handholding), remains on a task for five minutes or longer, and occasionally selects necessity cards (e.g., food, toileting, sleeping). At Phase 2, the child travels to and from activities with only verbal control necessary, rarely holds the hands of peers in play and travel, consistently chooses all necessity cards, frequently initiates activity selection verbally, and spends an hour or less total time each day in the playpen. When the child is successfully operating at Phase 2, he or she may be enrolled in the free choice program.

In the free choice program, the child selects activities to cover the school day. There are three major activity areas where the program takes place: (1) the learning center where academic tasks are undertaken, (2) the arts and crafts laboratory, and (3) the movement laboratory. Of the five periods in each child's school day, two must be in the learning center. Then, each day each child starts with a self-selected schedule indicating where he or she wants to spend each period.

Even though the selection has been made, if during a given period the child wishes to leave the activity and go to another, this is permitted. But the child must "wait for the bus." The school bus is actually a staff member who makes the rounds of the activity areas once an hour. Any child waiting by the door may "climb aboard" by lining up behind the staff member and following him or her to the desired new activity area.

Another innovative aspect of the free choice program is the "fix-it shop." Should a child become disruptive in an activity area, the teacher may send him or her out to wait for the bus to go to the fix-it shop. Here the staff member in charge may assign to the child order-type repetitive tasks which may be of low interest. Or the fix-it shop teacher may have the child "rehearse" more appropriate behavior or engage in relaxation therapy. If the child's disruptiveness continues, there is a time-out room nearby.

Each child in the free choice program wears a colored wrist band which he or she has made personally in the arts and crafts laboratory. These are kept on a large board with pegs after school hours. As long as the child is wearing a band he or she is eligible for surprise reinforcement (e.g., trip to local quick-food establishment). But if the child is not wearing a band, no such reinforcements are provided. The loss of one's wrist band comes about when the child's behavior has consistently fallen below expectations and the privilege to be allowed to wear it again must be earned.

The most prestigious wrist band is the blue band. Blue bands are awarded to children who accomplish the following:

1. No referrals to fix-it shop
2. Perfect bus rides five days in a row
   a) Waiting quietly in line until bus is ready to move
   b) Walking slowly and staying in one's own space
   c) Holding the door for the person behind
   d) Keeping eyes straight ahead
   e) Not talking without permission

The pay-off for being a blue-band wearer is "blue riderness" or the right to freely move from activity area to area without having to wait for the bus.

One of the Dejarnette posters informing students how to handle potentially physically explosive situations states the following:

Keep Cool Rules
1. Move
2. Politeness
3. Firm Voice
4. Reason

5. Ignore
6. Threaten to tell
7. Go tell

The Dejarnette program abounds in clever and highly motivating features. These are augmented by spacious facilities, a most enthusiastic staff, and a small staff-student ratio.

When the first edition of this book was written, there were very few established programs for severely disturbed children that were more educational than custodial. There was also very little research underway to study the learning characteristics of such children. Since that time, however, many programs have developed. In addition, an increasing number of research studies have been conducted. These developments are the result of federal funding of training and research programs in the field of special education, the increased number of trained leaders in special education that has emerged from the 1960s and 1970s, and a growing conviction that not only is every handicapped individual a learner ready to learn something but that he or she has a constitutional right to an appropriate education at public expense.

chapter 11

Working with Parents

A potent and significant force has emerged in the 1970s sending shock waves across the field of education: *parent power*. After years of frustration and rejection, parents of handicapped children are now not only asking, but demanding that the public schools in the nation provide a free, effective, and accountable school program for their children.

This is in marked contrast to earlier times when parents often stood "hat in hand" in a school district office requesting information about a school program for their handicapped child only to be told that the school had no special education services at all or none for children with their child's type of problem. This is in marked contrast to the time when a school district could administer an IQ test to a suspected retarded child and place the child in a self-contained class program for the retarded if the IQ score was below 80, sometimes without even informing the parents much less requesting permission for the testing and placement. This is in marked contrast to the time when children could be easily excluded for misconduct with the parents left to come up with a solution such as placement in a private school with a costly tuition. In this chapter, we will examine the rights of the parents of disturbed children with respect to Public Law 94–142, problems encountered in parent-teacher-school relationships, and guidelines for establishing a parents' citizens advisory committee for a public school special education program.

Parents' Rights

In Chapter 3 we discussed the formulation of an Individual Education Program (IEP). The IEP is actually developed by an appraisal team made up of a representative of the school or other service agency, the student's teacher, the student's parents, and the student if appropriate. There are six steps that constitute the actual development of the IEP and the process of instructional planning:

1. Referral of the Student to the School Appraisal Team. Teachers, local school or school district administrators, private professionals, concerned community members, school personnel, parents, or students themselves can all refer children or youths with possible exceptional needs to the school appraisal team. This team may be made up of the school psychologist, the principal, the special education teacher or other district representative with expertise related to the child's problem.

2. Assessment to Determine the Student's Learning Needs. First, the school must send a written notice to the student's parents, stating the reason for the assessment, the types of assessment to be done, and requesting their consent. Once parental consent is obtained, the appraisal team develops an assessment plan and team members are given assignments which must be completed within a specified time period. The purpose of the assessment is to determine the special learning needs of the student and to provide information about appropriate educational placement, special services, and instructional techniques. Typically, the team will consider the student's educational history, observe the student in his or her present placement, and determine the student's level of functioning in such areas as academic, social, self-help, psychomotor, and prevocational or vocational skills. Hearing and vision are also checked, as are cultural and language factors which may relate to the child's performance. For some students, the team will need to obtain more in-depth information about the student's developmental history, intellectual ability, and language functioning.

3. Appraisal Team Meeting (Formulating the IEP). The teacher(s) or specialists who have assessed the child, and who will carry out the student's plan, and the student's parents participate in this meeting. When appropriate, the student may also participate. The school must make an effort to conduct the meeting at a mutually convenient time and place and to assist parents in understanding the proceedings at the meeting.

The following should be accomplished in formulating the IEP:

Provide each member of the team (including the parents) with a clear picture of the student's areas of strength and weakness.

Identify, in order of importance, the student's educational needs and what goals can reasonably be accomplished within the school year.

Specify measurable instructional objectives leading to the accomplishment of each major goal.

Identify instructional strategies and materials likely to be needed by the student.

Provide a forum for exploring possible program and placement alternatives.

The IEP is sometimes called a total service plan, since it outlines the student's program for the school year and lists the special services which will be provided for the student.

The IEP should be developed cooperatively with the parents at the actual appraisal team meeting. We have found that many parents who are informed regarding their rights are offended if a fully written plan is presented for their signature. The essence of the meeting is that parents will have substantial input regarding their concerns, observations, objectives, and aspirations.

4. Placement. There is an ever-increasing range of placement options for disturbed children. It is unlikely that all possible placement alternatives will be available within a given school district. As a result, many school districts cooperate with other districts, and/or with the County Schools Office, to make a full range of services available to the handicapped children in a geographical area. Unlike the way in which placement decisions have often been made in the past, there are now fewer "hard and fast" rules and regulations about a child's eligibility for a particular class, program, or school placement. It is the responsibility of the team, with input from parents (and sometimes also from the student) to determine the placement or educational setting in which the student's learning needs can best be met and in which the child will be most able to function both as a student and as a person.

Some things which must be considered in making placement decisions are:

What are the student's primary learning needs?

What type of educational setting can most effectively help meet the child's needs?

What kind of activities can the student successfully do in the regular program?

Is the child able to be integrated successfully for all or part of the day?

If the child requires placement in a special class or center, are there any opportunities for interaction with nonhandicapped or less handicapped peers?

The term *least restrictive environment* has come to be equated with *mainstreaming,* or the integration of handicapped children into regular classrooms. The concept of least restrictive environment really means many things. It means that handicapped children have the *right* of access to appropriate public education programs, unimpeded by architectural, physical, financial, or attitudinal barriers. It also means that parents have the *right* of access to the school and the *right* to participate in the discussions and decisions concerning their child's placement, to examine the alternatives, and to give their consent. However, some parents of handicapped children, as well as some regular and special educators, are ambivalent about mainstreaming. In forming an opinion on mainstreaming, the following points are important to consider:

1. Mainstreaming is an approach that has been used successfully with mildly handicapped students in some school districts for many years.

2. Mainstreaming does *not* mean that special classes and centers will be abolished; these placements will still be provided for students who need them, but more thought will be given to how they can be made less restrictive.

3. Mainstreaming also means not removing students from the regular program unless it is absolutely necessary.

4. The application of the mainstreaming concept to more severely handicapped students is relatively new; however, when a given handicapped child stands to gain from involvement, even for a very short period of time, in a given regular classroom and does not restrict the other children's learning rights, the concept should be explored.

5. Students can be "mainstreamed" for a major part of the school day, or only for certain activities such as physical education, music, and

lunch. The degree of mainstreaming will depend on the student's skills and learning needs.

6. Integrated school settings allow the exceptional child to be a part of the real world, to learn to accept limitations, to observe and model appropriate behaviors, and to become more socially accepted by other children and adults. They also teach nonexceptional children valuable lessons regarding individual differences and the fact that there can be different right things rather than the same right things for all.

7. Mainstreaming is most successful when the child, the parents, the teacher, and the class are prepared in advance.

5. Instruction. Once the child's educational placement has been made, the special teacher, together with other professionals, may prepare an Individual Implementation Plan (IIP) which is something like a series of lesson plans. The IIP presents short-term instructional objectives and strategies related to each annual objective specified on the child's IEP or total service plan. While parents may also be involved in this step, it is not necessary to have an appraisal team meeting each time modifications or changes are made on the IIP. However, any changes on the longer-range IEP require parental consultation and approval. The short-term objectives on the IIP are usually written for a period of a few weeks. The plan includes a list of instructional resources and materials to be used to help the child obtain the desired level of performance. The teacher, and other professionals who work with the child, will make periodic checks of the child's progress and revise or change the short-term objectives and learning activities as necessary, Each short-term objective is intended as a step toward full attainment of the annual long-term instructional objectives. In our A-B-C approach for developing an IEP, which was presented in Chapter 5, we combined the IIP with the longer-range IEP.

6. Review. At least once every year, each child's IEP must be reviewed. The progress made toward stated goals and objectives is studied and, depending on the child's needs at that point in time, goals and objectives may be modified or changed, and alternative placements and services considered. The parents, teacher, or other involved school professionals may request a review of a child's progress at any point during the school year.

There is no hard and fast set of rules that will ensure successful interaction when problems arise between educators and parents. The appraisal team process, in which the parent is an *equal contributing team member* in seeking a solution, is one significant step in the right direction. This process must include a genuine effort to explore alternatives and flexibility on the part of team members. The movement away from the older, rigidly self-contained classroom where all students supposedly had the same deficits and were all labeled with the same self-fulfilling prophecy has made such flexibility possible.

Another characteristic of optimum appraisal team planning is to individualize the solution for each problem. Just as each student is guaranteed an Individual Education Program designed to capitalize on strengths and remediate deficits, each solution to a parental concern or problem can be individualized. This ability to individualize with parents as well as children is one means of problem solving. Each parent has unique concerns and priorities as well as anxieties and coping skills. The days when these can be ignored and a unilateral decision can be forced on parents is gone. We must now be aware of and exercise all due process procedures as well as all possible opportunities for participatory decision-making.

The public school administrator who is responsible for special education, as well as other school staff members, must be aware of the procedural safeguards guaranteed to parents under Public Law 94–142. This law provides an important mechanism by which parents may enforce their child's special education rights. A due process hearing is available whenever there is a dispute between parents and school officials regarding the identification, evaluation, or placement of an exceptional child. The following points are important to consider with respect to the parents' due process rights:

1. Whenever a dispute arises regarding the child's special education services, the parents have the right to promptly request a due process hearing.

2. A school district must provide the parents with reasonable notice whenever:
   a) it proposes to initiate or change the identification procedures, evaluation, or educational placement of the child.
   b) it refuses to initiate or change the identification procedures, evaluation, or educational placement of the child requested by the parents.

3. Failure to provide such notice renders any action taken by the school invalid.

4. Any action on the part of the school to refuse to change the special education program to conform to the parents' wishes may be halted as a result of a due process hearing. At the hearing the parents have the right to:
   a) be accompanied and advised by counsel and by professionals with expertise regarding the problems of exceptional children. However, this does not mean the parents must be represented by a lawyer. The parents are entitled to present their own case or be represented by a lay advocate such as another parent.
   b) present evidence to support their position, ask questions of any person supporting the school's position, and compel the attendance of any person whom they believe may be able to provide relevant information.
   c) obtain a written or electronic record of the hearing.
   d) obtain written findings of facts and decisions.

5. The due process hearing must be conductd by someone who is not

employed by the school district or involved with the educational services provided the child.

6. If the parents are dissatisfied with the results of the due process hearing, they may appeal to the State Department of Education.

7. All hearings must be conducted at a time and place which is reasonably convenient to the parents and the child.

8. School officials must proceed promptly on a request for a hearing. Hearings should be held and decisions rendered within forty-five days of the filing of a complaint (written request for a hearing).

Parent advocacy groups have formed in increasing numbers in the larger population centers across the country. In many instances, the forming of these groups is the direct result of dissatisfaction with existing special education programs and the slow and complicated bureaucratic processes operating in some school districts. In addition, parents are becoming increasingly aware of their rights and the right of their children to a free, equal education. In short, as we mentioned earlier, parent power has arrived.

Some parent advocacy groups send out literature to parents of exceptional children offering to provide an experienced parent to accompany a new parent to the appraisal team meeting. Some offer to provide legal aid should a due process hearing be held. Helpful hints for parents in dealing with school officials are as follows:

1. Communicate with school officials *in writing* whenever possible. If you must communicate orally (either in person or by telephone), you should *promptly* send a letter confirming your understanding of the issues discussed and commitments made during the conversation. Send carbon copies of your letters to the school district's superintendent and the State Department of Special Education. Keep copies of all correspondence sent and received in a central location.

2. Whenever you request a school official to take action with regard to *anything* related to the education of your child, specify a reasonable time (no longer than thirty days) by which you expect a response.

3. Do not assume the person with whom you have traditionally dealt (for instance, the director of special education) has the responsibility (or authority) to make the decision you are seeking. When in doubt, deal with the superintendent or principal.

4. Learn to recognize "bureaucratic" excuses for inaction. Be firm but not offensive.

5. Keep in touch with, and/or make use of, parent groups whenever feasible.

6. If your requests are denied or resisted, promptly *(in writing)* request a due process hearing.

There can be no question that we have entered an entirely new era with respect to parent and school relations in special education. It can become an era of mixed blessings if every effort is not made to establish and maintain honest and clear communication channels between the home and the school. On the one hand, school districts could assume an aloof and patronizing posture, "tokenizing" the parents' role or attempting to "railroad" through preprepared Individual Education Programs. On the other hand, parents could be overly demanding and critical using every legal trick in the book to force the district to pay full tuition for their child's placement in an exclusive private school.

The result of such discord could be both time consuming and very costly. Parents could invest considerable amounts in paying legal or consultant fees in order to protect their rights and the rights of their child. The schools could be forced to maintain a permanent staff of lawyers whose sole function would be to prepare defenses on the school's behalf in due process hearings. Hopefully, such extremes will not occur. If they do, it will be a clear indication of a lack of trust and adequate communication between the parents and the school. Both parties must work hard at building such trust and communication. Schools must be honest and reasonable. Parents must be honest and reasonable. It is in such a climate that the welfare of the individual child is most apt to be maximized.

In the next section, we will discuss some common problems that complicate parent-school interactions.

Problems Encountered in Parent–School Relationships

Working with parents of disturbed children, particularly the mildly disturbed, may be more difficult than working with parents of children with other exceptionalities. To begin with, the first assumption an individual may make when considering a behavior disordered child is: "No doubt, this problem is related to conditions at home." As a result, parents of disturbed children are put almost immediately on the defensive whether or not the child's problem stems from family difficulties. The parents of a deaf or blind child usually evoke immediate empathy on the part of others. After all, such conditions can be explained as "God willed," not "parent caused."

In addition, there are many individuals among the American lay public who have very definite ideas about how to deal with children who are not physically handicapped but who are rude, disruptive, bullying, demanding, loud, and destructive. Far from supporting special education programs in which such children are catered to on an individual basis, many would apply a simple formula: such children should "shape up or ship out." This punitive reaction toward rule breakers by many in our society explains in part why full-scale programs for disturbed children in the public schools have been slow to develop. It may also partially explain why PL 94–142 defines only severe emotional disturbance, not behavior disorders.

Before discussing problems that may exist in parent-school relationships further, we should examine what it means to be the parent of a disturbed child. Let's suppose Sue Billings, the teacher of Bobby Myron whom we met in Chapter 1, called Bobby's parents on the telephone to report the hectic morning she had had with him. Here are some of the parents' possible reactions:

Bobby is just "all boy" and his teacher wants him to be a sissy.

Bobby is the brightest child in the class, and his behavior is just an indication of the fact that he is bored.

That rotten brat. I'm going to beat the daylights out of him.

There's nothing wrong with Bobby. It's just that stupid teacher who can't teach worth a damn and the lousy school system.

Each of these reactions reveals some of the pain involved in having to deal with the problems created by a disturbed child. The first represents an attempt to deny there is a problem. The second goes even further and attempts to deny the problem by turning it into an indication of giftedness. The third is direct rejection and a lashing out at Bobby, while the fourth attempts to place total blame for the problem on the teacher and the school.

Underlying all of these reactions is probably a dynamic very often found among parents of exceptional children—*guilt*. Why did this happen to us? What did we do wrong? What must others think of us when our child behaves this way? Whose side of the family contributed most to this problem? Which parent is the real villain? Because these are very painful questions to answer, parents may seek to locate the blame for the problems outside the home or vent their frustration and anger directly on the child.

It is not difficult to see how conflicts may arise with parents who bring one or more of these attitudes with them to school, to an appraisal team meeting, or to a parent-teacher conference. Even the parent who considers Bobby a "rotten brat" and agrees with the school must be carefully dealt with for Bobby's sake in light of the possible reprisals that could occur at home. It should be noted that some parents with disturbed children may manifest still another reaction to a teacher's call.

Bobby's had another setback. We've got to check into some ways to help him. Maybe we can have a conference with Ms. Billings and have Dr. Brock examine him.

Just as we should not sell disturbed children short and expect only negative characteristics from them, we should by no means indict all parents of disturbed children as defensive and uncooperative. Most have a genuine desire to help their child, and they can be strong allies of the school if the school offers them the opportunity. Two important steps in accomplishing this alliance have been described by Kroth (1975): (1) determining the ownership of the problem, and (2) clearly identifying the problem.

Determining the Ownership of the Problem

Who is responsible for the misbehavior evidenced by Bobby Myron? In Chapter 2 we discussed various orientations that lodge the problem to various degrees in Bobby, in Bobby's environment, or in the interactions between Bobby and his environment. But when teacher and parent come face to face, we have no time for theoretical orientations. We must deal in a more direct and simplified manner with the question of ownership.

The question again: Who is responsible for the misbehavior evidenced by Bobby Myron? There will be cases where the ownership of a problem like Bobby's will rest solely with school, teacher, parent, or Bobby himself. A school district and principal that believe in liberal use of corporal punishment may trigger off problems like Bobby's. A dull, boring, unmotivated, critical, shaming teacher might do the same. Certainly, if Bobby's parents let him watch television until three or four in the morning every night and never fix him breakfast, blame might largely rest with them. And if Bobby clearly fits the "dificult child" temperamental pattern discussed in Chapter 1, we might say what happened in Sue Billings' room was out of any outsider's control.

But far more often, a joint ownership of problem behavior exists between the school, the home, and the child. It is the recognition that this joint ownership exists that is the first critical consideration at the appraisal team meeting or other parent-teacher conference. Disaster is assured if the teacher "grills" the parent regarding problems at home and then smugly says, "Well, we aren't going to be able to help your child until you etc." Disaster can also occur if the parent launches into a bitter attack against the teacher, principal, school district, or all three. It is in such situations that school personnel recognizing the pain that such an attack represents must exercise patience, tact, and nondefensiveness. Disaster is almost assured if a communication channel is not established between parent and school. Establishing this channel depends on reasonableness and a genuine concern for the child's welfare on the parts of the parents and the school personnel. Unreasonableness on the part of the parents, we have pointed out earlier, may lead to ridiculous demands in due process hearings. Unreasonableness on the part of the school may result in the loss of the parents' participation as an ally.

One of us was asked to serve as a member of a task force to investigate charges of child abuse in a program for severely disturbed children. In addition to the author, there was a psychologist, a special educator, and a parent of a severely disturbed child. Headlines had been made in the local newspaper concerning the alleged child abuse. An eight-year-old, severely disturbed boy who engaged in self-stimulatory behavior (i.e., constantly putting his hands up to his head and pulling at tufts of hair) was punished by means of an overcorrection procedure. The procedure resulted in welts developing on the child's wrists. The parent went to the superintendent of schools and angrily demanded that the teacher be fired.

The task force met with as many parties involved as possible, and from numerous reports (including one from a parent who watched the entire overcorrection episode) gleaned the following:

1. The child's parent was fully aware of the use of overcorrection procedures and had been heard to support their use with her son.

2. The overcorrection procedure was not abusively administered.

3. The issue was actually not whether or not the child had been abused, but a total parent-school-teacher breakdown of communication, trust, and cooperation.

The problem was further complicated by the fact that the parent had never actually signed or been asked to sign a consent form giving the school permission to apply overcorrection procedures. But in the final analysis, what was operating was a hostile, two-way, parent-school relationship that had been allowed to escalate until this unfortunate incident was used as a means for the parent to get back at the school. The boy's welfare was not central to the problem, although some may question the use of overcorrective procedures in general.

While this example may not be typical of the kind of problem likely to be encountered between parents and school, the importance of constantly striving for successful two-way communication is well illustrated.

Establishing an orientation of joint ownership of the child's problem during the appraisal team meeting or during any parent-initiated or school-initiated conference is apt to foster the working partnership relationship between parent and school that is so necessary if Public Law 94–142 is to be successful. This will probably never be an easy matter. But here are some considerations that may help:

Put the Parent at Ease. Coming to open house and chatting with the teacher of one's child is relatively stress-free for most parents. Setting up an appointment to see the teacher or being called at home regarding the child's school behavior may be somewhat more stressful. Walking into a conference room with five or six professionals, including the principal and a psychologist, staring across a table may be very stressful for a parent. In fact, it is not always easy to get parents of disturbed children to take advantage of their rights and appear at an appraisal team meeting.

Every effort must be made in advance to communicate to the parents that the meeting is not being called to criticize their child or their parenting but to put both the school and home-side view of the child's problem together to work out an effective course of action to help the child.

Invite the Parent to Participate. Because of the stress of the team meeting or, in some cases, of teacher-parent conferences, the parent may tend to "clam up" and feel intimidated by the school personnel. Before reviewing the school side of the problem, the parent may be asked:

How do you think she is doing in school?

How are things going at home?

This will allow the timid parent to contribute some specific thoughts or the accusatory parent to vent his or her feelings in an accepting climate.

Listen to the Parent. One of the most frustrating interpersonal experiences occurs when we pour our hearts out to someone trying desperately to get a point across, the other person nods and perhaps smiles attentively, and then later we discover that that person did not really hear one thing we said. This can occur in teacher-parent conferences, and it is important to not only tune-in on what the parent is saying but also to confirm that you have been both heard and understood by restating what has been said.

Avoid Lecturing. One teacher asked to have a tape recording of one of her parent conferences analyzed only to find out that she had talked 80 percent of the time (Kroth, 1975). This one-way communication approach prohibits the parent from really feeling involved, and although some parents may prefer it and actively reinforce the teacher's filibuster tendencies, the teacher must be aware of the limitations.

Clearly Identifying the Problem

After determining the joint ownership of the child's problems, the problems themselves must be defined. Kroth (1975) has suggested that the following steps be followed:

1. *Reduce the global problem into measurable problems.* The teacher telling the parent the child is poor in citizenship or the parent telling the teacher the child has a reading problem is unlikely to result in anything but a vague, frustrating communication exercise. The teacher needs to pin down the citizenship problem.
   a) What specifically does the child do (e.g., gets out of seat and bothers others)?
   b) How often does it occur?
   c) How long are these episodes?
The reason this specificity is important is that it establishes a reference for future use when the parent and teacher can get together again and reflect on the child's progress over time.

2. *List the specific problems on a sheet of paper.* Further pinning down the problems by writing them in numerical order will often keep the discussion focused on specifics and reduce the time devoted to wandering.

3. *Have the parent establish priorities.* Examining the list, the teacher and parent, or appraisal team member and parent, can mutually decide what problems need primary attention. Letting the parent take the initiative here further enhances the participatory involvement of the parent. Clarifying the parental priorities and perhaps suggesting differential focus based on the school's view can come later. Two extremely important terms and concepts must always be considered in parent-school relationships under Public Law 94–142—*flexibility* and *negotiability.* The school personnel who spell out a position with finality and rigidity will not be contributing to the mutualness so necessary in a school-parent working partnership. The parent who arrives at an appraisal team meeting with a lawyer and psychological consultant and who proceeds to present a list of nonnegotiable demands will also be violating the need for mutualness.

4. *Decide how many of the top priority problems can reasonably be selected as objectives and how changes in the child's behavior can be measured.* Once the target areas have been identified, there must be agreement as to how the child's progress can be measured. The days of such global evaluation gestures as "I think he's doing better in reading" are over. You had better *know* if he's doing better in reading and have the data to prove it. This is why it is so important to define global problems in terms of measurable behaviors. Both teacher and parent have a part to play in the evaluation process. The objective "improve in self-concept" can be measured by teacher observations and record-keeping as discussed in Chapter 3. But the parent may be asked to record favorable comments about school, evidence of increasing confidence, and even average number of smiles per week. The objective, "will read adequately in third-grade reader," will involve a specific number of permissible errors and a means of measuring comprehension.

The parent-school alliance era can mean the beginning of true mutualness between home and school. Hopefully, the roadblocks to trust, communication, and cooperation between the parents and the school will be worked through by a give-and-take partnership. Such a partnership may be enhanced on a more formal level by the establishment of a community advisory committee within the school district.

Establishing a Community Advisory Committee

A strong community advisory committee made up largely of parents of exceptional children can be very useful in communicating a district's special education program to the community and in communicating the concerns and needs of both handicapped children and their parents to the school district. Initially, a task force of eight to twelve parents needs to gather information on the feasibility of such a committee, to study how other successful committees have gotten started, and to begin to draft potential bylaws. They need to make such organizations as the PTA, YMCA, and YWCA aware of the formation of the committee, for these organizations may play an important role in future activities and programs sponsored by the committee.

Once the task force has spelled out the responsibilities of the committee and its precise relationship to the district board of education and school administration, such matters as committee size, membership qualifications, terms of office, schedule of meetings, operating procedures, and available resources are considered. The size of the committee needs to be large enough to provide for a cross section of community opinion, yet small enough to permit effective group processes in an atmosphere of relative informality. Although committees vary widely in size from twelve to as many as forty members, fifteen to twenty-five seems to be a workable size. In circumstances where it may be advantageous to have a large committee, as a means of giving voice to many social, economic, religious, ethnic, and geographical elements in an extended area, it might be wise to divide into working subcommittees under the direction and coordination of a small executive board.

The majority of the members of a typical advisory committee will be parents; approximately half of these will be parents of exceptional children. In addition, the members of the community advisory committee will be appointed by or approved by the district board of education. The board may appoint the members independently or base their appointments on a list prepared by a nomination committee of citizens.

It is often helpful to develop a list of desirable qualifications for use in considering each person for membership. These may include:

1. Concern for all children

2. Readiness to consider needs and interests of all parents and children

3. Sincere belief in the goals of the committee

4. Willingness to work for committee goals

5. Freedom from restrictive biases

6. Ability to participate in group processes

7. Integrity

8. Being representative of a segment of the community

While a one-year term may be too short to permit members to become familiar with their tasks, terms may need to be restricted to two or three years with no reappointment until several years have elapsed. Staggered terms are also a good idea as they ensure that at least half the members have had experience on the committee. Policies of this nature help ensure that the committee does not develop into a sedentary group with the same old ax to grind. It also helps to provide a broad base of representation, bring new ideas to the group, and increase the group's influence.

Support for the community advisory committee by the school district is vital if it is to be a positive influence. This usually means a school administrative representative serving in some capacity (e.g., executive secretary) on the committee. The district might also make available to the committee advice from consultants or administrators within the district. Professional consultants can be secured from a number of sources, such as the staff of other school districts, college and university faculties, the State Education Department, and the lay citizenry. Besides making professional consultants and assistants available to the advisory committee, the district board of education should make available clerical help, duplicating services, postage, and essential supplies. It should also provide pleasant and comfortable physical space for committee meetings and work sessions.

The following four endeavors are typical of what a community advisory committee might undertake: vocational training, mock appraisal team meetings, evaluations of parental reactions to appraisal team meetings, and revision of forms used by the appraisal team.

Vocational Training. A continuing concern of parents of exceptional children who approach the mid-teens is how can such children be helped to acquire the experience and skills they need to achieve some level of independence as adults. One project an advisory committee set up was to locate and contact various businesses in the community that required the kinds of job skills a wide range of exceptional children might realistically acquire. An arrangement was made to pay the business owner or manager $100 to $150 for a ten- to fifteen-hour training program during which the exceptional individual would learn how to do a job he or she might later be paid to do. Gasoline stations, fast-food establishments, upholstering shops, restaurants, hardware stores, nurseries, hotels, and supermarkets agreed to participate in the committee's project, and a large number of adolescent trainees were prepared for employment.

Mock Appraisal Team Meetings. Many committee members themselves will have appeared at appraisal team meetings and can share their reactions to the proceedings. A common concern is the technical language used by school personnel and the trepidation parents feel over being put in the spotlight in a room filled with professionals. By holding a mock team meeting, one committee analyzed its various aspects and later conveyed their recommendations to the special education supervisor. One recommendation was to have the special education teacher meet the parents before the team meeting and put them "at ease." This might be done over a cup of coffee with the teacher describing the various team members to be present and the usual routine of the meeting.

Evaluate Parental Reaction to the Appraisal Team Meeting. One community advisory committee sent out questionnaires to all parents who participated in appraisal team meetings on a regular basis. The questionnaire asked for the parents' candid opinions on how the meeting was handled, how satisfied they were with the deliberation and outcome, and a request for suggestions that might improve the entire appraisal team meeting process.

Revision of Forms Used by the Appraisal Team. A community advisory committee carefully examined the forms that the district used to record data concerning exceptional children, particularly the ones devoted to spelling out the Individual Education Program which the parent must sign for approval. They decided that the forms were too technical for most parents to understand. As a result, they suggested that on the reverse side of the main form a flow-chart be printed in pictorial form. This chart would cover the identification process through actual placement of the student in a special program.

The school district which strongly supports the formation and maintenance of a community advisory committee is making a very wise investment. Parents of exceptional children want to help and can bring to district personnel an understanding of "exceptionality" no individual who has not been the parent of an exceptional child can ever hope to acquire. In closing this chapter on working with parents, we are going to present a statement made by B. G. Greer, the father of an exceptional child, at Memphis State University.

> Many of the basic problems with which parents of handicapped children have to deal come directly from society. Such problems originate in society's perpetration of certain myths or frauds, to put it bluntly. We are especially susceptible to these myths as we are growing up. One myth encouraged by the romance magazines that teenagers read is that marriage is "eternal bliss." Another more pertinent myth is that out of this blissful union will come children who are both physically and mentally beautiful and perfect. Therefore, the parents of a handicapped child have not lived up to the "ideal" and have produced an imperfect replica of themselves. This may cause much unconscious, if not conscious, guilt as well as feelings of inferiority. At the same time, if parents are unfortunate enough to have a handicapped child (which society says subtly they are not supposed to do), society then hypocritically says they must be superparents. They must supply enormous additional amounts of care, love, and attention to their child. They must do this, additionally, on a 24 hour a day, 365 day a year basis; otherwise, they are superbad.

> As a professional evaluating a child's progress, I can be the most patient, empathetic person on earth for half an hour. I can look critically at the impatient, harried parent. Unfortunately many professionals encountered by parents of handicapped children do not take the 24 hours, 365 days a year responsibilities of parents into account in their evaluation of the parent. In the back of parents' minds, then, is a vague awareness that society is looking over their shoulders and judging if they are carrying out their prescribed duties, giving much love, attention, and devotion, not missing any

treatment appointments, providing the best available care, etc. This is a "goldfish bowl" type of existence which eventually takes its toll in energy, strength, and courage.

Parents of handicapped children must realize that fleeting moments of resentment and rejection of the burdens presented by a handicapped child are natural and are not indicative that they are bad parents. They need to seek help in solving their practical day to day problems. The best help can be found in interaction with parents who have experienced and solved such problems. Even though every family's situation is unique and what works for one family may not work for another, having someone with common problems with whom to interact is in itself therapeutic.

Parents must realize also that only by banding together can they bring about the changes in society which are needed. Legislators and other government leaders listen to groups when they might not listen to individuals. Therefore, in order to have their voices heard, parents of the handicapped must unite and seek common goals for their children's welfare.*

This chapter brings to a close the second edition of this book. We have provided theoretical, practical, and useful ways for viewing emotional disturbance, as well as some specific procedures for establishing instructional objectives for disturbed children and teaching them in the school setting.

There are two major developing eras in special education that will most certainly affect disturbed children over the coming years. First, we are probably not as committed or polarized with respect to theory or practice as we were a decade ago. Individual children and their unique characteristics, and individual teachers and their unique experiences and insight combine to determine what is actually done in the classroom. There is not a single theoretical approach. Second, we are accountable for what we do or do not do with disturbed children in the schools as never before. The disruptive child's disruption will have to be quantified on a pre- and post-behavioral basis so we can *document* changes. Self-concept, an ever slippery aspect of human personality, will only be accepted as improved if there is evidence (e.g., self-rating scale, sociometric measure, demonstrated confidence, increased rate of smiling). In general, this evidence will only have to pass muster at the local school level, but it is possible we may have to produce it, defend it, and let a court of law decide whether we are guilty or not guilty with respect to the adequacy of our educational efforts. Pivotal to this will be the success of our efforts to establish and maintain a working partnership and clear communication with the parents of the children with whom we work.

These two areas clearly constitute giant steps forward in the field of education of emotionally disturbed children. Developing and fulfilling them will take us well into the future.

*From a speech made at Memphis State University in 1974 by B. G. Greer. Reproduced by permission.

References

Achenbach, T. M. The classification of children's psychiatric symptoms: A factor analytic study. *Psychological Monographs,* 1966, *80* (Whole No. 615).

Achenbach, T. M. *Developmental psychopathology.* New York: Ronald Press, 1974.

Acker, L. *Errorless discrimination training in autistic and normal children.* Unpublished doctoral dissertation, University of California, Los Angeles, Department of Psychology, 1966.

Adelman, H. S. The concept of intrinsic motivation: Implications for practice and research with the learning disabled. *Learning Disabilities Quarterly,* 1978, *7,* 43–54.

Aichhorn, A. *Wayward youth.* New York: The Viking Press, 1965. (Originally published, 1925.)

Ayllon, T., & Haughton, E. Control of the behavior of schizophrenic patients by food. *Journal of Experimental Analysis of Behavior,* 1962, *5,* 343–354.

Baker, R. P., & Dreger, R. M. The preschool behavior classification project: A follow-up report. *Journal of Abnormal Child Psychology,* 1977, *5,* 241–248.

Bandura, A. *Aggression: A social learning analysis.* Englewood Cliffs, N.J.: Prentice-Hall, 1973.

Barrish, H. H., Saunders, M., & Wolf, M. M. Good behavior game: Effects of individual contingencies for group consequences on disruptive behavior in a classroom. *Journal of Applied Behavior Analysis,* 1969, *2,* 119–124.

Barsch, R. H. *A movigenic curriculum.* Madison, Wis.: Bureau for Handicapped Children, 1965.

Bartak, L., Rutter, M., & Cox, A. A comparative study of infantile autism and specific developmental receptive language disorder. I. The children. *British Journal of Psychiatry,* 1975, *126,* 127–145.

Bateman, B. *Young MR curriculum.* Paper presented to the Special Study Institute for Administrators of Special Education, sponsored by the California State Department of Education and the University of Southern California, Sacramento, October 1967.

Bayley, N. *Bayley scales of infant development.* New York: Psychological Corporation, 1969.

Bender, L. Schizophrenia in childhood. *Nervous Child,* 1942, *1,* 138–140.

Bender, L. Childhood schizophrenia: A review. *International Journal of Psychiatry,* 1968, *5,* 211–220.

Berkowitz, L. Control of aggression. In B. M. Caldwell & H. N. Ricciuti (Eds.), *Review of child development research* (Vol. 3). Chicago: University of Chicago Press, 1973.

Berkowitz, P. H. Pearl H. Berkowitz. In J. M. Kauffman & C. D. Lewis (Eds.), *Teaching children with behavior disorders: Personal perspectives.* Columbus, Ohio: Merrill, 1974.

Berkowitz, P. H., & Rothman, E. P. *The disturbed child: Recognition and psychoeducational therapy in the classroom.* New York: New York University Press, 1960.

Biddle, B. J., & Thomas, E. J. (Eds.). *Role theory: Concepts and research.* New York: Wiley, 1966.

Bijou, S. W. Theory and research in mental developmental retardation. *The Psychological Record,* 1963, *13,* 95–110.

Birnbrauer, J. S., Bijou, S. W., Wolf, M. M., & Kidder, J. D. Programmed instruction in the classroom. In L. P. Pullman & L. Krasner (Eds.), *Case studies in behavior modification.* New York: Holt, Rinehart, and Winston, 1965.

Bousfield, W., Esterson, J., & Whitmarsh, G. The effects of concomitant colored and uncolored pictorial representations on the learning of stimulus words. *Journal of Applied Psychology,* 1957, *41,* 165–167.

Bower, E. M., Lourie, R. S., Strother, C. R., & Sutherland, R. L. (Eds.). *Project Re–ED: New concepts for helping emotionally disturbed children. Evaluation by a panel of visitors.* Nashville, Tenn.: John F. Kennedy Center for Research on Education and Human Development, 1969.

Bradley, C. The behavior of children receiving benzedrine. *American Journal of Psychiatry,* 1937, *94,* 577–585.

Bradley, C., & Bowen, M. Behavior characteristics of schizophrenic children. *Psychiatric Quarterly,* 1941, *15,* 298–315.

Bridges, K. M. B. Emotional development in early infancy. *Child Development,* 1932, *3,* 324–341.

Bruininks, R. H., & Rynders, J. E. Alternatives to special class placement for educable mentally retarded children. *Focus on Exceptional Children,* 1971, *3*(4), 1–12.

Bryan, T. H., & Bryan, J. H. *Understanding learning disabilities.* Port Washington, N.Y.: Alfred Publishing, 1975.

Bucher, B. B., & Lovaas, O. I. Use of aversive stimulation in behavior modification. In M. R. Jones (Ed.), *Miami symposium on the prediction of behavior, 1967: Aversive stimulation.* Coral Gables, Fla.: University of Miami Press, 1968.

Buehler, R. E., Patterson, G. R., & Furness, R. M. The reinforcement of behavior in institutional settings. *Behavior Research and Therapy,* 1966, *4,* 157–167.

Buss, A. H. *Psychopathology.* New York: Wiley, 1966.

Carr, E. G., Newsom, C. D., & Binkoff, J. A. Stimulus control of self-destructive behavior in a psychotic child. *Journal of Abnormal Child Psychology,* 1976, *4,* 139–153.

Chandler, M. J. Egocentrism and antisocial behavior: The assessment and training of social perspective-taking skills. *Developmental Psychology,* 1973, *9,* 326–332.

Chandler, M. J., Greenspan, S., & Barenboim, C. Assessment and training of role-taking and referential communication skills in institutionalized emotionally disturbed children. *Developmental Psychology,* 1974, *10,* 546–553.

Chittenden, G. E. An experimental study in measuring and modifying assertive behavior in young children. *Monographs of the Society for Research in Child Development,* 1942, *7* (1, Serial No. 31).

Churchill, D. The relation of infantile autism and early childhood schizophrenia to developmental language disorders of childhood. *Journal of Autism and Childhood Schizophrenia,* 1972, *2,* 182–187.

Coaladarci, A. Presentation at School Psychology Conference [no title], University of California, Berkeley, 1967.

Coleman, J. C. *Abnormal psychology and modern life* (4th ed.). Glenview, Ill.: Scott, Foresman, 1972.

Colman, R., Ames, S., & Frankel, F. *The exceptional child as a teacher of cooperative play skills.* Paper presented at the 99th Annual Meeting of the American Association on Mental Deficiency, Portland, Oregon, 1975.

Cratty, B. J. *Motor activity and the education of retardates* (2nd ed.). Philadelphia: Lea & Febiger, 1974.

Cruickshank, W. M. The development of education for exceptional children. In W. M. Cruickshank & G. O. Johnson (Eds.), *Education of exceptional children and youth* (3rd ed.). Englewood Cliffs, N.J.: Prentice-Hall, 1975.

Cruickshank, W. M., Bentzen, F., Ratzeberg, F., & Tannhauser, M. A. *Teaching method for brain-injured and hyperactive children.* Syracuse, N.Y.: Syracuse University Press, 1961.

Cruse, D. The effect of distraction upon the performance of brain-injured and familial retarded children. In E. Trapp & P. Himmelstein (Eds.), *Readings on the exceptional child.* New York: The Free Press, 1970.

Csapo, M. Peer models reverse the "one bad apple spoils the barrel" theory. *Teaching Exceptional Children,* 1972, *5,* 20–24.

Deci, E. L. *Intrinsic motivation.* New York: Plenum, 1975.

Despert, J. L. *The emotionally disturbed child.* New York: Doubleday, 1965.

Dorward, B. A comparison of the competencies for regular classroom teachers and teachers of emotionally disturbed children. *Exceptional Children,* 1963, *30,* 67–73.

Douglas, K. The teacher's role in a children's psychiatric hospital unit. *Exceptional Children,* 1961, *27,* 246–251.

Drabman, R. S., Spitalnik, R., & O'Leary, K. D. Teaching self-control to disruptive children. *Journal of Abnormal Psychology,* 1973, *82,* 10–16.

Dupont, H. (Ed.). *Educating emotionally disturbed children.* New York: Holt, Rinehart, and Winston, 1969.

Eisenberg, L., & Kanner, L. Early infantile autism, 1943–1955. *American Journal of Orthopsychiatry, 1956, 26,* 556–566.

Epstein, L. H., Doke, L. A., Sajwaj, T. E., Sorrell, S., & Rimmer, B. Generality and side effects of overcorrection. *Journal of Applied Behavior Analysis, 1974, 7,* 385–390.

Erikson, E. *Childhood and society* (2nd ed.). New York: Norton, 1963.

Eron, L. D., Huesmann, L. R., Lefkowitz, M. M., & Walder, L. O. Does television violence cause aggression? *American Psychologist, 1972, 27,* 253–263.

Evers, W. L., & Schwarz, J. C. Modifying social withdrawal in preschoolers: The effects of filmed modeling and teacher praise. *Journal of Abnormal Child Psychology, 1973, 1,* 248–256.

Feagans, L. Ecological theory as a model for constructing a theory of emotional disturbance. In W. C. Rhodes & M. L. Tracy (Eds.), *A study of child variance: Conceptual models* (Vol. 1). Ann Arbor: University of Michigan Press, 1974.

Federal Register, Vol. 42, No. 163, August 23, 1977.

Fenichel, C. Carl Fenichel. In J. M. Kauffman & C. D. Lewis (Eds.), *Teaching children with behavior disorders: Personal perspectives.* Columbus, Ohio: Merrill, 1974.

Fernald, G. M. *Remedial techniques in basic school subjects.* New York: McGraw-Hill, 1947.

Forness, S. R. Behavioristic approach to classroom management and motivation. *Psychology in the Schools, 1970, 1,* 356–363.

Forness, S. R. Educational approaches to autism. *Training School Bulletin, 1974, 71,* 167–173.

Frankel, R., Chikami, B., Freeman, B. J., Ritvo, E. R., & Carr, E. *The reinforcing effects of photic stimulation upon the behavior of autistic and retarded children.* Paper presented at the 54th Annual Meeting of the Western Psychological Association, San Francisco, 1974.

Frankel, F., Ritvo, E. R., & Pardo, R. *The effects of environmental stimulation upon stereotypic behavior of autistic children at two levels of mental age.* Paper presented at the 99th Annual Meeting of the American Association on Mental Deficiency, Portland, Oregon, 1975.

Frankel, F., Tymchuk, A., & Simmons, J. Q. Operant analysis and intervention with autistic children: Implications of current research. In E. R. Ritvo, B. J. Freeman, E. M. Ornitz, & P. E. Tanguay (Eds.), *Autism: Diagnosis, current research and management.* New York: Spectrum Publications, 1976.

Freitag, G. An experimental study of the social responsiveness of children with autistic behaviors. *Journal of Experimental Child Psychology, 1970, 9,* 436–453.

Freud, S. *An outline of psychoanalysis.* New York: Norton, 1949.

Friedrich, L. K., & Stein, A. H. Aggressive and prosocial television programs and the natural behavior of preschool children. *Monographs of the Society for Research in Child Development*, 1973, *38* (4, Serial No. 151).

Frostig, M., & Horne, D. *The Frostig program for the development of visual perception.* Chicago: Follett Corporation, 1964.

Fulwiler, R. L., & Fouts, R. S. Acquisition of American Sign Language by a noncommunicating autistic child. *Journal of Autism and Childhood Schizophrenia*, 1976, *6*, 43–51.

GAP (Group for the Advancement of Psychiatry). *Psychopathological disorders in childhood: Theoretical considerations and a proposed classification.* New York: Group for the Advancement of Psychiatry, 1966.

Gallagher, P. A. *Teaching students with behavior disorders: Techniques for classroom instruction.* Denver: Love Publishing, 1979.

Glasser, W. Reality therapy. In V. Binder, A. Binder, & B. Rimland (Eds.), *Modern therapies.* Englewood Cliffs, N.J.: Prentice-Hall, 1976.

Glavin, J. P. Persistence of behavior disorders in children. *Exceptional Children*, 1972, *38*, 367–376.

Glidewell, J. C., & Swallow, C. S. *The prevalence of maladjustment in elementary schools.* A report for the Joint Commission on the Mental Health of Children, University of Chicago, 1968.

Goldfarb, W. Self-awareness in schizophrenic children. *Archives of General Psychiatry*, 1963, *8*, 47–60.

Goldfarb, W. Childhood psychosis. In P. M. Mussen (Ed.), *Carmichael's manual of child psychology* (Vol. 2). New York: Wiley, 1970.

Goldfarb, W., Braenstein, P., & Lorge, I. A study of speech patterns in a group of schizophrenic children. *American Journal of Orthopsychiatry*, 1956, *26*, 544–555.

Goldstein, H. *The social learning curriculum.* Columbus, Ohio: Merrill, 1974.

Graham, V. L. Educational approaches at the NPI school: The general program. In E. R. Ritvo, B. J. Freeman, E. M. Ornitz, & P. E. Tanguay (Eds.), *Autism: Diagnosis, current research and management.* New York: Spectrum Publications, 1976.

Graubard, P. Children with behavioral disabilities. In L. M. Dunn (Ed.), *Exceptional children in the schools* (2nd ed.). New York: Holt, Rinehart, and Winston, 1973.

Green, A. H. Self-mutilation in schizophrenic children. *Archives of General Psychiatry*, 1967, *17*, 234–244.

Griffith, R., & Ritvo, E. R. Echolalia: Concerning the dynamics of the syndrome. *Journal of American Academy of Child Psychiatry*, 1967, *6*, 184–193.

Hall, R. V., Fox, R., Willard, D., Goldsmith, L., Emerson, M., Owen, M., Davis, F., & Procia, E. The teacher as observer and experimenter in the modification of disputing and talking-out behaviors. *Journal of Applied Behavior Analysis,* 1971, *4,* 141–149.

Hall, R. V., Lund, D., & Jackson, D. Effects of teacher attention on study behavior. *Journal of Applied Behavioral Analysis,* 1968, *1,* 1–22.

Haring, N. G., & Phillips, E. L. *Educating emotionally disturbed children.* New York: McGraw-Hill, 1962.

Haring, N. G., & Phillips, E. L. *Analysis and modification of classroom behavior.* Englewood Cliffs, N.J.: Prentice-Hall, 1972.

Harris, B. Whatever happened to Little Albert? *American Psychologist,* 1979, *34,* 151–160.

Haubrick, P. A., & Shores, R. E. Attending behavior and academic performance of emotionally disturbed children. *Exceptional Children,* 1976, *42,* 337–338.

Hermelin, B., & O'Connor, N. *Psychological experiments with autistic children.* Oxford, England: Pergamon Press, 1970.

Hewett, F. M. *An investigation of the effect of pleasant and unpleasant affective tone on learning and recall of words among delinquent and nondelinquent adolescents with reading problems.* Unpublished manuscript, 1961.

Hewett, F. M. A hierarchy of educational tests for children with learning disorders. *Exceptional Children,* 1964, *31,* 207–214.

Hewett, F. M. Teaching speech to an autistic child through operant conditioning. *American Journal of Orthopsychiatry,* 1965, *35,* 927–936.

Hewett, F. M. *The emotionally disturbed child in the classroom* (1st ed.). Boston: Allyn and Bacon, 1968.

Hewett, F. M., & Blake, P. R. Teaching the emotionally disturbed. In R. W. Travers (Ed.), *Second handbook of research on teaching.* Chicago: Rand McNally, 1973.

Hewett, F. M., with Forness, S. R. *Education of exceptional learners* (2nd ed.). Boston: Allyn and Bacon, 1977.

Hewett, F. M., Hoffman, J., Kahn, N. T., Lahti, G., Peck, B. P., Reynard, C. L., Weller, E. L., Zoeller, C. J. *Project 3PI: Planned Positive Peer Interaction.* Special Project, Bureau of Education for the Handicapped, 1979.

Hewett, F. M., Mayhew, D., & Rabb, E. An experimental reading program for neurologically impaired, mentally retarded, and severely emotionally disturbed children. *American Journal of Orthopsychiatry,* 1967, *37,* 35–48.

Hewett, F. M., Taylor, F. D., & Artuso, A. A. The Santa Monica Project. *Exceptional Children,* 1969, *34,* 387–388.

Hewitt, L. E., & Jenkins, R. L. *Fundamental patterns of maladjustment: The dynamics of their origins.* Springfield, Ill.: State of Illinois, 1946.

Hobbs, N. Helping disturbing children: Psychological and ecological strategies. In H. Dupont (Ed.), *Educating emotionally disturbed children.* New York: Holt, Rinehart, and Winston, 1969.

Hobbs, N. Perspectives on re–education. *Behavioral Disorders,* 1978, *3,* 65–66.

Hunter, M. Humanism vs. behaviorism. In H. Goldstein (Ed.), *Readings in emotional and behavioral disorders.* Guilford, Conn.: Special Learning Corporation, 1978.

Hyman, I. *Corporal punishment in schools: America's officially sanctioned brand of child abuse.* Paper presented at the Second Annual Conference on Child Abuse and Neglect, Houston, April 18, 1977.

Ingraham v. *Wright,* 430 U.S. 651, 97 S.Ct. 1401 (1977).

Jacobson, S., & Faegre, C. Neutralization: A tool for the teacher of disturbed children. *Exceptional Children,* 1959, *25,* 243–246.

Jones, M. A laboratory study of fear: The case of Peter. *Pedagogical Seminary,* 1924, *31,* 310–311.

Josselyn, I. M. *Psychosocial development of children.* New York: Family Service Association of America, 1948.

Kanner, L. Autistic disturbances of affective contact. *Nervous Child,* 1943, *2,* 217–250.

Karraker, R. J. Self versus teacher selected reinforcer in a token economy. *Exceptional Children,* 1977, *43,* 454–455.

Kauffman, J. M. *Characteristics of children's behavior disorders.* Columbus, Ohio: Merrill, 1977.

Kazdin, A. E., & Klock, J. The effect of nonverbal approval on student attentive behavior. *Journal of Applied Behavior Analysis,* 1973, *6,* 643–654.

Keogh, B. K. Hyperactivity and learning disorders: Review and speculations. *Exceptional Children,* 1971, *38*(2), 101–109.

Keogh, B. K., & Barkett, C. An educational analysis of hyperactive children's achievement problems. In C. Whalen & B. Henker (Eds.), *Hyperactive children: The social ecology of identification and treatment.* New York: Academic Press, in press.

Kephart, N. C. *The slow learner in the classroom* (2nd ed.). Columbus, Ohio: Merrill, 1971.

Kirk, S. A., McCarthy, J. J., & Kirk, W. D. *The Illinois Test of Psycholinguistic Abilities* (Rev. ed.). Urbana, Ill.: University of Illinois Press, 1968.

Kirk, S. A., & Kirk W. D. *Psycholinguistic learning disabilities: Diagnosis and remediation.* Urbana, Ill.: University of Illinois Press, 1971.

Knobloch, P. *Field-based teacher training at Jowonio.* Paper presented at the Conference on Preparing Teachers for Severely Emotionally Disturbed Children with Autistic Characteristics, Advanced Institute for Trainers of Teachers for Seriously Emotionally Disturbed Children, University of Minnesota, May 22–24, 1977.

Koegel, R. L., & Covert, A. The relationship of self-stimulation to learning in autistic children. *Journal of Applied Behavior Analysis,* 1972, *5,* 381–387.

Koegel, R. L., Firestone, P. B., Kramme, K. W., & Dunlap, G. Increasing spontaneous play by suppressing self-stimulation in autistic children. *Journal of Applied Behavior Analysis,* 1974, *7,* 521–528.

Koegel, R. L., & Rincover, A. Treatment of psychotic children in a classroom environment: I. Learning in a large group. *Journal of Applied Behavior Analysis,* 1974, *7,* 45–59.

Kohn, M. The Kohn Social Competence Scale and Kohn Symptom Checklist for the Preschool Child: A follow-up report. *Journal of Abnormal Child Psychology,* 1977, *5*(3), 249–263.

Kraus, W., & McKeever, C. Rational-emotive education with learning disabled children. *Journal of Learning Disabilities,* 1977, *10,* 16–19.

Kroth, R. *Communicating with parents of exceptional children.* Denver: Love Publishing, 1975.

Kuypers, D. S., Becker, W. C., & O'Leary, K. D. How to make a token system fail. *Exceptional Children,* 1968, *35,* 101–109.

La Vigna, G. W. Communication training in mute autistic adolescents using the written word. *Journal of Autism and Childhood Schizophrenia,* 1977, *7,* 135–149.

Lenneberg, E. *Biological foundations of language.* New York: Wiley, 1967.

Lewin, K., Lippitt, R., & White, R. Patterns of aggressive behavior in experimentally created "social climates." *Journal of Social Psychology,* 1939, *10,* 271–299.

Lewis, W. W. Project Re-ED: Educational intervention in discordant child rearing systems. In E. L. Cowen, E. A. Gardener, & M. Zax (Eds.), *Emergent approaches to mental health.* New York: Appleton-Century-Crofts, 1967.

Lichstein, K. L., & Schreibman, L. Employing electric shock with autistic children: A review of the side effects. *Journal of Autism and Childhood Schizophrenia,* 1976, *6,* 163–174.

Long, N. J., Morse, W. C., & Newman, R. G. (Eds.). *Conflict in the classroom* (2nd ed.). Belmont, Calif.: Wadsworth, 1971.

Lovaas, O. I., Berberich, J. P., Perloff, B. F., & Schaeffer, B. Acquisition of imitative speech in schizophrenic children. *Science,* 1966, *151,* 705–707.

Lovaas, O. I., Koegel, R. L., Simmons, J. Q., & Long, J. S. Some generalization and follow-up measures on autistic children in behavior therapy. *Journal of Applied Behavior Analysis,* 1973, *6,* 131–165.

Lovaas, O. I., & Newsom, C. D. Behavior modification with psychotic children. In H. Leitenberg (Ed.), *Handbook of behavior modification and behavior therapy.* New York: Appleton-Century-Crofts, 1976.

Lovaas, O. I., Schaeffer, B., & Simmons, J. Q. Building social behavior by use of electric shock. *Journal of Experimental Research in Personality,* 1965, *1,* 99–109.

Lovaas, O. I., Schreibman, L., Koegel, R. L., & Rehm, R. Selective responding by autistic children to multiple sensory input. *Journal of Abnormal Psychology,* 1971, *77,* 211–222.

Lovaas, O. I., & Simmons, J. Q. Manipulation of self-destruction in three retarded children. *Journal of Applied Behavior Analysis,* 1969, *2,* 143–157.

Lovitt, P., Lovitt, T. C., Eaton, M., & Kirkwood, M. The deceleration of inappropriate comments by a natural consequence. *Journal of School Psychology,* 1973, *11,* 149–156.

Lovitt, T. C. Self-management projects with children with behavior disabilities. *Journal of Learning Disabilities,* 1973, *6,* 138–150.

Lovitt, T. C., & Curtiss, K. Academic response rate as a function of teacher- and self-imposed contingencies. *Journal of Applied Behavior Analysis,* 1969, *2,* 49–53.

MacDonough, T. S., & Forehand, R. Response-contingent time out: Important parameters in behavior modification with children. *Journal of Behavior Therapy and Experimental Psychiatry,* 1973, *4,* 231–236.

Macfarlane, J., Allen, L., & Honzik, M. *A developmental study of the behavior problems of normal children between 21 months and 14 years.* Berkeley, Calif.: University of California Press, 1955.

MacMillan, D. L., Forness, S. R., & Trumbull, B. M. The role of punishment in the classroom. *Exceptional Children,* 1973, *40,* 85–96.

MacMillan, D. L., & Morrison, G. M. Educational programs. In H. Quay & J. Werry (Eds.), *Psychopathological disorders of childhood.* New York: Wiley, 1979.

Madsen, C. H., Becker, W. C., & Thomas, D. R. Rules, praise, and ignoring: Elements of elementary classroom control. *Journal of Applied Behavior Analysis,* 1968, *1,* 139–150.

Madsen, C. H., Becker, W. C., Thomas, D. R., Koser, L., & Plager, E. An analysis of the reinforcing function of "sit down" commands. In R. K. Parke (Ed.), *Readings in educational psychology.* Boston: Allyn and Bacon, 1968.

Mahler, M. On child psychosis and schizophrenia: Autistic and symbiotic infantile psychosis. In *Psychoanalytic study of the child* (Vol. 7). New York: International University Press, 1952.

Mahler, M. On early infantile psychosis: The symbiotic and autistic syndromes. *Journal of the American Academy of Psychiatry,* 1965, *4,* 554–568.

Mahler, M., & Furer, M. Child psychosis: A theoretical statement and its implications. *Journal of Autism and Childhood Schizophrenia,* 1972, *2,* 213–218.

Martin, W. E., & Stendler, C. B. *Child behavior and development* (Rev. ed.). New York: Harcourt, Brace, 1959.

Mayhew, D., & Ferjo, J. *The use of in-patient adolescents as teacher assistants in an elementary classroom in a psychiatric setting.* Paper presented at the 45th Annual Meeting of the American Orthopsychiatric Association, Chicago, 1968.

McCaffrey, I., Cumming, J., & Pausley, B. *Emotional disturbances in schools: Some interim observations in a longitudinal study of elementary school children.* Paper presented before American School Health Associates and the American Republic Health Association, November 14, 1963.

Meehl, P. Schizotoxia, schizotypy, schizophrenia. In A. Buss (Ed.), *Theories of schizophrenia.* New York: Atherton Press, 1969.

Menyuk, P. *The acquisition and development of language.* Englewood Cliffs, N.J.: Prentice-Hall, 1971.

Mercer, J. The meaning of mental retardation. In R. Koch & J. Dobson (Eds.), *The mentally retarded child and his family.* New York: Brunner/Mazel, 1971.

Moore, R., & Goldiamond, I. Errorless establishment of visual discrimination using fading procedures. *Journal of Experimental Analysis of Behavior,* 1964, *7,* 269–272.

Morse, W. C. The crisis teacher. In N. Long, W. C. Morse, & R. Newman (Eds.), *Conflict in the classroom: The education of emotionally disturbed children* (2nd ed.). Belmont, Calif.: Wadsworth, 1976.

Morse, W. C. Serving the needs of individuals with behavior disorders. *Exceptional Children,* 1977, *44,* 158–164.

Mosher, L. R., Gunderson, J. G., & Buchsbaum, S. Special report: Schizophrenia, 1972. *Schizophrenia Bulletin,* Winter 1973, 12–52.

Moustakas, C. E. *Children in play therapy.* New York: McGraw-Hill, 1953.

Munroe, R. L. *Schools of psychoanalytic thought.* New York: Dryden Press, 1955.

Needels, F., & Jamison, C. Educational approaches at the Los Angeles County Autism Project. In E. R. Ritvo, B. J. Freeman, E. M. Ornitz, & P. E. Tanguay (Eds.), *Autism: Diagnosis, current research and management.* New York: Spectrum Publications, 1976.

Newell, P. (Ed.). *A last resort? Corporal punishment in schools.* Harmondsworth, England: Penguin Books, 1972.

Newman, R. G. The assessment of progress in the treatment of hyperaggressive children with learning disturbances within a school setting. *American Journal of Orthopsychiatry,* 1959, *29,* 633–643.

O'Connor, R. D. Relative efficacy of modeling, shaping, and the combined procedures for modification of social withdrawal. *Journal of Abnormal Psychology,* 1972, *79,* 327–334.

Oden, S. L., & Asher, S. R. *Coaching children in social skills for friendship-making.* Paper presented at the biennial meeting of the Society for Research in Child Development, Denver, 1975.

O'Leary, K. D., & Drabman, R. S. Token reinforcement programs in the classroom: A review. *Psychological Bulletin,* 1971, *75,* 379–398.

O'Leary, K. D., Kaufman, K. F., Kass, R. E., & Drabman, R. S. Effects of loud and soft reprimands on the behavior of disruptive students. *Exceptional Children,* 1970, *37,* 145–155.

O'Leary, K. D., & O'Leary, S. G. *Classroom management: The successful use of behavior modification.* New York: Pergamon Press, 1972.

Ornitz, E. M. Childhood autism: A disorder of sensorimotor integration. In M. Rutter (Ed.), *Infantile autism: Concepts, characteristics, and treatment.* London: Churchill, 1971.

Ornitz, E. M., Brown, M. B., Mason A., & Putnam, N. Effect of visual input on vestibular nystagmus in autistic children. *Archives of General Psychiatry,* 1974, *31,* 369–375.

Ornitz, E. M., Brown, M. B., Sorosky, A. D., Ritvo, E. R., & Dietrich, L. Environmental modifications of autistic behavior. *Archives of General Psychiatry,* 1970, *22,* 560–565.

Ornitz, E. M., & Ritvo, E. R. Neuropsychological mechanisms underlying perceptual inconstancy in autistic and schizophrenic children. *Archives of General Psychiatry,* 1968, *19,* 22–27.

Ornitz, E. M., & Ritvo, E. R. The syndrome of autism: A critical review. *American Journal of Psychiatry,* 1976, *133,* 609–621.

Patterson, G. R., Reid, J. B., Jones, R. R., & Conger, R. E. *A social learning approach to family intervention: Families with aggressive children* (Vol. 1). Eugene, Oregon: Castalia, 1975.

Peterson, D. R. Behavior problems of middle childhood. *Journal of Consulting Psychology,* 1961, *25,* 205–209.

Potter, H. Schizophrenia in children. *American Journal of Psychiatry,* 1933, *12,* 1253–1268.

Premack, D. Toward empirical behavior laws: 1. Positive reinforcement. *Psychological Review,* 1959, *66,* 219–233.

Quay, H. C. Patterns of aggression, withdrawal and immaturity. In H. C. Quay & J. S. Werry (Eds.), *Psychopathological disorders of childhood.* New York: Wiley, 1972.

Quay, H. C., Morse, W. C., & Cutler, R. L. Personality patterns of pupils in special classes for the emotionally disturbed. *Exceptional Children,* 1966, *33,* 297–301.

Quay, H. C., & Quay, L. C. Behavior problems in early adolescence. *Child Development,* 1965, *36,* 215–220.

Rabinow, B. The role of the school in residential treatment. *American Journal of Orthopsychiatry,* 1955, *25,* 685–691.

Rabinow, B. A proposal for a training program for teachers of the emotionally disturbed and socially maladjusted. *Exceptional Children,* 1960, *26,* 287–293.

Rank, B. Adaption of psychoanalytic technique for the treatment of young children with atypical development. *American Journal of Orthopsychiatry,* 1949, *19,* 130–139.

Redl, F. Strategy and techniques of the life space interview. *American Journal of Orthopsychiatry,* 1959, *29,* 1–18.

Reinert, H. R. *Children in conflict: Educational strategies for the emotionally disturbed and behaviorally disordered.* St. Louis: Mosby, 1976.

Rezmierski, V., & Kotre, J. A limited literature review of theory of the psychodynamic model. In W. C. Rhodes & M. L. Tracy (Eds.), *A study of child variance: Conceptual models* (Vol 1). Ann Arbor: University of Michigan Press, 1974.

Rheingold, H. L., Stanley, W. C., & Doyle, G. A. Visual and auditory reinforcement of a manipulatory response in the young child. *Journal of Experimental Child Psychology,* 1964, *1,* 316–326.

Rhodes, W. C. The disturbing child: A problem of ecological management. *Exceptional Children,* 1967, *33,* 449–455.

Rhodes, W. C. A community participation analysis of emotional disturbance. *Exceptional Children,* 1970, *37,* 309–314.

Richey, E. Educational approaches at the NPI school: The language program. In E. R. Ritvo, B. J. Freeman, E. M. Ornitz, & P. E. Tanguay (Eds.), *Autism: Diagnosis, current research and management.* New York: Spectrum Publications, 1976.

Riggs, M. Recall and organization of aggressive words under varied conditions of emphasis. *Perceptual Motor Skills,* 1956, *6,* 273–284.

Rimland, B. *Infantile autism.* New York: Appleton-Century-Crofts, 1964.

Rimland, B. Psychogenesis versus biogenesis: The issues and the evidence. In S. Plog & R. Edgerton (Eds.), *Changing perspectives in mental illness.* New York: Holt, Rinehart, and Winston, 1969.

Rincover, A., & Koegel, R. L. Research on the education of autistic children: Recent advances and future directions. In B. B. Lahey & A. E. Kazdin (Eds.), *Advances in clinical child psychology* (Vol. 1). New York: Plenum, 1977.

Rincover, A., Newsom, C. D., Lovaas, O. I., & Koegel, R. L. Some motivational properties of sensory reinforcement in psychotic children. *Journal of Experimental Child Psychology,* 1977, *24,* 312–323.

Rincover, A., Peoples, A., & Packard, D. *Sensory extinction and sensory reinforcement in psychotic children.* Paper presented at annual meeting of the American Psychological Association, Washington, D.C., 1976.

Risley, T. R. The effects and side effects of punishing the autistic behaviors of a deviant child. *Journal of Applied Behavior Analysis,* 1968, *1,* 21–34.

Ritvo, E. R., Freeman, B. J., Ornitz, E. M., & Tanguay, P. E. (Eds.). *Autism: Diagnosis, current research and management.* New York: Spectrum Publications, 1976.

Ritvo, E. R., Ornitz, E. M., & La Franchi, S. Frequency of repetitive behavior in early infantile autism and its variants. *Archives of General Psychiatry,* 1968, *19,* 341–347.

Ritvo, E. R., Ornitz, E. M., Tanguay, P. E., & Lee, J. C. *Neurophysiologic and biochemical abnormalities in infantile autism and childhood schizophrenia.* Paper presented at the meeting of the American Orthopsychiatric Association, San Francisco, March 1970.

Rogers, C. *Freedom to learn.* Columbus, Ohio: Merrill, 1969.

Rosenthal, D. (Ed.). *The Genain quadruplets: A case study and theoretical analysis of heredity and environment in schizophrenia.* New York: Basic Books, 1963.

Rothman, E. P. Esther P. Rothman. In J. M. Kauffman & C. D. Lewis (Eds.), *Teaching children with behavior disorders: Personal perspectives.* Columbus, Ohio: Merrill, 1974.

Russ, D. F. A review of learning and behavior theory as it relates to emotional disturbance in children. In W. C. Rhodes & M. L. Tracy (Eds.), *A study of child variance: Conceptual models* (Vol. 1). Ann Arbor: University of Michigan Press, 1974.

Russell, D. The Ginn Basic Readers: *My little red story book, My little green story book, My little blue story book, The little white house.* Boston: Ginn, 1957.

Rutherford, R. B. Theory and research on the use of aversive procedures in the education of moderately behaviorally disordered and emotionally disturbed children and youth. In F. H. Wood & K. C. Lakin (Eds.), *Punishment and aversive stimulation in special education.* Minneapolis: University of Minnesota Press, 1978.

Safer, D. J., & Allen, R. P. *Hyperactive children: Diagnosis and management.* Baltimore: University Park Press, 1976.

Scholl, G. T. The education of children with visual impairments. In W. M. Cruickshank & G. O. Johnson (Eds.), *Education of exceptional children and youth* (3rd ed.). Englewood Cliffs, N.J.: Prentice-Hall, 1975.

Schopler, E. Early infantile autism and receptor processes. *Archives of General Psychiatry,* 1965, *13,* 327–335.

Schreibman, L., & Lovaas, O. I. Overselective response to social stimuli by autistic children. *Journal of Abnormal Child Psychology,* 1973, *1,* 152–168.

Schultz, E. W., Hirshoren, A., Manton, A., & Henderson, R. Special education for the emotionally disturbed. *Exceptional Children,* 1971, *38,* 313–320.

Schwitzgebel, R. *The science of learning and the art of teaching.* Paper presented at the First Annual Educational Engineering Conference, University of California, Los Angeles, 1965.

Sevareid, E. Sign-off for Sevareid. *Time,* December 12, 1977, p. 111.

Shapiro, T., Roberts, A., & Fish, B. Imitation and echoing in young schizophrenic children. *Journal of American Academy of Child Psychiatry,* 1970, *9,* 548–567.

Sherman, M. The differentiation of emotional responses in infants: I. Judgments of emotional responses from motion picture views and from actual observation. *Journal of Comparative Psychology,* 1927, *7,* 265–284.

Shores, R. E., & Haubrich, P. A. Effect of cubicles in educating emotionally disturbed children. *Exceptional Children,* 1969, *36,* 21–24.

Shutte, R. C., & Hopkins, B. L. The effect of teacher attention on following instructions in a kindergarten class. *Journal of Applied Behavior Analysis,* 1970, *3,* 117–122.

Skinner, B. F. *Science and human behavior.* New York: MacMillan, 1953.

Skinner, B. F. Teaching: The arrangement of contingencies under which something is taught. In N. G. Haring & A. H. Hayden (Eds.), *Improvement of instruction.* Seattle: Special Child Publications, 1972.

Solnick, J. V., Rincover, A., & Peterson, D. R. Some determinants of the reinforcing and punishing effects of timeout. *Journal of Applied Behavior Analysis,* 1977, *10,* 415–424.

Solomon, R. W., & Wahler, R. G. Peer reinforcement control of classroom problem behavior. *Journal of Applied Behavior Analysis,* 1973, *6,* 49–56.

Sprague, R. L., & Sleator, E. Drugs and dosage: Implications for learning disabilities. In R. Knights & D. Bakker (Eds.), *Neuropsychology of learning disorders: Theoretical approaches.* Baltimore: University Park Press, 1976.

Sroufe, L. A. Drug treatment of children with behavior problems. In F. D. Horowitz (Ed.), *Review of child development research* (Vol. 4). Chicago: University of Chicago Press, 1975.

Sroufe, L. A., & Mitchell, P. Emotional development in infancy. In J. Osofsky (Ed.), *Handbook of infancy research.* New York: Wiley, 1977.

Stein, A. H., & Friedrich, L. K. Impact of television on children and youth. In E. M. Hetherington (Ed.), *Review of child development research* (Vol. 5). Chicago: University of Chicago Press, 1975.

Stevens-Long, J., & Lovaas, O. I. Research and treatment with autistic children in a program of behavior therapy. In A. Davids (Ed.), *Child personality and psychopathology: Current topics* (Vol. 1). New York: Wiley-Interscience, 1974.

Stevenson, H., & Odom, R. Effects of pretraining on the reinforcing value of visual stimuli. *Child Development,* 1961, *32,* 739–744.

Stewart, M. A., & Olds. S. W. *Raising a hyperactive child.* New York: Harper & Row, 1973.

Stewart, M. A., Pitts, F. N., Craig, A. G., & Dieruf, W. The hyperactive child syndrome. *American Journal of Orthopsychiatry,* 1966, *36,* 861–867.

Strauss, A. A., & Lehtinen, L. *Psychopathology and education of the brain-injured child.* New York: Grune & Stratton, 1947.

Sulzer-Azaroff, B., & Mayer, G. R. *Applying behavior analysis procedures with children and youth.* New York: Holt, Rinehart, and Winston, 1977.

Terrace, H. S. Discrimination learning with and without "errors." *Journal of the Experimental Analysis of Behavior,* 1963, *6,* 1–27.

Thomas, A., & Chess, S. *Temperament and development.* New York: Brunner/Mazel, 1977.

Thomas, A., Chess, S., & Birch, H. *Temperament and behavior disorders in children.* New York: New York University Press, 1969.

Thomas, D. R., Becker, W. C., & Armstrong, M. Production and elimination of disruptive classroom behavior by systematically varying teacher's behavior. *Journal of Applied Behavior Analysis,* 1968, *1,* 35–45.

Thompson, G. C. *Child psychology.* Boston: Houghton Mifflin, 1952.

Trotter, R. J. Behavior modification: Here, there, and everywhere. *Science News,* 1973, *103,* 260–263.

Wallin, J. E. *Education of mentally handicapped children.* New York: Harper & Row, 1955.

Watson, J. B., & Rayner, R. Conditioned emotional reactions. *Journal of Experimental Psychology*, 1920, *3*, 1–14.

Watson, R. I. *Psychology of the child.* New York: Wiley, 1959.

Weiss, H., & Born, B. Speech training or language acquisition? A distinction when speech training is taught by operant conditioning procedures. *American Journal of Orthopsychiatry*, 1967, *37*, 49–55.

Wender, P. H. *Minimal brain dysfunction in children.* New York: Wiley, 1971.

Werry, J. S. The childhood psychoses. In H. C. Quay & J. S. Werry (Eds.), *Psychopathological disorders of childhood* (2nd ed.). New York: Wiley, 1979.

Wolf, M. M., Hanley, E. L., King, L. A., Lachowicz, J., & Giles, D. K. The timer-game: A variable interval contingency for the management of out-of-seat behavior. *Exceptional Children*, 1970, *36*, 113–117.

Wood, M. M. *Developmental therapy teacher training program.* Paper presented at the Conference on Preparing Teachers for Severely Emotionally Disturbed Children with Autistic Characteristics, Advanced Institute for Trainers of Teachers for Severely Emotionally Disturbed Children, University of Minnesota, May 22–24, 1977.

Zeigarnik, B. On finished and unfinished tasks. In W. D. Ellis (Ed.), *A source book of Gestalt psychology.* New York: Harcourt, Brace, & World, 1938.

Index

Achenbach, T. M., 99
Achievement Place, ecological approach
    model, 84–88
Activity level, and temperament, 18
Adaptability, and temperament, 18
Adelman, H. S., 116
Aggression, and Id, 18
Aggressive behavior, 26
    and children's families, 34–35
    and permissiveness, 62
    and punishment, 34
Aichhorn, A., 57, 59
Allyon, T., 124
Alphabet mastery, and autistic children,
    311–312
American Educational Research Associa-
    tion, 10
Anal stage, 96
    fixation in, 30
Animals, in the classroom, 199
Anita Johnson System (language activities),
    265
Anxiety factors, and emotional disturbance,
    99
Appraisal teams, 334
    meetings of, 335, 347–348
Arithmetic skills
    and autistic children, 310
    and the special day class, 260–265
Art activities, 196, 218
    and order tasks, 193
Attention level, 134, 135, 138–140
    increasing, 71–73
    and learning competence, 97, 100
    and severely disturbed children, 291, 293
    tasks, 176
        and learning competence levels, 176–
        180
    and temperament, 18
    use of interventions, 222
Atypical children, 290
Auditory discrimination, and autistic chil-
    dren, 312
Autistic children, 6, 40, 290. *See also* Severely
    disturbed children
    and alphabet mastery, 311–312
    and arithmetic skills, 310
    attention levels of, 291–293
    and auditory discrimination, 312
    developmental therapy programs for, 67
    and Early Infantile Autism, 290
    as learners, 94
    and Los Angeles County Autism Project,
        296–297
    and neurological impairment, 27–28

and phrase writing, 312
and spelling, 311–312

Barkett, C., 52
Barnell Loft materials, 257
Barsch, R. H., 55
Bayley, N., 295
Behavior. *See also* Aggressive behavior
    and attention, 71–73
    disorders
        and active-type children, 26–27
        defined, 10–11
        and passive-type children, 26–27
        primary, 37
        psychosomatic, 37
        and role theory, 49–51
        teacher's tolerance and, 7
    disruptive
        ignoring, 70
        reducing, 69–71
        and self-recording procedures, 73–74
    and drug usage, 52
    games for good, 70
    labeling, 10
    learned, 31
    and learning competence, 97
    maladaptive, 68–78
    modification
        and Achievement Place, 84–88
        behavioral approach to, 76–77
        and ecosystem, 79–88
        and electric shock, 306, 307–309
        goals in, 77–78
        neurological approach to, 77
        psychodynamic approach to, 67, 77
        psychoeducational approach to, 67
        teachers as modifiers, 68–78
    praising good, 70, 71–72
    and punishment, 33–34
    reinforcement, and a child's peers, 71
    rewarding appropriate, 70, 71–72
    self-injurious, in severely disturbed chil-
        dren, 306–307
    self-stimulatory, in severely disturbed
        children, 293–295
    skills, 155
Behavioral
    definitions, 37, 39–41
    orientation, 69
    rating scales, 40
Behaviorism, 12
    and conditioning, 31
    and reinforcement, 32–33
Behavior Problem Checklist, 39

Disturbed children, 187–188. *See also* Severely disturbed children
and behavioral factors, 31
and behavior disorders, 11, 38–39
causes for, 57–58
and classrooms, 110, 176
and concrete experiences, 179
creating learning environment for, 214–215
and ecosystem, 79–88
emotional disturbance vs. behavior disorders, 10–11
and environment, 36
hyperactive, 28
    and brain damage, 28–29
    medication for, 51–54
    training, 54–56
incidence of, 41–43
as maladaptive behaviors, 68–78
placement options for, 335–337
psychodynamic factors, 29–30
Public Law 94–142, definition of, 40–41
rewarding behavior, 63
in student role, 220
systematic approach to, 122–123
testing, 53–54
time-out procedures with, 222–226
Dress up, 210–211
Drugs, 51–53
amphetamines, 52
and hyperactive children, 51
Due process rights, 104, 338–340

Early Infantile Autism, 290
Ecological approach, 36, 43. *See also* Psychoeducational approach
and Achievement Place, 84–88
and Project Re-ED, 80–84
Ecology. *See* Human ecology
Ecosystems, defined, 79
Educational programs, 62–67. *See also* Classrooms; Curriculum; Learning
Achievement Place, 84–86
and crisis teachers, 64
for disordered children, 62–67
and integrated schools, 64–65
Jowonio: The Learning Place, 64–66
and the learning triangle, 108–122
Los Angeles County Autism Project, 296–297
Madison School Plan, 279
Neuropsychiatric Institute (NPI) School, 94–96, 295–304
open-ended class meetings, 64
permissive, 62
programmed instruction in, 63
Project Re-ED, 80–84
psychoeducational approach in, 63–67
Rainier School, 318

and rewarding behavior, 63
and role perspective, 46–47
Rutland Center, 66
Santa Monica Project, 72
stimulation of fantasies in, 63
Education for All the Handicapped Act (1975), 10–11
classification of children, 40
Educators. *See* Teachers
Ego, and emotions, 18–21
Electric shock
ethical implications of, 122
and self-injurious behavior, 306–307
and tantrum behavior, 309
Elementary daily schedule, 246
Emotional development. *See* Emotions
Emotional disturbance
anxiety factors in, 99
vs. behavior disorders, 10–11
behavioral
    definitions, 39–41
    factors in, 31–33
biological factors in, 27–29
causes for, 57–58
clustering, 9
defined, 10–11, 36–41
developmental factors in, 21–24
ecological factors in, 35–36
frequency of occurrence, 7
functional description of, 92–105
and human ecosystem, 79–88
ignoring, 9
incidence of, 41–43
and learning competence, 96–103
prescribing drugs for, 51–53
and Project Re-ED, 81
psychodynamic factors in, 29–31
and Public Law 94–142, 103–105
rebellion factors in, 99
and role perspectives, 47
and social learning factors, 34–35
teacher tolerance of, 6–7, 8–9
temperamental factors in, 24–27
vagueness of term, 40
Emotions
development of, 12–21
and Id, 18–21
as innate, 12–13
and temperament, 16–18
theories of origin of, 18–21
Environment theory, 58
Erikson, E., 29, 30, 58, 96
Errorless training, 186, 314–318
Exploratory
center, and classroom design, 218
level, 135, 136, 144–146
    and learning competence, 97, 100
    and severely disturbed children, 307–308
    use of interventions, 221

use of interventions, 222
tasks, 183–188
   characteristics of, 183–188
   and grades, 183–184
   response-facilitating approaches,
     186–187
   stifling communication, 184–186
Response cost, and punishment, 118–119
Retention aids, 182–183
Rewarding, consequences of, 63, 116–117
Rhythmicity, 18
Riggs, M., 177
Rimland, B., 27
Rogers, C., 58, 61
Role
  perspective, 46
  taking, and social tasks, 207–209
  theory, 46
    and neurologically impaired children,
     48–49
    and role perspective, 46
    and teacher as diagnostician-trainer,
     49–57
Rothman, E. P., 59–60
Rutherford, R. B., 118
Rutland Center (Georgia), 66

Santa Monica Project, 72
Schedules
  daily, 246, 247
  routine daily, 109
  secondary daily, 247
Schizophrenia, 40, 290. *See also* Severely
    disturbed children
School Appraisal Teams, 334–335
Schools. *See* Educational programs; Learn-
    ing
Science, as exploratory tasks, 198–199,
    218–219
Science Research Association Reading Labs,
    254, 257
Secret code writing, as an order task, 191
Self-concept skills, and mastery level, 137,
    147
Self-help skills, and mastery level, 137,
    147–149
Self-injurious behavior
  and severely disturbed children, 306–307
  and use of electric shock, 306–307
Self-stimulatory behavior, 308
  in severely disturbed children, 293–295
Sensory perception
  and learning competence, 100
  and reinforcement, 115
  and self-stimulatory behavior, 308
Severely disturbed children, 290–331. *See*
    also Autistic children
  and attention level, 291–293
  Dejarnette Center for Human Develop-

ment, 327–331
and electric shock use, 306–307
and exploratory level, 307–308
and mastery level, 310–331
and modeling procedures, 309
and order level, 306–307
and overselectivity, 309
and Public Law 94–142, 40
and response level, 293–295
and stimulus overselectivity, 291–292
and underreaction, 291
vocabulary building, 320–321
Shaping, and operant conditioning, 124–
    126
Simmons, J. Q., 327
Singer Math Kits, 262
Skill
  development, in the special day class, 257
  training meetings, and resource
    specialists, 285
Skinner, B. F., 31, 32, 129
Social
  approval, as a positive consequence,
    113–115
  maladjustment, 10
  skill level, 135, 136–137, 146–147
    and learning competence, 97, 101
    and severely disturbed children, 308–
     310
    use of interventions, 221
  tasks, 202
    characteristics of, 202–211
    and coaching, 207–209
    and modeling, 207–209
    and role taking, 207–209
  workers, and schoolroom efforts, 95
Social learning theory, 43
  and learning theory, 34
Space reduction, and training disturbed
    children, 54
Special day class, 244–270
  arithmetic period, 260
  daily procedures of, 244–246
  exploratory period, 267–268
  and length of school day, 244
  listening period, 266–267
  physical education period, 269–270
  reading period, 249–257
  skill development, 257
  story-writing period, 257–260
Speech development, and learning compe-
    tence, 100
Spelling, 265
  and autistic children, 311–312
SRA Computational Math Kits, 262
Stewart, M. A., 52
Stimuli reduction, and training disturbed
    children, 54
Stimulus overselectivity, and severely
    disturbed children, 291–292